COMMUNICATION FOR TECHNICIANS

Reading, Writing, and Speaking on the Job

Ann Gregson Tench

President
The Training Exchange

Isabelle Kramer Thompson

Assistant Professor
Auburn University

PRENTICE HALL, Englewood Cliffs, New Jersey 07632

LIBRARY OF CONGRESS
Library of Congress Cataloging-in-Publication Data

Tench, Ann Gregson
    Communication for technicians : reading, writing, and speaking on
the job / Ann Gregson Tench, Isabelle Kramer Thompson
     p. cm.
    Includes index.
    ISBN 0-13-154246-X
    I. Communication of technical information.   I. Thompson, Isabelle
Kramer   . II. Title.
    T10.5.T46 1988
    808'.0666—dc19   87-29207
                             CIP

Editorial/production supervision and
  interior design: Jan Stephan
Cover design: Wanda Lubelska Design
Manufacturing buyer: Ray Keating

 © 1988 by Ann Gregson Tench and
    Isabelle Kramer Thompson

Printed in the United States of America

10 9 8 7 6 5 4 3 2 1

ISBN 0-13-15426-X

Prentice-Hall International (UK) Limited, *London*
Prentice-Hall of Australia Pty. Limited, *Sydney*
Prentice-Hall Canada Inc., *Toronto*
Prentice-Hall Hispanoamericana, S.A., *Mexico*
Prentice-Hall of India Private Limited, *New Delhi*
Prentice-Hall of Japan, Inc., *Tokyo*
Prentice-Hall of Southeast Asia Pte. Ltd., *Singapore*
Editora Prentice-Hall do Brasil, Ltda., *Rio de Janeiro*

CONTENTS

3 PLANNING, REVISING, AND PROOFREADING   24

4 ORGANIZING INFORMATION IN STANDARD PATTERNS   42

5 PARAGRAPHS, BEGINNINGS, AND ENDINGS   62

6 REVISING FOR READABILITY   73

7 SPECIAL FORMATTING FEATURES   89

8 VISUAL AIDS   105

9 INFORMAL REPORTS   130

10 PROPOSALS   184

APPENDIX B: COMMON PROBLEMS WITH WRITTEN ENGLISH

APPENDIX C: LANGUAGE OF EQUAL TREATMENT

PREFACE

TO THE INSTRUCTOR

This textbook is addressed to students enrolled in one- and two-year vocational and technical programs and their instructors. Because these students attend college to learn immediately applicable skills, they have special needs not met by textbooks designed for students in college-transfer programs or four-year colleges. This textbook intends to make the transition from the classroom to the workplace easier. It provides realistic instruction in the communication skills technicians use most often on the job.

The purpose of this textbook is to provide advice and practice in reading, writing, and speaking on the job. Besides discussion and assignments, the textbook has a range of examples taken from the documents technicians will read, write, and talk about. It also has a plan sheet for each type of technical writing and business correspondence considered. These plan sheets, which appear at the ends of Chapters 9, 10, 11, 12, and 13, will remind students what information should be included and how that information should be organized. Both the plan sheets and assignments in this textbook have been tested in technical writing classrooms. The plan sheets have also been used by writers in business and industry.

Chapters 1 and 2 give a general discussion of the different types of communication and the factors that influence successful reading, writing, and speaking. Chapter 1 describes the elements of the communication process and some common causes of breakdowns in communication. Chapter 2 discusses the importance of audience and purpose in communication.

Chapters 3, 4, 5, and 6 give guidelines that are important for most writing tasks. Chapter 3 discusses the writing process, how to plan, write a first draft, revise, and proofread. Chapter 4 explains how to organize information in standard patterns. Chapter 5 explains how to write the topic sentences and paragraphs that begin and end technical documents. Chapter 6 gives some guidelines for making written communication easy to read.

Chapters 7 and 8 tell how to present technical information. Chapter 7 discusses some special features used in technical writing, including white space, lists, headings, and supplementary materials at the front and the end. Chapter 8 gives some guidelines for using visual aids.

Chapters 9, 10, 11, and 12 discuss the written communication most technicians are responsible for. Chapter 9 discusses how to write some types of informal reports, while Chapter 10 considers proposals. Chapter 11 discusses the types of letters most commonly written on the job. Chapter 12 describes the most common types of manuals, both those that govern the operation of the company and those that explain the operation of equipment. Chapter 12 also explains how to write technical descriptions and instructions.

Chapters 13 and 14 discuss the job search. Chapter 13 explains how to write a letter of application and a résumé and how to fill in an application form. Chapter 14 gives advice about how to behave in an interview.

Chapters 15 and 16 discuss some common tasks which require technicians to be proficient at spoken communication. Chapter 15 explains how to train other technicians to be productive workers in a company and how to behave professionally in face-to-face conversations with supervisors and customers. Chapter 16 explains how to participate effectively in work groups and at company meetings.

The textbook also has three appendixes. Appendix A, "Conventions of Standard Written American English," and Appendix B, "Common Problems with Written English," are intended to give students help with proofreading. Appendix C, "Language of Equal Treatment," discusses some ways of avoiding sexist language.

The sequence of chapters in this textbook does not represent the sequence of assignments that we would suggest for a course syllabus. As you can see, Chapters 1–8 provide general guidelines for communication, while the rest of the chapters are concerned with particular communication tasks. The three appendixes at the end are intended to be used as references. We suggest that most of the assignments should come from Chapters 9–16, with the other chapters used where they are appropriate.

ACKNOWLEDGMENTS

The inspiration for this book came from the many vocational and technical students we have known. Besides those students, we would like to acknowledge the contributions of several other groups of people. First, we owe our examples to a number of professional and amateur writers. Some examples came from government documents, periodicals, and friends in industry and the service sector. The government documents include Army and Air Force technical manuals, Navy training manuals, *FDA Consumer*, and a range of pamphlets and brochures. The copyrighted materials from industry and the service sector are from the Society for Technical Communications, C.C. Mangum, Inc., Foxboro Company, and the Boulder Police Department. Other examples came from students and graduates of Wake Technical College in Raleigh, North Carolina, and from technicians currently working in business and industry throughout the United States.

Second, we have received assistance locating relevant information and technical advice from the Auburn University reference librarians, Boyd Childress, Yvonne Kozlowski, Harmon Straiton, and Lorna Wiggins and from the Wake Technical College librarian, James Grey. Third, our colleagues at Wake Tech, particularly Howard Blanton, and associates in business and industry, particularly David Levy, have offered advice about content and style. Fourth, we would like to acknowledge the important influence that our teachers have had on the composition of this book, especially Drs. Norma Rose and Ione Knight of Meredith College in Raleigh, North Carolina, and Dr. Ruth S. Smith.

Finally and most importantly, we could not have completed this textbook without the support of our families, Ben, Ben, Jr., and Bizzie Tench; Betty, Ray, and Maude Gregson; Warren Werner; and Wallace F. and Jane Thompson.

Isabelle Thompson

Ann Tench

1

THE COMMUNICATION PROCESS

When you complete this chapter, you should know the five major elements of the communication process, the most common forms for messages, and some causes of unsuccessful communication. You should learn about the following topics:

Elements of the communication process
Forms for messages
  Communication with words
  Communication without words
  Choosing an appropriate form
Breakdowns in communication
  Problems in sending the message
  Problems in receiving the message
  Problems in interpreting and replying to the message
Technicians as communicators

The purpose of this textbook is to teach you how to communicate effectively on the job. The reading, writing, and speaking skills you will learn are as vital for your success as the labs and lectures that make up your curriculum courses. The most competent technician will not be successful unless he or she can communicate with supervisors, customers, and other technicians. This chapter provides an introduction to the communication process on the job. It gives examples of the reading, writing, and speaking skills discussed later.

ELEMENTS OF THE COMMUNICATION PROCESS

Communication is the process of exchanging information between two or more people. On the job, communication often has practical goals. It usually provides information and influences behavior and attitudes. The five elements of the communication process are sender, channel, message, receiver, and response.

Sender. The person who starts the exchange of information. In communication on the job, the sender is the speaker or writer.

Channel. The method by which the sender chooses to communicate the message. The message can be verbal or nonverbal. If it is verbal, it can be written or spoken. If a message is nonverbal, it is sent through body movements, facial expressions, changes in voice, or other nonverbal channels.

Message. The information the sender wants the receiver to understand and respond to. In communication on the job, a message has a *purpose*. The purpose takes into account the changes in behavior or attitude that the sender hopes will result from the receiver's understanding of the message.

Receiver. The intended *audience* for the communication. In communication on the job, the receiver is the listener or reader.

Response. The receiver's interpretation and reply to the message. The response tells the sender whether the attempted communication has been successful or not.

Let's consider some examples of successful communication. Officer Simpkins is a member of the Elm City Police Department. At the moment, he is directing traffic to avoid further collisions at an accident site. When Officer Simpkins raises his hand and faces oncoming cars, the drivers stop. When he blows his whistle and lowers his hand with a quick motion, they go. As long as all the drivers obey Officer Simpkins' signals, the communication is successful—even though no words are spoken. In this example, the *sender* is Officer Simpkins. The *channel* is nonverbal, hand signals and a whistle. The *messages* are to stop or to go. The *receivers* are the drivers whom Officer Simpkins is directing. The *response* is what the drivers do based on Officer Simpkins' nonverbal directions.

Jan Rogers is a broker for Elm City Realty. After several months, she has finally found a house that may be appropriate for a young couple she represents. The realtor calls the couple and asks them to meet her at the house at 5:00 P.M. She gives them directions about how to find the house. If the couple arrives at the house at 5:00 P.M., the communication has been successful. The *sender* is Jan Rogers, the realtor. The *channel* is verbal, spoken communication over the phone. The *message* is the information about when to meet and how to get to the house. The *receivers* are the young couple, particularly the person who answered the phone. The *response* includes the comments made by the person who answered the phone and the couple's ability to follow the directions correctly. In this example, the receivers may understand the message but be prevented from reaching the house. Even though the couple may know where the house is, a flat tire or traffic accident could prevent their arrival at the house by 5:00 P.M. This problem would result not from a breakdown in communication but from circumstances unrelated to the message.

Herb Askew is another resident of Elm City. He is a recent graduate of Smith Technical College with training in electronics engineering. Herb writes a letter and sends a résumé to an IBM plant in California. On the opposite side of the United States from Elm City, California is a place where Herb has always wanted to live. If Herb gets a job or even an interview, the communication has been successful. The *sender* is Herb Askew. The *channel* is verbal, a written letter of application and a résumé. The *message* is a request for an interview that will lead to employment with IBM. The initial *receiver* is probably the personnel officer at IBM, but if Herb looks like a good prospect, the letter and résumé may be forwarded to other people in the company. The *response* is a phone call or letter inviting Herb for an interview or, if the company is not interested, a letter turning down Herb's request. Unfortunately, some companies do not respond at all to applicants they are not interested in hiring.

FORMS FOR MESSAGES

Messages can be expressed with or without words. When sent with words, they are either spoken or written. Communication can also take place without words. Facial expressions and gestures, changes in voice, and silence send messages without words. Often the same communication act uses both words and gestures.

Communication with Words

When a message is expressed with words, the communication is verbal. Spoken and written communications are verbal. Spoken communication includes face-to-face conversations, phone conversations, conference calls, interviews, classroom discussions or lectures, meetings, and speeches. Spoken communication ranges from the "Look out!" one member of a construction crew yells as the scaffolding shakes to the inaugural speech given by a newly elected president of the United States.

Written communication includes letters to friends, memoranda to supervisors, letters to customers, reports, and even this textbook. It ranges from the two-line Mother's Day poems written by second graders to the multivolume *Encyclopedia of Science and Technology*. Written communication is not just spoken communication in another form. Its use and circumstances are different, and few writers write the same way that they talk. Because the writer is often not available to answer questions about the message, written communication must conform to a strict system of rules.

Communication without Words

Along with words, a message can be expressed with gestures, movements, and changes in voice. This communication is nonverbal. In every face-to-face conversation, in phone conversations, and in other more formal situations where a person is speaking to a group, nonverbal communication occurs. The most familiar forms of nonverbal communication are body movements and facial expressions. Compare the nonverbal messages in these two examples of communication. Suppose Oscar gets an F on a math test. On his way to his next class, he walks quickly and forcefully down the hall. He kicks at every trash can he passes and hits a water fountain with his books. His eyes blaze; his cheeks are red; his teeth are clenched tightly. Although Oscar has not said anything about the math test, his anger is very obvious to those around him. On the other hand, consider Alex, who also received an F on the math test. Alex has failed the course three times, and he sees little hope of passing his fourth time around. Holding his math test in his hand, Alex stumbles into the instructor's office. His head is down and his hands are shaking. Like Oscar, Alex communicates his message without saying a word.

Besides body movements and facial expressions, other forms of nonverbal communication are the use of sounds and changes in voice. Sounds are noises that are not words: clearing the throat, sighing, laughing, and sneering. Sounds communicate approval or disapproval, happiness or sadness, boredom or excitement. For example, suppose Oscar and Alex return to math class the day after the test is returned. The instructor tells the class that since this was the first test in the quarter, it was the easiest. The tests that follow will be comprehensive and more difficult than this one. Oscar lets out a loud "Hrumph"—a sneer indicating his contempt for the instructor and the class. Alex just sighs, sadly and quietly. Changes in voice affect the manner in which a message is spoken. These changes occur in the tone, pitch, and tempo of the message. Different tones, pitches, and tempos are used to express attitudes toward the speaker and the message: sarcasm, questioning, joy, sadness, and arrogance. For example, Oscar approaches the instructor after class. "So I'm going to fail this course, huh?" he says loudly. The tone, pitch, and tempo of his voice as he speaks this sentence indicate sarcasm and intend to challenge the instructor. Alex's approach is different. The same sentence—"So I'm going to fail this course, huh?"—is said slowly and softly.

Silence is also a form of communication. When it is used deliberately, it gives a very clear message. For example, suppose Mary and Agnes have an argument, and Mary vows never to speak to Agnes again. Silence, rather than sarcasm or even physical assault, is the most awful punishment that Mary can imagine. Oscar's girlfriend does not answer her telephone and sends his letters back unopened. Oscar assumes from the silence that the romance is over.

Choosing an Appropriate Form

The selection of an appropriate form for a message depends on the content of the message and on the relationship of the sender and the receiver. Most communication is spoken, and often spoken words are accompanied with gestures and facial expressions. Except for formal occasions, such as the inaugural speech mentioned earlier, spoken communication is likely to be more relaxed and more personal than written communication. Speech allows senders to communicate their messages quickly and receive a quick response. However, unless it is recorded, it is not permanent or available for later reference. For example, instructors want to be certain that students understand their explanations. Therefore, they often discuss assignments as well as require readings from textbooks. Based on puzzled looks and blank stares, instructors repeat parts of an explanation or try a different approach. On the job, most work crews have daily or weekly meetings to discuss their progress on a current task and prepare for the new task. During these meetings, questions can be answered immediately and potential problems avoided. Spoken communication is an essential vehicle for getting routine things done both on the job and off.

Communication must be written when permanent documentation is needed, when the person to whom the message is directed is not present, or when the sender wants to establish a formal relationship with the receiver. Written communication leaves a permanent message that can be read when the sender is absent. It can be looked back on, studied, and reread. Speech disappears and can be forgotten completely or partly. The permanence of writing helps also to prevent legal complications. Some written communication is directed at receivers outside the company. For example, the closing agreement between the young couple and the realtor on the sale of the house is written. Technical manuals that accompany complicated pieces of equipment are written. Other written communication is directed at receivers inside the company. For example, most supervisors write evaluations of the people who work for them. These evaluations are used to determine raises and promotion. Their written form allows later reference and provides evidence that can be used in lawsuits, if necessary.

BREAKDOWNS IN COMMUNICATION

Communication on the job breaks down when the receiver does not understand the sender's message or give an appropriate reply. This unsuccessful communication does not achieve its practical goal, and time and money are wasted. This section examines the three most common causes for breakdowns in communication: problems in sending the message, problems in receiving the message, and problems in interpreting and replying to the message. It is not unusual for all three types of problems to occur with the same message.

Problems in Sending the Message

Senders want receivers to understand their message, but they do not always write or speak clearly. They are affected by the conditions that are around them and inside them. A sender's message can be affected by external conditions. These conditions include the weather, loud noises, and distractions from other people. The way the message is expressed can also be affected by internal conditions. These conditions include the sender's mental state, past experience with the receiver, attitude about the topic of the communication, and skill as a communicator. As most of you know, all kinds of factors that seem unrelated affect performance on the job. These same factors—some of which are related to the message and some of which are not—affect the sender's ability to say what he or she means.

Let's consider an example. Eric Burns is a crew chief for a large construction company. As part of his job, he has to write quarterly evaluations of the members of his crew. Ethan Floyd, a crew member, is a good worker. Floyd is always on time and never needs discipline. Burns intends to give Ethan an excellent evaluation each quarter. While he is writing the June evaluation, Burns is in a positive frame of mind: he is excited about his daughter's wedding that month, the weather is very pleasant, and his doctor has just told him that he has the body of an 18-year-old. Burns writes: "Ethan Floyd is an outstanding worker. If we have a job that I cannot personally supervise, I always send Floyd. He is capable and trustworthy." Three months later, while he is writing his September evaluations, Burns is in a negative frame of mind: His daughter's marriage is not happy, the weather is miserable, and he has a cold. Even though Ethan's work habits have not changed, Burns writes only: "Floyd is a good worker." His mental state and the conditions that surround him affect the message that Burns will send.

Problems in Receiving the Message

Since no two people are alike, the receiver will interpret the message from a viewpoint different from the sender's. Even if the message is clearly expressed, receivers may not understand it. Like senders, receivers are affected by external conditions and internal conditions. Misunderstanding can result from a number of factors. Some of these factors are conflicts with previous training or experience and poor listening or reading skills.

Consider an example from Burns' crew. Anson Weaver has worked as a concrete finisher in Florida for 20 years. Now, after divorcing his wife, he has moved to Michigan. Anson is the newest member of Burns' crew. The crew is currently at work pouring concrete in a subdivision. As his company requires, Burns gives Anson a brief training session. He begins by defining and explaining Anson's job. During the explanation Anson smiles and nods his head. He tries to appear interested and cooperative. However, Anson pays very little attention. He is thinking about sunny Florida—the white beaches and his ex-wife. Anson assumes that his 20 years of experience as a concrete finisher have trained him to do any task. When Burns has finished the explanation, he asks Anson to help finish a concrete basement. Anson is stunned: In Florida, houses do not have basements. Although no special techniques may be required, Anson is not certain. Burns has explained this part of the job, but Anson has not been paying attention. He has assumed that his previous experience has taught him everything he needs to know about construction. Burns' attempted communication has failed because Anson has not received the message.

Problems in Interpreting and Replying to the Message

The sender judges the success of communication by the response the receiver gives. A response is usually a second message based on the receiver's understanding and interpretation of the original message. It can be nonverbal or verbal, written or spoken. A response can be a nod of the receiver's head to indicate agreement, accompanied by a simple "Yes." It can also be a 300-page proposal to build a new store in reply to a request for bids sent out by a major grocery chain. If the receiver indicates understanding and agreement, the sender assumes that the communication is successful. If the receiver appears puzzled or disagrees, the sender can circle back and explain the points again. When the receiver does not respond to the sender or when an incorrect response is given, the sender cannot judge the reception of the message. The communication process breaks down.

Let's return to Burns' training session with Anson. As Burns explains the task, Anson is nodding his head and smiling to indicate that he understands. However, as we said before, Anson has not been paying attention, and he may not be able to do the job. His response is incorrect, and he is misleading Burns. The communication is unsuccessful, but Burns is unaware of the problem. The same situation can occur when Alex visits the math instructor. Listening attentively as the instructor explains the problems he missed on the math exam, Alex thinks that he understands. He nods his head, smiling at his success. On the next test, however, Alex finds that his understanding was incomplete, and he misses the same problems. In this case, the receiver thinks he is giving a correct response, but, again, he is misleading the sender. The communication is unsuccessful.

A delay in response is another potential source of difficulty. The lack of immediate response—no nod in agreement or puzzled look—prevents a sender from judging the success of the communication. It also delays the opportunity to revise or further explain the message. This delay is always present in written communication. The delayed response makes writing more difficult than speaking for most people. Writers prepare their messages away from their intended audiences. Although they may carefully consider the needs of their readers, they cannot be certain how readers will receive their ideas. They cannot expect a response for days, weeks, or sometimes even months.

TECHNICIANS AS COMMUNICATORS

For most of you, communication is an effortless part of a daily routine. You read a newspaper, write down a list of items to buy at the grocery store, or talk to friends and family. This communication is effortless because the message is familiar and the receiver is well known. Even though the setting is not as comfortable, the skills involved in communicating on the job are similar to those used at home or at a Friday night poker game. Instead of reading newspapers, you may read technical and administrative manuals, procedures, or trade magazines. Instead of writing down a grocery list, you may write memoranda and letters. Instead of talking with friends and family, you may help to train new workers, explain problems to supervisors, or justify costs to customers.

When you are promoted from an entry-level position, your new job may demand even more expertise as a communicator. Besides reading operating procedures and trade magazines, you may be in charge of writing those procedures or suggesting changes in methods based on what you know about the latest technical advancements. Besides participating as a member of a group, you may be in charge of one and be required to conduct group meetings. The higher you go in a company's organization, the more important effective communication becomes. This textbook will help you learn the skills required for successful reading, writing, and speaking on the job. The more you practice with the types of messages you will have to communicate, the easier communication will become.

SUMMARY

Communication is the process of exchanging ideas between two or more people. It has five elements: sender, channel, message, receiver, and response. Senders begin the communication process. They have some information, a message, that they want receivers to understand and respond to. Breakdowns in communication can result from three different sources: problems in sending the message, problems in receiving the message, and problems in responding to the message. To be a successful technician, you must be able to communicate effectively on the job. This textbook will teach you the skills required for successful reading, writing, and speaking on the job.

ASSIGNMENTS

Application 1:
Observing the Process of Communication

A. Write down three examples of nonverbal communication that you have used or seen in the past week. Beside each example, write down whether the message was received and interpreted according to the sender's intentions.

B. Write down three examples of a message that has been misunderstood. Beside each example, write down the reasons for the misunderstanding. Then explain what could have been done to make the message clearer.

Application 2:
Defining Key Words

This chapter introduces some important words that will be used throughout this textbook. To make certain you understand the concepts they refer to, write down definitions for the words on the list.

communication
sender
speaker
writer
channel
message
purpose
receiver
listener
reader
response
verbal communication
nonverbal communication

Application 3:
Practicing Voice Changes

Read the following sentences aloud in several different voices: factual, angry, sad, questioning.

1. The car won't start again.
2. Jon and Mary got married.
3. Agnes won the award.
4. Herb was recently hired by IBM.

2

AUDIENCE
AND PURPOSE

When you complete this chapter, you should know how audience and purpose affect your choices of content and style in communication. You should learn about the following topics:

> Audience
> Technicians
> Supervisors
> Customers
> Purpose
> Content and style
> Clarity
> Persuasiveness
> Formality

As you learned in the last chapter, communication is more than the transfer of information. Unless someone responds to the message, the attempt at communication has not been successful. In this chapter, you will learn more about two elements of the communication process: audience and purpose. These two elements have important effects on your choices of content and style. The audience is the intended receiver of the message. The purpose is the reason the message is sent. In communication on the job, the audience has some practical need for the message. To achieve its purpose, the message must meet that practical need. This chapter describes the three most likely audiences you will communicate with on the job. It also explains three important considerations in the choice of content and style: clarity, persuasiveness, and formality.

While you read this chapter, keep these comparisons in mind. A message is not like a home run ball hit into the stands at a baseball game. The home run ball is directed at no one in particular. Grabbed by a lucky fan as a souvenir, it is not returned to the hitter. Instead, a message is more like a tennis ball hit back and forth in a well-played match. The receiving player tries to return the ball to the opponent's court. Each time the ball is hit, its direction and speed change. However, playing tennis is different from communicating in at least one important way. Tennis is competitive, while communication is cooperative. Good tennis players know how to hit the ball so that their opponents cannot return it. Good communicators know how to explain the message so that their audience can easily understand and reply to it. They know how to direct their message so that it can be returned.

AUDIENCE

Before communication can be successful, the message must make sense to the intended audience. Regardless of the low sale price on a pair of handmade alligator boots, the boots will not be sold unless they fit some interested cowboy. Regardless of how loudly a message is yelled or how neatly it is typed, it will not achieve its practical purpose unless it fits its intended audience. The more you know about an audience, the easier it is to design communication that fits. Three sets of questions can help you learn about your audience.

1. What is your relationship to the audience?

    Is the audience a group or an individual?

    Do you know your audience personally?

    Is the audience employed by your company?

    If so, what rank does the audience have? Is the audience above you, below you, or at the same level in the company's organizational structure?

    If not, is the audience a customer?

2. What does the audience know about your field?

    How much classroom training does the audience have in your field? Is that training recent?

    How much work experience does the audience have in your field?

    Does the audience have more or less knowledge of the field than you?

3. What will the audience do with the information you are trying to communicate?

    Does the audience have to operate equipment or perform a task based on your communication?

    Does the audience have to make a management decision based on your communication?

    Does the audience have to decide about buying your product, selling you something you want, or hiring your company to provide a service based on your communication?

As a technician, you will have to communicate with at least three types of audiences: other technicians in your group at the company, your supervisor, and customers. The following discussion gives some advice about how to communicate successfully with each type of audience.

Technicians

Technicians make up the audience most like you. You both are members of the same group. You have similar training and experience. You also share the same rank in the company. In communicating with technicians, you can assume that they are familiar with current applications of technology in your field and with relevant company policy. Technicians in your group will know the particular equipment and procedures used in your company. They will also be familiar with common abbreviations and symbols.

Since technicians are hired to repair, install, and maintain systems designed by someone else, they are likely to be more interested in applications than theory. They are more concerned with the *how* than the *why* of new technology. When trying to communicate with technicians, you should emphasize applications. In a 20-minute presentation to your work group, you should spend no more than three minutes on theory and rationale. This theory should be used to introduce and explain the *why* of the applications that follow. In addition, you can increase the chances for successful communication by including some form of illustration. In a written message, the illustration may be a drawing of a new machine with the parts labeled. In a group presentation, you may demonstrate how to operate the new machine.

Supervisors

Even though supervisors work at your company, they are not members of your group. They rank higher than you in the organizational structure of the company. They have authority over you. The training and experience of supervisors vary from one company to the next. In some cases, supervisors are highly experienced, well-trained technicians promoted into management. In other cases, they are trained primarily in business and have learned a little about technology by working in the company for a long time. The distance that supervisors maintain from their crews of technicians also varies. Many first-line supervisors spend most of their time on the job site. They work along with their crews as well as write reports and perform other managerial duties. Second-line supervisors spend most of their time away from the job site, writing reports and attending meetings.

Regardless of their training and experience and their closeness to the crews who work under them, supervisors differ significantly from technicians in their responsibilities to the company. They are responsible for managing personnel and producing, buying, or selling a product or service. They are concerned with costs and benefits, personnel problems, and efficient production. Supervisors are interested in the benefits of new technology for the company. They are often not interested in the details of how to perform the latest procedure. Therefore, rather than explaining each step in a new procedure, you should discuss what this procedure can do to increase productivity at no extra cost to the company. You should also explain any special training needed to use the new procedure and any changes in personnel. When writing or talking to supervisors, you will probably need to use some common technical words. If the supervisor is not trained in your field, you may have to define those terms. However, you should avoid the shop talk you can use with other technicians. When necessary, you should reinforce your message with simple illustrations. These may range from a map quickly drawn on the back of an envelope to show where the road needs to be cut in a parcel of timberland to a neatly drawn bar graph that shows how much production can increase with your proposed purchase of new equipment.

Customers

Customers or clients make up the audience the least like you. They do not share your technical training and experience. They also have no obligation to your company. Customers consist of a wide range of people. Some of them are well educated, and some are not. Some know a lot about your field, and some know nothing. Like you, most customers are also professionals who sell products and provide services.

Customers' needs are practical and personal. Customers are not interested in learning about technology. Instead they want to use that technology to make their lives easier or more pleasant. Customers are willing to pay you for your technical skills so that they do not have to learn what you know. When you must explain technical information to a customer, you should keep the discussion as simple as possible. You may have to begin with some background information. A common application or a comparison to something familiar will let you start within your customer's existing knowledge. Then you can lead into the more complicated part of the discussion. If you must use technical words, you should provide simple definitions. Also, as for the other two audiences, you should include simple illustrations to reinforce your message. Drawings, pie graphs, or bar graphs are often helpful for untrained readers.

The table on page 14 compares the characteristics of the three types of audiences. As you see, technicians, supervisors, and customers are related to you in different ways. Each group has a different need for your message. To be successful, you must adapt your communication according to the characteristics of each group.

Sometimes you will have to communicate with two different audiences at the same time. In that case, you will have to decide who is the primary audience and who is the secondary audience. The primary audience usually consists of supervisors and managers. It includes those people who make decisions about buying new equipment, hiring new workers, or implementing a different production method. The secondary audience usually consists of tech-

Table: Characteristics of the Three Types of Audiences

AUDIENCE	CHARACTERISTICS		
	Relationship to You	Training and Experience	Need for Your Communication
Technician	same level in company	same as yours	to learn how to perform a task or how to operate equipment
Supervisor	level above you in company	possibly same as yours; possibly training in business	to learn what has been done and what can be or should be done
Customer	not in company	unknown; probably none in your field	to learn enough to buy or use your product or service

nicians, your peers who will use the new equipment and follow procedures based on the new method. After the primary audience approves suggestions for change, the secondary audience is responsible for putting that change into effect.

PURPOSE

Purpose is the reason the writer or speaker sends the message. It includes the changes in behavior or attitude that the message should bring about in the audience. Often communication has more than one purpose. For example, an electrical engineering technician working in a textile mill reads an article in a trade journal about the use of variable-speed AC drives to run the AC motors in mills. She realizes that these variable-speed drives could save her company a great deal of money. Therefore, the technician decides to write a proposal to management suggesting that a complete study be conducted. First, she explains her idea to her supervisor. Then she writes the proposal. The written and spoken communication in this example has several purposes. In the conversation with the supervisor, one purpose is to suggest the study of variable-speed AC drives. A second purpose is to demonstrate a willingness to use proper channels in making contact with higher management. In the written proposal, the first purpose is the same: to suggest the study of variable-speed AC drives. However, the second purpose is larger. The technician wants to gain recognition as an enterprising and dedicted employee. Eventually she wants to be promoted and receive a pay raise. Communication on the job offers you the chance to demonstrate your skills as a technician and your loyalty as an employee.

Along with its relationship to a larger career goal beyond a single message, the purpose for written or spoken communication is also connected to a technical purpose. For example, a technician who works for Dover Elevator Company *repairs* a broken elevator in a high-rise office building. Then he *ex-*

plains to the building's owner what he has done. The technical purpose is *to repair*; the purpose of the communication is *to explain*. While attending a professional convention, a nurse learns about a new way to organize the Intensive Care Unit so that the nurses in her hospital can watch the patients more carefully and reach dangerously ill patients more quickly. She *assesses* the potential benefits of this new organization and *decides* how to implement this organization in her hospital. Then she *recommends* the new organization to her supervisor and the hospital administration. The technical purposes are to *assess* the potential benefits of the new organization for the hospital and to *decide* how to implement it in the Intensive Care Unit; the purpose of the communication is to *recommend* the change. Some common purposes for written and spoken communication are as follows:

> to explain
> to instruct
> to describe
> to propose
> to request
> to recommend
> to suggest

The more you know about your purpose, the more likely you are to communicate successfully with your audience.

Let's consider one more example. A consulting forester is asked to submit a proposal for managing a large tract of timberland. If the landowner accepts the forester's recommendations, the forester not only will be paid for making the suggestions but also will probably be paid to implement those suggestions over a period of years. Before writing the timber management plan, the forester must perform several technical tasks. She must settle any boundary disputes, count how much timber is on the land, and inspect the timber for damage from insects or disease. She must decide what timber to cut (if any) and what to leave and determine how to clear away the underbrush and put in a road to gain access to the timber. Back in the office, the forester identifies special government programs that will help the landowner pay for reseeding if he decides to cut the timber and calculates how much the additional revenue from a timber sale may increase the landowner's taxes. Once she has completed all these tasks, the forester can *recommend* a plan for *managing* the timberland. The technical purpose is to *manage*; the purpose of the communication is to *recommend*.

While she is writing, the forester considers the needs of her audience in relation to her purpose. Her audience is a customer. If he owns other timberland, the customer may have some knowledge of forestry practices. However, he probably does not want a detailed description of how to eradicate the Southern Pine Beetle as explained in the latest pamphlet from the United States Forest Service. Nor does he want to know exactly how to put in the road or how to choose trees for select cutting. Instead, the landowner wants to know what can be done to get as much profit as possible from his timberland. This profit depends not only on the current condition of the trees but also on what the land will yield in the future and how added revenue from selling timber will raise the landowner's taxes. In other words, the landowner wants to know the *what* and the *how much*, but he does not want to know the *how to*. If the forester were writing a textbook on timber management for students training to become forestry technicians, she would include the *how to*. For the landowner, she describes the current conditions briefly, explains his options, and limits her recommendations to a single tract of land.

CONTENT AND STYLE

Audience and purpose determine the content and style of a message. Content is *what* information is included, and style is *how* that information is expressed. In choosing content and style appropriate for your audience and purpose, you need to consider clarity, persuasiveness, and formality. This section discusses those considerations.

Clarity

Clarity relates to how quickly and easily your readers or listeners can understand your message and how much they can remember. Clarity varies according to audience. Sometimes a message is not clear because the content is unfamiliar to the audience. For example, the average buyer of jeans produced at the textile mill mentioned earlier will not understand the technician's explanation of variable-speed AC drives. However, because he is familiar with the technology up to this point, the supervisor should be able to understand the explanation easily. Sometimes a message is not clear because it is badly expressed. The management at the textile mill will have trouble understanding the technician's proposal if it is poorly organized and full of long sentences with misspelled words and punctuation errors. On the other hand, if the proposal is well written, the message will be clear. In written communication, clarity is referred to as readability. If a piece of writing is clear, it is readable.

Below are two different ways of writing the same sections from *Principles of Automotive Vehicles*, a technical manual developed by the Departments of the Army and the Air Force.[1] These two versions are different attempts at explaining the same major ideas to the same audience. They have been written to achieve the same purpose. Which do you think is the more readable? Remember that readable writing is clear and easy to understand.

---

[1] The information about Ohm's Law is adapted from the Army and Air Force technical manual *Principles of Automotive Vehicles*. Washington: Government Printing Office, 1956.

Version 1

Ohm's Law

General statements about voltage, amperage, and ohms can all be related in a succinct statement, known since its discovery as Ohm's law, so named for the scientist Georg Simon Ohm, who first stated this important relationship. The law can be stated as follows in this sentence: voltage is equal to amperage multiplied by ohms. Or, it can be stated as follows in this mathematical formula:

$$E = I \times R$$

It is very important that you memorize and remember this important formula because it makes understandable many of the changing conditions that occur in an electric circuit. For instance, if the voltage remains constant, the current flow goes down if the resistance goes up.

Version 2

Ohm's Law

Ohm's law relates voltage, amperage, and ohms. Named for the scientist Georg Simon Ohm, who first stated the relationship, the law says that *voltage is equal to amperage multiplied by ohms.*

$$E = I \times R$$

where E is volts, I is current in amperes, and R is resistance in ohms.

This formula explains many of the things that happen in an electric circuit. For instance, if the voltage remains constant and the resistance goes up, the current flow goes down. Consider a lighting circuit that is going bad in a truck. Suppose the wiring circuit between the battery and the lights has deteriorated because the connections have become poor. Strands in the wire have broken, and switch contacts have become dirty. Therefore, the electron path is reduced, and resistance is increased. With this increased resistance, less current will flow.

By applying Ohm's law, you can calculate the size of the decrease. Regardless of the condition of the circuit, the voltage of the battery stays the same. For example, it may have 12 volts. When the circuit was new, the resistance was 6 ohms. At that time, 2 amperes of current flowed through the circuit. You are solving for I.

$$E = I \times R$$
$$I = E/R$$
$$I = 12/6$$
$$I = 2$$

But as the wiring deteriorates, the resistance increases. If resistance goes up to 8 ohms, only 1.5 amperes can flow. Again you are solving for I.

$$E = I \times R$$
$$I = E/R$$
$$I = 12/8$$
$$I = 1.5$$

The increased resistance cuts down the current flow. Consequently it decreases the amount of light from the headlights.

Although written to discuss the same concept (Ohm's law), the two versions are very different. The second is longer than the first. The difference in length comes from the explanation of the symbols in the formula and the extended example of the bad lighting circuit in the truck. This additional information increases the readers' understanding of the law being discussed. Moreover, a comparison of the number of words appearing in each version before the equation shows that the second version is actually more concise than the first. The second uses only 30 words to introduce the equation; the first uses 64. The second version also avoids difficult and unnecessary words such as "succinct." For most trainees, the second version will be more readable than the first. Chapter 6 discusses how to increase the readability of your writing.

However, clarity is more complex than the comparison of these two versions indicates. Clarity is affected by content as well as form. Some information is more difficult to understand than other information. Consider another situation. Suppose a student enrolled in an automotive repair curriculum is taking an introductory physics course. This is his first science course since tenth grade, when he got a D in biology. During the second class meeting, the instructor describes the parts of an atom. Protons, neutrons, and electrons rotate in confused orbits in the future automotive technician's head. He has never seen an atom, at least not up close. Therefore, he finds the lecture very difficult to understand. In the afternoon, the same student has an automotive repair lab. The car he is assigned to work on is a 1985 Camaro, just like the one he drives. The automotive instructor tells him what to do to the car. This time the student understands what the instructor means. The message is clear because the content is familiar. Regardless of how carefully the physics instructor explains the parts of the atom, the automotive repair student will not be able to understand the lecture as easily as he can understand the explanation in the lab. From the student's point of view, the second explanation is clearer than the first. On the other hand, if the physics instructor visits the automotive lab, he may experience the same confusion and frustration as the student experienced during the lecture about the atom. Unless he is familiar with the inner workings of Camaros, he may not understand the automotive instructor's explanation. Clarity varies with each different audience and in each different situation.

Persuasiveness

Like clarity, persuasiveness depends on audience. Communication is persuasive when the audience is convinced to accept the opinions expressed and to act accordingly. If the audience is not persuaded, the attempted communication does not achieve its purpose. All communication is persuasive to some extent. But the level of persuasion varies. Some messages are more persuasive than other messages. The line below shows the level of persuasion in some typical kinds of communication on the job. Notice the types of communication at various levels.

Highly Persuasive	↑ *persuasive*
	advertisements for products
	political speeches
	sales/service proposals
	planning proposals
	letters of application
	letters giving bad news
	scientific articles
	technical descriptions,
	specifications
	technical instructions,
	procedures
Not Highly Persuasive	↓ *informative*

Figure 2-1: Levels of Persuasion in Speech and Writing

At the highest levels of persuasion, a message may provide the fewest technical details. At the lowest levels, it may be the most factual.

Below are two pieces of writing about tires. Taken from *Principles of Automotive Vehicles*, the technical manual mentioned earlier, the first describes the parts of a tire.[2] A drawing is included to make sure the reader sees what the writer describes. The drawing is shown on page 20.

> The structural parts of a tire are the tread, breaker, cushion, plies, and bead. (See Figure 2–2) Each part of the tire serves a definite purpose.
>
> The tread is a layer of rubber on the outside circumference of the tire. It is the tire's wearing surface. With a nonskid design to provide traction, the tread protects cords from cuts, bruises, and moisture. Rubber extends down over the sidewalls for protection.
>
> Breakers are layers of rubber-covered cords. They are similar to plies, except that the cords are spaced farther apart. Breakers distribute road shocks and prevent separation of the tread from the tire.
>
> The cushion is soft, heat-resisting rubber. It absorbs road shocks and bonds plies and breakers together.
>
> Cord plies give strength to resist internal pressure, to support loads, and to absorb road shocks.
>
> The bead anchors the tire to the rim. It consists of two or more cables of steel wire surrounded with a hard rubber compound. The plies are wrapped around the rubber compound to tie the bead to the carcass.

This piece of writing is intended to teach trainees the parts of the tire. Therefore, it is almost entirely informative.

This second message, a television advertisement for Burnt Rubber

[2]This excerpt is adapted from the Army and Air Force technical manual *Principles of Automotive Vehicles*. Washington: Government Printing Office, 1956.

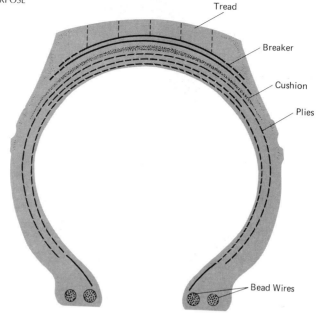

Figure 2-2:   Parts of a Tire

Tires, is intended to be highly persuasive. It is not concerned with giving information. Instead it is a sales pitch.

> Once seen rolling along on the fastest cars at Indy, Burnt Rubber Tires are now available for your family car. Made from heat-treated rubber with extra-thick tread and superelastic cushion, these special tires will give you a smooth ride over miles and miles of city streets and country roads. Although you might expect to pay more to get the durability and safety demanded by the leading racecar drivers, Burnt Rubber Tires come to you with this special introductory offer . . . . If you don't believe me, ask my friend, Rick Reverup, the winner of last year's Firecracker 2000.

Notice the lack of facts in this advertisement. No drawing shows the details of the tires. No explanation gives customers the details of the heat treatment or the superelastic cushion. As evidence of the safety and durability of the tires, the speaker refers to famous auto races and finally uses a racecar driver as an expert witness. He provides no statistics about the tires' performance. Finally, the speaker announces a "special introductory offer." This offer implies that the price will soon increase. The advertisement does not intend to let customers make thoughtful decisions based on facts. Instead, the purpose is to talk them into buying the tires.

As the line of persuasion indicates, most communication falls somewhere between the technical description and the advertisement. It intends to be both persuasive and informative. Most communication mixes a sales pitch with technical details. The level of persuasion varies from one message to the next. A memo recommending that a company sanction a men's softball team requires more deliberate persuasion than one describing the company's new policy on absenteeism. Neither is as deliberately persuasive as a speech by a political candidate.

Formality

Formality refers to how casual a message appears. Formal communication is not at all casual. The message is official. The sender does not try to make a personal connection with the receiver. Informal communication is very casual. The sender tries to make a personal connection with the receiver. At its most formal, communication is like a business suit. It looks official and impressive, but it is not very functional or comfortable. At its least formal, communication is like a pair of old jeans. It does not look impressive or sophisticated, but it is functional and comfortable. Informal communication is usually easier to understand than formal communication. Figure 2−3 shows the level of formality in some typical kinds of spoken and written communication.

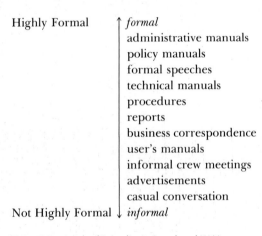

Figure 2-3:   Levels of Formality in Speech and Writing

At its most formal, communication is the most authoritative. At its least formal, communication is the least authoritative.

Consider two examples of formal and informal communication on the construction site we described in Chapter 1. Let's look back at Burns' training of the new crew member, Anson. As part of their orientation, new employees with Botsworth Construction are required to sign a copy of the company's drug and alcohol policy. Their signatures indicate that they are familiar with the policy. Burns gives Anson a copy of this paragraph from the Botsworth administrative manual.

> The possession or use of nonapproved drugs or alcoholic beverages on the Botsworth job site is contrary to company policy and will result in the immediate dismissal and/or barring of the possessor if the possession or use of the drugs and alcohol in any way affects that individual's safe and efficient work performance or the safety and efficiency of others.

The writing is very formal. It intends to sound authoritative and impersonal. The penalty applies to everyone, from the president of the company to the lowest-paid temporary employee. Yet the responsibility for writing and enforcing such a strict policy belongs to no single individual. The company, not Burns, developed the policy and will fire violators.

Beside appearing authoritiative, the writing is also difficult to read. To prevent any later claims of misunderstanding, Burns always explains the policy to new crew members. He says to Anson:

> I don't know what that company in Florida you worked for does, but here in Detroit we've got this rule against drinking and taking drugs on the job site. If you violate it, the company says I've got to fire you. Last week two boys went to that pizza place down the road for lunch and had a couple of beers. They weren't drunk, but you sure could smell the beer on their breath. I had to fire them. If the owner had come by . . . .

Level of formality varies according to how much respect or fear the communication intends to bring about. A president's inaugural address is ceremonial and formal. The voters in the audience are supposed to be respectful of the person they have elected to represent the country. A graduation ceremony is also formal. It is supposed to remind graduates and their families of their obligations to be productive members of society. The conversation at a lunchtime card game is informal. The players are equal in rank and status, and the occasion is not solemn or ceremonial. A classroom discussion is also fairly informal. Although the students respect the authority of the instructor, they are invited to participate in a free exchange of ideas. Chapter 12 provides more discussion of the formal writing that appears in manuals.

SUMMARY

Audience and purpose are two important elements of the communication process. Unless the intended audience responds to the message, the communication is not successful. In that case, you will not achieve your purpose. On the job, you will need to communicate with three different audiences: other technicians in your work group, your supervisor, and your customers. Each audience requires a unique message. Purpose is the reason a message is sent. Common purposes are to explain, to instruct, to describe, to propose, to request, to recommend, and to suggest. Audience and purpose determine the content and style of a message. Content is what information is included, and style is how the message is expressed. Three important considerations are clarity, persuasiveness, and formality. You will learn more about these considerations in other chapters of this textbook.

ASSIGNMENTS

Application:
Revising for Different Audiences

A. Bring to class a technical article describing an important advancement in your field. Rewrite it for an audience of supervisors with no technical training. Remember to consider what supervisors want to know about a product or process. Do not waste their time with needless technical details.

B. When you have completed your writing to the audience of supervisors, write a second description to an audience of customers. Again be certain to consider the needs of your readers.

3

PLANNING, REVISING, AND PROOFREADING

When you complete this chapter, you should know how to plan, write a first draft, revise, and proofread your writing. You should learn these skills:

Planning
  Methods of planning
  Types of plans
Writing a first draft
Revising
  Questions about content and organization
  Questions about paragraphs, sentences, and words
Proofreading

Experienced writers are like experienced automotive technicians tuning car engines. They fiddle around until they get the writing to run smoothly. Exactly what they do is impossible to describe. Because writing varies so much, we cannot give you a set of instructions to teach you how to communicate effectively all the time. However, we can discuss the tasks required for most writing. In this chapter, you will learn how to plan a piece of writing, turn that plan into sentences and paragraphs, revise your first draft, and proofread for errors in usage and spelling.

The tasks you will learn in this chapter are not steps in a rigid sequence. You do not often move easily and neatly from planning to writing the first draft to revising to proofreading. Instead, you may find during revising that the information you are writing about is incomplete. Then you will have to return to your plan to add the missing facts. Especially in long and unfamiliar pieces of writing, you will probably move back and forth from planning to revising. However, one task, proofreading, is always last. You should not waste time correcting spelling and usage errors until you decide exactly what you want to say and how to say it.

PLANNING

Plans show the preliminary decisions about content and organization that writers make before they try to write sentences and paragraphs. Planning a piece of writing is like planning a trip. Without deciding on their routes, drivers may get lost when they enter unfamiliar territory. Without deciding on destinations, they will wander around, wasting gas and going nowhere. Unless they make plans, the drivers may not accomplish the goals of their trips. The same is true for writers. Without planning content and organization, they will get lost. They will waste time and energy wandering around with words. Like the drivers, they will not accomplish their goals.

To ensure the success of their trips, drivers trace their routes on roadmaps before they leave home. These predetermined routes act as guides. Before beginning to write sentences and paragraphs, you should jot down plans for the same reason. Plans are predetermined routes which will guide you through the ideas you want to discuss. When the writing gets underway, plans can be changed. Initial plans show your best guesses before you start your car and back out of your driveway. As you drive along, you may find new routes. Plans can help you in two ways. First, they remind you of your purpose and clearly represent how content can be organized to achieve that purpose. They show an overview of the writing. Like routes traced on roadmaps, plans remind you of your destination and tell you how to get there. Second, plans trigger words and sentences. They help you move from an overview to the individual parts.

Methods of Planning

Before you can design a plan for your writing, you must identify your readers and define your purpose. Then you must gather information on your topic and organize that information in an arrangement appropriate for your purpose. Chapter 2 discusses how to identify your readers and define a purpose. This chapter is concerned with gathering and organizing information on a topic.

Information for writing can come from several different sources. It can come from outside sources—books and periodicals or the members of your work group. It can also come from your own memory. This inside source of information is most important for writing. You can usually base your writing on what you already know about a topic. Since human memory is very complicated, however, you may have difficulty deciding exactly what you know. Three methods can help you search your memory for information about a topic: brainstorming, freewriting, and filling in a form.

Brainstorming and freewriting can help you pull chunks of related information from your memory. Both methods help you concentrate on content without being distracted by organization. In brainstorming, you make lists of facts on a topic. Try to restrict the list to the facts that seem relevant for your readers. When the brainstorming is completed, look back through your list. Eliminate unnecessary facts and organize the remainder into an arrangement appropriate for your purpose. Besides being used by individuals writing alone, brainstorming is also a favorite method for group problem solving. It is an excellent method for pooling knowledge and talent in solving all kinds of problems, even those that do not require writing.

Consider this example of a writer on the job using brainstorming to get started. David, a Senior Instrument and Control Technician at a local utility, has been assigned to write a procedure for using a new piece of equipment. He sits at his desk, tapping his pencil furiously. He cannot get started. After a trip to the coffee machine and a brief stop by a friend's desk on the way back to his own, David decides to start slowly by jotting down relevant items in a random list instead of trying to write the procedure in its final form. His list includes the purpose of the procedure, the type of instrument discussed, design of the instrument, installation methods, troubleshooting techniques, repair of the instrument, cautions for potential damage to the instrument or harm to the user, and electrical hazards. After the list is complete, he can begin filling in details and organizing the writing.

Freewriting is similar to brainstorming. However, as its name implies, it is even less structured. In freewriting, you should jot down in sentences what you are thinking. Write as quickly as you can, with the understanding that you will stop after a certain length of time. When you finish freewriting, eliminate the unnecessary information and organize the remainder appropriately. You may have to freewrite several times before you gather all the information you need. Because freewriting encourages wandering around with words, it helps some writers get their memories unblocked. Writers know that they can stop after a given period of time, even if they have not finished the planning. Therefore, they are able to dive into the topic rather than staring helplessly at a blank piece of paper.

Filling in a form is different from brainstorming and freewriting. The form tells you what to pull out of your memory. Two types of forms are available in this textbook. First, Chapter 9 gives examples of the printed forms used in most companies for routine communication. Printed forms allow you to plan and write a first draft at the same time. When the printed form is filled in correctly and completely, the writing task is finished. Second, Chapters 9, 10, 11, 12, and 13 provide plan sheets for most technical writing and business correspondence. The plan sheets show what information is most typically included in the writing. Besides helping you gather information, printed forms and plan sheets also help you decide how to organize it.

Types of Plans

All plans require you to make decisions about the content and organization of your writing. However, these directions for writing vary greatly in their length and complexity and their shape. Writers differ in the types of plans that are most effective in inspiring sentences and paragraphs. Some writers prepare very detailed plans. Others can easily plan a 20-page proposal on a small index card. Some writers jot down their plan in words. Others use a combination of words, lines, and shapes. This section explains seven types of plans: lists, outlines, trees, arrows, hub and spokes, S curves, and rough sketches. Not all these types will be appropriate for you. As you read this section, pay close attention to those types that you think are the most useful.

Lists.   Lists include phrases or words that name important ideas in a piece of writing. These words and phrases trigger ideas. Lists show the relationships among ideas by indenting subordinate information under major ideas. Here is a list showing the ideas discussed in this chapter.

> *Purpose: to teach students how to plan, write a first draft, revise, and proofread their writing*
>
> Planning—preliminary decisions about content and organization
>   Methods of planning—how to gather information from memory and organize it
>   Brainstorming
>   Freewriting
>   Filling in forms
>   Types of plans
>   Lists—primarily words
>   Outlines—like lists
>   Trees—words and lines
>   Arrows—lines; used for steps in instructions, stages in a sequence, events in a narrative
>   Hub and spokes—circles and lines; used for factors, causes, examples
>   S curves—S; used for dos and don'ts, pros and cons, benefits and limitations, advantages and disadvantages
>   Rough sketches—plans for drawings
> Writing a first draft
> Revising
>   Questions about content and organization
>   Questions about paragraphs, sentences, and words
> Proofreading

Notice that the purpose is stated across the top to make the goal, or destination of the trip, clear. Notice also that ideas of secondary importance are indented and that the order of ideas shown in the list is the same as the order of the discussion in this chapter.

Outlines.   Outlines are lists with numbers and letters or numbers. In conventional outlines, Roman numbers (I, II, III) point to ideas of the first, most general, level; capital letters (A, B, C) the second level; and Arabic numbers (1, 2, 3) the third level. Fourth and fifth levels are also possible as indicated in this empty outline.

Purpose:

I. First Level
   A. Second level
      1. Third level
      2.
      3.
   B.
II.
   A.
   B.
      1.
         a. Fourth level
         b.
            (1.) Fifth level
            (2.)
         c.
      2.
III.

The list of major ideas in this chapter can easily be converted into an outline.

Purpose: to teach students how to plan, write a first draft, revise, and proofread their writing

I. Planning—preliminary decisions about content and organization
   A. Methods of planning—how to gather information from memory and organize it.
      1. Brainstorming
      2. Freewriting
      3. Filling in forms
   B. Types of plans
      1. Lists—primarily words
      2. Outlines—like lists
      3. Trees—words and lines
      4. Arrows—lines; used for steps in instructions, stages in a sequence, events in a narrative
      5. Hub and spokes—circles and lines; used for factors, causes, examples
      6. S curves—S; used for dos and don'ts, pros and cons, benefits and limitations, advantages and disadvantages
      7. Rough sketches—plans for drawings
II. Writing a first draft
III. Revising
   A. Questions about content and organization
   B. Questions about paragraphs, sentences, and words
IV. Proofreading

Four first-level ideas are "Planning," "Writing a first draft," "Revising," and "Proofreading." Second-level ideas name the two sections, "Methods of planning" and "Types of planning," under "Planning." Second-level ideas also name the two sets of questions involved in "Revising." Third-level ideas name the three methods of planning and the seven types of plans. As plans, outlines work like lists to remind you of content and organization and to provide words that trigger sentences and paragraphs.

In technical writing, outlines often have only Arabic numbers rather than a mixture of Arabic and Roman numbers and letters. Levels are indicated by the sequence of the numbers. A single number followed by a period and a zero (1.0) shows the first level. Two numbers, neither of which is a zero, are separated with a period between them (1.1) to show the second level. Three numbers with periods between each (1.1.1) show the third level. Like the conventional outline, the numbered outline can show as many levels as necessary.

Purpose:

1.0. First level
   1.1. Second level
      1.1.1 Third level
      1.1.2
      1.1.3.
   1.2.
2.0
   2.1.
   2.2.
      2.2.1.
         2.2.1.1. Fourth level
         2.2.1.2.
            2.2.1.2.1 Fifth level
            2.2.1.2.2
         2.2.1.3
      2.2.2
3.0

Trees. Trees show their ideas with a combination of lines and words. The most important idea appears at the top of the tree. Ideas of lesser importance are branches. The information shown in an outline can also be shown in a tree or a group of several trees. Figure 3–1 on page 30 shows a group of trees used as a plan for this chapter.

Purpose: to teach students how to plan, write a first draft, revise, and proofread their writing

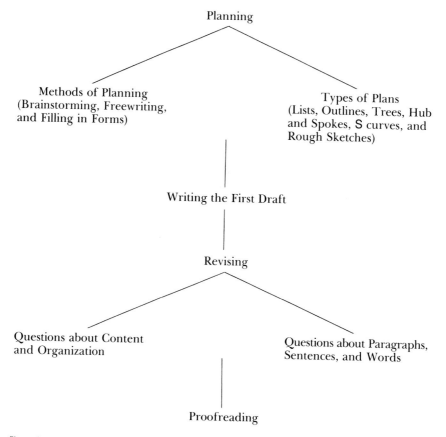

Figure 3-1:   Trees Showing Contents of the Chapter

Arrows.   Like the branches on trees, arrows point to the relationships among ideas. They can point to the sequence of steps in instructions or stages in a process. They can also show the sequence of events in a narrative. Arrows give direction from one step or event to the next and clearly indicate the correct order.

This set of instructions explains how to disinfect drinking water.[1]

Disinfecting Water for Drinking

When safe drinking water is not available, you can disinfect contaminated water by adding iodine tablets.

---

[1]The instructions are adapted from the Department of the Army Soldier's Manual *Ammunition Specialist*. Washington: Government Printing Office, 1980.

Materials: canteen, cup, iodine tablets

Steps:

1. Inspect iodine tablets for changes that may indicate decay. Iodine tablets should not be used if they are crumbled or stuck together or if their color has become gray.
2. Fill the canteen with water. Leave an air space of 1 in. below the neck of the canteen.
3. Add 1 iodine tablet to a 1-quart canteen of clear water. If the water is cloudy, add 2 iodine tablets.
4. Place the cap on the canteen loosely. Wait 5 minutes. Then shake the canteen well. Allow leaking water to rinse the threads around the neck of the canteen.
5. Tighten the cap and wait an additional 20 minutes before using the water for any purpose.

NOTE: If the water is very cold (45°F or below), wait 40 minutes.

Figure 3–2 shows a plan for the instructions. The arrows allow writers to see the steps separately and in sequence. The purpose is stated at the top.

Purpose: to explain how to disinfect water for drinking by using iodine tablets

inspect iodine tablets

fill canteen with water (1 in. from top)

add 1 iodine tablet
place cap on loosely, wait 5 minutes, shake

tighten cap, wait another 20 minutes
(If water is cold, wait 40 minutes.)

Figure 3-2:   Arrows Showing Steps in Instructions

In some cases, the sequence of events is continuous. The last step leads back to the first one. This excerpt discusses the phases of the moon.

The phases of the moon are determined by the positions of the moon, earth, and sun during the moon's 28-day orbit around the earth. The first phase is the new moon. In this phase, the moon is between the sun and the earth. Therefore, it is invisible from the earth. The second phase is the first quarter. In this phase, the moon has gone through a fourth of its orbit, and half its face can be seen from the earth. The third phase is the full moon. In this phase, the moon has completed half of its orbit, and its full face can be seen from the earth. The fourth phase is the third quarter. In this phase, the moon has finished three-fourths of its orbit. Half its face can be seen from the earth. The third quarter is like the first quarter, but a different part of the moon is seen. When the moon completes an orbit, it starts again. The moon begins its phases with the invisible new moon.

Figure 3–3 shows the plan for the excerpt. The arrows that circle back indicate that the moon's cycle is continuous. The fourth phase leads back to the first phase.

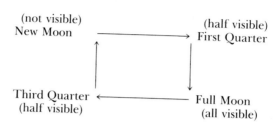

Purpose: to explain the phases of the moon

(not visible)
New Moon ⟶ (half visible)
First Quarter

Third Quarter ⟵ Full Moon
(half visible) (all visible)

Figure 3-3: Arrows Showing a Sequence that Repeats

Hub and Spokes. Hub and spokes[2] is another way of showing information with words, shapes, and lines. Hub and spokes can show the types of items that make up a group, the factors involved in an event, or the causes of a problem. In a slightly different use, hub and spokes can show a main idea supported by examples. All applications of the hub and spokes plan have a similar design. A general statement or category is the hub. Items that give specific information about the hub are spokes. These items are equally important, and they do not overlap.

This excerpt gives information about how to buy a computer. The writer describes three types of computers according to the most likely reason for purchase.

According to what you expect in return for your money, three types of computers are available: the computer designed to help you achieve a basic level of computer literacy, the computer designed to provide entertainment for you and your kids, and the computer designed to help you do work.

The "basic literacy" computer will help you get comfortable with computers and learn something about what computers do. These computers let you play games and practice simple programming. However, they do not provide for fancy word processing or elaborate financial spread sheets. At under $100 (not including the television display and other devices), "basic literacy" computers are best-sellers.

The "entertainment" computer allows you to play arcade games at home. These computers have colors, sound effects, and a choice of exciting recrea-

---

[2]The hub and spokes and the S curve are suggested by Susan Feinberg in "Visual Patterns: An Experiment with Technically Oriented Writers." *Technical Communication* 31 (1984): 20–22. With permission from the Society for Technical Communication, we have modified and expanded this discussion.

tional and educational games. Besides the video game console, some of these computers come with add-on keyboards. The keyboards allow the computers to be used in more serious ways. Prices range for "entertainment" computers from $100 to $500.

The "work" computer is designed to make the work of running a home or a small business easier. These computers can help you prepare financial statements, print out mailing lists, or even write a book. They help you get organized, and they play games too. The "work" computer starts at $1000.

The three choices of computer and the basis for their selection are shown in Figure 3–4. The hub contains the basis for establishing the types. The spokes point to the different items.

Purpose: to describe the types of home computers. Types are established according to most likely motives for buying

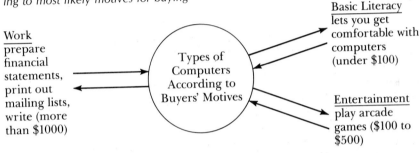

Figure 3-4: Hub and Spokes Showing Types

S *Curves.* A final combination of lines and words is the **S** curve. The **S** curve can show dos and don'ts, pros and cons, or benefits and limitations. The positive side (dos, pros, benefits) is usually laid out in the top of the **S**. The negative side (don'ts, cons, limitations) is usually laid out in the bottom. This excerpt explains the benefits and limitations of using clay pots for plants.

Clay pots are good containers for growing plants. They are easy to find in most stores, and they come in a variety of sizes and shapes. Since they are porous, they allow moisture to evaporate through their sides to keep plants from being overwatered. Clay pots are also durable and attractive. They blend in with most patios.

However, they do have some limitations. Compared to paper and wooden containers, clay pots are breakable and expensive. When filled with damp soil, they can be heavy and difficult to move. In addition, their porosity lets the potting mix dry out quickly so that plants in clay pots require frequent watering.

Figure 3–5 on page 34 shows the benefits and limitations discussed in this excerpt. Notice that the benefits (the pros) are listed in the top of the **S**, while the limitations (the cons) are listed in the bottom. This order is the same as the order of the excerpt.

Rough Sketches. Rough sketches are plans for drawings that will appear in the final version of the piece of writing. These plans for drawing often provide

Purpose: *to explain the benefits and limitations of clay pots*

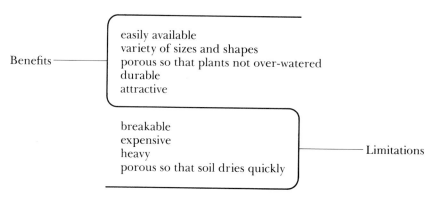

Benefits
- easily available
- variety of sizes and shapes
- porous so that plants not over-watered
- durable
- attractive

- breakable
- expensive
- heavy
- porous so that soil dries quickly

Limitations

Figure 3-5:   S Curve Showing Benefits and Limitations

useful guides for writing. If the piece of writing is short and the content is familiar, rough sketches may be the only type of preliminary planning needed. For example, a technical writer is writing a discussion of a four-stroke diesel engine as a part of a Navy training manual. He wants to explain what happens during intake, compression, power, and exhaust. Before he begins writing words and sentences, the writer draws four rough sketches. The sketches remind the writer of the content and organization of the passage, and the final versions will appear in the finished manual. To be useful as plans, the sketches must show the positions of the piston; the changes in the intake valve, the injector, and the exhaust valve; and the rotated positions of the crankshaft for each stroke. The writer labels the parts of the piston on the first drawing.

WRITING A FIRST DRAFT

When you have completed your plan, you can begin to write a first draft. You express the ideas you want to communicate to your readers in sentences and paragraphs organized according to your plan. You can complete the writing task most efficiently if you write your first draft quickly. In this draft, get your thoughts down in sentences. However, do not worry about choosing exactly the right words or about correcting misspelled words and incorrect punctuation. This first attempt at writing sentences and paragraphs will later be revised extensively. Although no two pieces of writing are the same, you probably can write more successfully if you prepare a plan and if you revise according to an established procedure.

REVISING

Revision acts as a control on the ideas created during planning. It checks earlier choices of content and style. Revision helps you shape your drafts into convincing messages. The checking and shaping may lead to major changes in the plan and minor changes in paragraphs, sentences, and words. This section explains a procedure which will help you learn what to look for when you revise. It will help you decide when to revise your plan and begin a new draft and when to revise sentences or change words without revising your plan.

The procedure contains two sets of questions that you should ask yourself each time you try to revise a piece of writing. When you read the questions for the first time, you may not know what some of them mean. However, with practice, the questions will become easier to understand and more helpful as guides for revision. Each set of questions has references to other chapters in this textbook. At the end of the chapter is a set of guidelines. You should use these guidelines as the basis for revision with all the writing assignments in this textbook.

The goal of the procedure is simple: Revision is more efficient if you start with the major considerations (those that may require you to revise your plan) and move to the minor ones (those that do not require you to revise your plan). With this general goal in mind, you should begin revising a piece of writing by carefully examining its content and organization. When you think that you have included all the necessary information and organized that information in an arrangement that will achieve your purpose, you should then examine the paragraphs, sentences, and words used in the writing.

Questions about Content and Organization

The first consideration in revising is to ensure that the content and organization are correct and appropriate. You should think back to your readers and your purpose. Answer the following questions:

1. Do I discuss ideas appropriate for my reader? My reader is _____.
   My reader (1) knows as much as I do about my topic (2) knows more than I do about my topic (3) knows nothing about my topic. (See Chapter 2.)
2. Why does my reader need this piece of writing? My reader needs this piece of writing so that _____ . (See Chapter 2.)
3. Does my content achieve my purpose? My purpose is _____ . (See Chapter 2.)
4. Do I support and explain my purpose with sufficient and appropriate details and examples? Put a check beside each. (See Chapters 4 and 6.)
5. Do my conclusions, recommendations, or questions follow logically from what has gone before? Draw arrows from conclusions and recommendations to supporting information.

6. Do I include only necessary information? Do I discuss only what my reader needs to know and will understand? (See Chapter 2.)

7. Do I organize my information in an arrangement appropriate for my purpose? (See the plan sheet provided for the piece of writing.)

If you cannot answer these questions or if the answer to any of them is no, you should rethink your reasons for writing. You should ask yourself what you intend to accomplish. You should then examine your plan closely. In some cases, you may have to scrap the first plan, design a new plan, and begin a new draft. In other cases, you may be able to take apart an existing plan, put it back together in a different way, and shift around paragraphs in current draft. All kinds of changes are possible: You can add or delete information, change minor points to major ones, and include summaries or examples.

Questions about Paragraphs, Sentences, and Words

The second consideration in revising is to ensure that the paragraphs are developed logically, the sentences are easy to read, and the words are appropriate for the intended readers. Answer the following questions:

1. Do I develop my paragraphs logically? Put an X beside the topic sentence in each paragraph or section of closely related paragraphs. (See Chapter 5.)

2. Do I relate my sentences clearly to each together? Do I build new ideas on top of what the reader already knows? Do I use signal words and phrases to name connections that the reader may not understand? (See Chapter 6.)

3. Are my sentences easy to read? Have I eliminated any unnecessary words? (See Chapter 6.)

4. Do I use words appropriate for my reader and purpose? If your reader is a customer, cross out all technical words that are not necessary. If any technical words are necessary to the understanding of your message, define them. (See Chapter 6.)

If you cannot answer these questions or if the answer to any of them is no, you should examine the paragraphs, sentences, and words in your draft. Since you have decided on your content and organization, you probably do not need to revise your plan. You have decided what to say, and now you are concerned with how to say it. However, while you are looking closely at your paragraphs, sentences, and words, keep in mind that sometimes small changes can reveal larger problems. You may think that your content and organization are correct and appropriate but later find that when you start fiddling with paragraphs, sentences, and words, important information is missing.

You should begin your assessment with the largest of this second group of considerations: paragraphs. You should examine your paragraphs for topic sentences. Although every paragraph does not need a topic sentence, paragraphs that introduce new ideas use these general statements to connect to old ideas and to summarize the new content and forecast its arrangement. After checking for topic sentences, you should be sure that each sentence connects clearly with the one before and after. Once you are sure that your paragraphs are logically and clearly developed, you should try to cut out any unnecessary words to make the sentences as easy to read as possible. Finally, you need to be sure that you have defined any technical words that your reader may not understand. As a test for your revision, read the writing aloud. If it does not "sound right," your revision is probably not finished.

PROOFREADING

Proofreading ensures that your writing is correct according to the rules of standard written American English. It requires you to check for errors in usage, punctuation, and spelling. These errors are like gnats on a hot summer day. Although they do not change the meaning of your message, they irritate your readers. They may detract from your content. Proofreading is the last task in the writing process. You should not begin to proofread until you have finished revising and your draft is ready to be copied neatly or typed. Proofread the last revision carefully, copy or type it, and proofread the writing one last time before you submit it to your readers.

To proofread effectively, you need to examine your writing sentence by sentence and word by word. Begin by reading each sentence separately. Identify the main clauses and subordinate clauses to check for sentence fragments, comma splices, and fused sentences. Check the subjects and verbs in each clause to see that they agree, and be sure that the pronouns refer clearly to the nouns that name them. After your sentence-by-sentence check, examine any punctuation marks that you may have missed. Then proofread word by word. Force your eyes to stop and focus on each word to check spelling. Some writers claim that reading backwards forces them to proofread word by word. Others use their finger or the tip of their pencil to point to each word and slow down their normal reading rate.

Here is a set of questions to help with proofreading. If you do not understand the terms used, refer to the discussion of standard written American English in Appendixes A and B.

1. Have you proofread sentence by sentence?
   Check main clauses and subordinate clauses.
      fragments   yes _____ no _____
      comma splices   yes _____ no _____
      fused sentences yes _____ no _____
   Check subjects and verbs.
      errors in subject-verb agreement   yes _____ no _____
   Check pronouns and the nouns they refer to.
      errors in pronoun reference   yes _____ no _____
      errors in pronoun-antecedent agreement   yes _____ no _____
2. Have you checked your punctuation?
      periods   yes _____ no _____
      question marks   yes _____ no _____

semicolons   yes _____ no _____
commas   yes _____ no _____
others   yes _____ no _____

3. Have you proofread word by word?
   errors in spelling   yes _____ no _____
4. Has the writing been neatly copied or typed?
   yes _____ no _____
5. Have you proofread this final, neat version?
   yes _____ no _____

SUMMARY

Plans are preliminary decisions about content and organization made before you begin to write sentences and paragraphs. Brainstorming and freewriting can help you gather information for your plans. Filling in forms can help you organize as well as gather information for planning. Plans can be shown with words; or they can use a combination of words, lines, and shapes. Lists and outlines rely on words. Trees, arrows, hub and spokes, and S curves show content and organization with lines and shapes as well as words. Rough sketches, which serve as preliminary designs for drawings, can also act as plans for writing. Based on your plan, you should jot down a first draft as quickly as possible. Then you can revise that draft. Revision acts as a check on planning. It requires you to consider two sets of questions. The first set asks about changes in content and organization. The second set asks about changes in paragraphs, sentences, and words. When you have finished revising your draft, proofread it carefully for errors in standard written American English. Then neatly type or copy the draft and proofread it once more before submitting the piece of writing to your reader.

ASSIGNMENTS

Application:
Designing Plans

Below are three excerpts. Based on the types of plans described in this chapter, design at least two ways of showing the information in each excerpt. Choose lists, outlines, trees, arrows, hub and spokes, or S curves. Use as many different plans as necessary to show a single excerpt. Remember that your design must allow the writer to remember all the content and to organize the passage. Also be certain to write down the purpose at the top of each plan.

A. This excerpt gives the history of the evolution of ketchup.[3] It begins with a discussion of where ketchup was first made and ends with a description of the condiment's current version.

Ketchup was first made in the Orient. According to the H. J. Heinz Company, its ancestor is one of the fermented fish sauces that have been popular in the Far East for centuries. After its discovery by British sailors, ketchup slowly changed from a smelly fish sauce to the tomato sauce that appears on so many hamburgers today.

In the late seventeenth century, British sailors sailed to all parts of the globe to establish an empire for their country. During their travels, they found the natives of Singapore and Malaysia using "kechap." This sauce was a tangy blend of fish brine, herbs, and spices. When they returned to England, they tried to copy the sauce. However, they did not have the ingredients available in the Far East, and they had to make do with a sauce of mushrooms, walnuts, and cucumbers.

Soon ketchup became popular in England. Recipes for it appeared in a 1748 cookbook and later in Mrs. Breeton's *Book of Household Management*. Mrs Breeton offered a number of recipes for ketchup. She advised young homemakers: "This flavoring ingredient, if genuine and well prepared, is one of the most useful sauces to the experienced cook, and no trouble should be spared in its preparation." American housewives were also cooking up batches of ketchup. They used more or less the same ingredients as the British: spices and vinegar. To this base, Americans added grapes, berries, or lobsters. No sugar was added. When the sauce was cooked, the solids were discarded. Since no tomatoes were used, the early English and American ketchups were not like our ketchup. Instead, they resembled today's Worcestershire sauce.

Finally, someone put the fish sauce, minus the fish, and the tomato together. The result was a sauce similar to the ketchup we know today. By the 1870s, ketchup contained both tomatoes and added sugar. H. J. Heinz first produced bottled ketchup in 1876.

B. This excerpt describes the types of life insurance available and makes suggestions about selecting the policy that best suits a potential buyer.[4]

Most people buy life insurance to protect someone who depends on them for financial support. In the past, men bought life insurance to protect their wives and children. Now many wives also bring in salaries essential to maintaining a family's financial lifestyle. Therefore, women also buy life insurance. The three basic types of life insurance are term insurance, whole life insurance, and endowment insurance. Most other policies are variations of these types.

Term insurance protects your family for a specified period of time. Usually the period of time ranges from one to 20 years or until you are 65. Term insurance pays only if you die during the period covered by the insurance. At the end of the term the coverage agreed upon earlier stops. However, another term can often be established if you are willing to pay a higher rate.

[3]The information about ketchup is adapted from "The Evolution of Ketchup." *FDA Consumer* July-August, 1984:27.
[4]The information about life insurance policies is adapted from a pamphlet published by the American Council of Life Insurance, *A Consumer's Guide to Life Insurance*.

Whole life insurance protects your family for an indefinite period. In the beginning whole life is more expensive than term insurance. However, the premium does not increase as you grow older. The costs are averaged out over your lifetime. Also unlike term insurance, whole life insurance has a "cash value." Cash value is the sum you receive if the insurance is cancelled. Cash value increases through the years.

Endowment insurance protects your family by building up the money that is invested. After a certain number of years or when you reach a certain age, the endowment matures. It then pays the amount of the policy. If you die before the endowment matures, the money is paid to your beneficiary. Endowment insurance is the most expensive of the three types.

In deciding which type of insurance to buy, you should consider your particular needs. Consider these examples. Fred Janzasik is 25 years old. He is married and has two small children. To protect his wife and children in case of his unexpected death, Fred should probably buy term insurance. Since he is young and healthy, this type is the least expensive. Fred's father, Elbert Janzasik, may make a different choice. He is 45 years old and smokes two packs of cigarettes a day. Even though Fred is no longer dependent on him, Elbert still supports two children and a wife. He should probably buy whole life insurance. Although whole life insurance is expensive in the beginning, it has a fixed rate and a cash value accumulates. Reginald Hawkins III owns the garage where Fred works. He is 55 years old and has just inherited a large sum of cash from his mother. Reginald invests this cash in endowment insurance to plan for his retirement.

C. This excerpt discusses the benefits and limitations of word processors.

Word processors have many important time-saving benefits for their users. One time-saving benefit is that they make typing easier and faster. Word processors allow minor and major revisions without retyping the entire document. Many users also claim that with the fear of error reduced, their typing speed increases. A second time-saving benefit is that word processors encourage writers to learn to compose without a handwritten draft. The lack of noise and the ease of correction on word processors make it possible for many users to move from their plan to the keyboard. In addition, many software packages have a thesaurus and a spell checker to help writers find words and spell them correctly. Some even have a grammar checker.

In spite of their many benefits, word processors have some limitations. A major limitation is the time required to learn how to use the machine and its software. This initial investment of time will be paid back easily as soon as the user becomes proficient. A second limitation is the lack of flexibility of some software packages. Unlike typewriters, some word processors use software packages that do not allow the addition of a few words at the bottom of a page or indention in some unprescribed place. A final limitation is the initial cost of most word processors. A good word processor and a letter-quality printer cost about $2000, and many systems are three or four times that price. Good electric or electronic typewriters are cheaper.

We have not included any applications that provide practice with the revision procedure described in this chapter. As indicated in the two sets of questions, you will learn more about the procedure in the chapters that follow. While you work the applications at the end of those chapters, think back to the revision procedure. The Guidelines for Revision will be directly referred to in later chapters.

GUIDELINES FOR REVISION

Content and Organization

1. My purpose is

2. My reader is _____ .
   These readers need the writing because

3. I have filled in the plan sheet for this piece of writing to make decisions about content and organization. yes _____ no _____ .

Paragraphs, Sentences, and Words

1. I have underlined the topic sentence in each paragraph or section of related paragraphs. yes _____ no _____

2. I have checked to be sure that my sentences relate clearly to each other. yes _____ no _____

3. I have eliminated an unnecessary words. yes _____ no _____

4. I have defined any technical words that my reader may not understand. yes _____ no _____

5. I have read my writing aloud and listened for anything that breaks the smooth flow. yes _____ no _____

WHEN YOU FINISH YOUR REVISION, PROOFREAD YOUR WRITING CAREFULLY. COPY OR TYPE IT NEATLY. PROOFREAD AGAIN BEFORE SUBMITTING THE FINAL VERSION TO YOUR READER.

4

ORGANIZING INFORMATION IN STANDARD PATTERNS

When you finish this chapter, you should know how to organize information according to seven patterns. You should learn these patterns of organization:

Definition
  Sentence definition
  Expanded definition
Description
Classification and division
Comparison
Cause and effect
Time sequence
  Narrative
  Process
Details and examples

Standard organizational patterns are methods for arranging information to achieve a purpose. These patterns allow you to present your major points in an order that is familiar to most readers. This chapter will discuss seven patterns for arranging information: definition, description, classification and division, comparison, cause and effect, time sequence, and details and examples. Although this chapter will consider each pattern separately, they seldom appear alone. Most often, they are used together. The assignments at the end of the chapter show how these patterns work together.

DEFINITION

Definitions provide concise, but exact, meanings for unfamiliar words and explain special meanings for familiar words. The words may name a process, object, or concept. Used with other methods of development, definitions introduce new ideas. They are often used to explain technical words and concepts. Definitions can be informal or formal. Informal definitions are synonyms (words that share the same meaning) or explanatory phrases that appear in the same sentence with the unfamiliar word. As shown in parentheses in the previous sentence, an informal definition can be used when the reader does not need much information about the word. Formal definitions are found in dictionaries and glossaries. They also introduce paragraphs or longer sections in a piece of writing. Occasionally they appear as explanatory notes at the bottom of the page. This section is concerned primarily with formal definitions.

What to define and what information to include in a definition depend on the needs of the reader and the purpose of the communication. For customers, you should avoid technical words as often as possible. Customers are interested in hiring someone to do a job for them or in buying a product. They are not interested in learning the special technology of a field. If technical words are essential to justify cost or explain a method, they should be quickly and simply defined. For technicians, you should also avoid needless technical words and their definitions. You should keep definitions of new words and the related explanations of new technology as simple as possible. When asked to remember too many definitions at one time, readers get so tangled in the words that they miss the point of the writing. Depending on the needs of the reader and the purpose of the communication, definitions may be limited to single sentences or expanded to several paragraphs.

Sentence Definition

Sentence definitions are written according to an established form: WORD + is + CLASS + DIFFERENCE. WORD is the name of the object, process, or concept defined. "Is" or "are" make the definition into a sentence. CLASS is the general group to which the object, process, or concept belongs. All members of the same CLASS share certain common characteristics. For example, a chair is "a piece of furniture," and changing the oil is "a maintenance procedure." DIFFERENCE is the distinctive feature that separates the object, process, or concept from other members of its class. A chair and a table are both pieces of furniture. However, a chair is different from a table because it has four legs, a seat, and a back and is used by one person for sitting. Changing the oil is different from rotating the tires, another maintenance procedure, because it requires that the dirty, old oil be replaced with new, clean oil.

Look at the class and difference for the words on page 44.

Word	Class	Difference
time efficiency incentive	promised reward	that encourages a worker to finish a task on schedule or ahead of schedule
embryo transfer	medical procedure	in which a fertilized egg is removed from the reproductive tract of a donor animal and inserted into the womb of a recipient animal
no-tillage planting	farming procedure	in which a crop is planted without turning up the seedbed
acid rain	secondary pollution	that occurs when certain chemicals in the air combine with atmospheric water vapor and fall to the earth as rain

These definitions are easier to read when they are written as sentences.

Time efficiency incentive is a promised reward that encourages a worker to finish a task on schedule or ahead of schedule.

Embryo transfer is a medical procedure in which a fertilized egg is removed from the reproductive tract of a donor animal and inserted into the womb of a recipient animal.

No-tillage planting is a farming procedure in which the crop is planted without turning up the seedbed.

Acid rain is secondary pollution that occurs when certain chemicals in the air combine with atmospheric water vapor and fall to the earth as rain.

Three general rules are important in writing sentence definitions.

○ The definition must be less technical than the word. A sentence definition will not help a reader understand an unfamiliar word if it is made of equally unfamiliar words.

○ The class must not be eliminated. Many writers are tempted to skip the class and jump into the difference. They replace the class with the less exact words "where" or "when." For example, "Acid rain is when certain chemicals in the air combine with atmospheric water vapor" leaves out the important information that acid rain is secondary pollution.

○ Most often, the definition should not contain the word that is defined. When the word is repeated in the class or difference, the definition is circular. For example, "embryo transfer is a medical procedure for transferring embryos" is not informative. In some cases, however, repeating the word is less confusing and more exact than supplying a synonym. In the definition of no-tillage planting, replacing the word "planted" with a phrase such as "put into the ground" lengthens and confuses the sentence. Awkward attempts to avoid repeating a common word—"No-tillage planting is a farm procedure in which impregnation by seeds can occur without turning up the ground"—are often difficult to understand as well as silly.

For more examples of sentence definitions, you can consult a dictionary of technical words used in your field. Sentence definitions are also found in manuals, standards, procedures, and textbooks.

Expanded Definition

When the reader needs more than a brief explanation, a sentence definition can be added to or expanded. Usually an expanded definition is a paragraph or two long. It gives a general discussion of an object, process, or concept. The methods for expanding a sentence definition include other standard patterns of organization explained later in this chapter. Below is a list of the most typical methods of expansion.

> *Explanation of use or function.* How the object, process, or concept is used, and its benefits and limitations can be given.
>
> *Description of parts.* If the word defined is an object, the object's parts can be listed and briefly described.
>
> *Basic operating principle.* If the word defined is an object, a brief explanation of how the object works can be included. If the word defined is a process, the explanation can tell what happens during the process or how the process is performed.
>
> *Comparison.* The object, process, or concept can be compared to something familiar to the reader. Likenesses and differences can be pointed out.
>
> *Origin of the word.* The historical background for the word can be given. This method of expansion is particularly effective with medical words or other words derived from Latin roots. It is also effective for new words that name recent technical advancements. For example, osteoporosis is a bone disease which weakens the skeleton and can lead to fractures of the hip, back, or legs. The word "osteoporosis" comes from two Greek words. *Osteo* is the root of the Greek word for bone. *Porosis* is a Greek word that means passage. Literally, osteoporosis is a disease caused by abnormal passageways in the bone.
>
> *Examples.* Examples of how the object, process, or concept is used or where it occurs can be included. This method of expansion helps readers understand the function.
>
> *Negation.* This method of expansion tells readers what the word does *not* mean or what the object, process, or concept is *not*. It can be used to warn readers not to confuse the word defined with a similar word.
>
> *Visual aids.* If the word defined is an object, the object can be illustrated with diagrams or sketches; or, if it is a process, it can be shown with a flowchart.

An expanded definition of a relief valve appears on page 46.[1] This type of introduction to technical words and the devices they name is often found in training manuals. The reader does not read the definition to satisfy a general interest but to gain knowledge that can be used on the job.

---

[1] The information and drawing of the relief valve are adapted from the Naval Education and Training Command Rate Training Manual *Fireman.* Washington: Government Printing Office, 1982.

Relief valves are controlling devices that open automatically to reduce pressure when it has become dangerously high. They are installed in water, oil, and air lines and in certain machines. Relief valves protect piping much the same way that fuses protect electrical equipment and wiring in a house. They release pressure that could overload the system.

Most relief valves operate with either a disk or a steel ball acting against a coil spring. The disk-type relief valve is shown in Figure 4-1A. It consists of a valve body, a valve disk, a stem, and a steel spring. The spring pushes down on the disk and keeps the valve closed. The force on the bottom of the disk is exerted by the pressure of the fluid in the line. When this force becomes greater than the compression of the spring, the disk is pushed off the seat. The valve opens. The ball-type valve is shown in Figure 4-1B. It operates on the same principle as the disk-type valve. However, instead of a stem and disk, it has a ball. When the ball is pushed off the seat, the valve opens. Then the pressure in the line is released.

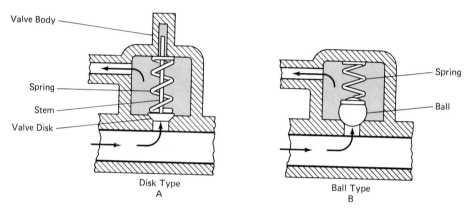

Figure 4-1:   Two Types of Relief Valves

Notice the first sentence. It is a sentence definition that establishes a clear focus for this excerpt. Also notice the methods of expansion used: explanation of use, comparison with a familiar item (fuse), list of parts, basic operating principle, and visual aid.

Here is another expanded definition. Unlike the technicians who read the first example, these readers do not need this writing to perform their jobs. Instead, they are similar to the customers who ask for general information about your products.

Aspirin is an over-the-counter drug used to reduce pain, swelling, and fever. The technical name of aspirin is acetylsalicylic acid. Aspirin belongs to a family of drugs called salicylates. It is a relative of the willow bark Hippocrates gave patients 2300 years ago. Willow bark's principal ingredient is salicin. Salicin occurs in many other trees and shrubs, including the spirea plant. In the nineteenth century, scientists learned to extract salicylic acid from its natural sources. They prescribed salicylic acid to lower fevers and reduce pain. But salicylic acid irritated the mouth, throat, and stomach. In the late 1890s a less harsh compound, acetylsalicylic acid, was developed. Acetylsalicylic acid was called "aspirin." "A" stands for "acetyl" and "spir" for the *Spiraea* genus of plants.

Soon aspirin was being used all over the world. Its major uses today are still for fever, headache, and muscle ache, and the pain and swelling of arthritis. Aspirin lowers fever temperatures rapidly although it does not affect normal temperatures. For a patient with fever, aspirin resets the body's temperature to normal. It also releases the body's excess heat by increasing sweating and blood flow in the skin.

Again notice that the expanded definition begins with a sentence definition. It continues with an explanation of the word's origin along with a brief history of the development of aspirin, examples of its use, and its basic operating principle.

DESCRIPTION

In writing on the job, description is most often used to point out the physical characteristics of an object. What should be described and how much detail should be included are determined by the readers and the purpose of the description. Depending on the needs of the readers, descriptions can be one paragraph or several hundred pages long. Chapter 12 explains how to write a technical description of an object by describing each individual part. This section offers only a general explanation.

Often a description is introduced with a sentence definition to classify the object and point out its most important features or functions. Then the rest of the description is organized according to the order in which you want the audience to "see" the object: from left to right, top to bottom, inside to outside. Information about the shape, size, color, and parts of an object is included. If necessary, the material the object is made of is identified. The information must be exact. Here are some examples.

Shape: square; round; octagonal; rectangular
Size: 16 ft 3 in. × 14 ft 2 in.; 250 lb; about 4 inches longer and 50 pounds heavier than the old copier it replaces
Color: gray; black; red; white with $\frac{1}{2}$ inch black tips; 3 inches long with a black body and six orange legs
Parts: A stop valve is a controlling device used to close off a pipe or opening so that fluid cannot pass through. The typical stop valve consists of the body, an opening through which the fluid flows (port), a movable disk for closing this opening, and some means to raise and lower the disk.

Plaster is composed of the following ingredients: aggregate (usually sand), water, and a binder to hold the other two ingredients together.
Material made of: 100 percent cotton; steel; carbon dioxide and water vapor

Besides specific information about these five characteristics, descriptions often contain comparisons. Comparisons tell readers how the object described is like or how it is not like a more familiar object. Descriptions are also often accompanied by drawings of the object.

Here is a short description giving the characteristics of a field pack.[2] The intended audience is Navy Seabees, who may have to carry the pack during field operations.

The field pack is a cotton duck bag used to carry rations and equipment essential during field operations. The front and back are shown in Figure 4-2. When it is full, the field pack is approximately 9 inches wide, 8 $\frac{3}{4}$ inches high, and 5 inches deep. It has a waterproof throat at the top. Also at the top is an expandable flap kept in place by two web straps and buckles. A handle is located on the flap so the pack can be carried in your hand as well as on your back. A plastic identification card is also located on the flap. The field pack has two web straps on the bottom. These straps allow items to be attached to the pack. On the back are two attaching clips and eyelets so the pack can be attached to your suspenders and pistol belt.

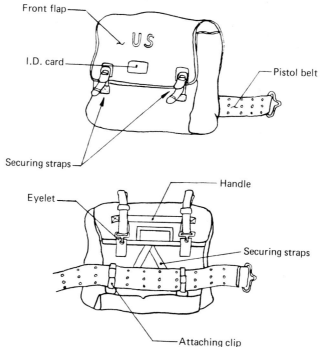

Notice that in this excerpt, the writer helps the reader see the field pack by giving the overall dimensions and describing the object from top to bottom and front to back. He also includes a drawing of the field pack. The writer begins with a sentence definition to classify and to explain the pack's major function.

[2] The information about the field pack is adapted from the Naval Education and Training Command Rate Training Manual and Nonresident Career Course *Seabee Combat Handbook*. Washington: Government Printing Office, 1976.

The second description is slightly different from the first. Rather than describing an object's appearance, this excerpt describes the six components of flour.[3]

Composition of Flour

Wheat flour is used to make bread. It has six ingredients that are essential to the bread-making process: moisture, starch, proteins, fat, minerals, and enzymes.

Moisture. Wheat flour usually contains from 9 to 15 percent moisture. Flour either absorbs moisture or loses it in storage, depending on atmospheric conditions.

Starch. Wheat flour contains from 70 to 75 percent starch. When flour is used to make bread, starch supplies food for the yeast. The yeast is the ingredient that makes the bread rise. Before it can be used by the yeast, the starch must be changed to sugar. This change is a natural part of the bread-making process.

Proteins. Five different proteins are found in wheat flour. When combined with water, these proteins become a tough elastic substance called gluten. Gluten forms the structure of bread. It gives dough the necessary strength and elasticity to rise without allowing the air bubbles from the yeast to break through.

Fat. Wheat flour contains approximately 1.5 percent fat.

Minerals. Minerals in wheat flour are commonly referred to as "ash." Ash consists of the phosphates of lime, magnesium, and potassium. Ash content in wheat flour runs from 0.4 percent to about 0.48 percent. Enriched flour has a higher ash content than flour that is not enriched.

Enzymes. The two principal enzymes in wheat flour are diastase and protease.

Diastase. Diastase converts starch to sugar for the yeast to feed on. Since diastase performs a vital function, it is a necessary component of flour. However, too much diastase makes dough sticky.

Protease. Protease softens gluten and makes it elastic. Flour usually has a high protease content.

According to this description, flour has six major components: moisture, starch, proteins, fat, minerals, and enzymes. The two enzymes present are diastase and protease. These components give flour its unique characteristics and make it different from cornmeal or sugar.

CLASSIFICATION AND DIVISION

Classification and division are methods for organizing information in groups or classes. These patterns operate like filing systems to sort through ideas and establish relationships. Each file is composed of information grouped according to some common feature. Although both classification and division are concerned with forming groups, they operate differently. Classification organizes

[3] The information about the composition of flour is adapted from the Army and Air Force technical manual *Pastry Baking*. Washington: Government Printing Office, 1966.

forward, while division looks backward. Classification *brings together* related items. It begins with the most specific and moves toward the most general. For example, as patients are admitted to a hospital, they are classified according to the treatment they need. Pregnant women are put together in the Obstetrics Unit; people undergoing surgery are placed in the Surgical Unit. Critically ill patients who need constant attention are placed in the Intensive Care Unit, while less seriously ill patients are assigned beds in a Medical Unit. On the other hand, rather than bringing together related items, division *breaks apart* a large group into smaller groups. According to how they operate, pumps fall into five categories: reciprocating, rotary, centrifugal, propeller, and jet. Classification forms groups from individual items. Division breaks down a large group into subgroups. The two organizational techniques have similar goals, and they often arrive at the same place.

Four major rules are important in classification and division.

○ The groups must be established according to a consistent principle. For example, the custodian of a toolroom decides to classify tools according to use. He cannot place a level in the same group as a pair of cable cutters, even if the tools are almost the same size. Whether classifying separate items into groups or dividing a large group into subgroups, you must base your decision on a single factor. Some factors are size, location, method of operation, cause, and effect.

○ The names given to the groups must be similar in form. The five types of pumps cannot be labeled "reciprocating," "rotary," "pumps that are centrifugal," "pumps that operate with propellors," and "jet." "Pumps that are centrifugal" and "pumps that operate with propellors" are written in forms that differ from the other three.

○ The groups must be large enough to include a significant number of items. The custodian of a toolroom should not divide tools so that one group contains only one tool while all the other groups cover five or six different tools. At the same time, he should also avoid very large groups. A group that includes 20 different tools covers three or four times as many items as the other groups. Groups should be proportional.

○ The groups must not overlap. For example, two types of tools cannot be "measuring instruments" and "measuring gages" because the second group should be included in the first.

This excerpt discusses the types of bricks according to grade.[4]

Brick Masonry

Brick masonry is a type of construction in which units of baked clay or shale of uniform size are laid next to each other with mortar joints. Unlike concrete blocks, bricks are small enough to be placed with one hand. They are laid on top of and beside each other to build walls of unlimited length and height. Bricks are made from clay and shale mixtures. They are baked in kilns until

[4] The information about brick masonry is adapted from the Naval Training Command Rate Training Manual *Builder I & C*. Washington: Government Printing Office, 1973.

they reach the desired hardness. The chemical and physical characteristics of the clay and shale vary considerably. These characteristics along with varying kiln temperatures produce brick in a range of colors, hardnesses, and grades. The more common grades are those designed for exposure to severe, moderate, and negligible weather conditions. The bricks are designated SW, MW, and NW.

Grade SW is brick designed to withstand exposure to below-freezing temperatures in a moist climate. This climate occurs in the northern regions of the United States.

Grade MW is brick designed to withstand exposure to below-freezing temperatures in a drier climate.

Grade NW is brick intended primarily for interior or backup brick. However, it may be used exposed in regions where no frost occurs. It may be used as exterior brick in regions where frost occurs occasionally but the annual rainfall is less than 15 inches.

The dimensions of the standard U.S. building brick are 2½ inches × 3¾ inches × 8 inches. The actual dimensions of brick may vary a little because of shrinkage during burning.

The principle of division is the effects of weather on the brick. Based on this principle, three classes of brick—SW, MW, and NW—are established. Notice that the excerpt begins with a sentence definition.

COMPARISON

Comparison is used to explain how two or more items are alike and how they are different. Before they can be compared, all the items must be members of the same class, and the criteria for the comparison must be established. Some comparisons are short, two opposing sentences. Some are long, several paragraphs or pages.

Three rules are important in comparisons.

○ The items compared must be members of the same class. It is difficult to imagine what an automotive technician could accomplish by trying to compare a carburetor to an oil can.

○ Criteria for comparison are established in advance. For example, the criteria used to determine the purchase of office copy machines may include initial cost, ease of operation, availability of maintenance, and cost for yearly maintenance. The office manager responsible for making the comparison will establish the criteria before she looks at any machines.

○ Once the criteria are established, two ways of arranging the comparison are possible. One way focuses on the items being compared. The other way focuses on the criteria. The two methods of arrangement are shown in the two excerpts on page 52.

In the first excerpt, each item is discussed separately. The emphasis is on the items. The comparison is between two artificial sweeteners, saccharin and aspartame (trade name Nutrasweet). Saccharin is discussed first, and aspartame second.

> Diabetics, dieters, and other people interested in reducing the amount of sugar they consume have two choices of artificial sweetener: saccharin and aspartame. Saccharin is the older of the two products. It has been linked to cancer in rats. Aspartame is the newest artificial sweetener available today. It seems to have few ill effects.
>
> *Saccharin* is approximately 300 times sweeter than sugar. It has no calories. However, it has been linked to cancer in laboratory animals. When saccharin was fed in large quantities to laboratory rats, the animals suffered a higher number of bladder cancers than usual. Saccharin has also been linked to cancer in the blood-forming and reproductive systems. The most recent findings suggest that saccharin may be a *promoter* of cancer rather than a *cause*. Unlike cigarettes and ultraviolet rays, it does not have a direct connection with cancer. Instead, the use of saccharin may increase the risk of developing cancer from other sources. Because of its potential danger, saccharin has been banned in the United States. However, in response to public support for the artificial sweetener, Congress has temporarily stopped enforcement of the ban.
>
> *Aspartame* is approximately 200 times sweeter than sugar. It has as many calories per gram as sugar. However, since it is so much sweeter, $\frac{1}{200}$ gram of aspartame can replace one gram of sugar. Aspartame adds a few calories to the products it becomes a part of, but the increase is very small. Unlike saccharin, it has not been linked to cancer. As stated on the warning label, the only proven dangers from aspartame relate to sufferers of a rare metabolic disorder called PKU (phenylketonuria). Testing of this new artificial sweetener continues, but aspartame has been approved for use in soft drinks since 1983.

The criteria are number of calories, safety, and current status. Notice that the discussion of each sweetener is arranged with the criteria in the same order.

In the second excerpt, the information is arranged according to the criteria on which the comparison is based. This arrangement takes the reader's attention away from the individual items and places it on the criteria. The comparison is again between saccharin and aspartame, but it focuses on the benefits of each artificial sweetener over the other according to certain criteria.

> Diabetics, dieters, and other people interested in reducing the amount of sugar they consume have two choices of artificial sweetener: saccharin and aspartame. Both sweeteners are effective at adding a sweet taste to soft drinks, baked goods, and other foods, but questions about their safety remain unanswered. Below is a comparison of saccharin and aspartame based on the number of calories each has, its safety, and its current legal status.
>
> *Calories.* Saccharin is approximately 300 times sweeter than sugar. It has no calories. Aspartame is approximately 200 times sweeter than sugar. Per gram, it has as many calories as sugar. However, since aspartame is 200 times sweeter, $\frac{1}{200}$ gram can replace one gram of sugar. Aspartame adds very few calories to the foods it is used in.
>
> *Safety.* Saccharin has been linked to cancer in laboratory animals. When it was fed in large quantities to laboratory rats, the animals suffered more bladder cancers than usual. Saccharin has also been linked to cancers in blood-forming

and reproductive systems. However, the most recent studies have concluded that saccharin is not a *cause* of cancer. Instead it may be a *promoter*. It may increase the risk of developing cancer from other sources.

Aspartame has not been linked to cancer. As stated on the warning label, the only proven dangers from aspartame relate to sufferers of a rare metabolic disorder called PKU (phenylketonuria).

Current Status. Because of its link to cancer, saccharin has been banned in the United States. However, its removal from the market created such a public outcry that Congress temporarily stopped enforcement of the ban. Aspartame was approved for use in soft drinks in 1983. Although testing continues, there is no current threat of a ban on aspartame.

Notice that within each criterion the arrangement is consistent. Saccharin is always discussed first. Aspartame is discussed second.

CAUSE AND EFFECT

Cause and effect are opposite patterns for organizing information according to reasons and results. Causes are the reasons that an effect occurs. Effects are the results. As patterns of organization, cause and effect have similar goals. However, their arrangements are different. Cause moves forward, with the reasons stated before the results. For example, Jan constantly overeats during meals. Between meals, she eats junk food, such as candy bars and potato chips. She also drinks beer and gets no exercise. One effect of this unhealthy life style will be excessive weight gain. Because Jan overeats, particularly high-calorie, low-nutrition foods, and does not exercise, she will become fat. Effect moves backward. The result is stated before the reasons. Consider the previous example in reverse. Jan is fat. Her excessive weight gain was caused by overeating, consuming high-calorie foods, and refusing to exercise. The effect is stated first and the causes last.

In this short excerpt, the causes are given before the effect.

After the eye of the hurricane passed, winds increased to over 100 miles per hour. Some gusts were as high as 120 mph. Waves crested at 50 feet above normal. Rain poured down. Many ocean-front cottages were badly damaged or destroyed.

The causes are high winds, large waves, and pouring rains. The effect is damage to cottages. This excerpt can be revised to state the effect first and the causes second.

Many ocean-front cottages were badly damaged or destroyed. After the eye of the hurricane passed, winds increased to over 100 miles per hour. Some gusts were as high as 120 mph. Waves crested at 50 feet above normal. Rain poured down.

Usually the cause and effect pattern is not as simple as these examples show. The excerpt on page 54 discusses the effects of radiation exposure. It begins by explaining the effects of radiation exposure on the cells in the human body. Then it describes a second group of effects that can occur because of these damaged cells.

When exposed to radiation, the cells that make up the human body can be damaged. The cell membrane can be broken or its structure permanently changed. Chromosomes can be altered. The cell's ability to divide can be hampered. The extent of cell damage depends on how much exposure to radiation is received, how quickly the radiation is absorbed by the cells, and which cells are affected. Cell damage can result in leukemia, which may appear years after the exposure to radiation, and birth defects in future generations. If the cells absorb a large amount of radiation, immediate death can occur.

The cause is radiation exposure. The effect is damage to the cells in the human body. The effects these damaged cells can bring about are leukemia, birth defects in future generations, and immediate death.

TIME SEQUENCE

The time sequence pattern organizes information according to the order of events. It is concerned with what happened. The sequence begins with the first event and continues until the last one. Time sequence is the organizing principle for two important types of writing: narrative and process. We will briefly discuss both types here and provide more details about process in Chapter 12.

Narrative

Narratives use time sequence to provide a historical overview. The events have occurred in the past, and they will not be repeated. They are arranged in order according to what happened. Time sequence can be used to discuss the employment history for an individual with a company or the events that led to the bombing of Pearl Harbor or the signing of the Declaration of Independence. This excerpt discusses the development of CPR, cardiopulmonary resuscitation.[5]

During their pioneering work with the defibrillator in the 1950s, researchers at Johns Hopkins University discovered that blood could be moved through the body of a patient suffering cardiac arrest by pressing forcefully on the chest. This discovery went on to become cardiopulmonary resuscitation, now used and taught throughout the world as CPR.

The technique was discovered accidently by Guy Knickerbocker, a graduate student working with Dr. William Kouwenhoven. As professor of electrical engineering at Johns Hopkins, Kouwenhoven had long been interested in the effects of electricity on the human body. He had shown that an electric current applied directly to the heart could restore the heartbeat, but this method of

[5] The information about CPR is adapted from Richard C. Thompson's "The Lifesaver Known as CPR." *FDA Consumer* February 1986: 17.

resuscitation required opening the chest. By 1957, he had perfected the defibrillator, a small box cabinet with two insulated cables. The device became standard equipment at the Johns Hopkins Hospital and elsewhere for use in cardiac arrest.

Knickerbocker continued his experiments with the defibrillator. One day in 1958, he noticed that simply placing heavy copper electrodes on the chests of anesthetized animals caused the blood pressure to rise. Pressing down with the electrodes made it rise even higher. Based on this discovery, he and others at Johns Hopkins speculated that a forceful, rhythmic pressure on the chest could cause enough blood to move through the body to sustain the vital organs. A year of testing showed they were correct. Closed-chest massage could maintain up to 40 percent of normal circulation. Satisfied that closed-chest massage worked, the researchers announced their discovery. Within months it was combined with mouth-to-mouth resuscitation to become cardiopulmonary resuscitation, now known as CPR.

The sequence of events begins with the invention of the defibrillator, a device that uses electricity to revive heart attack patients, and ends with the final testing and development of CPR in its present form. The events are discussed in the order that they occurred.

Process

Process uses a time sequence to show how something occurs or how to perform a certain task. Unlike the sequence of events in a narrative, the sequence of stages or steps in a process can be repeated. The events, stages, or steps have happened previously and can occur again. The process can be natural—for example, the sequence of events that form a hurricane in the southern Atlantic. It can be mechanical—for example, the sequence of events that occur in the ignition of an automobile. The process can also be done by a human—for example, the sequence of steps for taking a blood sample from a patient.

Process is a very important organizational pattern in technical writing. It appears in several different forms. The discussion can be aimed at the reader either as an observer or as a doer. With the reader as an observer, the purpose of the writing is to explain what happens during the process so that the reader can understand. This type of writing is often called process description. The observer does not have to perform the process. With the reader as doer, the purpose of the piece of writing is to explain how to perform the process so that the reader can do the task correctly and safely. This type of writing is referred to as instructions or procedures. Examples of instructions and procedures are given in Chapter 12. The excerpts that follow are process descriptions. They are intended for observers rather than doers.

This excerpt describes a natural process, the forming of a thunderstorm. Because one event results in another, this paragraph shows the cause and effect pattern as well as process.

A thunderstorm is a small storm, always accompanied by thunder and lightning. It usually has gusts of wind and heavy rain and sometimes hail. Thunderstorms form when a cumulus cloud develops into a thunderhead. Air currents inside the cloud force it upward, higher than 25,000 feet. The upper parts of the cloud reach the cool air in the upper part of the earth's atmosphere. Some parts of the cloud are as high as 50,000 feet. In the upper atmosphere, the cool air condenses the moisture in the cloud to rain drops or ice crystals. This condensed moisture falls and cools the air in the lower part of the cloud. While the thunderhead is cooled, rain falls. Lightning occurs because the electrical charges that build up in the cloud are different from those that collect in the earth below. When this difference becomes large enough, an electrical discharge, a lightning bolt, is formed. Thunder occurs because the air is heated very rapidly by the lightning. The noise associated with thunder is produced all along the lightning stroke.

The reader is an observer interested in learning how natural events occur.

This excerpt describes the basic operation of an internal combustion engine. Again cause and effect are important in the process.

The power of an internal combustion machine comes from burning a mixture of fuel and air in a small enclosed space. It comes from the forced movement of the piston in the cylinder. When the fuel-air mixture in the cylinder burns, it expands greatly. Pressure is created. This pressure moves the piston down in the cylinder. As the piston moves down, it rotates the crankshaft. The straight-line (reciprocating) motion of the piston is changed to circular (rotating) motion.

The reader of this discussion is not expected to learn how to repair an internal combustion machine. The excerpt discusses only the most general information about the operation of the machine. It may be followed by detailed instructions or procedures.

DETAILS AND EXAMPLES

Details and examples make general statements believable. Used along with other patterns of organization, details and examples bring realism, concreteness, and interest to writing.

This excerpt intends to convince its readers about the nutritional value and the importance of potatoes.[6] The writer backs up her general statements with details and examples.

Potatoes are frequent visitors on dinner tables in most Western countries. They were previously condemned as foods that weight watchers should avoid, but potatoes are now considered beneficial ingredients in most diets. They are important vegetables because of their nutritional value, their popularity, and their willingness to grow almost anywhere.

Nutritionally, potatoes offer ingredients vital to a balanced diet. They have significant amounts of carbohydrate, vitamin C, thiamine, potassium, iron, and

[6] The information about potatoes is adapted from Evelyn Zamula's "Potatoes: Delicious, Nutritious and Almost Fat-Free." *FDA Consumer* March 1984: 10-12.

other nutrients. One-third of the nutrients are found under the skin in the cortex (the ring visible in potato chips). Therefore, the most nutrition comes from eating the whole potato, including the skin. Potatoes are almost fat-free and contain only about 95 calories.

As a world food crop, potatoes are very important. In 1982, the world grew 252 million metric tons of potatoes (555,660,000,000 pounds). Europe and the Soviet Union produced 75 percent of the world's crop. The United States produced only 6.3 percent. The 1982 worldwide production of potatoes averages 119 pounds for every person on earth.

Besides their nutritional value and popularity, potatoes are easy to grow. They prefer low humidity and cool weather. However, they grow well in all the temperate regions of the world. They can be planted from below sea level up to altitudes of 14,000 feet. Some wild potatoes even grow near glaciers where there is a permanent layer of frozen subsoil.

The writer makes three general statements to support her idea that potatoes are important vegetables. First, at the beginning of the second paragraph, she says they are nutritional. Second, at the beginning of the third paragraph, she says they are popular. Third, at the beginning of the fourth paragraph, the author says potatoes are easy to grow. Each statement is backed up with examples and details. Chapter 6 provides more information about the use of details and examples.

SUMMARY

Standard organizational patterns allow you to present information in arrangements familiar to most readers. Seven patterns are particularly important: definition, description, classification and division, comparison, cause and effect, time sequence, and details and examples. Definition explains the meaning of specialized terms and introduces new concepts. Description gives the physical characteristics of an object, including its shape, size, color, parts, and the materials it is made of. Classification and division establish and discuss groups, or classes, of related items. Comparison points to likenesses and differences between items of the same class. Cause and effect explain the reasons or the results. Time sequence describes events as they occur in either a narrative or a process. Details and examples give support to general statements, adding interest and realism. These organizational patterns seldom appear alone but usually are found in combination.

ASSIGNMENTS

Application 1:
Reading Standard Patterns

As you learned in this chapter, the standard patterns of organization seldom occur alone. Instead they usually appear together. Read each of these excerpts carefully and answer the questions that follow. Write down your answers.

A. This is a brief discussion of collapsed stars known as black holes. Black holes have confused space watchers around the world.

A black hole is the remains of a collapsed star with an extremely strong gravitational field. A star collapses after millions of years of generating nuclear reactions because it runs out of fuel. When the nuclear reactions stop, the star's gravity pulls inward and crushes the mass of the star. A black hole has two properties. The first property, gravitational force, traps particles from space and draws them toward the hole. The particles rotate in a spiral pattern much like a tornado. The second property, rotation, is related to the first. To the viewer in space, a black hole looks like a disk of particles surrounding a hole. The hole is black because the intense gravitational force has an escape velocity (the speed needed to overcome the force) greater than the speed of light.

Write down answers to these questions.

1. What is a black hole? Where does the *sentence definition* appear in the excerpt?
2. What is the *informal definition* that appears in this excerpt?
3. What are the properties of a black hole?
4. What does the black hole look like? What pattern of organization does the word "like" often introduce?

B. This excerpt explains the basic differences in the operation of internal and external combustion engines.

In the internal combustion engine, the burning of the fuel takes place *inside* the engine. In the external combustion engine, combustion takes place *outside* the engine. In the internal combustion engine, combustion occurs inside the cylinder. This combustion is directly responsible for moving the piston down. In the external combustion engine, combustion occurs in the boiler. This combustion causes water to boil and to produce steam. The steam passes to the engine cylinder under pressure and forces the piston to move down. Therefore, in an external combustion engine, combustion is indirectly, rather than directly, responsible for moving the piston.

Write down answers to these questions.

1. What two things are being *compared*? What is their major difference?
2. What *causes* the piston to move down in an internal combustion engine?
3. What *causes* the piston to move down in an external combustion engine?

C. This excerpt discusses polio.[7] Before the 1950s, this disease killed or crippled American children every summer. One famous president, Franklin D. Roosevelt, caught polio as an adult. Although he survived, Roosevelt suffered from the effects of the disease for the remainder of his life.

> Poliomyelitis is an acute, infectious disease that can result in paralysis. Polio is found throughout the world, especially in warm regions. It most often affects children.
>
> Polio is caused by a virus that can affect the central nervous system. When the virus reaches the brain and the spinal cord, muscles no longer receive strong signals to tell them how and when to move. The result is paralysis. If the paralysis affects breathing and swallowing, it can be fatal. In addition, the patient suffers painful muscle spasms in the arms and legs. Recovery from a serious case of polio is slow. Some effects such as weakness and paralysis can last a lifetime.
>
> Vaccines to prevent polio were introduced in the 1950s and 1960s. These vaccines were developed by Dr. Salk and Dr. Sabin. They have almost eliminated polio in the United States, and they have reduced the number of new cases throughout the world. Until the vaccines were developed, 20,000 cases of paralytic polio occurred each year in the United States. About 5 percent of these cases resulted in death. Now fewer than 10 cases of polio a year are found in this country.

Write down answers to these questions.

1. What is poliomyelitis? Where does the *sentence definition* appear in the excerpt?
2. What *causes* polio?
3. What are the *effects* of polio?
4. Until the vaccines were developed, how widespread was polio in the United States? How widespread is the disease now? (comparison and details)

D. This excerpt discusses two antidotes for poisons.[8] The two antidotes are syrup of ipecac and activated charcoal. If you have small children, you should keep both antidotes in your home.

> Each year approximately two million children under the age of five are victims of accidental poisonings. They get into the drain cleaners, medicines, paints, perfumes, or vitamins that parents think have been safely put out of reach. Even the most careful households risk accidental poisonings. If such an accident occurs, prompt action must be taken. Depending on the type of poison eaten, two at-home antidotes can save the child's life when there is not enough

[7] The information about polio is adapted from "What is Polio?" *FDA Consumer* December 1985-January 1986: 28.

[8] The information about antidotes for poisons is adapted from Roger W. Miller's "At Home Antidotes for Poisoning Emergencies." *FDA Consumer* March 1986: 27, 29.

time to get to a hospital. These two antidotes are syrup of ipecac and activated charcoal.

Syrup of ipecac is a chemical substance used to cause vomiting and rid the stomach of the swallowed poison. It comes from a South American plant and was originally used to treat diarrhea. Ipecac contains two substances: cmetine and cephaeline. It works by irritating the stomach and by stimulating the vomiting center in the brain. Dosage is 1 to 2 teaspoons for children under one year old. After swallowing the syrup, the child should drink a half to a full glass of water. Dosage is 1 tablespoon for older children and adults. It should be followed by one to two glasses of water. Vomiting should occur within 30 minutes.

Syrup of ipecac should not be given if the swallowed poison is caustic. When vomited, caustic substances can burn the esophagus, throat, and lips. Common caustic substances are cleaning compounds, petroleum solvents, and turpentine. In addition, syrup of ipecac should not be used to cause vomiting when the victim is not fully conscious.

Activated charcoal is specially treated charcoal that can absorb poisonous substances. It binds with the substances and prevents the poison from getting into the bloodstream and the rest of the body. At the drugstore, activated charcoal is sold in liquid form in 30-gram doses. Children under five should receive a dose of 30 grams. Older children and adults should receive a dose of 50 grams. Like syrup of ipecac, activated charcoal should be used only on conscious victims. Unconscious victims should be treated in a hospital by professionals.

Both syrup of ipecac and activated charcoal can be purchased without a prescription. However, as their labels point out, they should not be used without first consulting a doctor or the poison control center in the area. The two antidotes work in different ways. Syrup of ipecac causes vomiting to rid the body of the poison. Activated charcoal absorbs the poison to prevent it from being spread through the body. The two should not be used at the same time because the charcoal will absorb the ipecac. However, charcoal can be given after the vomiting caused by the ipecac has stopped. It will then absorb any remaining poison.

Write down answers to these questions.

1. How many children under the age of five are victims of accidental poisoning each year? What are some *examples* of the poisonous substances they eat?

2. What is syrup of ipecac? Where does the *sentence definition* appear?

3. How does syrup of ipecac work? (principle of operation)

4. What are the *instructions* for taking syrup of ipecac?

5. What is activated charcoal? Where does the *sentence definition* appear?

6. How does activated charcoal work? (principle of operation)

7. Can syrup of ipecac and activated charcoal be taken together? Why not? (comparison)

Application 2:
Writing Sentence Definitions

Define five words from your field of study. Assume that you are defining these words for customers. Use the technical definition pattern you learned in this chapter: WORD + is + CLASS + DIFFERENCE. Underline the word once, circle the class, and put brackets around the difference. If necessary, refer to a specialized dictionary. Below is a list of words that customers may be unfamiliar with.

compact disc	hypodermic	stethoscope
videotape player	micrometer	speedometer
ac current	disk	electron
lathe	filter	ignition switch
pump	calipers	breathalyzer
capacitor	cortisone	microchip
laser	fan	cam
thermostat	x-ray	vise
accelerator	beaker	fuel injector
electrode	pressure	turbocharger
computer software	computer hardware	blueprint
electronic typewriter	radar	series circuit

5

PARAGRAPHS, BEGINNINGS, AND ENDINGS

When you complete this chapter, you should know how to organize information in paragraphs and how to write the special paragraphs that act as beginnings and endings. You should learn how to write three different types of paragraphs:

> Paragraphs in the body
> Beginnings
> Endings

A paragraph is a group of related sentences on the same topic. Different types of paragraphs serve different functions in a piece of writing. Paragraphs at the beginning and end tell readers what the writing is about and remind them of what they have read. Paragraphs in the body present most of the details. This chapter explains how to write the paragraphs that make up the body of a piece of writing and how to write beginnings and endings.

PARAGRAPHS IN THE BODY

The body of a piece of writing is sometimes called the discussion. It is usually the longest and most complex section of the writing. Paragraphs in the body are established for two reasons. First, starting a new paragraph shows a change in topic. When a new topic is introduced, the paragraph begins with a topic sentence. This sentence introduces the new content and its arrangement. Second, starting a new paragraph allows a break for readers. If the discussion of a topic is too long to be explained in one paragraph, it may be broken into several paragraphs.

The topic sentence is like a playmaker on a basketball team. It announces the goal, decides on the strategy, and positions the content. The topic sentence tells readers in advance what a paragraph or a group of several paragraphs on the same topic is about.

Let's look at some topic sentences. Here is a short paragraph from the body of an article discussing the diagnosis of allergies. The purpose of the article is to offer general information to readers without medical training. The topic sentence is underlined.

> <u>Doctors have two important tools for diagnosing allergies.</u> First, they can ask patients to keep a diary describing the severity of symptoms and the length of time they last, the amount of medication needed to get relief, and other important factors. They compare the diary with the time of the year substances suspected of causing the allergic reaction typically bloom and the amount of pollen these substances produce. Second, besides common-sense guesses based on a patient's records, doctors can use "skin tests." To do skin tests, they inject a tiny drop of the substance under the skin of the patient. If a rash occurs, they assume the patient is allergic to that substance.

Notice that the topic sentence is the most general statement in the paragraph. It introduces the topic, tools for diagnosing allergies. It also tells the reader to prepare for a discussion of more than one tool. The paragraph describes two tools, patients' records and skin tests.

Now let's look at a longer excerpt with several paragraphs. Notice how topic sentences help readers move from one group of related but different ideas to the next. This excerpt is from the body of an article about pica.[1] Pica is an eating disorder that seems to be connected to iron deficiency. The victims of pica often have cravings for nonfood items, such as clay, dirt, or laundry starch. They may also crave large quantities of a single food, such as Life Savers or raw potatoes. Again the topic sentences are underlined.

> <u>Pica is a widespread disease.</u> It occurs in both sexes, in all races, in all parts of the world, and in animals as well as humans. It was reported as early as 40 B.C. and is still with us today. Both children and adults can be pica victims. What they eat may range from the strange to the disgusting. In many cases, poisonous substances, like lead, are eaten. The results of eating these poisonous substances can be tragic—brain damage, epilepsy, even death.
>
> <u>Though pica is widespread, its detection is not easy because both children and adults cover up their strange cravings.</u> Many mothers know that their children eat dirt or sand regularly. They do not report this habit to the doctor because they expect the children to outgrow it. Usually they are right, and children do outgrow the habit. However, in some cases, children try to hide

[1]The information about pica is adapted from Evelyn Zamula's "The Curious Compulsion Called Pica." *FDA Consumer* December 1985. January 1986: 29−32.

pica—especially if it involves something particularly nasty. They are afraid they will be punished. Most doctors do not ask about pica except when they suspect lead poisoning. Parents usually seek medical help because the pica is causing the child to become destructive, ill, or cry too much. Out of shame, adults also try to keep their strange cravings hidden. Pica is sometimes discovered when a victim complains to the doctor of abdominal pain, vomiting, or some other problem. It is also sometimes discovered when an x-ray shows an unexplained lump in the stomach.

<u>Doctors throughout history have suggested different kinds of treatments for pica</u>. In some cultures, doctors took for granted that pregnant women would have pica. In other cultures, doctors thought pica was a form of insanity. They thought that victims should be tied down or put in prison to keep them from eating what they wanted. One seventeenth-century doctor recommended mixing a drug that would cause vomiting with the desired substance. He hoped that the desired substance would become associated in the patient's mind with the resulting sickness. From time to time a smart doctor realized that pica in some people was caused by something missing in their diet. Avicenna, who lived about 1000 A.D., was the first to recommend treating pica with doses of iron. Boezo made the same recommendation in 1638. But the pica-diet connection was not completely accepted until this century.

As you can see, the topic sentences in this excerpt set up the paragraphs. They tell readers what to expect and what to look for as they read.

Topic sentences can have three functions.

- ○ They can serve as transitions to show the relationship between an old topic and a new one.
- ○ They can summarize the information to be given on the topic they introduce.
- ○ They can point to the organization of that information.

Not all topic sentences fulfill all three functions. To be effective, however, they should at least summarize the information they introduce. Let's look at the topic sentences from the pica excerpt.

First Topic Sentence

Pica is a widespread disease.

This topic sentence summarizes the information that will be discussed in the paragraph.

Second Topic Sentence

Though pica is widespread, detection is not easy because both children and adults cover up their strange cravings.

The first part of the sentence, "Though pica is widespread," refers back to the previous paragraph. The rest of the sentence summarizes the information to be given on the topic. The last part, ". . . because both children and adults cover up their strange cravings," points to the arrangement of that information: Pica in children is discussed first, and pica in adults is discussed second.

Third Topic Sentence

Doctors throughout history have suggested different kinds of treatments for pica.

This topic sentence summarizes the new information to be given and its arrangement. The phrase "throughout history" tells the reader that the information will be arranged in a time sequence.

Topic sentences are important aids for readers. Therefore, you should pay special attention to writing them. Although you probably should not worry about the form of topic sentences while writing your first draft, you should examine them closely while you are revising.

BEGINNINGS

Beginnings, or introductions, usually tell what a piece of writing is about. Beginnings are important for clarity in all kinds of writing. They give readers an overview of the content and its arrangement. Depending on what readers already know, introductions provide the following information:

    Background of the writing task
    Problem to be solved (if any)
    Purpose
    Major topics discussed in the piece of writing
    Summary of conclusions and recommendations (if any)

Unlike the paragraphs in the body, beginnings do not have topic sentences. Instead they attempt to connect with what the reader already knows about the content and explain what new information will be discussed. To establish a connection with the reader, the first few sentences of a beginnning provide any necessary background. Then writers can get to the point, the purpose of the writing. This introduction is from a 10-page report that discusses turbocharging. The purpose statement, which appears on page 66, is underlined.

    The turbocharger, or turbo, is an exhaust-driven air compressor that force-feeds extra air into an engine. This force feeding greatly increases the power and efficiency of automobile powerplants. Currently used by every major automaker worldwide in a large diversity of applications, turbos can be found on the Porsche 930, Buick Regal, Volvo stationwagon, Dodge Colt, and Chrysler New Yorker. Worldwide sales for turbocharged vehicles reached the two million mark in 1986, with American market sales exceeding one half million vehicles. However, even though turbos command a large market share, their principles of operation remain largely unknown to automotive enthusiasts.

<u>This report is a brief introduction to turbocharging</u>. It will describe the parts of the turbocharger, discuss its operation, and project future developments in turbocharging.

The first paragraph from the report begins by providing necessary background. It tells what a turbocharger is and how it is currently being used. The second paragraph begins with the purpose statement. The purpose statement is followed by a forecast of the major sections in the report. The report does not make recommendations; therefore, no summary statement of recommendations is included.

Now let's examine an introduction from a short memorandum report. In this example, the head of a work crew is reporting to her supervisor about the causes of habitual (very frequent) absenteeism on Monday mornings. The supervisor has requested this report. Again the purpose statement is underlined.

Here is the report you requested last week. <u>My purpose is to recommend a way to end habitual absenteeism on Monday mornings</u>. Based on interviews with employees, my suggestion is to implement a system of flextime. This system will offer incentives for working on Monday mornings but allow those who cannot work to make up the time later in the week.

Because the reader expects the report, little background is required. The first sentence reminds the reader that the report is assigned. After the purpose is stated in the second sentence, a summary of the major recommendation is given. The last sentence points to the benefits of the recommendation. The memorandum is short, only two pages. If the supervisor agrees with the suggestion to implement flextime, the head of the work crew may have to write a much longer report explaining exactly how to set the system up.

Beginnings can vary in length, in the amount of background information that is included, and in the type of purpose statement they use. However, they all tell readers what to expect in the piece of writing. Beginnings introduce the content and its arrangement.

ENDINGS

The ending is the last section of a piece of writing. It explains and summarizes the information for the reader. It often answers the question "So what?" As its name suggests, the end is a final opportunity to restate opinions and to persuade readers. In a long report, the end frequently contains several paragraphs or even separately headed sections. Some present conclusions, some make recommendations, and some act as a summary for the entire report.

Beginnings and endings should work together to set up a piece of writing and to remind the readers of what they have read. In this excerpt from a

10-page report, the writer announces his purpose, major topics, and general recommendation in the beginning. He discusses the details of his conclusions and recommendations in the ending.

[BEGINNING]

Purpose and
Major Topics

    As you requested, I have studied the feasibility of locating a remote ATM (Automated Teller Machine) on the campus of Greenville Community College. This report discusses the legality of building an ATM, possible locations for the machine, costs, and expected clientele.

Summary of
Conclusions and
Recommendations

    My investigation shows that Greenville Union Bank will benefit from locating an ATM on the college campus. However, I suggest that we proceed cautiously with the construction. We should begin by determining the legality of establishing a new ATM. Then we should meet with the directors of Greenville Community College to decide on a location.

[ENDING]

Conclusions

Summary

    If Greenville Union Bank decides to enlarge its ATM system, then Greenville Community College offers a feasible location. Greenville Community College has a student population, which falls into the age group most easily introduced to automatic banking. It also has accessible, highly visible places to locate an ATM. Finally, enrollment at Greenville Community College is increasing, and the school believes that this trend will continue.

Benefits

    If we locate an ATM on the campus of Greenville Community College, we can possibly accomplish several goals. First, we will have an edge on capturing the new accounts on campus. Second, we will be able to provide service to our existing customers who attend Greenville Community College. Third, we may take over accounts from other banks.

Recommendations

General
Recommendation

    I recommend that Greenville Union Bank locate an ATM on the campus of Greenville Community College. However, I suggest that we proceed cautiously in the following sequence:

List

1. We should ask for a definite ruling from the State Banking Department on the legality of building a remote ATM after December 31, 1987.
2. We should coordinate meetings with the President of Greenville Community College to determine the school's needs and capabilities. At that time, we can discuss site preferences and costs.

3. We should ask our Marketing Department to determine the most feasible site for locating the ATM.
4. We should file for permits from the Federal Reserve and the State Banking Department. We can later cancel these permits if we decide not to construct the ATM.
5. We should order a remote ATM from Diebold.

Final Urging   This report indicates that Greenville Community College is a feasible location for an ATM. We should work efficiently and swiftly to lead our competitors in this project.

Since the readers are expecting the report, the writer offers almost no background. Instead he moves immediately to his assigned task: to report on the possible benefits of establishing an Automated Teller Machine on the campus of Greenville Community College. After stating his purpose, he mentions the topics the report will cover. Then he summarizes his conclusion that the ATM is potentially profitable and his recommendation to begin the building. With this brief summary statement, the writer tells his readers what to expect in the report. At the end of the report, the writer discusses his conclusions and recommendations in detail. He defends his conclusion that Greenville Community College is a feasible location for the ATM by summarizing the information presented in the discussion section of the report. Then he points out the possible benefits of the recommendations that will follow. In the last section, the writer makes his recommendations. First, he gives his general recommendation that an ATM be established on the campus. Then, he gives specific recommendations for implementing his general recommendation. Finally, the writer urges his reader to accept his recommendations. Other examples of beginnings and endings are found in later chapters.

SUMMARY

A paragraph is a group of related sentences. The organization of a paragraph depends on its use in the body, in the beginning, or in the ending. In the body, paragraphs give the details of the discussion. New paragraphs in the body introduce a new topic or provide a break for the reader. When a new topic is introduced, the paragraph begins with a topic sentence. Beginnings introduce a piece of writing. They include information about the background of the writing, the problem, the purpose, the arrangement of the content, and a summary of the conclusions and recommendations. Endings conclude a piece of writing. They explain and summarize the content. Endings may consist of conclusions and recommendations as well as summaries.

ASSIGNMENTS

Application 1:
Organizing Paragraphs

The three paragraphs that follow have been broken down into lists of facts. The topic sentence for each appears at the beginning. Combine the lists of facts to write a paragraph that fits the topic sentence. Two kinds of clues have been provided. First, groups of related facts that can be combined into single sentences have been numbered. Second, signal words (See Chapter 6) have been placed in the margins. Use these clues to help with the organization of the facts in the paragraphs. Write down your final versions.

Manometers[2]

Topic Sentence: A manometer is an accurate, inexpensive instrument used to measure low pressure.

1. A manometer consists of a U-tube.
   The U-tube is glass.
   It is uniform in diameter.
   It is filled with liquid.
2. The liquid can be water.
   It can be oil.
   It can be mercury.
   These liquids are most common.
   They are used in U-tubes.
3. One end is open to the atmosphere.
   The end is of the U-tube.
   The other end is connected with the pressure.
   The pressure is to be measured.

Sulfites

Topic Sentence: Sulfites are chemicals used as preservatives in a number of foods and drugs.

1. Sulfites delay or prevent changes in color.
   They delay or prevent changes in flavor.
   They delay or prevent changes in texture.
   An example of these changes is browning.
   Another example is fading in color.
   The fading is caused by oxidation.
2. Sulfites keep fruits looking fresh. [*because*]
   They keep vegetables looking fresh.
   Their use has increased.
   They are used in restaurants.
   Their increased use is related to the popularity of salad bars.

[2]The information about manometers is adapted from the Naval Education and Training Command Rate Training Manual *Fireman.* Washington: Government Printing Office, 1982.

3. Sulfites are used in other restaurant foods.
   They are especially used in seafood and potatoes.
4. Sulfites are also used in many processed foods.
   These foods include fruit drinks.
   They include beer.
   They include wine.
   They include baked goods.
   They include vegetables.
   They include dried fruits.

The Turbine[3]

Topic Sentence: A Greek mathematician, Hero, built a small steam turbine almost 2000 years ago to demonstrate that steam power could be used to operate other machinery.

1. Hero's turbine consisted of a sphere.
   The sphere was hollow.
   The sphere carried nozzles.
   The nozzles were bent.
2. The sphere rotated freely on tubes.
   There were two tubes.
   The tubes carried steam from the boiler.
3. Steam passed upward through the tubes.
   It passed into the sphere.
   It passed out through the nozzles.
   The steam was generated in the boiler.
4. The steam left the nozzles. [as]
   The sphere rotated rapidly.
5. The turbine principle has been applied to machines.
   The machines are of many different types.
   The application has occurred through the ages.
6. The waterwheel is an example of the turbine principle.
   The waterwheel operated the flour mills.
   These mills existed in colonial times.
   The windmill is also an example of the turbine principle.
   The windmill pumped water.
7. In both examples, the power is derived.
   It is derived from the effect of flowing water on a set of blades.
   It is derived from the effect of the wind on a set of blades.
   The blades are attached to a wheel.
8. Steam can act like the flowing water.
   It can act like the wind.
   Steam generates power in the steam turbine. [to]

---

[3]The information about turbines is adapted from the Naval Education and Training Command Rate Training Manual *Fireman*. Washington: Government Printing Office, 1982.

Application 2:
Identifying New Paragraphs

The following excerpts need to be divided into paragraphs. Indicate where each new paragraph should begin with a >. Remember to start a new paragraph for each new topic and to provide a break in a long discussion.

A. This excerpt explains three kinds of heat stress and the symptoms of each.[4]

Heat Stress

When a person works in an environment that is hot and humid, heat builds up within the body. The body automatically reacts to cool itself through sweating. Sweating reduces the body temperature by evaporation. It is a normal body function; however, this process takes away the body's liquid and salt. If these essential ingredients are not replaced, heat cramps, heat exhaustion, or even heat stroke can result. Heat cramps are caused by excessive sweating, which leads to the loss of liquid and salt. An overheated person may develop cramps by drinking too much cold liquid. Heat cramps are often an early warning sign of approaching heat exhaustion. Heat exhaustion is a more serious problem. The sweat control mechanism is overloaded and cannot cope with the heat buildup in the body. The blood flow is disturbed, and dizziness, headache, and nausea may result. These symptoms are accompanied by gray, cold skin. They are similar to the symptoms of shock. The victim should be taken to a hospital as soon as possible. Heat stroke is less common but far more serious than heat exhaustion. In about 20 percent of its cases, it is fatal. Heat stroke occurs when the sweating mechanism has completely broken down. The body is unable to rid itself of the excessive body heat. The body temperature may rise as high as 105° Fahrenheit. If the high temperature lasts more than a few minutes, it can cause failure of the brain, kidneys, and liver. The early symptoms of heat stroke are similar to those of heat exhaustion: headache, nausea, and dizziness. At first breathing is deep and rapid, but as the symptoms progress, the breathing becomes shallow, almost absent. The skin appears flushed, dry, and very hot. The pupils are constricted to pinpoints. The pulse is fast and strong. Victims of heat stoke must be taken to a hospital immediately. Awareness of the factors which can cause heat stress will decrease the possibility of your becoming a victim.

B. This excerpt discusses the rise in popularity of the tomato.[5] The discussion begins with the tomato's first mention in history and ends with its current use. The paragraphs may not be as easy to establish here as in the previous assignment. Be prepared to explain your decisions.

Although the tomato is now very popular, it has not always been so widely enjoyed. In fact, Americans lagged behind Europeans in accepting this vegetable. The tomato is native to South America. It was first found in the area that

[4]The information about heat stress is adapted from the Naval Education and Training Command Rate Training Manual *Fireman.* Washington: Government Printing Office, 1982.

[5]The information about the tomato is adapted from Evelyn Zamula's "Tale of the Tomato: From Poison to Pizza." *FDA Consumer* July-August 1984: 24, 28–29.

is now Peru, Bolivia, and Ecuador. By the first century A.D., however, the to-mato had been carried to Mexico and Central America. In Mexico, it was dis-covered by Spanish soldiers. The soldiers took the tomato to Europe. The to-mato was particularly popular in Italy. Written references indicate that Italians enjoyed tomatoes as early as 1554. The vegetable quickly became a major ele-ment in Italian sauces. By the eighteenth century, Italians had developed new varieties and were growing tomatoes as a crop. The tomato was not as popular in the United States as it was in Italy. Colonial Americans thought tomatoes were poisonous. Most Americans remained suspicious even though famous people like Thomas Jefferson grew them in gardens. Finally, in 1820 Colonel Robert Gibbon decided to end the false rumors about the tomato. He stood on the courthouse steps in Salem County, New Jersey, and ate a tomato in front of a large crowd of people. Much to everyone's surprise, Colonel Gibbon did not drop dead. Today the tomato is the most frequently used processed vegetable in the United States. We consume almost all our processed tomatoes. However, American producers cannot meet the demand for the vegetable. We import processed tomatoes from other countries.

6

REVISING
FOR READABILITY

When you complete this chapter, you should know how to revise your writing to increase its readability. You should learn the following techniques for making your writing easy to read:

> Choosing words that are appropriate for readers
> > Technical words
> > Cover-up words
> Eliminating unnecessary words
> Addressing readers
> Using details and examples to support general statements
> Building new ideas on something already said
> Using signal words and phrases to show how one idea relates to another

As you learned in Chapter 2, readability depends on how quickly and easily your readers can understand your writing and how much they can remember. Besides the content of a message, readability is affected by the word choice, the sentence structure, and the unity of the ideas expressed. Often readers can figure out difficult words and long sentences. However, the struggle causes them to waste time. Readable writing is efficient. It is as easy to understand as its content allows. This chapter discusses some revisions that can make writing easier to read. It considers the selection of appropriate words for your readers and your purpose and suggests techniques for revising sentences and paragraphs.

CHOOSING WORDS THAT ARE APPROPRIATE FOR READERS

Language that is effective for certain readers and situations may be ineffective in other circumstances. The words selected to communicate with technicians are different from those chosen to communicate with supervisors and customers. This section offers advice about how to choose words that readers will understand and respond to favorably. It discusses technical words and cover-up words.

Technical Words

A language, such as English or Spanish, develops because people who live in the same area need to communicate. They need to find food and shelter and companionship. Along with the rules for punctuation and use, a language is made of words. The words are a common vocabulary for the language's speakers and writers. After they go to school and are employed, most people add a specialized vocabulary to the common vocabulary they share with their family and friends. These special words allow technicians to discuss topics not a part of daily conversation outside their profession. As it is discovered, each new machine, disease, and technique is given a name by the inventor. This name becomes a part of a profession's technical vocabulary.

A technical vocabulary is the group of specialized words associated with a profession. From their training and experience, heating and air conditioning technicians, nurses, and child care technicians have learned technical vocabularies unique to their fields. If used in discussions with members of the same profession, technical words make communication more efficient. In fact, two automotive technicians discussing the benefits of fuel injection will find conversation over the phone impossible if they have to point to each part of the system. The phone call will be expensive if the speakers have to refer to each part as "that thingamabob over on the right side, you know the one."

Because they lack the training and experience, outsiders cannot understand these technical vocabularies. Without training, a Mexican cannot understand English. In comparison, a nurse will not understand the specialized vocabulary of an automotive technician; and an automotive technician cannot name the diseases and body parts so familiar to a nurse. Therefore, technical words should be avoided in talking to or writing for customers. If a technical word must be used, it should be clearly defined. For example, suppose an automotive technician visits his doctor for a routine physical. After running some tests, the doctor reports that the automotive technician suffers from "hypertension caused by pheochromocytoma." Unless the doctor provides further explanation, the patient may not know that he has high blood pressure caused by a tumor on the adrenal glands. The automotive technician may be frightened by the specialized words of medicine. Therefore, he may never learn that his tumor is probably not cancerous (benign) and that its removal may end his high blood pressure. In this example, the doctor is responsible for explaining the automotive technician's illness as simply and clearly as possible.

When technicians use technical words in conversations with customers, they risk losing sales or commissions. Put yourself in this situation. Suppose you decide to buy a home computer for keeping household accounts and for doing simple typing tasks. As soon as he greets you, the salesman begins discussing "microprocessors." He describes the "input" and "output" of certain machines. He talks about "memory" in "bytes," "kilobytes," and "megabytes." He shows you computers that use various kind of "disks," which hold "files" of your input. If you use a computer at work, you probably will have no trouble understanding what the salesman is saying. As long as he avoids words like "RAM" (random access memory) and "ROM" (read-only memory), you can maintain your end of the conversation. In that case, the salesman has a chance of convincing you to buy his computer. However, if you do not know the difference between hardware and software, you are likely to be very confused. You may leave the store without buying anything.

A good salesperson will determine the customer's level of technical knowledge and use this level as a starting place for the sales pitch. The same is true for writers. A good writer begins with what readers know and then builds slowly and carefully on this existing knowledge.

Cover-up Words

Cover-up words are expressions that are carelessly or intentionally unclear. They include the unfamiliar words and unnecessarily long phrases that confuse rather than inform readers. For example, politicians are infamous for creating words to cover up what could be an unpopular decision. During the Vietnam War, fighter pilots flew "antipersonnel missions." Soldiers participated in an "active combat phase" when they fought the enemy. More recently, the invasion of Grenada was called a "predawn vertical insertion." If the government pays $400 for a pen, the common ballpoint may become a "hand-held, tubular writing machine." These words intentionally add confusion to writing.

Cover-up words receive the most publicity when they appear in statements released by government officials. However, the selection of language to cover up rather than to clarify can be found in all kinds of writing. Consider these examples.

Example 1

The department's underutilization of its support staff led to termination of one member.

Translation

One secretary was fired because the department did not need her.

Example 2

   With deepest regret, President Hamilton must decline the invitation to address your banquet. Every Wednesday afternoon, he interfaces with high-level executives in a contest of physical prowess at Highland Racquet Club.

Translation

President Hamilton cannot speak at your banquet because he plays racquetball with his friends every Wednesday afternoon.

Cover-up words often fall into two categories:

○ They may be long and sound scholarly. For example, when they want to be impressive, writers use words like "cognizant" rather then "know," "remuneration" rather than "pay," and "utilize" rather than "use." However, sometimes a long word that is unfamiliar to most people is necessary for a writer's message. To make certain that they get the correct chemical, serious gardeners will ask for "dichlorophenoxyacetic acid" rather than simple "weed killer."

○ They may be technical words taken out of context. In one of the examples above, a human being "interfaces" with other human beings in a racquetball game. The word "interface" generally refers to connections between computers and peripheral devices. Another word borrowed from language about computer is "input." "John inputted his opinions into the conversation" not only missapplies a word used to discuss technology into a human context but also changes a noun ("input") into a verb ("inputted").

   Cover-up words make writing very difficult to read. Although you may never write reports with cover-up words, you need to learn how to translate these expressions into "plain" English. This skill will protect you from being misled by writing that is carelessly or intentionally unclear.

ELIMINATING UNNECESSARY WORDS

   Unnecessary words clutter writing. They make sentences long and difficult to read. Let's examine some cluttered sentences.

Example 1

There is a lot of discussion about the fact that frequent oil changes lead to long and trouble-free engine life.

As it now appears, the sentence contains 20 words, and the reader really does not know what it is about until the end.

Example 2

Most of our electrical products seem to be designed, tested, and built so that they are safe. However, sometimes, on occasions, a defect in the aforementioned product or improper use can cause hazardous situations to arise, resulting in either electrical shock or fire.

This one has 43 words.

Example 3

It has been pointed out that valves can be classified in three types: stop valves, check valves, or combination stop-check valves.

This one has 21 words.

Now that you have seen some examples of wordy sentences, let's consider how to revise them. We suggest a very simple method with only three steps.

1. Determine the "real" subject of the sentence. (Usually you can ask yourself "Who is doing the action?" or "What is causing the action to occur?")
2. Determine the "real" verb. (Usually you can ask "What is happening?")
3. Throw away all the unnecessary words.

Let's apply this method to the sentences shown previously. Underline the "real" subjects and verbs and cross out unnecessary words. In Example 1, the subject is "frequent oil changes" and the verb is "lead."

1. There is a lot of discussion about the fact that <u>frequent oil changes</u> <u>lead</u> to long and trouble-free engine life.

The unnecessary words are the first part of the sentence, "There is a lot of discussion about the fact that . . . "

The sentence can be rewritten as follows:

Frequent oil changes lead to long and trouble-free engine life.

The selection of the appropriate revision depends on the sentences before and after and the purpose of the piece of writing. In all revisions, however, words that do not add information should be deleted whenever possible.

Example 2 can be revised in a similar way. The subject of the first sentence is "electrical products," and the verbs are "designed," "tested," and "built." The subjects of the second sentence are "defect" and "improper use," and the verb is revised to "can result." Again words that do not add information are deleted. Question marks indicate indecision. Often they point to phrases that are too long and bulky but that cannot be fixed by simple deletion. These phrases need revising so that they can be shortened.

2. Most of our <u>electrical products</u> seem to be <u>designed</u>, <u>tested</u>, and <u>built</u> so that they are safe. However, sometimes, on occasions, <u>a defect</u> in the aforementioned product or <u>improper use</u> <u>can</u> cause hazardous situations to arise, <u>resulting</u> in either electrical shock or fire.

The expressions "Most of our" and "seem to be" are not very informative here. The phrase "to be designed, tested, and built" is simplified to serve as the verb in the first sentence. The words "So that they are" can be changed to "to be." In the second sentence, the expression "on occasions" is the same as "sometimes." "Aforementioned product" refers unnecessarily to the product mentioned earlier. The "hazardous situations" that "arise" need not be mentioned because the "results"—"electrical shock or fire"—are named.

> Electrical products are designed, tested, and built to be safe. However, sometimes a defect or improper use can result in electrical shock or fire.

These two sentences, which once had 43 words, now have only 24.

Let's look at the last sentence. It is about the three types of valves. The subject is "three types of valves," but the verb "can be classified" seems unnecessarily long and complicated and can be revised to "are." Delete the words that do not add information.

> 3. It has been pointed out that <u>valves</u> can be classified in <u>three types</u>: stop valves, check valves, or combination stop-check valves.

The expression "It has been pointed out that" does not add information to the sentence. The word "valves" need not be repeated in the list at the end.

> Three types of valves are stop, check, or combination stop-check.

Using these three steps for revising sentences allows you to cut away unnecessary words, to clean out the clutter, and to produce short sentences that are easier to read.

ADDRESSING READERS

In the same way that you chose words appropriate for discussing your content, you also must make decisions about how to address your readers. The choices include personal forms of address, such as direct commands and the advisory "you." They also include less personal forms, such as sentences that imply but do not mention you or the reader. The decision about how to address your readers is based on how much distance you want to establish. When direct commands and the advisory "you" are used, a close, informal relationship is established. The writing almost sounds like talk. It is like a one-sided spoken conversation over the phone. When directions are given or recommendations are made without reference to the reader or to you, a more distant, formal relationship is established. The writing is impersonal. This section offers some examples of forms of address in several different situations.

Direct commands are the least formal and most personal way of addressing readers. They strip communication down to a straightforward verb. Direct commands allow you to stand next to your readers and guide them through a set of instructions. Direct commands come from your knowledge in a particular area. They represent your authority over the reader. Because they are very clear, direct commands are used to write instructions and rules. In Chapter 12, you will learn how to use direct commands in writing instructions. The example below shows direct commands in rules. Here are the Ten Commandments of Safety.

LEARN the safe way to do your job before you start.
THINK safety.
ACT safety at all times.
WEAR proper clothing and protective equipment.
CONDUCT yourself properly at all times.
OPERATE only the equipment you are authorized to use.
INSPECT tools and equipment before starting work.
ADVISE your superior promptly of any unsafe conditions or practice.
REPORT any injury immediately to your superior.
SUPPORT your safety program and take an active part in safety meetings.

Notice the closeness that is assumed between the writer and the reader. To replace the direct commands with expressions like "you should learn" or "you should think" would add unnecessary words. This change would also decrease the feeling of authority. To write "one should learn" or "one should think" would make the writing seem impersonal.

The advisory "you" will also allow you to establish a personal relationship with readers. The writer is "I" and the reader is "you." The advisory "you" intends to act like a hand stretched out from the writing and offered in friendship to the reader. Consider this example. A customer wants to modify a personal computer she just bought and connect a new printer. The modifications are complicated, and there is no dealership in her town. Therefore, she writes the main office for advice. An employee in the customer relations department sends her a booklet of detailed instructions with a polite letter. Here is the last paragraph.

By following the instructions *we* have enclosed, *you* should be able to modify the computer as *you* suggested and connect the daisy-wheel printer. If *you* have further questions, do not hesitate to write or call.

Notice the familiarity the writer assumes. "We" refers to the computer company, and "you" refers to the customer. With these personal pronouns, the writer tries to establish an informal relationship with the reader. Look at what happens when the "you" is changed to the formal "one" and the "we" is eliminated.

> By following the instructions enclosed, *one* should be able to modify the computer as suggested and connect the daisy-wheel printer. If there are any questions, *one* should not hesitate to write or call this office.

Most often, responding to letters from customers does not require extreme formality. Although the second version is correct, it is not appropriate in the situation described. Throughout this textbook, we have used the advisory "you" because we want to make our relationship with you as close as possible. Since there are two of us, we refer to ourselves as "we."

In a more formal style, more distance is established between you and your readers. A procedure can be explained without direct commands or the advisory "you." The focus is on the procedure rather than the person who is doing the procedure.

> Tick removal should be done with care. The fingers can be used but tweezers are recommended. Care should be taken to avoid crushing the tick because the rickettsiae (contamination that leads to Rocky Mountain spotted fever) may enter through broken skin. Proper removal calls for grasping the tick as close as possible to the point of attachment. Then the tick should be pulled repeatedly and gently until it is freed from the skin. The bitten area should be treated with an antiseptic and the hands washed thoroughly.

Notice that neither "I" nor "you" appears in this paragraph. The writer does not seem to be standing over the reader's shoulder. He is not directing the removal of a particular tick.

When an even more formal style is required, the distance between the reader and the writer can be increased. This formality seems to release the writer from responsibility for what is written. Here are recommendations to cut the existing benefit program for employees in the computer firm described earlier.

> It is recommended that the health insurance deductible be raised to $150.00.

> It is recommended that dental coverage be eliminated from the health insurance policy.

> It is recommended that the price of routine eye exams and prescriptions for eyeglasses be excluded from the health insurance policy.

> It is recommended that the employees' life insurance fund be eliminated.

Notice the impersonal "It is . . ." that introduces each recommendation. This formal beginning offers the writer a convenient hiding place. Most likely, these decisions were made by a committee rather than an individual. However, even if a single high-level manager is responsible for these cuts, he or she does not intend to step forward and listen to the complaints.

USING DETAILS AND EXAMPLES
TO SUPPORT GENERAL STATEMENTS

General statements without supporting details or examples are not informative. Consider this general statement.

> Data show that some people die from electrocution.

Readers may ask "what data?," "how many people?," "where?" They also may simply chuck that report aside and go on to the next one. Notice the difference a few details can make.

> Data collected by the U.S. Consumer Product Safety Commission show that 600 persons die each year from electrocution in residential accidents.

Let's look at another general statement.

> Cordless phones work when they are away from their base units.

Since it lacks details, the sentence is not very informative. Before buying cordless phones, most customers will want more details. Among other things, they will probably want to know how far the handset can pick up signals from the base unit. These two sentences provide those details.

> When interference is low, some cordless phones allow users to receive and make calls up to 1000 feet from the base unit. However, they are most reliable at distances of 200 to 300 feet.

If the reader is unfamiliar with the operation of cordless phones, the first sentence may provide a simple introduction and lead to the second two. If the reader already knows this basic information, the first sentence may be left out. The information in the first sentence is stated or implied in the two that follow.

Along with statistics and names of places or people, you can use examples to explain generalities. This sentence is the first one in a paragraph.

> Every known civilization has searched for a way to avoid the morning-after hangover.

To anyone who has ever drunk too much beer or any other alcoholic beverage, this subject may be interesting. However, if the sentence is left alone or followed by some equally general statement about the treatment of arthritis, it is not effective. It should be followed by examples.

> Every known civilization has searched for a way to avoid the morning-after hangover. The Romans used remedies such as owlets' eyes and raw owls' eggs. They also wore garlands of celery the night before to ward off hangovers. The Greeks wore parsley for the same reason. The Assyrians ate a spoonful of swallow-beak ashes with a dash of myrrh. Haitian voodoo worshipers stuck pins in the cork of the bottle from which they drank.

The examples refer to the range of methods for treating hangovers. They refer to methods used by the Romans, the Greeks, the Assyrians, and the Haitian voodoo worshipers. Details and examples make writing interesting as well as informative.

BUILDING NEW IDEAS ON SOMETHING ALREADY SAID

Besides the choice of appropriate words and forms of address, the elimination of unnecessary words, and the use of details and examples, readability is also affected by coherence. Coherence is what makes a paragraph different from a list. If writing is not coherent, readers will read each idea separately, like the items on a grocery list. If writing is coherent, readers will read a message with connected ideas, like a meal prepared from the separate items bought in the grocery store. Unless they learn how one idea relates to another, readers will not understand the writer's message. In coherent writing, each idea is built on something the reader already knows, and connections between ideas are clear. This section discusses the building process. The next section describes some common words and phrases that signal the connections between ideas.

Paragraphs are built by connecting new ideas with old ones. Readers understand new ideas according to what they already know. Writing is like laying bricks. Each new idea should be laid on top of what has been written previously. The building occurs with repeated words, pronouns, or synonyms. Consider the repeated words, pronouns, and synonyms in this description of headaches. Pay particular attention to the underlined words.

> All headaches have different characteristics. Some are not very painful; others are so painful that they drive the sufferer to thoughts of suicide. A headache may be a steady pain, or it may be a throbbing pain. Some headaches come on suddenly, like lightning bolts; others come on slowly. The pain may be concentrated on just one side of the head, may center around the eyes and sinus areas, or may fill the entire area from the eyebrows to the back of the neck.

The purpose of the paragraph is to describe headaches. Therefore, the word "headache" is the subject of the first sentence. Some reference to headache appears in the subject position of each sentence that follows. The building of new information on old is shown with pronouns like "some," "other," and "it" and with synonyms like "the pain." The topic of the paragraph, headache, is the foundation of the building. Frequent reference to the topic makes the paragraph coherent for the reader.

Now that you have examined a coherent version of the paragraph, let's look at some ways writers can go wrong in writing descriptions.

> <u>All</u> <u>headaches</u> have different characteristics. <u>Some</u> are not very painful; <u>others</u> are so painful that they drive the sufferer to thoughts of suicide. <u>I always get</u> a <u>headache</u> when I read too long, especially when I read my physics textbook. <u>A headache</u> may be a steady pain . . . .

The sentence describing the writer's headache interferes with the coherence of the paragraph. It breaks the unity of the paragraph because the focus changes from a general description of a headache to the particular headache of the writer. Let's look at one more example.

> <u>All</u> <u>headaches</u> have different characteristics. When my Uncle Jed gets a <u>head-ache</u>, Aunt Mary hangs a bag of garlic around his neck. In ancient Rome, doctors thought <u>headaches</u> were caused by . . . .

Even though the word "headache" appears in each sentence, this paragraph is not coherent. It is simply a collection of general sentences.

USING SIGNAL WORDS AND PHRASES TO SHOW HOW ONE IDEA RELATES TO ANOTHER

Besides building new ideas on top of old ones, you can also make connections with signal words and phrases. Signal words and phrases are labels that can be used to name the relationship between one idea and the next and to identify the importance of certain concepts. They help to make writing coherent for readers.

First, signal words and phrases can link ideas across or within sentences. These signal words and phrases are transitional expressions and coordinate and subordinate conjunctions. Consider the signals, the underlined words, in this example.

> <u>When</u> properly cooked, all the flesh of the polar bear is safe to eat. <u>However</u>, the liver should never be eaten <u>because</u> its oversupply of vitamin A may be fatal to the consumer.

Signal words and phrases that link can name four major kinds of relationships within or between sentences:

> *Addition:* "for example," "moreover," "and"
> *Opposition:* "however," "but," "or," "in contrast"
> *Time:* "after," "now," "first . . .second"
> *Cause:* "therefore," "thus," "because"

Second, signal words and phrases can also point out the importance of certain ideas. In some cases, signals tell the reader outright that an idea is important. Expressions such as "The most important benefits of the plan are . . . ," "The purpose of this study is . . . ," and "The point is . . ." make sure readers do not miss the major information.

Like all the other advice in this chapter, the suggestion to use signals must be followed with care. Too many signal words and phrases will increase the length of the paragraph. These added words decrease, rather than increase, readability. Consider the underlined signals in this example.

> <u>The point to be emphasized is that after</u> they begin jogging, smokers often cut down <u>or</u> quit. <u>It is likely that they attribute their decision to two reasons. The first reason is because</u> it is difficult for smokers to exercise vigorously. <u>The second reason is because</u> the noticeable improvement in physical condition encourages further positive changes in lifestyle.

The first version has 59 words, but the second, which has only 40 words, gives the same information in a more readable style.

> <u>After</u> they begin jogging, smokers often cut down <u>or</u> quit. <u>They attribute their decision to two reasons. One</u>, it is difficult for smokers to exercise vigorously. <u>Two</u>, the noticeable improvement in physical condition encourages further positive changes in lifestyle.

SUMMARY

Readable writing is as easy to understand as its content allows. Along with the information included in the writing, readability is affected by the choice of appropriate words, elimination of unnecessary words, use of the proper form of address, use of details and examples, and use of appropriate techniques for showing coherence. Readability is increased when you use words familiar to your readers. Technical words name the complex pieces of equipment, procedures, and concepts familiar to technicians but unfamiliar to customers. They are not appropriate in writing for customers. Cover-up words either carelessly or intentionally hide the truth from readers. Besides the selection of exact and familiar words, readability is also increased by the elimination of unnecessary words and by the use of the appropriate form of address. To make sentences concise, you can use a three-step procedure to identify the "real" subject and verb and throw away uninformative words. You should also select the form of address that best establishes your relationship to your readers. Forms of address include direct commands, the advisory "you," or implied address. Finally, readability is affected by elements beyond the word and the sentence. General statements are more informative and persuasive when they are illustrated with details and examples. Coherence is an important characteristic of readable writing. You can help readers understand how ideas are coherent by building new ideas on top of old ones. You can use signal words and phrases to name difficult connections.

ASSIGNMENTS

Application 1:
Identifying Technical Words

Make a list of 10 technical words frequently used in your field. Beside each word, name the type of audience who will not understand the word. Assume that your audience of *technicians* is the people in your curriculum at college, that your audience of *supervisors* has no formal training in technology but 20 years' experience as managers at the company where you both work, and that your audience of *customers* knows nothing about the field. Explain each decision you make.

Application 2:
Revising to Eliminate Unnecessary Words

Revise the following items to eliminate unnecessary words. Write down your revisions.

A. There are a number of warts caused by viruses. Besides the common wart, there are juvenile warts, plantar warts, and genital warts.

B. As a rule, the fact is that vegetarians as a group may be a whole lot healthier than people who eat meat.

C. The army cook must recognize and pay attention to the fact that preferences for hot food in the Arctic are the most natural result of desires created by the environment in which the troops are operating and stationed in and must make every effort to cook and serve food that satisfies both the taste buds and the needs of the human body.

D. Most good diet plans involve teaching dieters to burn off calories through some type of daily exercise as well as to reduce the amount of food that is high in calories that they eat.

E. It seems that a response is possible for a victim of electrocution if that aforementioned victim is rendered resuscitation in the form of artificial respiration.

F. It has been pointed out several times that the aforementioned heaters are really not very safe as per Consumer Product Safety guidelines.

G. It must be borne in mind that the deenergization of the main supply circuits by the opening of the supply switches will not necessarily or even probably "kill" or disable all circuits in a given piece of equipment.

H. In the past, it had been hoped that persons who were exposed to or who were believed to have been exposed to rabies could be treated with a vaccine that required a very long series of immunization shots, 23 in number, which were very, very painful.

Application 3:
Revising to Eliminate Unnecessary Words

Now revise this paragraph for wordiness. Can you reduce it to one or two sentences?

Extreme caution should be exercised and taken when installing and removing batteries. The fact is that the nature of battery construction is such that the batteries are heavy for their size and somewhat awkward and hard to handle even though they are not large in size. These characteristics seem to dictate the extreme importance of using proper safety precautions. There is the distinct possibility of acid causing extensive damage to equipment or injury to personnel and the very real danger of an explosion that may be caused from the gas that is produced as the previously mentioned battery is charged. Always be sure to follow the prescribed safety precautions in working with batteries.

Application 4:
Identifying Details and Examples

Write down the topic or put brackets around the topic sentence. Then underline the details and examples in the paragraphs below.

A. Studies indicate that Americans often eat out in fast food restaurants. A Gallup study over a three-year period (1984–86) showed that 30 to 42 percent of those polled had eaten out the day before. Mostly, they ate lunch away from home, and 28 percent ate at a fast-food restaurant. Another study showed one out of every five working women eating at a fast-food establishment four times a week.

B. In general, about 10 to 20 percent of all varieties of mushroom can be eaten. About 5 to 10 percent are poisonous to humans. The remaining 70 to 85 percent are not poisonous. However, people cannot eat them because they smell or taste bad.

C. Margarine is the leading table spread in the United States. Its use passed that of butter in 1957. By 1981 Americans were eating 2.5 times more margarine than butter. By 1981, margarine was being consumed at an average rate of 11.2 pounds per person each year. The average person ate only 4.4 pounds of butter. By contrast, in 1887, the earliest year of which figures are available, each person ate an average of 0.4 pound of margarine and 19 pounds of butter.

Application 5:
Identifying Details and Examples

First, fill in the blanks in the sentences below. Then, list the details and examples needed to develop convincing paragraphs.

A. The _____ is a simple machine that has many uses.

B. Americans drink more_____ (or eat more_____) than any other people in the world. (Use your imagination.)

C. _____ are the best cars on the road today.

D. Repairing _____ can be dangerous.

Application 6:
Identifying Topics in Coherent Paragraphs

Write down a noun that names the topic of each paragraph below. Underline the words in the paragraph that refer to that topic.

A. The FDA's Total Diet Laboratory checks for unwanted materials in our food supply. Located in Kansas City, Missouri, it is responsible for the analyses required by the Consumer Protection Agency's Total Diet Study. The 20 chemists and technicians assigned to the Total Diet Laboratory analyze chocolate milkshakes, quarter-pound hamburgers, beer, bologna, lasagna, frozen pizza, dill pickles, watermelon, chocolate chip cookies, and more than 200 other foods Americans eat each year. They are interested in what should not be in those foods: unsafe amounts of pesticides, industrial chemicals, and toxic elements such as arsenic, lead, cadmium, and mercury. In addition to testing for unwanted materials, they also measure the quantities of several essential minerals.

B. Unlike grasses, shrubs, and trees, fungi cannot make their own food from sunlight. They steal their food from living plants and animals, from dead plants and animals, and even from substances such as paint and wallpaper paste. Some fungi can infect humans and cause disease. A few can cause allergic reactions such as sneezing, runny nose, asthma, and serious lung ailments.

C. Shock occurs when electric current flows through the body. It can happen when a person comes in contact with an energized electrical circuit or with something that conducts electricity from an energized circuit. The effect can range from a slight tingle to a severe burn and even death by electrocution. The effect depends on the amount of current flowing through the body, the path of the current, and the length of time exposed.

Application 7:
Identifying Signals

Circle the signal words and phrases in these paragraphs. Write down the type of connection they name.

A. Rocky Mountain spotted fever is a very serious disease caused by a tick bite. However, it is not as feared as it once was. At the turn of the century, when it was called "black measles," the fever carried a death rate of 80 percent in some areas of the Rocky Mountains. By comparison, the death rate today is 3 to 8 percent.

B. Sudden infant death syndrome (SIDS) is the sudden, unexpected, and unexplained death of an apparently healthy baby. Until the 1960s, this syndrome did not have an official name. In fact, it was not entered as cause of death on death certificates until the mid-1970s. Instead unexplained deaths were given causes, such as pneumonia, viral illness, or health and respiratory failure.

7

SPECIAL FORMATTING FEATURES

When you complete this chapter, you should know how to use some special formatting features to increase the readability of your writing. You should learn how to use these features:

> White space
> Lists
>   Use
>   Form
> Headings
>   Use
>   Form
> Supplementary parts
>   Front matter
>   End matter

In Chapter 6, you learned how readability is affected by the selection of familiar words, the elimination of unnecessary words, the use of details and examples, and the careful building of a coherent message. This chapter describes some other features that affect readability. These features have special uses in formats for technical writing. Special formatting features operate like display racks. They show off information in much the same way that racks show off merchandise in a store. They help readers see what a writer considers important. Therefore, they make reading easier and faster. Special formatting features include white space, lists, headings, and supplementary parts at the front or back of a report.

WHITE SPACE

White space is the blank area on a page. In the same way that silence affects understanding in spoken communication, white space affects the meaning that readers understand from a written message. If white space were eliminated from a piece of writing, the pages would be almost entirely black. Only a few white specks would show at the tops and bottoms of letters. White space appears on every page of writing. It makes up the margins between the written text and the end of the page, the indentions for paragraphs, and the blank areas between lines and paragraphs. Typical dimensions for standard white space are as follows:

- The left margin can be 1 to 1½ inches, and the other three margins—right, top, and bottom—must be at least 1 inch.
- When paragraphs are indented, the indention is usually set in five spaces from the left margin.
- When the page is single-spaced, no blank space appears between lines. When it is double-spaced, blank space appears between lines.
- When writing is single-spaced, a double space appears between paragraphs.

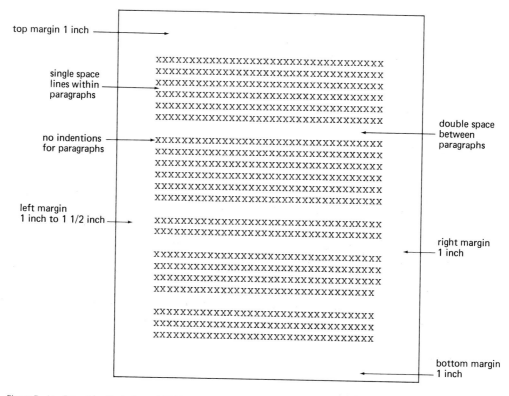

Figure 7–1:   Format for Single-Spaced Writing

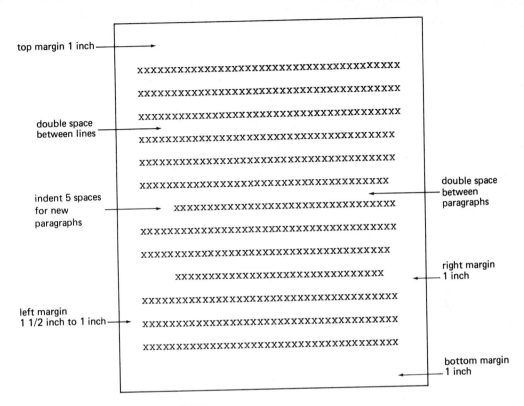

Figure 7−2:   Format for Double-Spaced Writing

Figures 7−1 and 7−2 show the standard white spaces used on a typical page. Figure 7−1 shows a single-spaced page. Single-spaced writing can be presented either without indentions for paragraphs or with five-space indentions. In Figure 7−1, the paragraphs are not indented. Single-spaced formats are used most frequently for short pieces of writing, such as letters and memoranda.

Figure 7−2 shows a double-spaced page. In writing that is double-spaced, white space appears between each line. The paragraphs are indented five spaces. However, as you can see, the margins are the same for both single- and double-spaced writing. Double-spaced formats are used most frequently for long pieces of writing. Most readers find that double-spacing helps them read efficiently for long periods of time.

Besides its standard place on every typed page, white space is also used with the special features you will learn about in the rest of this chapter and visual aids you will learn about in Chapter 8. It appears around lists to set them off from the rest of the writing. It also appears around each item to set that item off from the one before and the one after. White space sets off headings so that readers can skim quickly to pick out the major topics without having to read each paragraph. Finally, white space is used to set off visual aids. It makes tables and figures easier to see and read. Examples of the use of white space are given in the discussions of the other special features.

LISTS

Lists present equally important ideas in equal forms. They make writing more readable by grouping together related ideas. Lists can be used to present various kinds of information. For example, listed items may be parts of a machine in a technical description or steps in a set of instructions. They may also be recommendations or conclusions. Regardless of content, however, lists must have three major characteristics.

○ They must have a clearly stated introductory sentence.
○ They must be made of items of the same type.
○ They must present these similar items in the same form.

This section explains the use and form of lists.

Use

This paragraph is taken from a proposal for a report on the Southern Pine Beetle. The purpose of the report will be to recommend a method for preventing infestation by these destructive insects. How many sections will the report have? What is each section about?

Several areas of research will be covered to determine a pest-management system for controlling Southern Pine Beetles. First, I will cover the life cycle and behavioral characteristics of the Southern Pine Beetle. The next area of research includes a section on host susceptibility to the Southern Pine Beetle. The next area of research to be covered will deal with the methods of identifying Southern Pine Beetle infested stands. The fourth area of research will be control methods. Preventative control methods will also be discussed in the control section.

Let's convert this paragraph to a list.

Four areas of research will be covered in developing an integrated pest-management system for controlling Southern Pine Beetles:

○ Life cycle and behavior of the beetle
○ Host susceptibility to the beetle
○ Identification of infestations
○ Methods of control and prevention

Notice that the sections in the proposed report are much easier to identify in the list than in the paragraph. The separations allowed by white space and the bullets (○) point to each section. The list changes not only the appearance of the information but also the sentence structure. When he makes a list, the writer is forced to write the four items in similar forms. He also cuts out unnecessary words and cleans up awkward sentences. The paragraph version has 89 words, while the list has only 39. In this example, the list encourages a more concise as well as a more readable presentation of the information.

Form

A list must have a general statement that acts as an introduction. In addition, its equal items must be stated in similar forms. Each item must clearly relate to the one before and after. All the items must provide the specific information related to the general statement. Consider this example that lists the factors required for perfect combustion.

> In theory, perfect combustion is simple. Each particle of the fuel is brought into contact with the correct amount of oxygen. Four factors are involved.

- Sufficient air must be supplied.
- The air and fuel particles must be thoroughly mixed.
- Temperatures must be high enough to maintain combustion.
- Enough time must be allowed for the process to be completed.

The introductory sentence, "Four factors are involved," tells readers that the list will consist of four items. By reading the first two sentences of the paragraph, readers learn that these four factors relate to combustion. Each item on the list has an equally important place in achieving perfect combustion. No item is more general than the introductory sentence. The items are presented in similar ways: SUBJECT + MUST BE. For three of the items the "must be" is followed by a VERB + ED, "supplied," "mixed," and "allowed."

To show their relationship, the items in a list are set off from each other by numbers, bullets, or other means of identification. They are also separated by white space. Numbers indicate that the items are related in a sequence. Often they point to steps in a process or in a set of instructions. As shown in the two examples that appear in this section, another frequently used identifying device is the bullet. Some bullets are open (○). Some are closed (●). Some are even decorative (☞).

HEADINGS

Headings, like the one above, make the organization of writing easy to see. Headings allow readers to skim quickly to find the part they are most interested in reading carefully. They also increase readability for readers interested in the entire piece of writing. Each company and each professional organization adopts its own format, but headings share certain common characteristics.

- They appear in different levels or degrees to show the relationships among sections in a piece of writing.

- ○ They summarize the content of the sections they introduce.
- ○ Within the same level, they are written in the same form.

The section explains the use and form of headings.

Use

Placing headings in a report is like laying a formal outline over a piece of writing. Like the numbers and letters in a conventional outline, headings tell readers which are main topics and which are subordinate ones. The form for a heading is based on its degree. There are first-degree headings, second-degree headings, and third-degree headings. First-degree headings introduce major sections in a piece of writing. They are the same level as Roman numbers (I, II, III) in a conventional outline. Second-degree headings introduce sections at the next level of importance. They are the same level as capital letters (A, B, C) in a conventional outline. Third-degree headings introduce sections which are immediately below the second-degree sections in importance and two steps beneath the first-degree sections. They are the same level as Arabic numbers (1, 2, 3) in a conventional outline.

No limit is put on the number of levels that can be used, but three levels of headings are sufficient for most reports. If too many levels of headings appear, readers may have trouble remembering where they are in a piece of writing. In this case, the headings will decrease rather than increase readability. Usually the length of a piece of writing and its use in a company or organization determine how many different levels of headings are needed. A manual will probably have more levels of headings than a brochure.

Headings also tell readers what the section is about. Again, like the words and phrases in a conventional outline, headings summarize the contents in each section. To be effective, headings should be as specific as possible. Uninformative headings, such as "Discussion," should be revised. The revision should tell readers exactly what the section covers. "Problems with Current Procedure" and "Discussion of the Three Procedures" are more informative headings. At the lowest levels, headings become the most specific. For example, a health physics technician at a nuclear facility describes the types of respirators so that management can decide which ones to buy. Her discussion section may be titled with a first-degree heading, "Types of Respirators." Two second-degree headings might be "Atmosphere-Purifying Respirators," and "Atmosphere-Supplying Respirators." Under "Atmosphere-Purifying Respirators," three third-degree headings name brands: "Ultravue," "Ultratwin," and "Scott-O-Vista." Here is a list.

Types of Respirators
　Atmosphere-Purifying Respirators
　　Ultravue
　　Ultratwin
　　Scott-O-Vista
　Atmosphere-Supplying Respirators

As you can see, the third-degree headings are much more specific than the first-degree heading.

Form

To increase readability, headings in the same piece of writing should appear in the same form. Within each level in each section, they should be similar in length and word choice. Let's look at some examples.

The same general form should be used for all headings in a certain piece of writing. Depending upon the readers and the purpose of the writing, headings will most likely appear as either noun phrases or questions. Noun phrases assume that readers are interested in the entire piece of writing. At the least, readers will skim the writing to get an overview of the information. Noun-phrase headings work like titles summarizing the contents of each section. They all share the same form with many repeated words.

These headings are from an excerpt about pollution.[1] The excerpt is taken from a general discussion of environmental controls.

> Pollution (First-degree heading)
>   Oil and Chemical Pollution (Second-degree heading)
>   Oil Spill Prevention (Third-degree heading)
>   Oil Spill Removal (Third-degree heading)
>   Noise Pollution (Second-degree heading)
>   Noise Measurement (Third-degree heading)
>   Noise Hazards (Third-degree Heading)
>   Noise Control (Third-degree heading)

"Pollution" is a first-degree heading. It has two second-degree headings, "Oil and Chemical Pollution" and "Noise Pollution." These second-degree headings are written in the same form. The word "pollution" appears in each. The second-degree heading, "Oil and Chemical Pollution," has two third-degree headings, "Oil Spill Prevention" and "Oil Spill Removal." Like the second-degree headings, they also have repeated words. In addition, these two headings are exactly the same length. The other second-degree heading, "Noise Pollution," has three third-degree headings, "Noise Measurement," "Noise Hazards" and "Noise Control." All three are the same length and share the word "noise."

Besides being written in similar forms, headings must be used in pairs. If it is divided at all, a section must have more than one subsection. A first-degree section must have more than one second-degree heading, and a second-degree section must have more than one third-degree heading. When only one heading is possible, the section should not be divided at all. As long as it has two equal subsections, a section may have as many subsections as necessary to

---

[1] The headings are taken from the Naval Education and Training Command Rate Training Manual *Fireman*. Washington: Government Printing Office, 1982.

make its contents easy to understand. No rule requires that a section have the same number of headings as the one before.

Often, noun-phrase headings appear alone, without numbers. For example, like the excerpt about pollution shown above, this textbook uses noun-phrase headings without numbers. When used in procedures, specifications, technical manuals, and certain kinds of reports, however, noun-phrase headings often have numbers to signal their relationship to each other. This example shows the headings from an engineering report that makes recommendations to meet future transportation needs in an area. The excerpt describes the existing conditions on the site.

1.0 DESCRIPTION OF AREA
   1.1   Physical Setting
   1.2   General Land Use
   1.3   Neighborhoods
      1.3.1 Housing
      1.3.2 Schools
      1.3.3 Parks
  1.4 Transportation
      1.4.1 Roads and Streets
      1.4.2 Bus Stops
2.0 DESCRIPTION OF PROPOSED CHANGES

Although the format varies from one company to the next, this example offers a typical presentation of numbered headings. The numbering system is the same as that used for the numbered outline described in Chapter 3.

The noun-phrase form is the most frequently used general type of heading. However, other forms are also available. In some cases, readers will use the writing to find answers to certain questions. Therefore, headings are written in the form of the questions readers will most likely ask. Questions assume that readers are not interested in the entire piece of writing but that they will use it as a reference. For example, a pamphlet describing the benefits paid by a health insurance plan may contain these headings:

> What is covered by our policy?
> Who is eligible to file a claim?
> How can a claim be filed?

Notice that like the noun-phrase headings, question headings are specific. They are not in the form most typically used for titles, but they serve the same function by telling readers the contents of their sections. Question headings are used most frequently in writing for customers.

SUPPLEMENTARY PARTS

Supplementary parts are additional pieces of writing placed at the front and end of a report. Supplementary parts before the beginning section of the report are front matter. Those after the ending section are end matter. Most companies have established forms for front and end matter. This section describes the use of both types of supplementary parts and gives examples of the front matter for a sales proposal from Lakeside Docks, Incorporated. Excerpts from the proposal are shown in Chapter 10.

Front Matter

Front matter introduces a report to the reader. The report it appears with should be at least six pages long and discuss an important project or try to sell a product or service to a customer. Placed first, before readers see the report, the front matter is written last, after you are sure of what you want to say and how the information will be organized. Although it can include a variety of supplementary materials, front matter usually consists of four related pieces of writing: letter or memorandum of transmittal, title page, table of contents, and summary. It is numbered with lower-case Roman numerals (i, ii, iii). The counting begins with the title page, but Roman numerals do not appear until the page for the table of contents.

Letter or Memorandum of Transmittal.   The letter or memorandum of transmittal is addressed to the receiver of the report. When the receiver works in the same company as the writer, a memorandum is used. When the receiver is a potential customer, a letter is used. Regardless of its intended audience, the letter or memorandum of transmittal introduces or "covers" the report. It begins by explaining the purpose of the report, with a brief mention of the situation that prompted its writing. Then it discusses in more detail what the receiver can expect to find in the report. Both the letter and memorandum of transmittal end politely, usually with an offer to supply more information if necessary.

The letter of transmittal from Lakeside Docks, Incorported, begins by explaining that the writer is responding to a request for bids and by describing the contents of the proposal. The second paragraph discusses the company's qualifications, and the third paragraph gives a brief sales pitch. If the proposal had been longer and more complicated, more discussion of the contents of the report would have been necessary. That discussion would have carried over to the second paragraph.

As result of the bid let March 1, I am forwarding a proposal to build a dock at Lot 27 on Lake Gaston. The proposal describes the methods of installation we would use and gives a breakdown of costs for labor and materials.

As you are aware, my company has installed 42 docks in the Lake Gaston area in the past two years; and I can say, without reservation, that we have 42 satisfied customers. I will be glad to furnish the name of any one of them so that you may call to verify the quality of our work. In addition, I would be delighted to take you to see several of the docks we have constructed.

We look forward to building a quality dock for you so that you can enjoy the pleasures of boating on Lake Gaston right from your backyard. If you have any questions or if any parts of this proposal require further explanation, please call me at 467-1200.

This letter follows the rules of business correspondence. It is typed on letterhead stationery with a dateline, inside address, salutation, complimentary close, and signature. For questions about the formats for letters, see Chapter 11; for questions about the format for memoranda, see Chapter 9.

Title Page.   The title page of a report is a cover sheet, which states the title, the name of the individual or company for whom the report is being prepared, the name of the individual or company preparing the report, the location of the company, and the date of submission. It is very similar to the title page for lab reports. Figure 7–3 shows a title page from the sales proposal for the dock.

The title of a report should provide two types of information for readers. It should identify the type of report that is being submitted and the topic. Here are some examples.

Not Complete

Bovine Embryo Transfer for Small Cattle Ranchers in Alabama
Turbocharging
Biological Phosphorus Removal from Wastewater

Complete

An Evaluation of Bovine Embryo Transfer for Small Ranchers in Alabama
A Description of Turbocharging
A Proposal for Removal of Biological Phosphorus from Wastewater

Table of Contents.   The table of contents lists all the headings in the report and the pages they are found on. It also lists any front matter that comes after it and any appendixes at the end of the report. It does not list tables and figures. The table of contents provides a summary of the topics covered in the report and acts as a locating device. It should allow readers to determine the relationships among headings at a glance. Often a system of indenting, capitalizing, and underlining is used to distinguish among first-, second-, and third-degree headings, front matter, and appendixes.

Figure 7–4 on page 100 shows the table of contents in the proposal for the dock. The summary is written in capital letters. First-degree headings are written in capital and lower-case letters and underlined. Second-degree headings are written in capital and lower-case letters without underlining and indented five spaces. If third-degree headings had been used in the report, a different system of capital letters, underlining, and indenting could have been developed. Notice that the tables and figures in the proposal are listed separately at the bottom of the page. The number, the title, and the page number for each are given.

PROPOSAL

FOR THE

CONSTRUCTION OF A LAKESIDE DOCK AT

LOT 27, LAKE GASTON

prepared for

Clyde L. Anderson

prepared by

Larry Williams, President

Lakeside Docks, Incorporated

Tar Landing, North Carolina 27514

April 10, 1988

Figure 7–3:   Title Page

TABLE OF CONTENTS

LIST OF ILLUSTRATIONS

ii

Figure 7–4:   Table of Contents

Summary.   The summary, also called an abstract, is a brief preview of the in-for-mation found in the report. It gives the most important facts organized as they appear in the report. The summary should be no more than 10 percent of the length of the report or less than 250 words, regardless of how long the report is. The first sentence announces the purpose of the report, and the rest of the summary briefly presents the major details related to the purpose. The summary does not evaluate the information in the report, and personal pro-nouns such as "I" and "we" should be avoided. The reader should be able to detach the summary from the report and read it separately as a complete piece of writing.

The summary for the Lakeside Docks proposal includes the name of the product or service offered, the amount of time it will take to provide the product or service, and the total cost. Since the proposal is short, the summary is also short.

> Lakeside Docks, Incorporated, will build a 30-foot dock at Lot 27, Lake Gaston for a total cost of $1,292. The dock will be constructed of top-quality materials and be completed approximately five days after construction begins. Lakeside Docks will supply the carpenters and electricians necessary to do the job and subcontract the dredging and pile driving to another company. Before the con-struction can begin, Lakeside Docks will ask for a 25 percent down payment ($323), with the rest of the costs paid after completion and final inspection of the project.

End Matter

As its name implies, end matter appears at the end of a report. It includes appendixes and attachments. Appendixes and attachments present information that readers do not need to see while they are reading the body of a piece of writing. In some cases, the information may be unnecessary for the first reader of the report, but it may be essential for a second one. In other cases, informa-tion is placed in appendixes or attachments because it is bulky. For example, fold-out drawings, product brochures, or detailed sets of instructions are too big to fit neatly in the main text of a report. Although the function is the same in both cases, these unifying features are called "appendixes" in long pieces of writing and "attachments" in short pieces of writing. Appendixes appear in textbooks, manuals, and long reports. Attachments appear in memoranda or letter reports.

Each company and professional organization has its own format for labeling appendixes and attachments. However, most formats require two kinds of identification: a title and a number or letter. The title tells what the appendix or attachment presents: "Upstairs Floor Plan for Townhouse 44." If more than one appendix or attachment is used, a number or letter gives its location in the sequence. This book has three appendixes: Appendix A, "Con-ventions of Standard Written American English"; Appendix B, "Common Problems with Written English"; and Appendix C "Language of Equal Treatment." A letter proposal to landscape a large yard may have two attachments. Attachment A, "Lawn Enhancers," lists the proposed changes in the lawn, such as new plants, rock gardens, or walkways. Attachment B, "Costs," gives the charges for labor and materials. You will learn more about appendixes and attachments in Chapter 8, which discusses visual aids.

SUMMARY

Special formatting features increase the readability of technical writing. They include white space, lists, headings, and supplementary parts at the front and end of a report. White space is the blank area that appears on every page of writing. It is margins, indentions for paragraphs, and spaces between lines. White space is also used around lists, headings, and visual aids. Lists present equal items in equal forms. They group together related ideas for readers. Headings tell readers what a section is about and how that section relates to the ones before and after. Supplementary parts are front matter and end matter. Front matter introduces a report to the readers. It includes a letter or memorandum of transmittal, a title page, a table of contents, and a summary. End matter includes appendixes and attachments appearing after the concluding section of the report. Appendixes and attachments include supplementary information that may not be important to all readers of the report or that may be too big to fit neatly with the paragraphs and sentences.

ASSIGNMENTS

Application1:
Revising

Revise the following excerpts as indicated.

A. This excerpt would be easier to read if parts of it were written as a list.[2] Indicate where the list should be used and how the listed items should be presented. Do not revise the excerpt for word choice or sentence structure.

Laws Of Gases

In the middle of the seventeenth century, Robert Boyle, an English scientist, made some interesting discoveries concerning the relationship between the pressure, the temperature, and the volume of gases. In 1787, Jacques Charles, a Frenchman, proved that all gases expand the same amount when heated 1 degree if the pressure is kept constant. The relationships that these two men discovered are summarized as follows. First, when the temperature is held constant, an increase in the pressure on a gas causes a proportional decrease in

[2]The information about the laws of gases is adapted from the Naval Education and Training Command Rate Training Manual *Fireman*. Washington: Government Printing Office, 1982.

volume. A decrease in the pressure causes a proportional increase in volume. Second, when the pressure is held constant, an increase in the temperature of a gas causes a proportional increase in volume. A decrease in the temperature causes a proportional decrease in volume. Third, when the volume is held constant, an increase in the temperature of a gas causes a proportional increase in pressure. A decrease in the temperature causes a proportional decrease in pressure. Consider a boiler in which steam has been formed. With the steam stop valves still closed, the volume of the steam remains constant while the pressure and the temperature are both increasing. When operating pressure is reached and the steam stop valves are opened, the high pressure of the steam causes the steam to flow to the turbines. The pressure of the steam thus provides the potential for doing work. The actual conversion of thermal energy to work is done in turbines.

B. This excerpt is from a report written by a student on the benefits of working as an intern with the Federal Land Bank. The information could have been presented more effectively in a list than in this series of short, choppy paragraphs. Revise the excerpt to present the information in a concise, readable list.

There are several benefits you can look forward to if you decide to work as an intern with the Federal Land Bank.

For one thing the internship gives you a chance to earn five hours of school credit while working during the summer.

The salary for an intern is not too bad either. You will earn $200/week salary and another $100/week for living expenses.

The Federal Land Bank will teach you more about the Farm Credit System than you could ever learn in a textbook. Without credit, farming would not exist. Most all of the farmers in the United States are dependent on some form of farm credit to be able to buy land, equipment, and fertilizer to plant their crops.

If you do a good job during your internship, it will enhance your ability for employment with the Federal Land Bank after you graduate. The Federal Land Bank will hire you before it hires anyone else because it has already spent money and time on training you.

C. These headings are taken from a discussion of valves in a training manual. They are not parallel. Correct the problems with parallelism.

Valves

Stop Valves
   Globe Valves
   Valves That Act as Gates
   Plug Valves
   Needle Valves
   Butterfly Valves
Check Valves
Stop/Check Valves
Valves That Throttle
Relief Valves
Valves for Safety

D. These headings are taken from a short report on the potential benefits of establishing a McChicken franchise in Hickory, Virginia. Hickory is a small town. The company is concerned about the size of the market for its product, the possible competition, and the availability of a suitable location. Revise these headings to make them appropriate for the report.

> Market Size
>   Surveying the Market
>   Results of Survey
> The Possibility of Competition
>   Joe's Barbeque
>   Chicken Sold in Hamburger Restaurants
>   Competition from Kentucky Fried Chicken
> Possible Location
>   Oak Street

Application 2:
Examining Special Features

Copy and bring to class articles from a trade journal and a popular magazine that you enjoy reading. Examine both periodicals for the special features discussed in this chapter. Look at the use of white space, headings, and lists.

Consider these questions.

1. Do the two periodicals use lists? If so, what kinds of items are listed? How does the use of lists differ between the trade journal and the popular magazine?
2. Do the two periodicals use headings? If so, how are the headings used? Give examples of headings from each periodical.

8

VISUAL AIDS

When you complete this chapter, you should know how to use visual aids in written and spoken communication. You should learn about the following topics:

  Use
  Explaining visual aids
  Placement and labeling in writing
    Placement
    Labeling
  Types of visual aids
    Tables
    Graphs
    Charts
    Drawings
    Other figures

Visual aids present information without sentences or paragraphs.[1] When used appropriately, visual aids allow information to be presented clearly, precisely, and effectively. They can illustrate a description of a machine or an explanation of a process. They can also point up comparisons between two or more related groups of numbers. This chapter explains how visual aids increase clar-

___

[1]We wish to thank Walter Straub for his careful editing and drawing in this chapter.

ity in spoken and written communication and offers a few guidelines about designing and using them.

Most visual aids are classified as either tables and figures. Tables present information in columns and rows. They allow exact comparison of information either in words or in numbers. Figures are anything else: graphs, charts, drawings, and photographs. They usually rely on lines and shapes to present their information. For students who want more information, a few books about visual aids are listed at the end of this chapter.

USE

Visual aids are used to make information easier to understand and more appealing. The choice of visual aid is determined by the audience and purpose of the communication. For customers, a drawing may omit details about tiny parts. Customers are interested in an overall view to buy or use a product but not to repair it if it breaks down. For technicians, even the smallest details are important. Technicians need a clearly labeled drawing and discussion of each part that might have to be replaced or repaired. Different visual aids are used for each type of audience.

Here is a series of drawings designed for three types of audiences. Notice how the drawings change for each audience. Figure 8-1 is taken from a brochure intended to give farmers some tips on the safe operation of a loader. Figure 8-2 is taken from a set of instructions in an Army training manual designed for Ammunition Specialists. The purpose of the instructions is to explain how to drive a forklift to move ammunition from one place to another. The writer includes a drawing of the pedals and control devices inside the forklift. Figure 8-3 on page 108 is intended for the Army personnel responsible for repairing forklifts or at least for those who order the parts. It is from a manual which shows a breakdown of each major part of the forklift into its

**NEVER LEAVE
LOADER WITH
RAISED BUCKET**

FIGURE 8-1: Drawing of loader
Source: United States. Department of Labor, Occupational Safety and Health Administration. *Safety with Front-End Loaders*. Washington: Government Printing Office, 1976.

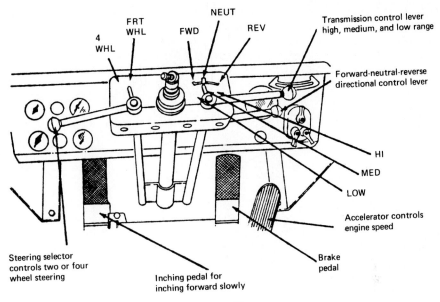

A. Pedal and control levers.

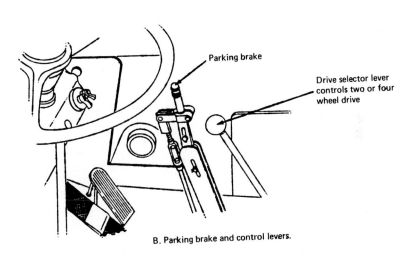

B. Parking brake and control levers.

FIGURE 8-2: Drawing of Control Panel of Forklift
Source: United States. Department of the Army. *Ammunitions Specialist.*
Washington: Government Printing Office, 1980.

subparts: screws, bolts, wires, and pieces of metal. This drawing shows an exploded view of one part of the control panel.

In Figure 8-1 the type of machine is barely recognizable. In Figure 8-2 the purpose is to show trainees how to operate the machine. In Figure 8-3 every wire and bolt is important.

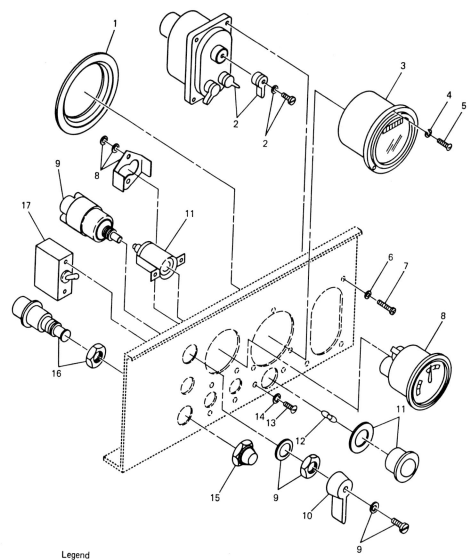

Legend

1. Damper
2. Switch Bank
3. Meter
4. Washer, Lock
5. Screw, Machine
6. Washer, Lock

7. Screw
8. Meter
9. Switch, Rotary
10. Handle, Switch
11. Light, Indicator
12. Lamp, Incandescent

13. Screw
14. Washer
15. Starter Button
16. Engine Start Button
17. Switch, Toggle Light

FIGURE 8-3:   Exploded View Drawing of Control Panel on Forklift
Source: United States. Department of the Army *Technical Manual,*
Organizational, Maintenance, Repair Parts, Special Tools Lists.
Truck, Lift, Fork, Diesel Engine. Washington: Government Printing Of-
fice, February 1985.

When used appropriately for an audience, visual aids increase clarity by making the presentation more appealing and by condensing information. They also emphasize important points. Readers and listeners are more likely to remember information presented in drawings than in words.

Visual aids are attractive. They add interest to written and spoken communication. One of the most popular features of magazines like *Sports Illustrated* or *National Geographic* is the photographs. The professionals who explain "how to" on television often demonstrate the procedure while they talk. If a demonstration is not possible, they use drawings. Shows like *Sesame Street* use a range of visual aids to appeal to children. Reports and oral presentations to work groups are not intended to be entertaining, but they should be as appealing and interesting as money and time allow.

Besides their use as decoration, tables and figures act as convenient summaries for information that may be difficult to understand when explained in sentences. Sometimes a long, confusing discussion can be made into a table. Consider this example.

In 1970, American farmers produced 4.2 billion bushels of corn. In 1975, production rose to 5.8 billion bushels. The rise continued in 1980 and 1982, with 6.6 and 8.4 billion bushels respectively. Wheat production was below corn production and did not experience as much increase. In 1970, American farmers produced 1.4 billion bushels of wheat. In 1975, they produced 2.1 billion bushels. Production in 1980 and 1982 was 2.4 and 2.8 billion bushels respectively. Increases in soybean production are comparable to those in wheat production and not as large as increases in corn production. In 1970, American farmers produced 1.1 billion bushels of soybeans. Production increased slightly to 1.5 billion bushels in 1975. In 1980, they produced 1.8 billion bushels. In 1982, production increased to 2.3 billion bushels.

Notice how the 120 words can be replaced by numbers in concise rows and columns.

Table: Corn, Wheat, and Soybean Production, 1970 to 1982

Crop	1970	1975	1980	1982
		(billions of bushels)		
corn	4.2	5.8	6.6	8.4
wheat	1.4	2.1	2.4	2.8
soybean	1.1	1.5	1.8	2.3

Often the same information can be presented in either a table or a figure. If readers or listeners need exact numbers, a table is used. If they need quick overall comparisons, a figure is used. Figure 8-4 on page 110 represents the same information as the table above. Notice how easy it is to see the increases in production for each crop and to determine the large differences between production in corn and production in wheat and soybeans.

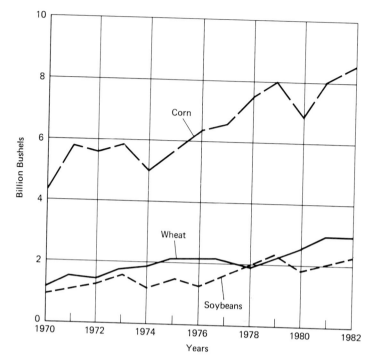

FIGURE 8-4: Corn, Wheat, and Soybean Production, 1970 to 1982
Source: United States. Bureau of the Census. *Statistical Abstract of the United States*.
104th ed. Washington: Government Printing Office, 1983.

EXPLAINING VISUAL AIDS

To be effective, visual aids must be explained. In both written and spoken communication, visual aids must be introduced and then discussed.

The introduction is usually a general statement explaining what the visual aid shows. In writing, the introduction includes a number for the visual aid. In an oral presentation, a number usually is not necessary. Instead of referring to a number, the speaker simply points to the table or figure. Here are some examples of introductions.

As shown on Figure 8-4, corn production has increased . . . .

As you can see, corn production has increased . . . .

When you compare production of corn, wheat, and soybeans, you can see that corn is the most popular of the three crops among American farmers. (See the table on page 109.)

Figure 8-4 shows that wheat production has increased . . . .

This graph shows that wheat production has increased . . . .

After the visual aid is introduced, it must be discussed. The most important details or comparisons should be pointed out. Information essential to the discussion should be mentioned.

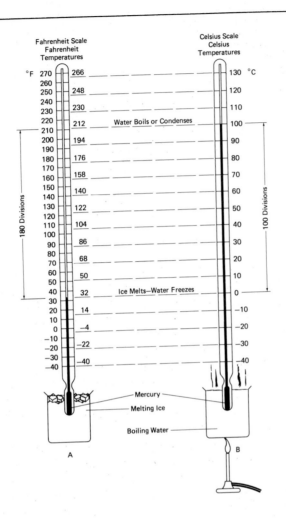

Figure 8-5 shows the two temperature scales in comparison and also introduces the simplest temperature measuring instrument, the liquid-in-glass thermometer. The two thermometers shown are exactly alike in size and shape; the only difference is the outside markings, or scales, on them. Each thermometer is a hollow glass tube which has a mercury-filled bulb at the bottom and which is sealed at the top. Mercury, like any other liquid, expands when heated and will rise in the hollow tube. The illustration shows the Fahrenheit thermometer with its bulb standing in ice water (32°F), while the Celsius thermometer is in boiling water (100°C).

The essential point to remember is that the level of the mercury in a thermometer depends only on the temperature to which the bulb is exposed. If the thermometers were exchanged the mercury in the Celsius thermometer would drop to the level at which the mercury now stands in the Fahrenheit thermometer, while the mercury in the Fahrenheit thermometer would rise to the level at which the mercury now stands in the Celsius thermometer. The temperature would be 0°C for the ice water and 212°F for the boiling water.

FIGURE 8-5:   Visual Aid with Text
Source: United States. Department of the Navy. *Fireman*. Washington: Government Printing Office, 1982.

Figure 8-5 on the previous page is taken from a Navy training manual. It shows a drawing and its written discussion. The writer is attempting to explain some fundamental principles of engineering to the trainees. Here he shows the comparison between Fahrenheit and Celsius scales. At the same time he demonstrates the operating principle of the thermometer. A major point is that the liquid-in-glass thermometer operates according to the same principle regardless of the scale marked on it.

PLACEMENT AND LABELING IN WRITING

When they are used in reports, manuals, or other pieces of writing, visual aids must be convenient and clearly labeled for the reader to use. A hard-to-find visual aid that lacks a title and identification of its major parts is useless.

Placement

Depending on the information shown on a table or figure and its size, a visual aid can appear immediately after it is mentioned or as an appendix or attachment.

As soon as it is introduced, the visual aid can be inserted on the same page. It appears as near the discussion as possible. In this case, the visual aid is closely integrated into the words and sentences and very easy for the reader to use. When a table or figure is too big to fit immediately after it is mentioned, it can be placed on a separate page. A note, "Insert Figure 8-1 here," is written on the page where the visual aid should appear.

If visual aids incorporated into the discussion take away from the ease of reading and using the writing, they are placed as appendixes in a long piece of writing and as attachments in a short piece of writing. Visual aids appear as appendixes or attachments for the three major reasons discussed in Chapter 7. First, they may be too big and bulky to be included in discussion. Second, they may show information that a reader needs throughout the entire piece of writing. Third, visual aids may present information not immediately relevant for the reader but very important for later readers.

Labeling

Besides being conveniently placed, most visual aids should be identified with a title and a number. The parts should also be appropriately labeled. These two types of labeling help readers easily and quickly relate visual aids to their discussion. Several considerations are important in labeling visual aids.

Clearly Stated Title. Visual aids should have clear titles. Sometimes the title identifies the type of visual aid as well as its content. For example, "Assembled View of Articulating Wheel Brake" is not the same as "Exploded View of Articulating Wheel Brake." It is not always necessary to identify the type of visual aid used, but it is important to tell readers exactly what the visual aid shows. Consider the table shown earlier: "Corn, Wheat, and Soybean Production, 1970 to 1982." This title names the three crops shown and the time period considered. "Crop Production" or even "Crop Production for 12 Years" does not provide much information for readers.

Number. Visual aids are numbered consecutively through the text. Usually Arabic numbers are used, and tables and figures are numbered separately. For example, a report may have five visual aids, two tables and three figures. The labeled sequence may be

   Figure 1
   Figure 2
   Table 1
   Figure 3
   Table 2

In a book or manual with several chapters, the numbers on visual aids include the chapter number first and the number for the visual aid second. For example, Figure 8-1 is the first figure in this chapter. Since most short writing does not have multiple chapters, visual aids often have only single numbers.

Correctly Placed Title. According to most style manuals, tables should have their numbers and titles at the top. Figures should have their identification at the bottom. Sometimes a publisher adopts a style different from what is most frequently used. In these cases, the labeling may be changed. Some of the figures shown in this chapter were labeled at the top in the books and magazines where we found them.

Listed in Front of Document. When three or more visual aids are included in a piece of writing, the titles and numbers and the page numbers on which the visual aids appear are listed at the bottom of the page that contains the table of contents. If all the visual aids are figures, the list may be called "List of Figures." If they are all tables, the list may be called "List of Tables." If both tables and figures appear, the list is called "List of Illustrations."

Parts Identified. Besides the title and number, the visual aid should have its parts clearly labeled. On a graph, the vertical and horizontal lines should be named. On a drawing, the parts should be named.

TYPES OF VISUAL AIDS

As mentioned earlier, the two general types of visual aids are tables and figures. Tables present information organized in columns or rows. Figures include any visual aid that is not a table. They can be graphs, charts, drawings, or photographs.

   Even though many companies have drafting or art departments to put figures in their final forms, technicians are responsible for deciding when and how to use visual aids. They are also responsible for explaining their ideas for visual aids to the professionals who draw them. In addition to their concern about the design of visual aids, technicians must be able to read and understand tables and figures to fulfill the demands of their jobs. Anyone who has tried to repair a broken forklift, wire a house, give a shot, or maintain a new car knows the importance of understanding information presented in tables and figures.

Tables

Tables show information in columns and rows to allow exact comparisons. They present their information very concisely and conveniently. Tables emphasize the details rather than the size of a comparison. Because of their detail, tables do not let readers make comparisons at a glance. Unlike graphs and charts, tables allow precise but not very quick understanding. Here are some guidelines for designing and using tables.

- Each vertical column has a heading which identifies the type of items listed. Each horizontal row is also labeled.
- If the table shows comparisons involving numbers, the same unit of measurement is used throughout. That unit is stated at the top of the column or the beginning of the row.
- The table stands out with lines at the top and at the bottom. At the top, one line separates the table from the rest of the text, and a second separates the heading from the information in the table. At the bottom only one line is used. Instead of lines, white space between rows and columns inside the table emphasizes the separation. Usually lines to indicate left and right margins are not necessary.
- Numbers are vertically aligned. If present, decimal points serve as guides for alignment.
- Footnotes can be used to explain items that a reader may not understand.
- If the table is taken from a secondary source, a notation appears at the bottom. This same form of citation is used to give proper credit for figures as well as tables borrowed from another writer. Examples of source notation appear throughout this chapter.

Figure 8-6 shows an empty table. Notice the boxed-in section for labels used to identify vertical columns and the section at the left for the labels used to identify horizontal rows. As you can see, tables have lines at the top and the bottom.

Figure 8-7 on page 116 shows a table representing the number of cars manufactured in the United States after 1965 that have emission controls of various types or that lack emission controls completely. In reading this table, notice that the total cars manufactured and the year they were manufactured serve as column headings. The type of emission control is identified on the row. The numbers in each column add up to the total in the heading. Notice also the use of footnotes and source notations to further explain the numbers and identify their originator.

The hyphens in the table should be read as "not applicable." They indicate that no cars were manufactured with a particular emission control during the year named. They suggest that the emission control was not used because it was not required. As users study this complex table, they can make exact com-

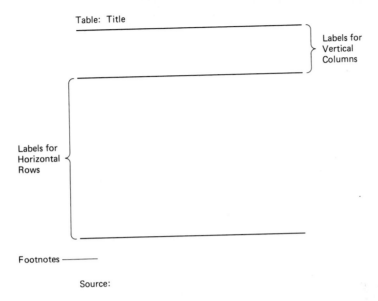

Table: Title

Labels for Vertical Columns

Labels for Horizontal Rows

Footnotes ———

Source:

FIGURE 8-6:   Empty Table

parisons and determine when certain kinds of emission controls were first required.

Graphs

When writers or speakers want to emphasize the size of a comparison rather than exact amounts, they are likely to use graphs rather than tables. Details may be lost in this change from numbers to lines and shapes, but the relationships will be much easier to understand quickly. Three common graphs are line graphs, bar graphs, and pie graphs. The line graph is the most exact and the least decorative of the three, while the pie graph is the least exact and the most decorative. Line graphs are likely to be used for audiences that consist of technicians or supervisors. Pie graphs are more likely to be used for customers interested in only the most general comparisons.

Line Graphs.   Line graphs are constructed from plotting points as they relate to an *x*-axis and a *y*-axis. They are used to show trends. Although they often point to changes over time, line graphs can also show other kinds of relationships. For example, in a report to the company's stockholders, a boat manufacturer may plot the sales record of a certain model from 1980 to 1987. This graph will allow stockholders to judge the success of that particular model. It shows change over a period of time. In an advertisement for potential customers, the boat manufacturer may plot the boat's speed against its gas mileage. This graph shows at what speeds the operation of the boat is most economical. It shows change according to speed. Time is not included in this example.

Some line graphs show changes in a single item. Others, called multiple-line graphs, show changes in as many as three items. Since their pur-

No. 1021.   Cars in Operation with Emission controls: 1965 to 1982

(As of July 1, figures show cars with emission controls whether or not the controls are in operation)

Emission Controls	Cars (Millions)							
	1965	1971	1975	1978	1979	1980[1]	1981	1982
Total cars	68.9	83.1	95.2	103.0	104.7	104.6	105.8	106.9
No emission controls	46.0	12.8	4.0	2.3	1.7	1.4	7.4	6.4
Crankcase control[2]	22.9	35.8	21.4	11.0	8.9	7.2		
Exhaust and crankcase controls[3]	—	27.7	24.6	17.8	14.9	12.1	10.2	8.6
Fuel evaporation and above controls[4]	—	6.8	18.5	16.3	14.8	13.0	11.5	10.0
Nitrogen oxide and above controls[5]	—	—	22.0	21.0	19.9	18.5	17.3	15.8
Catalyst and above controls[6]	—	—	4.7	34.6	44.4	52.3	59.4	66.1

—Represents zero
[1] Beginning 1980, passenger vans (approx. 1.4 million) were reclassified from passenger cars to trucks.
[2] Installed nationwide, starting with 1963 models, to reduce emissions of hydrocarbon.
[3] Exhaust controls introduced nationwide on 1968 models to accelerate the reduction of hydrocarbon emissions and emissions of carbon monoxide.
[4] Begun on 1971 models to eliminate losses from gasoline tanks and carburetors.
[5] Available on some 1971 and 1972 models and all 1973 and later models to lower emissions of nitrogen oxides.
[6] Catalyst or equivalent control systems introduced on cars in 1975 to meet tougher emission levels for hydrocarbons and carbon monoxide.

Source: Motor Vehicle Manufacturers Association of the United States, Inc. Detroit, Mich. Motor Vehicle Facts and Figures, annual. Computed from R. L. Polk & Co. data.

vertical labels

horizontal labels

alignment with decimal points

footnotes

source note

FIGURE 8-7:   Table Showing Cars in Operation with Emission Controls
Source: United States. Bureau of the Census. *Statistical Abstract of the United States.* 104th ed. Washington: Government Printing Office, 1983.

pose is to show trends, line graphs are not intended to allow a clear comparison of the size of one amount with another. Here are some guidelines for designing and reading line graphs.

○ The horizontal line (*x*-axis) lists items whose value is fixed (independent variable). The vertical line (*y*-axis) lists values that change (dependent variable).

○ On a multiple-line graph, different line types are often used to distinguish one line from another. For example, one line may be solid, another may have dashes, and a third may have dots and dashes.

○ When the lines are not labeled, a legend is often used to explain the line types. A legend shows readers a small sample of the different lines that appear on the graph. It is also used to identify symbols on bar graphs, schematic diagrams, and other kinds of figures. A line graph with a legend is shown in Figure 8-10.

Figure 8-8 shows an empty line graph. Notice that the horizontal line (*x*-axis) goes left to right, and the vertical line (*y*-axis) goes up and down. This same arrangement of vertical and horizontal axes is used in bar graphs, the next type of graph discussed in this chapter. The difference between the two graphs is obvious: Line graphs show their comparisons with lines, and bar graphs use bars.

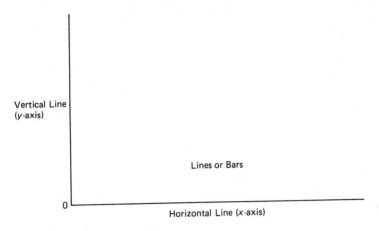

FIGURE 8-8:   Empty Line Graph or Bar Graph

Figure 8-9 is a line graph with a single line representing John Hanson's salary from 1982 to 1986. As the graph shows, John's salary has steadily increased during the five-year time period. He received a large raise in 1983.

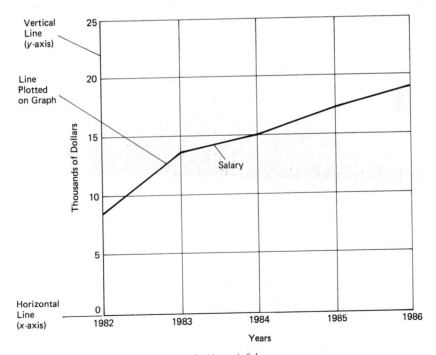

FIGURE 8-9:   Single-Line Graph Showing John Hanson's Salary

The single line on Figure 8-9 shows a trend toward a higher salary. However, the graph does not indicate how much John profited from the increase. A multiple-line graph will allow readers to see if the increase in salary is reflected in John's savings. Figure 8-10 shows that as John's salary has increased, his cost of living has also increased. His savings have not increased very much over the five-year period.

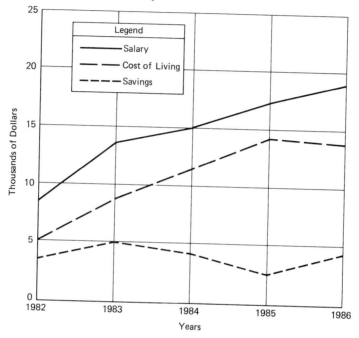

FIGURE 8-10:   Multiple-Line Graph Showing John Hanson's Finances

Notice the legend on the multiple-line graph. It gives readers a sample of each line used. John's salary is shown with a solid line. His cost of living is shown by a line with large dashes and small dashes. His savings are shown by a line with small dashes. When labeling will make a graph cluttered and difficult to read, legends are used to identify the lines.

Bar Graphs.   Bar graphs show change in size or amount. Two types of bar graphs are single-aspect bar graphs and multiple-bar graphs.

Single-aspect bar graphs have only one set of bars. Figure 8-11 is a single-aspect bar graph. It allows comparison of changes in an item over time. Figure 8-11 shows farm population measured each 10 years from 1950 to 1980 and in 1982. Notice the large decrease. A line graph could have shown the trend in declining population. However, the bars help readers see the size of the decline. The bar associated with 1950 is at least three times the size of the one associated with 1982. Multiple-bar graphs have several sets of bars. Like multiple-line graphs, they are used to compare related aspects of the same item.

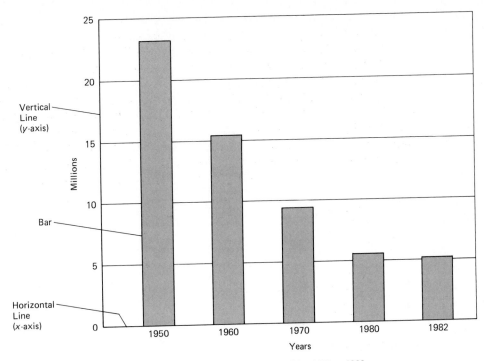

FIGURE 8-11:   Bar Graph Showing the Decrease in Farm Population from 1950 to 1982
Source: United States. Bureau of the Census. *Statistical Abstract of the United States*. 104th ed. Washington: Government Printing Office, 1983.

Here are some guidelines for designing and reading bar graphs. For questions about the scale on a bar graph, refer to Figure 8-8. Figure 8-8 shows the vertical and horizontal lines used as scales on both line graphs and bar graphs.

- A consistent scale will allow proper proportions on the graph.
- Depending on the items displayed, bar graphs can be vertical or horizontal.
- Bars can be emphasized or defined by shading, coloring, or cross-hatching. Bars or groups of bars that make up one item can often be separated with white space. Bars should be the same width. If they are separated with white space, the separations should be consistent.
- A legend is often used to explain the color or cross-hatch pattern that defines a bar.

Pie Graphs.   Pie graphs are used to show the relative proportion of items that make up a whole. All of the items shown on the pie add up to 100 percent. Each item takes up some portion of the whole. The purpose of the graph is to show how those portions compare with each other. Pie graphs are often accompanied by tables showing exact amounts. Here are some guidelines for designing and understanding pie graphs.

○ The first cut on the pie occurs at the 12:00 position. The largest piece is cut first. The other pieces are cut according to size.

○ Pies have at least three but no more than seven pieces.

○ Small segments are often combined in a last piece called "Others."

○ Percentages and labels are included on each piece. If a piece is too small for this information, the percentage and the label are written nearby and connected to the piece with a straight line. A legend is not usually necessary.

Figure 8-12 shows an empty pie graph. Notice that the first cut begins at the 12:00 position. The pieces are cut clockwise, from largest to smallest.

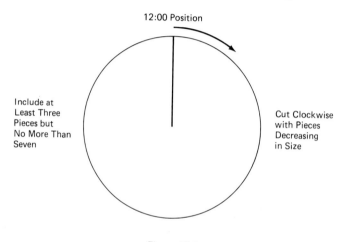

Figure: Title

FIGURE 8-12:   Empty Pie Graph

Charts

Charts are used to present information that is not in numbers and that cannot be presented in a table. They show the relationships among steps in a process and the relationships among parts or people in a system. Two kinds of charts are flowcharts and organizational charts.

Flowcharts.   Flowcharts show the steps involved in a process from the beginning to the end. They give an easy-to-see overview of the process. Flowcharts show how each movement leads to another and how it relates to the whole process. One kind of flowchart shows the decision-making process. Figure 8-13 outlines the procedure for troubleshooting a tail light. This flowchart is intended for untrained car owners rather than experienced automotive technicians. It shows the questions to ask in finding out what is wrong with the tail light and how to fix the problem once it is found. The questions are shown in diamonds and the actions in rectangles.

Flowcharts can also be used to represent a natural process or a mechan-

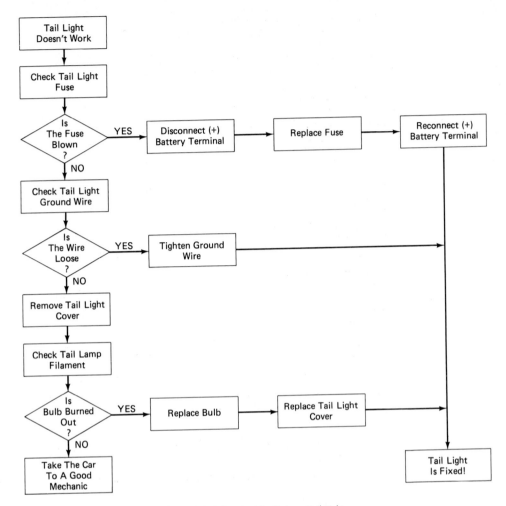

FIGURE 8-13:   Flowchart Showing the Decisions Required for Fixing a Tail Light

ical process that goes on without human decisions. For example, a flowchart can show coolant moving through a refrigeration system. Once the refrigeration system is set up and working properly, no human intervention is required.

Organizational Charts.   Organizational charts are used to show the relations of divisions and the hierarchy of positions in an organization. Rank in an organization is based on authority or responsibility. Each individual or position in an organization is ranked according to the other members. Boxes enclose the names and titles. Lines connect the boxes to show the hierarchy. Figure 8-14 on page 122 is an organizational chart of Joe's TV Sales and Service Center. Joe Alexander, Sr. is the owner and president, and the two locations are managed by his sons, Joe Jr. and Fred. Notice that Fred's store has a delivery staff, a sales staff, and a service staff, while Joe Jr.'s has only a sales staff.

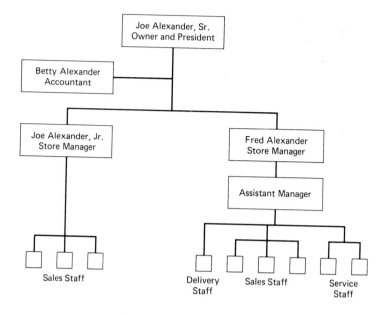

Joe's TV Sales and Service Centers

FIGURE 8-14:   Organizational Chart for Joe's TV Sales and Service Centers

Drawings

Drawings include diagrams and sketches used to show the parts of an item or other descriptive information. Some drawings are diagrams of parts, exploded-view diagrams, cutaway diagrams, cross-section diagrams, sketches, and maps. The production of these complex visual aids is usually the responsibility of an artist or draftsperson rather than a technican, but it is important for technicians to recognize the various types of drawings and read them correctly.

Diagrams of Parts.   Technical descriptions of equipment are often accompanied by diagrams of parts. These drawings let readers and listeners see the item that has been described. The amount of detail shown is determined by how the drawing will be used.

Figure 8-15 is a diagram that shows the parts of an electromechanical winch, a device used for moving or lifting heavy loads. This diagram appears in a Navy training manual. It will not be useful for readers who want to learn how to repair the device, because it lacks detail. However, it will help the trainees learn what a winch is.

Exploded-View Diagrams.   When the audience needs a detailed description of a piece of equipment, exploded-view diagrams of the parts are more useful than diagrams of the completed item. These detailed drawings appear frequently in

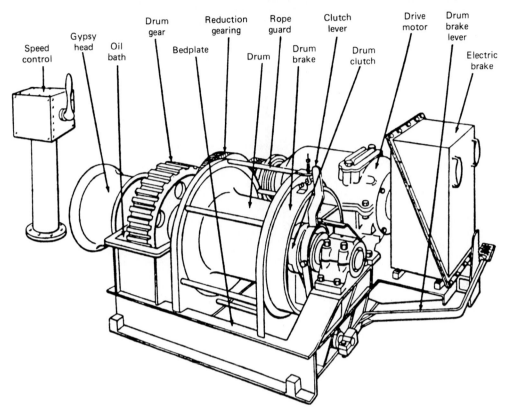

Speed control — Gypsy head — Oil bath — Drum gear — Bedplate — Reduction gearing — Drum — Rope guard — Drum brake — Clutch lever — Drum clutch — Drive motor — Drum brake lever — Electric brake

FIGURE 8-15: Diagram of the Parts of an Electromechanical Winch
Source: United States. Department of the Navy. *Fireman*. Washington: Government Printing Office, 1982.

technical manuals. They show the parts of a piece of equipment pulled slightly away from each other so that a technician can see how the equipment should be assembled. To save clutter, the parts are usually numbered and identified on a legend or list that accompanies the drawing. Figure 8-3, on page 108 at the beginning of this chapter, is an exploded-view diagram of the control panel from a forklift.

Cutaway Diagrams. Cutaway diagrams show both the inside and outside of an object in one drawing. A portion of the outside is broken away to allow a view of the inside.

Cross-Section Diagrams. Cross-section diagrams also show the inside of an item. However, instead of cutting away part of the outside covering to allow a peek at the inner workings, cross-section diagrams show slices of the inside. Figure 8-16 on page 124 is a cross-section diagram of a solar collector. It is taken from a government pamphlet for homeowners interested in low-cost passive designs using solar energy.

Solar Collectors on Earth Berms

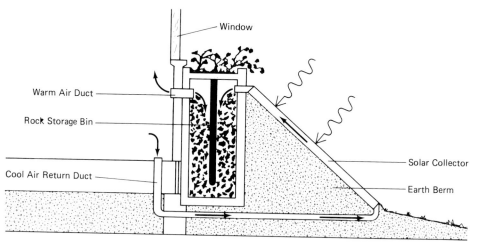

FIGURE 8-16:   Cross-Section Diagram of a Solar Collector on an Earth Beam
Source: United States. Department of Housing and Urban Development.
Passive Design Ideas for Energy Conscious Consumers. Washing-
ton: Government Printing Office, n.d.

Sketches.   Instead of photographs, sketches are often used to focus on various
aspects of an object or a procedure. They do not have the complex background
and the recognizable faces found in photographs. Therefore, they allow concentration on the object or procedure. Sketches include a large group of varied
drawings. They include the realistic sketches that illustrate instructions and
procedures as well the schematic diagrams that show connections in electrical
circuits.

Figure 8-17 accompanies a set of instructions on how to use hand grenades. The sketches demonstrate the grip.

Maps.   Maps can show geographical features such as mountains or rivers and
boundaries such as state lines. They can also present information such as population, outbreaks of disease, or housing starts according to geographical
distribution.

Other Figures

Besides graphs, charts, and drawings, photographs and samples are also considered figures. Photographs are used instead of sketches when realism is required or when the important part of an item is too complex to draw. Samples
include a piece of the material an item is made of, the product a machine can
make, or anything else that allows a "taste" of the item.

Proper grip of the grenade
(right-hand thrower).

Figure 1.

Proper grip of the grenade
(left-hand thrower).

Figure 2.

1. Throwing hand grenades

    a. The grip. The safest and easiest way to grip a hand genade for throwing is to hold it so that the safety lever is held down by the thumb while keeping the pull ring (and safety clip if present) free and facing the nonthrowing hand. (See Figures 1 and 2).

FIGURE 8-17:   Sketch Showing How To Hold a Hand Grenade and Explanation
Source: United States. Department of the Army. *Ammunitions Specialist.*
      Washington: Government Printing Office, 1980.

SUMMARY

Visual aids present information without using sentences and paragraphs. They are used to show relationships, provide summaries, or to make exact amounts easy to see. Most visual aids are classified as either tables or figures. To be effective, tables and figures must be designed to meet the needs of the intended audience. They should provide the information that is necessary but not add unnecessary technical or artistic clutter. They should also be correctly labeled and conveniently placed in written communication.

    Two types of visual aids are tables and figures. Tables present their information in columns and rows. They allow comparisons of exact amounts. Figures usually present their information with a combination of lines and numbers. They allow quick comparisons or show relationships at a glance. Figures include graphs, charts, and drawings. The design and use of tables and figures is a highly specialized, complex task. It is often a job for professional artists or draftspeople. If you want more than a general introduction, you should consult the sources listed on the next page.

Textbooks and Handbooks about Technical Writing

BRUSAW, CHARLES, GERALD J. ALRED, and WALTER E. OLIU. *Handbook of Technical Writing.* 3rd ed. New York: St. Martin's Press, 1987.

MARKEL, MICHAEL. *Technical Writing: Situations and Strategies.* New York: St. Martin's Press, 1984.

MATHES, J. C., and DWIGHT STEVENSON. *Designing Technical Reports: Writing for Audiences in Organizations.* Indianapolis: Bobbs-Merrill, 1976.

ROUNDY, NANCY. *Strategies for Technical Communication.* Boston: Little, Brown, and Company, 1985.

WARREN, THOMAS L. *Technical Writing: Purpose, Process, and Form.* Belmont, CA: Wadsworth Publishing, 1985.

Special Handbooks about the Design of Visual Aids

ENICK, NORBERT LLOYD. *Effective Graphic Communication.* Princeton: Auerbach, 1972.

KATZENBERG, ARLENE CHMIL. *How to Draw Graphs.* Chicago: R. R. Donnelley and Sons, 1975.

MACGREGOR, A. J. *Graphics Simplified: How to Plan and Prepare Effective Charts, Graphs, Illustrations, and Other Visual Aids.* Toronto: University of Toronto Press, 1979.

MEYERS, CECIL H. *Handbook of Basic Graphs: A Modern Approach.* Belmont, CA: Dickenson Publishing Company, 1970.

SELBY, PETER H. *Using Graphs and Tables: A Self-Teaching Guide.* New York: John Wiley and Sons, 1979.

TUFTE, EDWARD R. *The Visual Display of Quantitative Information.* Cheshire CT: 1983.

ASSIGNMENTS

Application 1:
Understanding Visual Aids

Figure 8-18 shows a table from *FDA Consumer.* It gives average energy

Mean Heights and Weights and Recommended Energy Intake

Category	Age (years)	Weight (pounds)	Height (inches)	Energy Needs (with range) (calories)	
Children	1-3	29	35	1300	(900-1800)
	4-6	44	44	1700	(1300-2300)
	7-10	62	52	2400	(1650-3300)
Males	11-14	99	62	2700	(2000-3700)
	15-18	145	69	2800	(2100-3900)
	19-22	154	70	2900	(2500-3300)
	23-50	154	70	2700	(2300-3100)
	51-75	154	70	2400	(2000-2800)
	76+	154	70	2050	(1650-2450)
Females	11-14	101	62	2200	(1500-3000)
	15-18	120	64	2100	(1200-3000)
	19-22	120	64	2100	(1700-2500)
	23-50	120	64	2000	(1600-2400)
	51-75	120	64	1800	(1400-2200)
	76+	120	64	1600	(1200-2000)
Pregnancy				+300	
Lactation				+500	

Source: Recommended Dietary Allowances, *National Academy of Sciences,* 1980.

FIGURE 8-18:   Table Showing Weight and Height Differences Between Men and Women
Source: Willis, Judith. "The Gender Gap at the Dinner Table." *FDA Consumer* June 1984: 13–17.

needs for the average person of a certain age, sex, height, and weight. Energy needs are measured according to how many calories a person should eat each day.

Write down the answers to these questions.

1. How much does the average 20-year-old woman weigh? How tall is she? How many calories per day, on the average, does she need? What is the range of calories required to meet her average energy needs?
2. How much does the average nine-year-old weigh? How many calories should he or she have each day?
3. How many more calories should a pregnant woman have than a woman who is not pregnant?
4. How much does the average 23-year-old male weigh? How tall is he? How many calories should he have each day?
5. How much does the average person of your age weigh? How tall is he or she? How many calories should he or she have each day?
6. What are the limitations of this table? How should you use the information displayed here?

Application 2:
Writing about Visual Aids

Taken from a Navy training manual, Figure 8-19 is a drawing of the mercurial barometer. Along with the visual aid, the writer offers a brief description and discussion of the general operating principle of the barometer. The audience is trainees unfamiliar with the fundamentals of engineering. Referring to the drawing below, arrange the sentences on page 128 in a paragraph. Delete any unnecessary words, and use signal words and phrases to

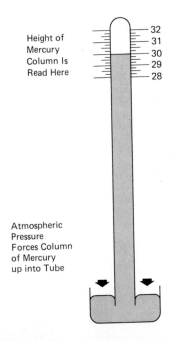

Height of
Mercury
Column Is
Read Here

32
31
30
29
28

Atmospheric
Pressure
Forces Column
of Mercury
up into Tube

FIGURE 8-19:   Drawing of Mercury Barometer

name the connections among ideas. (See Chapter 6.) Be certain to introduce and explain the drawing to the reader.

1. A barometer is used to measure atmospheric pressure.
2. Atmospheric pressure is the force exerted by the weight of the air in the atmosphere.
3. A barometer is made by filling a tube with mercury and then inverting the tube so that the open end rests in a container of mercury.
4. The container of mercury is open to the atmosphere.
5. There is no pressure at the closed end of the tube. This lack of pressure causes the pressure in the air, acting upon the surface of the mercury, to support the mercury in the tube.
6. The resulting height of mercury corresponds to the pressure being exerted.

Application 3:
Designing Visual Aids

This section asks you to design some simple tables and graphs based on the information given.

A. Figure 8-20 is a table from an article that discusses the amount of

Caffeine Content of Beverages and Foods

Item	Milligrams Caffeine	
	Average	*Range*
Coffee (5-oz. cup)		
Brewed, drip method	115	60−180
Brewed, percolator	80	40−170
Instant	65	30−120
Decaffeinated, brewed	3	2−5
Decaffeinated, instant	2	1−5
Tea (5-oz. cup)		
Brewed, major U.S. brands	40	20−90
Brewed, imported brands	60	25−110
Instant	30	25−50
Iced (12-oz. glass)	70	67−76
Cocoa beverage (5-oz. cup)	4	2−20
Chocolate milk beverage (8 oz.)	5	2−7
Milk chocolate (1 oz.)	6	1−15
Dark chocolate, semi-sweet (1 oz.)	20	5−35
Baker's chocolate (1 oz.)	26	26
Chocolate-flavored syrup (1 oz.)	4	4

Source: FDA, Food Additive Chemistry Evaluation Branch, based on evaluations of existing literature on caffeine levels.

FIGURE 8-20: Table Showing Caffeine Content of Foods
Source: Lecos, Chris. "The Latest Caffeine Scorecard."
    FDA Consumer March 1984: 14.

caffeine in beverages Americans commonly drink. To emphasize comparisons, the writer has decided to show the information by using graphs rather than tables. Design graphs that are appropriate for Figure 8-20. (Hint: All the information in the table cannot be shown on a single graph. You will probably have to draw several.)

    B. Below is a paragraph discussing the amount of personal electronic equipment produced in the United States in 1983, 1984, 1985, 1986, and 1987. Draw a figure to show clearly the trends indicated by these numbers.

> The production of personal electronic equipment increased greatly from 1983 to 1987. In 1983, total production was 53,638. In 1984, production was 67,441. In 1985, production was 74,230. In 1986, production was 113,524. In 1987, production was 142,838.

    C. Below is a paragraph discussing the average ages for male and female students enrolled in Holton Community College from 1970 to 1985. First, design a table to allow exact comparisons. Second, design a graph to allow readers to see relationships quickly.

> In 1970, the average age of male students at Holton was 25; the average age of females was 22. In 1975, the average age of male students was 24; the average age of females was 21. In 1980, the average age of male students was 20; the average age of females was 23. In 1985, the average age of male students was 19; the average age of females was 22.

9

INFORMAL REPORTS

When you complete this chapter, you should know how to write the informal reports required for most jobs. You should learn about the following formats and types of reports:

> Formats for reports
>> Printed forms
>> Memoranda reports
>> Letter reports
> Types of reports
>> Progress reports
>> Incident reports
>> Inspection reports
>> Field trip reports

Informal reports are routine communication for most jobs. They provide needed or requested information and make recommendations. Technicians may write informal reports to discuss progress on a job, request travel, report accidents, or explain the results of an inspection or the findings of a field trip. Some companies provide printed forms for this routine communication. Others require technicians to write memoranda or letters reporting the information. This chapter describes three formats for reports: printed forms, memoranda, and letters. It also discusses the four most common types of informal reports technicians write on the job: the progress report, the incident report, the inspection report, and the field trip report.

FORMATS FOR REPORTS

Information is reported on the job using printed forms, memoranda, and letters. As the name implies, printed forms are specially prepared by the company to save time in writing the most routine reports. They are most often sent to give information or make requests within a company, but sometimes they can be sent to customers. When a printed form is not available, memoranda or letters are used as formats for reports. Memoranda are always sent "in house," that is, within the company. Letters are sent to customers.

Printed Forms

Printed business forms are developed by companies so that employees can easily prepare certain kinds of typical reports. Standard formats ensure that the reports always contain appropriate information presented in a readable way. For technicians, the most common printed forms are travel authorization forms, purchase orders, expenditure requisitions, invoices, and time sheets.

Travel Authorization.   A travel authorization form is used to obtain approval and funding to make a trip related to company business. It is filled out and submitted 10 to 20 days prior to the date the trip is to be made. This amount of time is necessary to obtain approval from management and to allow the accounting department to issue funds for you to make the trip. If you are attending a conference or convention, a copy of the brochure listing dates, events, and hotel accommodations is attached to the form when it is sent in. Figure 9-1 shows a travel authorization form.

Expenditure Authorization Request.   An expenditure authorization request or purchase order is used to obtain approval to purchase items required for the job. This form may vary in complexity from company to company. However, most expenditure authorization requests and purchase orders require the name and address of the vendor or company you are ordering equipment or materials from, your name and the department or section you work in, and the reason you need to purchase the materials. You are usually required to list each item, the quantity or total number you need, the unit (whether the item comes as a single item or as part of a set or a package), a description of the item, and the total price for the number of items desired. The description of the items should include the catalog numbers and the unit price (price for one item). Figure 9-2 on page 133 shows an expenditure authorization request.

Purchase Order.   A purchase order is a form used to order materials, equipment, and supplies. When you fill in a purchase order, you include the name and address of the company supplying the goods, a billing address and a delivery address, as well as the items to be ordered. The purchase order is then sent to the accounting department for processing. Purchase orders are generally

TRAVEL AUTHORIZATION

DATE SUBMITTED

ACTION REQUESTED:

☐ OUT-OF-STATE TRAVEL
☐ OUT-OF-COUNTRY TRAVEL
☐ REIMBURSEMENT AUTHORIZATION FOR NON-STATE EMPLOYEE

☐ CONFIRMATION OF VERBAL APPROVAL
☐ * BLANKET TRAVEL AUTHORIZATION
☐ SPECIAL AUTHORIZATION ALLOWABLE
☐ REQUEST FOR ADDITIONAL INFORMATION

☐ IN-STATE EXCESS
☐ INITIAL REQUEST
☐ REVISED REQUEST
☐ OTHER _____

TRAVELERS:

TRAVEL TO:

SOURCE OF FUNDS:

MODE OF TRANSPORTATION:

SUBSISTENCE EXPENSES
MAXIMUM PER DAY $

CONVENTION REGISTRATION
$

REQUESTING DEPARTMENT

DEPARTMENTAL APPROVAL

DIVISION HEAD   DATE

DEPARTMENT HEAD   DATE

TOTAL ESTIMATED EXPENDITURE

DATES OF TRAVEL:
PERIOD BEGINNING   PERIOD ENDING

FOLD

PURPOSE AND EXPLANATORY REMARKS

(THIS SECTION FOR STATE OFFICE USE ONLY)

☐ REQUEST APPROVED
☐ REQUEST DENIED
☐ REQUEST RETURNED

COMMENTS OR REPLY:

APPROVAL FOR THE PRESIDENT   DATE

Figure 9-1:   Travel Authorization Form

numbered and printed on carbon-backed paper to make an original and a copy. Figure 9-3 on page 134 shows a purchase order form.

Invoice.   An invoice is used by a company to bill customers for services or materials provided. Invoices may be short and handwritten, with only the name and cost of the service or item. They may also be long, complex documents which have the goods and services provided by the company already printed on

EXPENDITURE AUTHORIZATION REQUEST
(Print Neatly Or Use Typewriter)

PURCHASE ORDER NO. ....

ACCOUNT CODE NO. ....

REQUESTED BY ....

REQUIRED FOR ....

DATE ....

DATE REQUIRED ....

VENDOR ....

ADDRESS ....

....

RECOMMEND APPROVAL:

..............................(DIRECTOR)

CONTRACT NO. ....

ITEM	QUANTITY	UNIT	DESCRIPTION OF ITEM OR SERVICES	UNIT PRICE	TOTAL PRICE
				SUB-TOTAL	
				3% STATE SALES TAX	
				ESTIMATED TRANSPORTATION	
				TOTAL	

BALANCE AVAILABLE IN COMMITMENT LEDGER: CODE ....$ ....

APPROVED ....   POSTED TO LEDGER ....
PRESIDENT   INITIALS

Figure 9-2:   Expenditure Authorization Request

them. Invoices are generally numbered, and copies are retained until the customer makes payment and clears the account. Figure 9-4 on page 135 shows an invoice used by C.C. Mangum, Grading and Paving Contractors.

Work or Job Order.   A work or job order form, sometimes called a trouble or repair ticket, is used by a company to give directions to its employees on a job

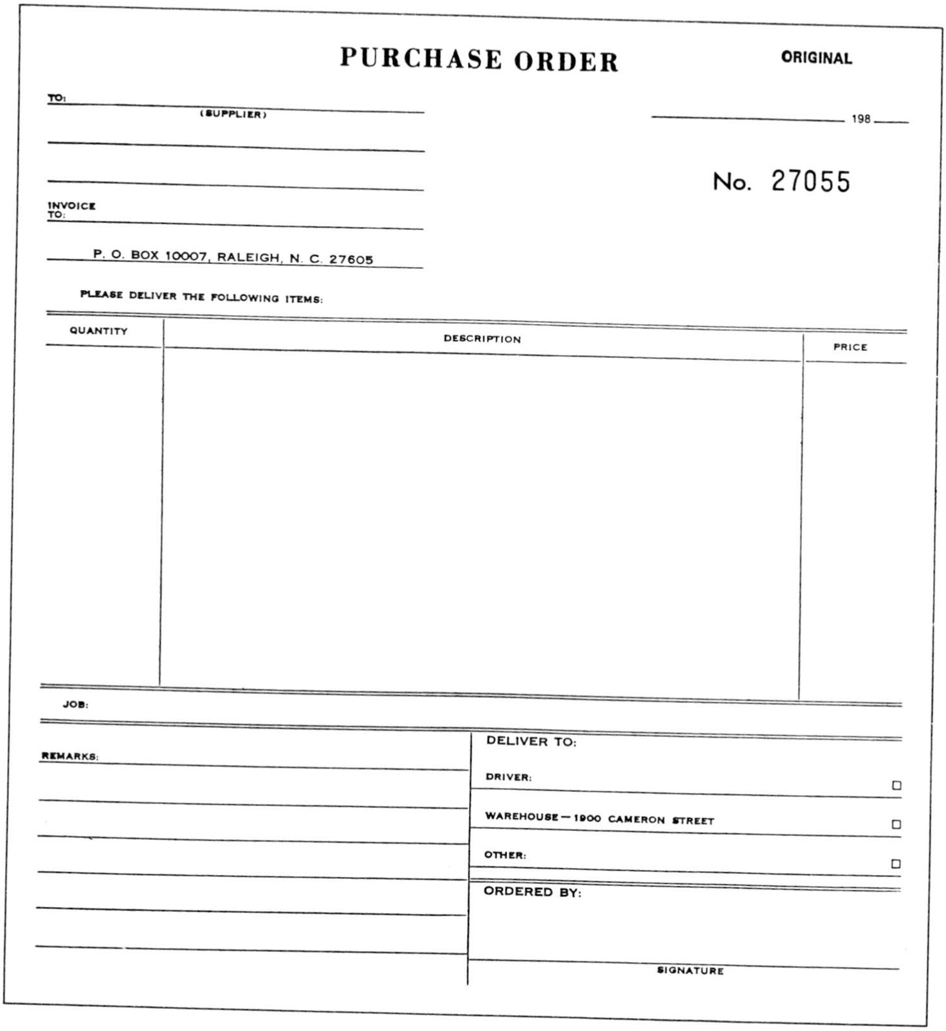

PURCHASE ORDER

ORIGINAL

TO: ______________________ (SUPPLIER)

______________________ 198____

No. 27055

INVOICE TO:

P. O. BOX 10007, RALEIGH, N. C. 27605

PLEASE DELIVER THE FOLLOWING ITEMS:

QUANTITY	DESCRIPTION	PRICE

JOB:

REMARKS:

DELIVER TO:

DRIVER: ☐

WAREHOUSE—1900 CAMERON STREET ☐

OTHER: ☐

ORDERED BY:

SIGNATURE

Figure 9-3: Purchase Order

to be done. Work orders are generally divided into two main sections. The first section describes the job to be done and gives the name of the employee assigned to the job and the job location. It is filled in by the employer. The second section lists the conditions found, the amount of time and materials required, and the results of the assignment. As the employee, you complete this section. Work orders are generally numbered and kept on file. At large companies, computerized work order forms enable the company to document your skills in getting the job done, to identify recurring problems, and to track the use of materials, equipment, and supplies. Figure 9-5 on page 136 shows a work order form.

C. C. MANGUM, INC.

GRADING & PAVING CONTRACTORS

3016 HILLSBOROUGH ST. — P. O. BOX 5936
RALEIGH, NORTH CAROLINA 27650

PHONES: 833-1831
833-7508

Estimate No. _____
For Period Ending _____
Job No. _____
Project _____
Date _____
Invoice No. _____

TO _____

Account No.	ITEM	Unit	Previous Quantity	Current Quantity	To Date Quantity	Unit Price	Current Amount	Current Retainage	Retainage To Date	Amount To Date

		CURRENT	TO DATE
Complete to Date			
Less Retainage _____ %			
Balance (1)			
Less Previous Estimates			
NET AMOUNT DUE			

Figure 9-4: Invoice

135

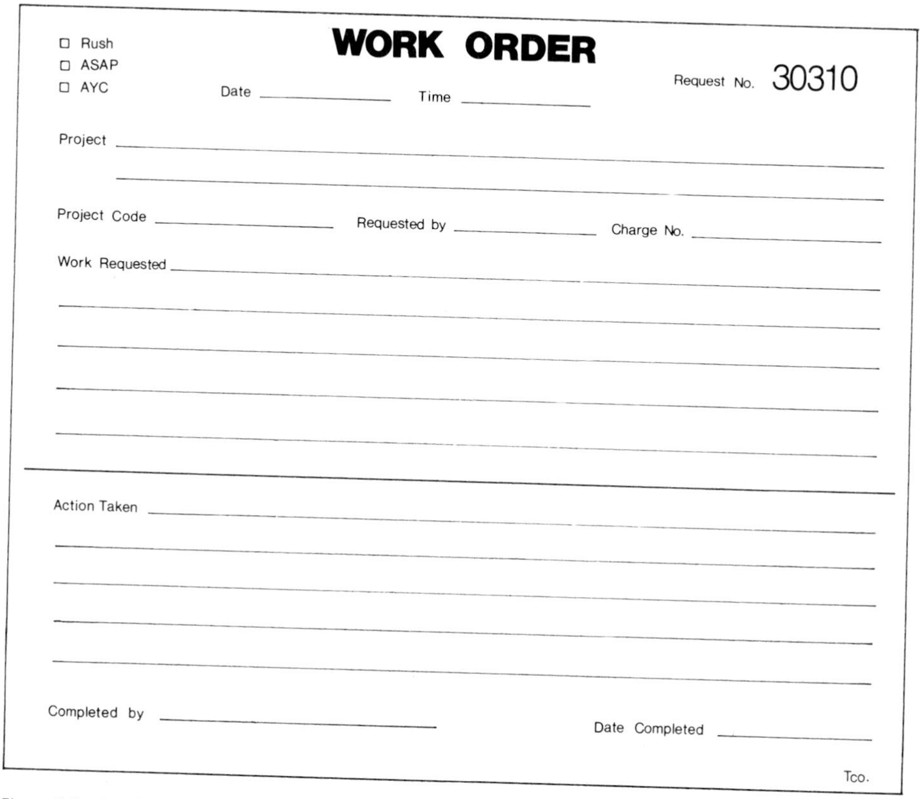

WORK ORDER

☐ Rush
☐ ASAP
☐ AYC

Date ________ Time ________ Request No. 30310

Project ________

Project Code ________ Requested by ________ Charge No. ________

Work Requested ________

Action Taken ________

Completed by ________ Date Completed ________

Tco.

Figure 9-5: Work Order Form

Time Sheet. A time sheet or card is used to document the time an employee spends on the job. Time sheets include a computerized punch card that you insert in a clock at the beginning and end of each day. They also include extremely complex forms that you fill in to document the time and overtime spent on a number of job assignments completed over a period of time. In addition, time sheets are used to accumulate information on your sick time and vacation time.

Memorandum Reports

Memoranda, or "memos," are used to report information or make requests and recommendations within a company. To be sure they are read by the correct person and to provide advance notice about their purpose, memos have "To," "From," "Subject," and "Date" labels at the top. Beside these labels, you should write the name and the title of the person receiving the report (To), your name and job title (From), a brief statement of the type of report and what it is about (Subject), and the date (Date). If your company does not supply special forms for memos, type the word "Memorandum" across the top of a blank piece of paper, and type in the labels yourself.

Filling in the To, From, and Date labels on a memo is easy, but deciding what to write on the subject line is more difficult. The subject line usually identifies the type of report and its topic. By glancing quickly at the subject line, a reader should be able to determine the purpose of the report. For example, Bernie, a trainer at Biggs Corporation, is working on a big project called "Training and Qualification Program." He sends several memos weekly to his supervisor. Below are subject lines from three of Bernie's memos for this project. Notice that each subject line identifies the type of report and the topic.

> Recommendations for Instructional Personnel in the Training and Qualification Program
> Inspection Report of Temporary Classroom Facilities
> Progress Report on the Training and Qualification Program

From reading these subject lines, Bernie's supervisor knows immediately what the memo concerns. In addition, the subject line serves as an identifier to use in filing the memo. Examples of memo reports appear throughout this chapter.

Letter Reports

Letter reports are used to provide information to individuals or agencies outside a company. They may be progress reports telling customers how much work has been completed on a job, or they may be short proposals offering to do some task for a certain amount of money. Letter reports follow the standard rules of business correspondence discussed in Chapter 11. They also use many of the special formatting features that appear in technical writing. Unlike most business correspondence, letter reports may have headings, lists, tables, and attachments.

TYPES OF REPORTS

In most companies, simple routine communication is sent on printed forms. However, as communication becomes more complicated and longer, it may not fit on these specially printed forms. When a printed form is not available, information is reported within a company in memo format. This section discusses the four most common memo reports: progress, incident, inspection, and field trip.

Progress Report

A progress report, sometimes called a status report, shows how much work has been completed on a project or assignment. Two types of progress reports are the occasional progress report, written at unscheduled intervals, and the periodic progress report, written at scheduled intervals.

The occasional progress report is a single report. It is either requested by management or initiated by the writer. For example, Jane is a field representative for an electronics firm that is not satisfied about the way customer service calls are being handled. The company puts her in charge of changing the customer service program. After the first week, management might ask her to write a progress report on how much work she has done in getting this new program underway and how much more time she will need to implement the program. On the other hand, Jane might decide that she should let management know the progress she has made on an assigned project. If she has encountered a problem in meeting the deadline, she needs to inform her supervisor about the delay.

The periodic progress report is one in a series of reports written at scheduled intervals. It discusses the progress made on a long-term project or assignment. Regardless of how much work has been done, periodic progress reports are submitted on predetermined dates. For example, David owns a hauling and grading company that has been awarded a contract to clear and grade a 20-acre site for a shopping center. One of the clauses of his contract stipulates that he submit a periodic progress report every two weeks. Even if it rains for a week and David and his crew get little work done, he still must submit the report.

Both types of progress reports require you to give specific information about what tasks have been completed and what tasks remain to be done.

Summary. As explained in Chapter 7, the summary is a condensed statement of all the information in the memo. It provides the reader an immediate overview of the situation. Usually written last and presented first, the summary explains the progress made, problems encountered, if any, and projected completion date. This summary statement is from the occasional progress report Jane wrote.

The new customer service program is on schedule and will be fully implemented by August 17, our target date.

Background. The background includes the identification of the project or assignment, the date assigned, the purpose, the overall requirements, the time limits, and the required equipment and supplies. If the report is one in a series of periodic progress reports, you must indicate its number.

Discussion Section. The discussion section describes the progress. If the project requires multiple tasks, the information is presented in tables. The first table shows the tasks completed, the date each was completed, and the time required for completion. The second table lists the tasks remaining, the date each should be finished, and the time projected for completion of each. If the tasks completed and tasks remaining can be briefly discussed, tables may not be necessary.

Ending Section. The ending section discusses the problems encountered. Common problems are equipment breakdowns, personnel absences, or bad weather—anything that might prevent meeting the deadline. The projected completion date is included in this section.

Figure 9-6 on page 140 is an occasional progress report written by Stanley Worth, an air conditioning and heating technician, to his supervisor, George Bryan. George is a project coordinator, not a specialist in the air conditioning and heating field, so Stanley limits the technical information in his report to a very general discussion, particularly in the "Work Completed" section. As you can see, Stanley's summary states the problem that is preventing completion of the job and informs George what to expect in the rest of the report. The discussion section describes work completed and work remaining to be done.

Incident Report

An incident report is written to inform management of some event that has occurred to either stop or disturb the normal flow of work. An incident report is concerned with such events as a breakdown in equipment, chronic absenteeism, accidents, and loss or theft of parts or equipment. Incident reports require you to explain what has happened and why and, if possible, make suggestions about how similar incidents can be avoided in the future.

Summary. The summary explains what kind of incident has occurred and gives a brief evaluation of the effect the incident will have on the company. This summary is from a report of an accident which occurred in an automotive repair shop:

> Fred Williamson suffered a compound leg fracture in an accident in the service bay July 8. He was hospitalized and will be out of work for approximately two months. His injury leaves us unable to fill our current work orders on time.

Background. The background gives the details of the incident. It answers the questions who, what, when, where, and why. This section explains exactly who was involved in the incident, what happened, when and where it occurred, and why it happened at that particular time.

Discussion Section. The discussion section explains the results of the incident: damages, injuries, costs, and possible consequences. Will the incident affect a production schedule? Will costs rise? Will new equipment be required?

Ending Section. The ending section generally describes changes in processes or practices and makes recommendations. It lets management know what changes have been made because of the incident. Then it makes recommendations that require management's approval. This section is omitted if there are no recommendations to make.

MEMORANDUM

TO: George Bryan, Assistant Project Coordinator

FROM: Stanley Worth, Air Conditioning & Heating Technician

SUBJECT: Progress Report on Installation of Air Conditioning (AC)
           Equipment in Room 6412

DATE: April 20, 1988

Summary

For the past five weeks we have met the schedule for installation of the AC
equipment in the Computer Control Center. However, we have encountered a major
problem in running lines from the compressor unit to the cooling fountain.
Because of these problems, we will have to shift our project completion date to
May 15, two weeks behind schedule.

Background

On January 12, a decision was made to install our own computers in Room
6412 to replace computer services leased from Compumac. The project began on
March 15. We had six weeks to install the AC equipment and test the area for
appropriate climate control before installing the computers on June 1.

Work Completed

As of this date, we have completed the following major tasks:

1. Installation of Ventilation Duct and Control lines; completed in
    80 hours on March 31.

2. Installation of the 20 ton Air Handling Unit; completed in 97 hours
    on April 5.

3. Installation of Compressor Unit; completed in 70 hours on April 20.

Work Remaining

The only task remaining is to install the lines running from the compressor
to the small fountain we are using as a heat sink. We cannot dig the required
trenches until representatives of the Galax Gas Company pinpoint the location of
gas lines running in the same area. Galax indicates that it will be a minimum
of ten days before it can send a representative to the site because of the
general strike by the gas utility workers.

Projected Completion

Because of the delay caused by Galax, we will be unable to do the required
operational tests of the unit by the due date. The ops tests, which take a
minimum of 16 hours, will be run during the first week in May, requiring re-
scheduling of the technical representatives from the computer company. Unless
we experience another delay, we will complete the project on May 15, approximately
two weeks behind schedule.

Page 1 of 1

Figure 9-6: Occasional Progress Report

Figure 9-7 on page 142 shows an incident report written by Mike Stadtler, foreman, to Bill Harvey, a vice-president of a steel fabricating company. One of Mr. Harvey's duties as a vice-president is to serve as chairperson of the company Safety Committee, which issues a monthly safe practices report. He is also responsible for informing senior management about delays in production and cost overruns. Mike's memo very specifically addresses both of these important topics. In addition, as a foreman, Mike is responsible for the safety of his co-workers. Therefore, he makes several recommendations for improving safe practices in his shop.

Inspection Report

The inspection report is written to explain the suitability, location, condition, availability, or adequacy of a specific area, item, or series of items. An inspection report can describe a small storage room to determine whether or not the space is adequate for the installation of a copy machine, or it can describe every nut and bolt in a huge bulldozer. Regardless of what is inspected, exact details about the current condition of the item or the area are required.

Summary. The summary explains briefly the condition of the area or item inspected. This summary is from a student's report on an electronics lab at a college.

> The electronics laboratory, located in Room 207 in Smithson Hall, is adequately equipped to handle 16 students at one time.

Background. In an *area report*, background identifies the area or location inspected including the building, address, or room number, if applicable. It also gives the reason for the inspection and the names of the personnel involved. In an *item report*, background identifies the item or items to be inspected, with the brand name and model number, if applicable. It also tells where the item or items are located and gives the purpose of the inspection.

Discussion Section. In an *area report*, the discussion section provides an overall description of the area. Depending upon the type of inspection, this section of the report includes information about the size of the area; the type of lighting; the number and location of doors and windows; the dimensions and materials of the flooring, walls, ceiling; and any decorative elements. A diagram of the floor plan may show the location of furnishings or items. Information about furniture and equipment may also be presented in a table. Type, quantity, condition, and location should be stated. In an *item report*, the discussion section generally includes an extensive table. The table lists the items inspected, their location, quantity, and condition.

MEMORANDUM

To: Mr. Bill Harvey, Vice President

From: Mike Sadtler, Foreman

Subject: Report of Accident in Welding Lab

Date: February 29, 1988

Summary

On February 29, 1988 the "T" fitting from work order 1135 for Bullock's Crane Service fell approximately four feet to the floor of our welding shop when the lifting eye tore into two pieces. Three of the support legs will have to be replaced. This accident will put our delivery date to Bullock's back one week and the replacement steel will cost us approximately $2400.

Background

Welder Juan Cruz welded a 4 x 6 x 3/8 inch lifting eye to the fitting so that it could be moved. However, when crane operator Jim Bates hoisted the fitting, the eye split, dropping the fitting and twisting the legs on impact. After inspection, I found that Mr. Cruz had made the lifting eye from an alloy with a low tensile strength instead of steel. This alloy could not support the 11-ton lift.

Damages from the Accident

As a result of the incident, three of the legs will have to be replaced. Because it will take a week for us to get replacement steel, we will be one week late on delivery to Bullock's Crane Service. The replacement steel will cost us $2400. Fortunately, no one was injured in the accident.

Recommendation

I have ordered the replacement steel and instructed all welders and fitters to have their projects inspected by Bill Jones or me before moving them.

I recommend that we put together a seminar on the identification and uses of the steel and alloys in our shop. We could present the seminar at one of our weekly safety meetings.

Figure 9-7: Incident Report

Ending Section.   The ending section for both types of inspection reports varies according to the reason for making the inspection. It may make recommendations to management concerning the appropriateness and condition of the location or items. It may also suggest repairs, replacements, additional materials, new equipment, or new furniture.

Figure 9-8 on pages 144—146 is an inspection report of an electro-hydraulic control drive unit. The report gives a description of the item, including a drawing, and a table listing the findings of the inspection. This detailed report has far more technical information than the two previous reports because Fred Carmichael, the senior technician, needs to make sure that the manager of engineering services fully understands the depth of the inspection. The manager of engineering services has the responsibility for informing the Foxworth representative that improper equipment has been installed in the plant and that Foxworth is responsible for replacing it. Fred explains the problem with the equipment after he reports his careful inspection. His recommendation is based on the fact that his company is not at fault.

Field Trip Report

A field trip report discusses an assignment or project completed away from the primary work location. Field trip reports fall into three general categories: business/industry, social institutions, and convention/conference. For example, a supervisor might assign an industrial engineering technician to visit a tool and die maker at a local plant and ask about the possible design and production of a part for repairing antique automobiles. A technician or a salesperson may be required to visit a social institution, such as a prison or a hospital, to report on how the company can help design rehabilitative or recreational facilities. Technicians may also have to report on sales conventions that they attend as representatives of their company. No matter which of these field trips is taken, the findings must be reported to management.

Summary.   The summary tells what the writer has found out. It includes a brief description of the assignment and results or recommendations. This summary is from a field trip report to a local hospital.

> After visiting McLane Memorial Hospital July 3—5 to examine the staff-patient interaction, I recommend a reevaluation of staff assignments to free health care professionals so that they can perform critical patient care duties.

Background.   The background explains the purpose of the field trip, the location, the individuals involved, and the dates and times involved. It also gives a brief overview of the activities.

MEMORANDUM

TO: William Holt, Manager of Engineering Services

FROM: Fred Carmichael, Senior Technician

SUBJECT: Report of the Inspection of Electrohydraulic Control Drive,
          Unit 2

DATE: July 20, 1988

Summary

On July 19, the Unit 2 Electrohydraulic Control Drive was
inspected. I found that a 10 horsepower (hp) motor had been installed
instead of the 20 hp motor that the unit requires. I am recommending
that we call the manufacturer's representative and request the
appropriate 20 hp motor be installed

Background

On July 19, Yon Stams, Senior Electrician; Tim Bradley, Electrical
Trainee; and I inspected the Unit 2 Foxworth Electrohydraulic Control
Drive, Model 777A located at level 374, Air Control Room A. The
purpose of the inspection was to determine why the motor has failed
three times in the past month.

Description of Foxworth Model 777A

The Foxworth Model 777A is 50 x 20 x 30 inches in an enclosed steel
cabinet. It weighs 215 pounds and has three access doors and a
lift-off cover for maintenance. The figure shows a sketch of its
component parts.

Page 1 of 3

Figure 9-8: Item Inspection

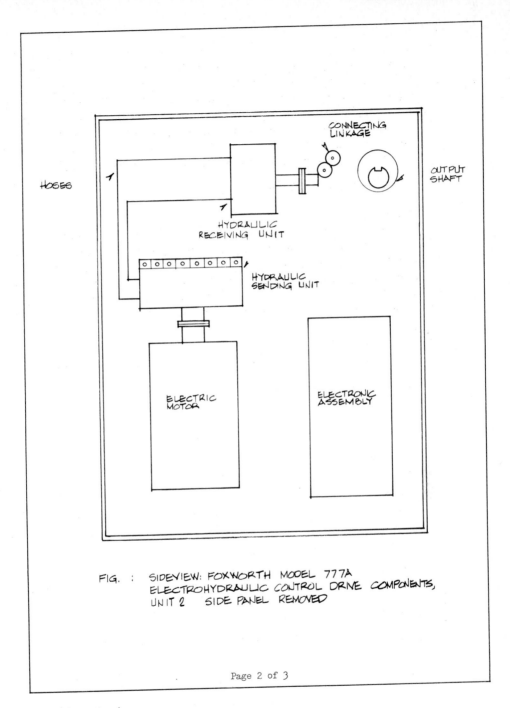

FIG. : SIDEVIEW: FOXWORTH MODEL 777A
ELECTROHYDRAULIC CONTROL DRIVE COMPONENTS,
UNIT 2   SIDE PANEL REMOVED

Page 2 of 3

Figure 9-8   *continued*

The results of the inspection are shown in the Table below.

Table: Condition of Electrohydraulic Control Drive Components

Component	Items Inspected	Condition
Output shaft	Straightness, rotation & bearing points	Normal
Connecting Linkages	Pivot points	Normal
Hydraulic Receiving Unit	Input, shaft rotation	Normal
Hoses	Crimping, size, output	Normal
Hydraulic Sending Unit	Shaft rotation	Normal
Three-phase Induction Motor	Overheating, placement, ventilation, lubrication	Normal

After reviewing the tech specs for the Foxworth, we found that the motor is sized at 10 hp. Model 777A requires a 20 hp motor to power the unit. Model B uses a 10 hp motor.

Recommendations

I am recommending that the Foxworth representative for this area be called to inspect the unit and install a new 20 hp motor at no cost to the company. The error was in the assembly at the Foxworth plant, not the manner in which we have made repairs.

Page 3 of 3

Figure 9-8: *continued*

Discussion Section.   The discussion section varies according to the destination of the trip. Three destinations are possible: a business or industry, a social institution, and a conference or convention.

In the report of a field trip to a *business* or *industry*, the discussion section is divided into two major parts. The first, a brief history, is written in paragraph form. It may describe the date the company was founded, the type of business or industry, and the product or service offered. It may also include an overview of the company's organization. The first part may give information about the number of people employed and the number of branches or subsidiaries of the company. The paragraph gives the history of LeMatre Corporation.

> LeMatre Corporation, founded in Beaumont, Texas, in 1918, manufactures high-tech surgical equipment. The headquarters are currently located in Dallas with subsidiaries in Houston, Phoenix, and Tulsa. Each subsidiary is headed by a vice-president reporting to the company president in Dallas. LeMatre has 2,500 employees and is planning to add another 200 with the expansion of the Phoenix plant.

The second part of the discussion section contains more specific information about the company's operation. It may include a detailed organizational chart which shows the top levels of management. If a facility is being described, a diagram to show the layout may be included. If a process is being described, a flowchart may be included. In addition, if the equipment on hand is extensive, it may be listed in a table.

In the report of a field trip to a *social institution*, the discussion section is also divided into two parts. The first is a brief history of the institution. It includes the founding date, purpose, population served, total population, personnel employed, and a brief overview of the organization. This paragraph gives the history of Yates Country Correctional Center.

> Yates County Correctional Center, constructed in 1979, houses 200 individuals between the ages of 15 and 18 who have been convicted of a felony in the State of North Carolina. The Center employs 30 correctional officers who rotate in three eight-hour shifts, two psychologists, and two rehabilitation counselors. The Center is headed by a Warden who reports directly to the Director of Corrections in the State Attorney General's office.

The second part discusses the facility itself. It gives a general description of the environment of the facility. Then it lists specific areas, such as the library, recreation room, and classrooms. The type of area, the location, the purpose, and the condition are explained. Often a table or a drawing is included. Besides a description of the area, this part of the discussion section may include a flowchart of the lines of communication.

In the report of a trip to a *conference* or *convention*, the history section is omitted. In its place, major business meetings or seminars are listed. A brief overview of each is given, with particular attention paid to those activities most important to the company. This list discusses some seminars from a convention the writer attended.

The "Training for Tomorrow" program is attached to this report. Of the seminars listed, I attended the four below:

1. Interviews—A review of the structured interview including purpose, procedure, and administration.
   Speaker: Phil Hollis.

2. Employee Selection Systems—Alternative methods of selecting employees including panel and telephone interviews.
   Speaker: Burt Willis

3. Cost Analysis—Methods of minimizing interview costs by using an effective selection process.
   Speaker: Anita French

4. Equal Employment Opportunity—An overview of recent federal and state court cases and their impact on hiring practices.
   Speaker: Jane Edleston

The second part may include a table listing the companies at the conference or convention, the names of their representatives, and the products or services offered. Another table may be included to list new products on exhibit, the manufacturing company, the wholesale and retail cost of the product, and an explanation of the value of these products for the writer's company.

Ending Section.   The ending section of all three types of field trip reports tells what has been learned. Also, depending on the assignment, it may list recommendations to tell how this new information may benefit the company.

Figure 9-9 on pages 149–151 shows a report written by Robert Paul, a senior mechanical engineering technician, who has been given the responsibility to make recommendations concerning valve replacement production. In order to justify his recommendation that Brockhurst be given the opportunity to quote production costs for the replacement valve, he is very thorough in his assessment of the corporation. Additionally, his supervisor must have this type of detail to send his own recommendations to the purchasing group. The language is technical and presumes a working knowledge of the way valves are manufactured and the equipment required to manufacture them.

Figure 9-10 on pages 152–155 shows a report written by a student nurse to her instructor as part of a course assignment. While the language is not technical, Susan's report is very thorough. The "Background" section presents the history of a private facility for acutely emotionally disturbed adolescents and summarizes the day she spent visiting the facility. To be sure that her instructor understands the organizational structure of Ashbury Center, she includes an organizational chart. Because this report is for her instructor's information only, she makes no recommendations; but she does draw conclusions about the effectiveness of the center in comparison to other facilities of this type.

MEMORANDUM

TO: Mr. George Mather, Supervisor, Design Engineering

FROM: Robert S. Paul, RP Mechanical Engineering Technician

SUBJECT: Report on Visit to Brockhurst Manufacturing Corporation to
         Assess Replacement Valve Production

DATE: February 25, 1985

Summary

This report summarizes my meeting with BMC and reviews plant layout and capital equipment. Brockhurst manufactures high-quality, dependable products, and I recommend that we ask the company to quote a price for production of the replacement valve.

Background

In our meeting on January 20, 1985, you suggested that I assess the Brockhurst Manufacturing Corporation (BMC) for possible production of the #309 solenoid replacement valves. As a result of that request, I met with Mr. Robert L. Perry, senior design engineer with BMC, on February 1, 1985. His tour through the Raleigh, North Carolina plant allowed me to review capital equipment, plant layout, and support departments.

General Description

BMC manufactures high-temperature, high-pressure cast iron valves. Materials used include iron, low-carbon steel, aluminum, bronze, and stellite (a cobalt-chromium-tungston metal that stays hard in extremely high temperatures). BMC's products are used in four main areas:

1. Power plants   60%

2. Ships   20%

3. Transmission of gas (pipelines)   10%

4. Petrochemicals   10%

Plant Layout

Plant layout at BMC maximizes station flow and minimizes material flow. One central receiving area serves all departments of the plant. Manufacturing is divided into Large Parts Manufacturing and Small Parts Manufacturing. Separate welding and inventory departments serve each of these areas.

Page 1 of 3

Figure 9-9: Field Trip Report, Business and Industry

Equipment

BMC is primarily a lathe machine shop. Ninety percent of the equipment purchased in the last five years is computer controlled. The following capital equipment is on-line at BMC:

Table: Capital Equipment

Equipment	Description and Function
Radial drill press	Basic milling
Milling machines	Keyways, slots, squares
Horizontal slotter	Square lots
Vertical turret lathe	Transition station
Horizontal boring mills	Modified facing head for combination table/head feed angle
NC turret lathe	47-inch chuck - 280 - RPM capable of machining all set ups
Mitsubishi lathe	144 inch chuck
Pull broaching machine	Keyway slotting
CNC vertical machining center	Two vises, two chuck machines, two spheres

Departments

I visited three departments at BMC: Welding, Assembly and Test, and Defects Testing.

Welding Department

The welding department functions as a separate unit and is used in the following areas:

1. Upgrading: improvement of commercial sand castings

2. Fabrication: components

3. Seat welding: stellite seat

Figure 9-9 *continued*

All types of welding are employed in the shop, including TIG, MIG, shielded arc, plasma, and submerged arc. The submerged arc welding machine is capable of welding two sides simultaneously at high speeds. It operates at 90 in/min with 1/8 inch wire electrodes.

<u>Assembly and Test Department</u>

All products are tested at 1.5 times working pressure. Three tests are performed on each part. These include the shell test, over-the-seat test, and under-the-seat test.

<u>Defects Testing Department</u>

Strict quality control is enforced at BMC because of the applications of its products. All valves are tested for defects by three or more of the following methods:

1. Red dye

2. Liquid penetrant

3. Radiography

4. Ultrasonic

5. Magnetic flux

<u>Traveler System</u>

The traveler system is used in the plant for the purpose of controlling the various steps in the manufacturing cycle. Manufacturing Engineering is responsible for compiling this package. High-specification require-ments include complete drawing sets, bill of materials, operator numbers, and parts lists.

<u>Recommendation</u>

BMC produces a precision-made, high-quality valve. Because power plant requirements are stringent, we require a product that has proven reliability. BMC is capable of manufacturing a valve that fits well into the tolerances and specs required. I recommend that we supply BMC with a package of our requirements for the #309 solenoid replacement valve so that a quote for production may be forwarded to us.

Figure 9-9   *continued*

MEMORANDUM

TO: Jane Wilshire, RN Instructor

FROM: Susan Fuller, Student Nurse

SUBJECT: Report on Private Care Facilities For Acutely Emotionally
         Disturbed Adolescents

DATE: May 15, 1988

Summary

On May 5, as part of my assignment to assess public and private
facilities for the acutely emotionally disturbed adolescent, I visited
Ashbury Center in Chapel Creek, South Carolina. Ashbury Center is a
model psychiatric unit with the most up-to-date facilities and
equipment in the Southeast. Staffing over the three shifts is on a
one-to-two ratio with one staff person per two clients.

Background

Ashbury Center was established in 1970 by a group of physicians
because no nearby facility adequately served acutely emotionally
disturbed adolescents from the ages of 12 to 18. Adolescents are sent
to the Center at Chapel Creek from four major surrounding cities with a
population base of 250,000. The Center houses 40 adolescents who stay
an average of one month at the cost of $125 per day. Approximately 500
adolescents are served by the facility annually.

On May 5, I met with Edward Johnson, Social Worker, and Dr. Mary
Douglas, Director of Psychiatry at 10:00 a.m. After a brief overview
of the function of the Center, I was taken on an extended tour of the
facility by Janet McLawhorn, Dr. Douglas' Administrative Assistant, and
had lunch in the cafeteria with the staff and clients. After lunch we
continued our tour which ended at 3:30 p.m. with a short closing visit
with Dr. Douglas.

Staffing

Ashbury is professionally staffed in three eight-hour shifts. The
first shift, which runs from 7 a.m. to 3 p.m. has the following
personnel on site:

5 Registered Nurses
3 Psychiatric Technicians
2 Social Workers
3 Classroom Instructors
1 Director of Psychiatry
2 In-Residence Psychiatrists
1 Director of Nursing
1 Chief Administrative Officer

Figure 9-10: Field Trip Report, Social Institution

Second shift, which runs from 3 p.m. to 11 p.m., has the following personnel:

    3 Registered Nurses
    2 Psychiatric Technicians
    1 Social Worker
    1 In-Residence Psychiatrist
    2 Occupational Therapists
    1 On-Call Administrator

Third shift, which runs from 11 p.m. to 7 a.m., has the following personnel:

    2 Registered Nurses
    1 Psychiatric Technician
    1 In-Residence Psychiatrist
    1 On-Call Administrator

The personnel charged with maintaining hospital services such as grounds and maintenance are not included in this listing.

The chart below shows the lines of communication and authority of Ashbury Center.

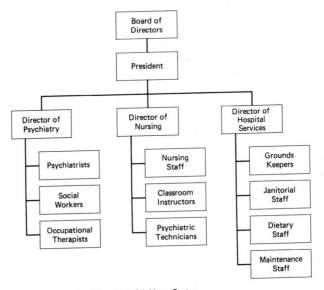

Figure: Organizational Structure of Ashbury Center

Figure 9-10   *continued*

<u>Facilities</u>

The Center is designed in an H-shape with nursing services, classrooms, library, and occupational therapy areas located in the center of
the H. The branches of the H house the adolescent population. Each
client is assigned to a private room with bath. Outside doors are
locked on a 24-hour basis with total freedom of movement inside the
facility and supervised movement outside the facility. All windows are
dual thermopane with embedded wire mesh and cannot be opened.

The table shown below lists all facilities, furnishings and available equipment.

Table: Facilities at Ashbury Center

Type	Number	Location	Equipment
Occupational Therapy	1	Room 101	Woodworking Painting Pottery Sewing
Classroom	3	Rooms 103, 105 & 107	14 standard desks 1 teacher's desk and chair 3 bookcases
Cafeteria	1	Room 102	12 four-person tables 48 chairs
Library	1	Room 104	2 six-person tables 2 sofas 2 easy chairs
Conference Room	2	Room 106A, 106B	1 chair 1 desk 1 side chair 1 sofa
Recreation Room	1	Room 108	3 card tables 12 chairs 1 TV 1 sofa
Basketball court	1	gymnasium	standard
Swimming pool	1	gymnasium	standard
Volleyball court	2	outside of gym	standard
Tennis court	2	outside of gym	standard

Figure 9-10: *continued*

General Environment

The general environment at Ashbury Hall is warm and bright. Primary colors predominate in activity areas. Muted shades of the same colors are used in restful areas and clients' rooms. Hanging baskets and potted plants abound in all areas of the facility, lending an atmosphere of hominess and comfort. All floors are carpeted in muted primary colors, and music is piped into all areas. The whole effect is designed to elevate mood without exciting the clients.

The clients are at the center of a group effort at rehabilitation with the social worker, nursing staff, psychiatric technicians, psychiatrists, instructors, and occupational therapists available at a moment's notice night and day.

Conclusion

Ashbury Center is a model treatment center for the emotionally disturbed adolescent. It is available to a limited clientele who can afford its services. The success rate is approximately 40 percent, similar to that found in most institutions, both private and public.

Page 4 of 4

Figure 9-10:   *continued*

Figure 9-11 on pages 157–159 shows a report written by Jennifer Bowen, the administrative assistant to the office manager, Jean Feathers. Jennifer has been sent, at company expense, to a convention in Atlanta to evaluate word processing equipment. Like the report of the student nurse, she gives a fairly extensive background and then describes and evaluates each of the presentations she attended. So that her supervisor might evaluate the different systems more easily, she summarizes her information in a table. She also lists and numbers her recommendations so that they are clearly defined.

SUMMARY

Printed forms, memoranda, and letters are the most commonly used formats for reporting information. Printed forms are developed by companies to handle routine communication that most commonly stays within the company, but sometimes they are sent to customers. The most frequently used printed forms are the travel authorization, expenditure authorization request, purchase order, invoice, work order, and time sheet. The memorandum is used to communicate with people inside the company. The letter is used to report to clients and customers outside the company. Unless their employers use printed forms, technicians will write several kinds of informal reports. The most common of these are progress, incident, inspection, and field trip reports. The progress report explains how much work has been completed on a project or assignment. The incident report is written to inform management of some event or situation that has either stopped or disturbed the work flow. The inspection report explains the suitability, location, condition, and availability of a specific area, item, or series of items. The field trip report presents information based on an assignment or project that is completed away from the primary work location.

ASSIGNMENTS

FORMATS FOR REPORTS

Application 1:
Analyzing Work Forms

Using any one of the examples of forms shown in this chapter, examine the form to determine its purpose. Write the purpose down, and be prepared to tell the class whether or not the form meets its purpose and why.

Application 2:
Designing Work Forms

Design a work form that would be used on the job you may have after you graduate or in your curriculum at the technical college. It could be a form

MEMORANDUM

TO: Jean Feathers, Office Manager

FROM: Jennifer Bowen, Administrative Assistant

SUBJECT: Report on Word Processing Product Exhibition, Atlanta
          Convention Center

DATE: July 10, 1988

Summary

On July 7 and 8, I attended the Word Processing Product Exhibition at the Atlanta Convention Center in Atlanta, Georgia. As a result of that visit, I am recommending that we purchase the "Easy Writer" word processing program offered by Office Systems, Inc. at a total cost of $10,000 for six word processing stations and one ICU (Integrated Control Unit).

Background

On June 12, I was assigned to visit the Word Processing Product Exhibition in Atlanta to compare word processing equipment so that we can purchase a six-station system for our current typing pool.

I arrived in Atlanta on July 7 and was met at the Convention Center by John Williamson, one of the coordinators of the Exhibition. After a general welcome held in the Center Auditorium at 11:00 a.m. and luncheon, participants were invited to tour the 10 exhibits and sign up for demonstrations to be held on July 8 between 8:00 a.m. and 5:00 p.m.

At 7:00 p.m., I attended a dinner and heard the keynote address, "Automated Office Systems of Tomorrow," delivered by Maxine Seawell, President of ILLC Corporation. The central theme of the address was the revolution of the secretarial function in two major areas: oral communication and written communication.

Presentations

On July 8, I attended presentations of the companies shown below. A synopsis of each is included.

1. RCN Company - John Brooks, Representative
    Explanation of functions of system; spelling correction component built in; word search and indexing functions included. Opportunity to operate system for 30 minutes. Poor instruction manuals.

Figure 9-11: Field Trip Report, Conference-Convention

2. Office Systems, Inc. - Trudy Williamson, Representative
   Explanation of system; spelling correction component built in;
   word search and indexing functions included. Three assistants
   to aid in one-hour hands-on experience. System easy to operate.
   Excellent instruction manuals.

3. Word Consultants, Inc. - Cynthia Allen, Representative
   Explanation of system; hands-on experience with partners;
   participated as well as observed. Highly technical instruction
   manuals.

4. Communications, Inc. - Elizabeth Wells, Representative
   Explanation of system; word search and indexing functions;
   vertical, horizontal, linear capabilities; no hands-on participation allowed; observed Communications, Inc. employee using
   system. Instruction manuals appeared to be excellent.

The attached table summarizes the four systems which I viewed and
includes storage capacity, advantages and disadvantages, and costs for
six work stations and one ICU.

Recommendations

Based on the equipment, software, and costs, I am recommending that
we purchase the "Easy Writer" system offered by Office Systems, Inc. for
the following reasons:

1. The cost of $10,000 is midrange and reasonable.

2. The size of the system allows installation with minimum modification of our existing facilities.

3. The 4000-page storage capacity is sufficient for our current
   needs, and the capability for adding more storage is available
   at a reasonable cost.

4. Office Systems, Inc. will send an area representative to our
   facility for one week to train our personnel on the system.

5. Office Systems, Inc. offers a three-year maintenance program
   at no extra cost.

6. The one disadvantage of the system, the lack of a contrast
   setting, can be offset by the purchase of the new "Display
   Screen Contrast" at a minimum cost.

Conclusion

The trip to the Word Processing Product Exhibition was definitely
worthwhile. Because of the variety of the systems available, the methods of
demonstration, and opportunity for hands-on applications, it was much
easier to compare the product lines.

Figure 9-11 *continued*

Table :   Comparison of Word Processing Systems*

Company	System	Maximum Storage Capacity	Advantages	Disadvantages	Cost
RCN	Systematic Word	3,500 pages	Tilting Display Screen	Oversized keyboard	$ 8,250
Office Systems, Inc.	Easy Writer	4,000 pages	Small keyboard Tilting keyboard No cost maintenance for three years	No contrast setting	10,000
Word Consult-ants, Inc.	WCI	4,500 pages	Compact ICU	Restricted printing capabilities	12,000
Communications, Inc.	Communications 6000	6,000 pages	Multiprinter capability	Space requirements restrictive	15,000

*Based on 6 work stations/one Integrated Control Unit

Page 3 of 3

Figure 9-11   *continued*

for reporting the results of a laboratory exercise, ordering new equipment, or conducting an inventory of a classroom or lab. Before you begin, decide on a purpose and determine what you need to ask for to get the information that you want.

Application 3:
Filling in the Work Form

Using the expenditure authorization request and the purchase order forms included in the examples in this chapter, prepare a purchase order for five pieces of equipment that would be used in your course of study. Fill in all parts of the form neatly.

TYPES OF REPORTS

Progress Report

Application 1:
Revising The Progress Report

Using the Progress Report Plan Sheet and the Guidelines for Revision in Chapter 3, revise this progress report. Address your revised version to Ms. Ella Bingham, English Instructor. The writer is Eric Owens, a student in Ms. Bingham's class. Fill in the appropriate plan sheet before you write a revised draft.

It looks like I'm not going to be able to finish up the self-paced English 1102 that I started on at the first of the semester. As you know, I have had to miss class a bunch of times for a total of 12 hours in order to work to go to school. I have decided to miss English class rather than Electrical class because the English isn't all that important. In spite of all of that, I have completed the following stuff I was assigned: one comparison paragraph, ten sentence revisions, one inspection report, and one technical description. I finished these up and turned them in on time. Now I have technical instructions, a proposal, six business letters, a resume, an oral report, and an interview as well as a field trip report left to do and they are all due in the next two weeks and there is no way I can get them done. I think I had better drop English and try to take it next quarter. I'm real sorry that I haven't done all the stuff I was supposed to do and it isn't because of you because you are a good teacher. Maybe I will get you next semester when I have a little more money and a little more time. I don't think I can pass this course right now.

Application 2:
Writing the Progress Report

Write a progress report about a project you are currently working on. Below are some possible topics.

Rebuilding a car engine
Redecorating your house, room, or apartment

Working on a laboratory project
Revising a work schedule
Preparing a research report

Fill in the appropriate plan sheet before you write a draft.

Incident Report

Application 1:
Revising the Incident Report

Using the Incident Report Plan Sheet and the Guidelines for Revision in Chapter 3, revise this report on the theft of copper wire. Address the report to Gene Robertson, Supervisor, from Alan Tenn, Foreman. Fill in the appropriate plan sheet before you write a revised draft.

Since long about August 10, a lot of copper wire has disappeared from the eight service trucks and the supply warehouse. Prior to that time we had a little bit of pilfering but in the last three weeks, it's really gotten a bit out of hand. I'm not sure exactly why we are having the problem but I'd be willing to bet that half of it is because we have poor distribution practices on the trucks. The other half is poor security.

Nobody's gotten hurt yet but it is costing us right much money to replace all that missing wire. As you know the cost of copper has shot sky-high and we are taking a real beating. We spent $1,001.77 to replace 10,000 feet of AWG 14 last month.

We are having real problems getting the construction work done on time and we will wind up having to pay for construction overruns if we are not careful. The guys are having a morale problem, too, because everybody is suspicious of everybody else and our normally good work situation is deteriorating pretty bad.

I figure we can solve the problem if we hire a local security service to check on the warehouse and put the trucks inside the chain link fence at night. We should get the foremen to record the amount of wire assigned to each truck each day and the amount of wire used during the day's job. If we catch one of the guys stealing, we better fire him.

Application 2:
Writing the Incident Report

Determine an appropriate audience and write an incident report based on an occurrence that happened or could have happened on your job or at school. Below are some possible topics.

A student slipping on an ice-covered walk and fracturing an elbow
A piece of very expensive equipment stolen from a lab
The failure of an employee or fellow student to show up for work or class on time nearly every day

Inspection Report

Application 1:
Revising the Inspection Report

Using the appropriate Inspection Report Plan Sheet and the Guidelines for Revision in Chapter 3, revise the inspection report shown below. Address your memo to Robin Edwards, Skaterama Manager, from one of her employees, Elmer Finch. Fill in the appropriate plan sheet before beginning a revised draft.

Summary

Due to the anticipated increase in employees in the fall of 1985, this report was conducted to evaluate the present employee lounge areas. The employee lounge is located beside the snack bar. The employees use this area to sit, eat, drink, and punch in and out on a time clock. The lounge is 12 feet long and 7 feet wide, with a tile floor and ceiling. The walls are white plastic covering. The lighting is created by 8 fluorescent bulbs. The lounge has only one entrance and exit. Its decorative elements include a bulletin board and posters dealing with employee morale. The following chart represents the equipment in the employee lounge and its condition.

Type	Quantity	Condition
Chairs	3	Fair
Refrigerator	1	Good
Time Clock	1	Good
Trash Can	1	Fair

To conclude, this report finds no need for major changes in the existing lounge. The following repairs should be made: one chair reupholstered. The following materials should be added: telephone and a coatrack.

Application 2:
Writing the Inspection Report

Write an inspection report appropriate for the situation discussed below. Address the memorandum to David Hooker, Supervisor of Training, from Fred Smith, Training Facility Coordinator. Remember to fill in all sections of the plan sheet before you begin your first draft.

Once a year, Fred Smith is required to inspect the company training facility for safety and first aid equipment. After his inspection, he writes an inspection report to his supervisor, David Hooker.

As a guide, he uses the floor plan of the facility shown in Figure 9-12. The legend shows the type and symbol for the various items of safety and first aid equipment located throughout the facility.

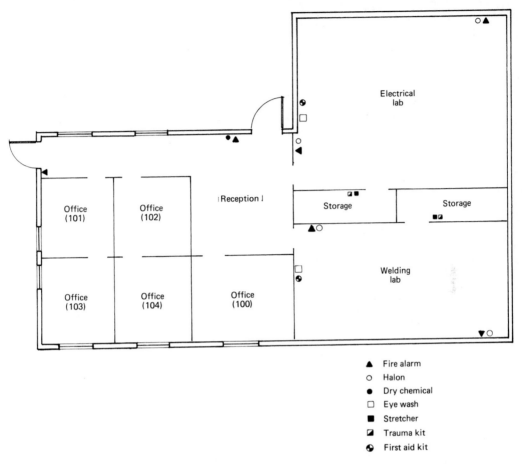

Figure 9-12:   Inspection Report Assignment

Field Trip Report

Application 1:
Revising the Field Trip Report

Using the appropriate Field Trip Report Plan Sheet and the Guidelines for Revision in Chapter 3, revise the field trip report written by Jack Walker, Technical Support Specialist, to Trent Edwards, Supervisor of Test Engineering, describing a microprocessor seminar he attended. Fill in the appropriate plan sheet before you try to write a draft.

Summary

On January 10, I attended a training seminar at the Telecommunications, Inc. Training Center to learn how to use the Winfield Micro-System Troubleshooter. Three tech support specialists and 5 technicians from the product test department went, too. The seminar lasted from 8:30 - 4:30 and we saw a demonstration of the equipment, then had time to do a hands-on work session, then a question and answer session, then a seminar evaluation.

Discussion

At the seminar, we divided up into 4 groups of 2 persons each and rotated between 6 set-ups of equipment to test the following functions: input of data, troubleshooting, mode keys, programming, register manipulation, and tape operations. The equipment had in-place circuit boards with "bugs" to test equipment accuracy.

The Winfield provides guided fault isolation on microprocessor based circuit packs and advanced controls logic. Unfortunately, the demonstration circuits malfunctioned at 3:00 o'clock so each group did not have a chance to perform all 6 functions described above.

Conclusion

I learned the basic use of the Winfield and elementary programming, specifically how to input data, mode keys, register manipulation, and troubleshooting. I didn't have a chance to try tape operations because of the equipment failure. The training manual that accompanied the equipment was good.

Application 2:
Writing the Field Trip Report

Write a report of a field trip either on or off your college campus. If you have not been on a field trip lately, write about a trip that you think would benefit the students in your curriculum. Below are some possible topics.

Trip to a correctional youth center for criminal justice class
Trip to Student Government Association Annual Conference
Trip to a mental institution for nursing class
Trip to a manufacturing company for industrial engineering technology class
Visit to the college computer center for a business data processing class

Progress Report
Occasional/Periodic
Plan Sheet
Long Form with Tables

MEMORANDUM

TO:

FROM:

SUBJECT:

DATE:

SUMMARY

Choose an appropriate heading, probably "Summary."

Progress Made: (briefly).

Problems Encountered:

Projected Completion Date:

BACKGROUND

Choose an appropriate heading.

Identification of Project or Assignment: (Include number if it is a periodic progress report.)

Date Assigned:

Purpose:

Overall Requirements:

Required Equipment and/or Supplies: (if applicable)

Time Limits:

DISCUSSION SECTION

Choose appropriate headings for all required subsections. Some typical headings are "Tasks Completed" and "Tasks Remaining."

The following tables indicate tasks completed and those remaining to be done.

Table: Tasks Completed

Task	Tasks Completed	Date Completed	Time Required
TASK 1:			
TASK 2:			
TASK 3:			
TASK 4:			
TASK 5:			
TASK 6:			
TASK 7:			
TASK 8:			
TASK 9:			
TASK 10:			
		Total Time Required_____	

Table: Tasks Remaining

Task	Tasks To Be Completed	Due Date	Completion Time
TASK 1:			
TASK 2:			
TASK 3:			
TASK 4:			

Table: Tasks Remaining

Task	Tasks To Be Completed	Due Date	Completion Time
TASK 5:			
TASK 6:			
TASK 7:			
TASK 8:			
TASK 9:			
TASK 10:			

Total Time Needed To Complete Work _____

Note: The "TASK" column does not appear on final memorandum.

ENDING SECTION

Choose an appropriate heading. Some typical headings are "Assessment," "Problems," and "Projected Completion." If your project is on schedule and you have encountered no problems, some of this information is not necessary.

Problems Encountered:

Supplies, Equipment Needed:

Extra Time Needed:

Projected Completion Date:

**Incident Report
Plan Sheet**

<u>MEMORANDUM</u>

TO:

FROM:

SUBJECT:

DATE:

SUMMARY

Choose an appropriate heading, probably "Summary."

Incident:

Brief Evaluation of the Incident's Effects:

BACKGROUND

Choose an appropriate heading.

Who:

What:

When:

Where:

Why:

DISCUSSION SECTION

Choose an appropriate heading. Some typical headings are "Damages," "Costs," "Consequences of the Incident."

Damages:

Injuries:

Costs:

Consequences:

ENDING SECTION

Choose an appropriate heading. Some typical headings are "Actions Taken" and "Recommendations." Omit any topics listed below that are not relevant for your report.

Action Taken:

Recommendations:

New Safety Precautions:

New/Improved Equipment:

New Inspection Techniques:

New Employee Training:

Employee Supervision:

Disciplinary Action:

Inspection Report
Plan Sheet 1
Area Report

<u>MEMORANDUM</u>

TO:

FROM:

SUBJECT:

DATE:

SUMMARY

Choose an appropriate heading, probably "Summary."

    Site:

    Results of Inspection:

    Summary of Recommendations (if applicable)

BACKGROUND

Choose an appropriate heading.

    Location: (Building, room number, street address)

    Purpose of Inspection:

    Other Individuals Involved in the Inspection: (if any)

DISCUSSION SECTION

Choose appropriate headings for all required subsections. Some typical headings are "Description of the Area" and "Plant Layout." Omit any topics listed below that are not relevant for your report.

Dimensions:

Lighting:

Windows:

Doors:

Flooring:

Walls:

Ceiling:

Decorative Elements:

Sketch of floor plan and location of items:
(Use a separate sheet of paper)

Table   : Items

Type of Item	Location	Quantity	Condition

ENDING SECTION

Choose an appropriate heading. Some typical headings are "Recommendations" and "Assessment of Area." Omit any topics listed below that are not relevant for your report.

Replacements Needed:

Repairs Needed:

Additional Furniture Needed:

Additional Equipment Needed:

Recommendations:

Inspection Report
Plan Sheet 2
Item or Series of Items

<u>MEMORANDUM</u>

TO:

FROM:

SUBJECT:

DATE:

SUMMARY

Choose an appropriate heading, probably "Summary."

    Item(s):

    Results of Inspection:

    Summary of Recommendations (if applicable):

BACKGROUND

Choose an appropriate heading, probably "Background."

    Item(s) Inspected (Brand Name, Model Number)

    Location:

    Purpose of Inspection:

    Other Individuals Involved in Inspection: (if any)

DISCUSSION SECTION

Choose appropriate headings for all required subsections. Some typical headings are "Description of Items" and "Existing Conditions."

Sketch of Floor Plan and Location of Items (if applicable):
(Use a separate sheet of paper.)

Table   :Items

Type of Item	Location	Quantity	Condition

ENDING SECTION

Choose an appropriate heading. Omit any topics listed below that are not relevant for your report.

Replacements Needed:

Repairs Needed:

Additional Parts Needed:

Additional Equipment Needed:

Recommendations:

Field Trip Report
Plan Sheet 1
Business/Industry

<u>MEMORANDUM</u>

TO:

FROM:

SUBJECT:

DATE:

SUMMARY

Choose an appropriate heading, probably "Summary."

Assignment:

Results or Recommendations:

BACKGROUND

Choose an appropriate heading.

Purpose of Field Trip:

Persons Involved:

Location:

Dates and Times Involved:

Activities:

DISCUSSION SECTION

Choose headings for all required subsections. Some typical headings are "Description of _____ ," "General Organization," "Employees," "Facilities," "Plant Layout," and "Equipment." Omit any topics listed below that are not relevant for your report.

Brief History:

Date of Founding:

Type of Business/Industry:

Product or Service Offered:

General Organization:

Number of Employees:

Branches/Subsidiaries:

Detailed Organizational Chart:
(Use a separate sheet of paper.)

Diagram of Physical Layout:
(Use a separate sheet of paper.)

Flowchart of Work Process:
(Use a separate sheet of paper.)

Equipment:

Table: Title		
Type	Number	Location

ENDING SECTION

Choose an appropriate heading. Some typical headings are "Comments," "Assessment," and "Recommendations."

What You Learned:

Recommendations:

Field Trip Report
Plan Sheet 2
Social Institution

<u>MEMORANDUM</u>

TO:

FROM:

SUBJECT:

DATE:

SUMMARY

Choose an appropriate heading, probably "Summary."

   Assignment:

   Results or Recommendations:

BACKGROUND

Choose an appropriate heading.

   Purpose of Field Trip:

   Persons Involved:

   Location:

   Dates and Times Involved:

   Activities:

DISCUSSION SECTION

Choose headings appropriate for the required subsections. Some typical headings are "History," "Goals," "Organization," and "Facilities." Omit any topics listed below that are not relevant for your report.

Brief History:

Date of Founding:

Purpose:

Population Served:

Total Number of Inmates, or Patients, or Population:

Personnel Employed:

General Organization of the institution:
(Use a separate sheet to draw an organizational chart, if necessary.)

General Description of the Environment:

Description of Facilities:

Table: Title

Type of Area	Condition	Location	Purpose

ENDING SECTION

Choose an appropriate heading. Some typical headings are "Comments," "Assessment," and "Recommendations."

What You Learned:

Recommendations:

Field Trip Report
Plan Sheet 3
Conference/Convention

<u>MEMORANDUM</u>

TO:

FROM:

SUBJECT :

DATE:

SUMMARY

Choose an appropriate heading, probably "Summary."

  Assignment:

  Results or Recommendations:

BACKGROUND

Choose an appropriate heading.

  Purpose of Field Trip:

  Persons Involved:

  Location:

  Dates and Times Involved:

Activities:

DISCUSSION SECTION

Choose appropriate headings for required subsections. Some typical headings are "Meetings Attended," "Companies Represented" and "Products on Exhibit." Omit any topics listed below that are not relevant for your report.

Major Business Conducted/Seminars Attended in a list with summary statement.

1.

2.

3.

4.

5.

6.

Companies Represented:

Table   :Title

Company	Product/Service	Representative

Products on Exhibit:

Table :Title			
Product	Company	Wholesale Price	Retail Price

Value of these products for your company:

ENDING SECTION

Choose an appropriate heading. Some typical headings are "Comments," "Assessment," and "Recommendations."

    What You Learned:

    Recommendations:

10

PROPOSALS

When you complete this chapter, you should know how to write two important types of proposals. You should learn how to plan and revise sales/service and planning proposals:

> Sales/Service proposal
> > Beginning section
> > Discussion section
> > Ending section
> Planning proposal
> > Beginning section
> > Discussion section
> > Ending section

Proposals are offers to do something or suggestions for change. These special reports are used to make recommendations to potential customers or to management in the writer's company. They can range in length from a few sentences quickly written on an employee suggestion form to a 300-page document offering to build a new industrial complex. In this chapter, the sales/service proposal and the planning proposal will be discussed. The sales/service proposal is an attempt to sell a product or service to a customer. A planning proposal is a suggestion for change in the writer's company.

SALES/SERVICE PROPOSAL

A sales/service proposal is a report in which a company or individual offers to provide a product or service to a potential customer. It is a bid to do work or to supply materials or equipment. For example, the owner of a radio-television sales center sends a bid to a local motel which has let a contract for the installation of televisions in 240 rooms. The owner is competing with the other television sales centers in the area. He tries to win the contract by emphasizing the quality of his product and the fairness of his price. Like an advertisement, a sales/service proposal is intended to be persuasive. It includes detailed descriptions of products and services, information about the qualifications and reputation of his company, and projections of item costs and total costs. For many large companies, sales/service proposals are routine correspondence. Therefore, they have designed a printed form for these reports.

The guidelines on the next few pages and the plan sheet at the end of the chapter explain how to organize information in a sales/service proposal. A sales/service proposal from Lakeside Docks, Incorporated is used as an example. Responding to a request from John L. Fitzgerald, a property owner, the company president, Clyde Anderson, submits a bid to build a dock. Because Mr. Fitzgerald is not an expert at building docks, Mr. Anderson is very thorough in his proposal. He describes the dock and even includes a topographical map to show its location on Mr. Fitzgerald's property. Mr. Anderson carefully presents the costs, down to the last nail, so that his prospective customer will not be surprised when he receives the bill. Mr. Anderson concentrates on the benefits of contracting with his company, explaining how many docks he has built in the area and offering to take Mr. Fitzgerald on a visit to a satisfied customer. Mr. Anderson is a salesman as well as a contractor; he is selling his company and his product.

Mr. Anderson's proposal is submitted to Mr. Fitzgerald with a letter of transmittal, a title page, summary, and table of contents. Refer to Chapter 7 for a discussion of these important parts of the proposal.

Beginning Section

The beginning section, or introduction, explains the purpose of the sales/service proposal, the location of the bidder's business, and the extent of the guarantee for customer satisfaction. The proposal from Lakeside Docks, Incorporated begins with the terms of the contract.

Introduction

Lakeside Docks, Incorporated, located in Tar Landing, North Carolina, proposes to build a dock at Lot 27, Lake Gaston for John L. Fitzgerald. Lakeside furnishes all materials and labor except for dredging and pile-driving services, which are subcontracted. Docks constructed by Lakeside are guaranteed for 20 years with the exception of any natural disasters. Construction will begin within 10 working days after a contract is signed.

Discussion Section

The discussion section of the sales/service proposal describes the product or service offered. It also explains tasks, time requirements, personnel requirements, costs for labor and materials, costs for subcontractors, and method of payment. Headings introduce each new topic.

General Description of Service or Product. The discussion section usually begins with a general description of the product or service offered. A diagram of parts should be included if a product is proposed. A flowchart should be included if a service is proposed. For example, the proposal from Lakeside Docks, contains a brief description of the dock to be built. It also has a map showing a topographical view of where the dock is located.

Description of Dock

The dock for Lot 27, Lake Gaston will be made of pressure-treated posts and weather-treated lumber and rest on four nonfloating creosote pilings. Six outdoor spotlights will be spaced at nine-foot intervals on each side of the dock. The dock will extend 30 feet into the water at an angle of 32 degrees to the shoreline. The dock will meet all safety and navigational requirements and regulations for pier construction on inland bodies of water for the State of North Carolina. See the figure for a topographical view of the location of the dock.

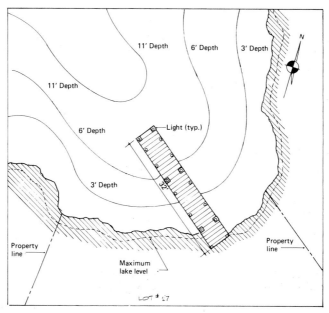

TOPOGRAPHICAL VIEW OF LOCATION OF DECK

Task Breakdown and Time Schedule.   The task breakdown and time schedule are usually given in a table. The table includes the steps that the company will take in fulfilling the contract, the time required to complete each step, and the total time required for completion. A summary sentence introduces the table and its contents. Another statement gives the starting and projected completion date of the project. If there are only one or two tasks, this information is written in a short paragraph. The proposal from Lakeside Docks contains a schedule of construction. There are seven tasks which will take over a week to accomplish, so Mr. Anderson includes a short introductory paragraph and a table showing the proposed construction schedule. The table lists the services his company and the subcontracting company perform. Notice that the heading names the service being provided.

Schedule of Construction

The schedule of construction for the dock at Lot 27 is shown in Table 1 below. Times are approximate and assume good weather conditions. We will begin work on the installation of your dock on May 4 with a projected completion date of May 8, 1988.

Table 1:   Construction Schedule

Task	Hours for Completion
Landscaping	4
Dredging	10
Pile Driving	4
Setting Posts	10
Framing	3
Planking	8
Wiring and Light Installation	8
Total time required	47 Hours

Personnel.   Personnel includes the number of workers who will be assigned to the project and their qualifications. The names of subcontracting companies also appear in this section. If only a few workers will be involved in the project, this information is written in a short paragraph. However, if the job requires a large number of workers, the information is presented in a table that lists the job title and the qualifications of each worker; or a separate appendix with résumés may be included in the proposal. Since Lakeside Docks will send only three people and subcontract portions of the project, a paragraph is appropriate.

Personnel

Two of Lakeside Docks' experienced carpenters will oversee and take part in the total construction effort, and our electrician will do the wiring. The dredging and pile driving will be subcontracted to Gaston Dredging Services, and the actual construction of the dock will be accomplished by the Lakeside Dock construction crew.

Cost of Materials.   A detailed table lists the cost of the materials required to do the job. The table shows the item number, the quantity required, a brief description of the item, the unit cost (the cost of one of the items), and the total cost. At the end of the table, a grand total is shown for the cost of all required materials. The table below lists the materials required to build Mr. Fitzgerald's dock.

Cost of Materials

The cost of the materials to build the dock are shown in Table 2. These prices are subject to minor change depending upon the availability of materials.

Table 2:   Cost of Materials

Item	Quantity	Description	Unit Cost	Total Cost
1	6	8′ × 6″ Pressure-treated posts	$ 7.95	$ 47.70
2	4	14′ × 6″ Pressure-treated posts	14.95	59.80
3	6	19′ × 6″ Pressure-treated posts	19.95	119.70
4	20	2″ × 4″ by 8′ Lumber	1.20	24.00
5	30	1 1/2″ × 6″ × 8′ Planks	1.40	42.00
6	250 ft	3 wire w/ground UL cable		67.50
7	6	Outdoor lighting fixtures	9.95	59.70
8	2	15-Amp light switches	2.50	5.00
9	1	15-Amp breaker switch	12.50	12.50
10	5 lbs	16-Penny nails	.90	4.50
			Total	$442.40

Cost of Subcontractors.   If subcontractors have been hired to do part of the job, a statement of their fees must be given. If several subcontractors have been hired, the name of the subcontractor, the service the subcontractor performs, and the cost of the service are listed on a table. If only one is hired, a sentence is appropriate. The cost of subcontractors in the Lakeside Dock project can be stated in a short paragraph.

Cost of Subcontractor

Gaston Dredging Services charges a standard flat rate of $25 per hour to dredge and drive pilings. Based on the approximate time required for this project, the subcontractor cost will be $350.

Cost of Labor. The cost of labor can be discussed in different ways. Some companies charge a flat rate for labor and will quote a single price. However, if the project is a large one, if a large number of people will be employed, if the contract may be extended, or if overtime costs may be incurred, a table is used. This table lists the job title by position, hourly rate of pay, overtime rate of pay, and an approximate total cost for labor per classification of worker. Since the Lakeside Docks project is a small one, a flat rate for labor is charged.

Cost of Labor

The total cost of labor for the construction of dock will be $500.

Total Cost. If several complicated cost factors are in the project, a short summary gives the total cost for the complete project. The summary may be omitted with only one cost factor. The proposal from Lakeside Docks has three subsections dealing with costs. Therefore, a statement of the total cost is necessary.

Total Cost

The total cost for the installation of your dock is as follows:

Materials	$ 442.40
Subcontractor	350.00
Labor	500.00
Grand Total	$1292.40

Method of Payment. The method of payment is how the company will be paid for the job. If the project is a short one, a sentence or two will be sufficient. If the project is an extremely long one, lasting over a period of months or even years, a much more detailed explanation is required. For a large project, often a company's lawyers decide and explain the method of payment. The proposal from Lakeside Docks discusses the method of payment.

Method of Payment

Lakeside Docks requires a 25 percent down payment ($323.10) upon delivery of materials to the site with the remainder ($969.30) to be paid in full upon completion and final inspection of the project.

Ending Section

The ending section of the sales/service proposal briefly mentions the benefits of hiring the company to do the job. It may include the names of satisfied customers; the number of years the company has been in business; and the enjoyment, pleasure, savings, or convenience the customer will receive. The ending section also explains what actions the customer should take to get the project under-way. The proposal from Lakeside Docks ends with a sales pitch.

Conclusion

Lakeside Docks, Incorporated will provide you with a high-quality dock for your boating pleasure. Forty-two satisfied customers at Lake Gaston attest to our high standards, economy, and efficiency in getting the job done. A simple telephone call will have the job under way in a matter of days.

The proposal from Lakeside Docks is typical of bids submitted for a project of moderate size. However, it does not show you all the possible varia-tions. The length and the complexity of sales/service proposals depend on the size of the job. The information included depends on the audience and pur-pose. The plan sheet will help you become more familiar with the range of possibilities for sales/service proposals.

PLANNING PROPOSALS

A planning proposal is a report in which a change in management, company organization, or procedure is suggested or a solution to a company problem is proposed. Planning proposals frequently save companies a great deal of money. Therefore, writers are often rewarded for their suggestions with pro-motions, bonus pay, or extra leave. Consider an example. Suppose a printer knows of a new brand of ink which dries three times faster than the brand currently used. Although the new brand costs more than the old brand, it al-lows faster completion of jobs so that the printing company can serve more customers. The printer writes a proposal to management recommending that the company try this quick-drying ink. His suggestion saves the company money, and he is awarded a $500 bonus. To convince management to accept the recommendations, a planning proposal describes the problem it is address-ing in detail and explains how to implement the suggested solution.

Like the sales/service proposal, the planning proposal is important rou-tine correspondence for many large companies. Printed forms such as the one shown on Figure 10-1 are often available. However, when printed forms are not available, you will have to develop your own proposal. The guidelines on the next few pages and the plan sheet at the end of the chapter will help you with that task. A planning proposal from a police lieutenant, Lt. Bartles, a member of the campus security staff at a small college, is used as an example. The proposal is addressed to Chief Wilson, the head of campus security. It suggests that the Student Security Patrol be increased to stop the rise in crime in a certain area on campus. Like Mr. Anderson, Lt. Bartles is attempting to sell something. However, Lt. Bartles is selling a solution to a problem—the problem of increased crime. He describes the seriousness of the problem, pro-vides statistical data to back up his position, and then proposes a reasonable, cost-effective solution. His primary concern is obtaining approval for his idea.

Suggestion
Employee Suggestion System

brain storm

INSTRUCTIONS:

1. BE SURE TO READ THE ELIGIBILITY REQUIREMENTS AND RULES ON THE REVERSE OF THIS FORM BEFORE YOU BEGIN.
2. Type or print with ink.
3. Attach additional pages if necessary (be sure to indicate the question number you are continuing).
4. Put only one suggestion on each form.
5. If you need help, ask your supervisor or a member of your department awards committee.

Name:	Title or Position:
Department or Agency:	Unit:
Work Address:	Work Telephone:
Home Address:	Home Telephone:

I. What is the subject of your suggestion ?

II. Describe the situation, condition, method, procedure, etc., to be improved. Be specific - what is wrong ?

III. What is your suggestion ? Be specific - describe the improvement and tell how it can be made.

Figure 10-1:   Employee Suggestion Form

Lt. Bartles' proposal is sent with a memorandum of transmittal, title page, table of contents, and summary. Refer to Chapter 7 for a discussion of these parts of the proposal.

Beginning Section

The beginning section, the introduction, introduces the reader to the content of the proposal and its arrangement. Generally, the beginning section explains the problem, the background, and the scope of the proposal. Depending on how much discussion is required, these topics may or may not be introduced by headings.

Description of Problem.   The problem that prompted the proposal should be stated directly and exactly. A clear statement of the problem justifies the writer's proposed solution.

Background.   The background tells what caused the problem to occur.

Scope.   The scope of the proposal explains the limitations placed on the project. Limitations may include the period of time the project will be in effect; the number of people involved; the locations; and the equipment, machinery, process, or procedures required to solve the problem.

Purpose.   The purpose is a brief statement of the change the writer proposes. This change will be justified and explained in the rest of the report.

Here is the introduction from Lt. Bartles' planning proposal. It gives a brief statement of the problem, offers an explanation of why the problem has occurred, and mentions a solution. The discussion section of the proposal will provide more details about both the problem and the solution.

Introduction

Statement of the Problem	Since the construction of the three high-rise dormitories on West Campus in 1972, vandalism and petty theft in the dorms and the parking area have been problems. However, last year we had a sizable increase in both the number and severity of crimes committed. Statistics from 1985 show an annual increase of 26 percent. The greatest increase has been in serious crimes such as felony, burglary, and, assault.
Background	The three dormitories—West, Hill, and Hudson—are located over one mile from the central or main portion of the campus in a dimly lit section of countryside as shown in the accompanying drawing. Bounded by woods, a low-income neighborhood, and a major railway line, the West Campus area lacks the student traffic prevalent in other parts of the campus. In addition, parts of the campus are deserted during weeknights and allow clandestine activities to take place. Student residents of the three dormitories have expressed concern about their own personal safety and loss or damage to their property.
Scope and Purpose	An increase in the number of students in the Student Security Patrol assigned specifically to the three dorms on West Campus for one semester would serve as a deterrent to the theft and assault and considerably lower the crime rate in that area. Student Security Patrols have been effective in other, limited situations.

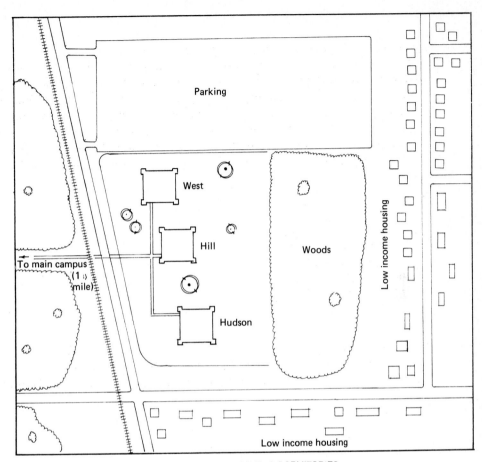

LOCATION OF WEST CAMPUS DORMITORIES

Discussion Section

The discussion section of the planning proposal tells who, what, when, why, how, and to what degree. It also justifies the proposed solution and explains how to implement it. Implementation often requires establishing a time schedule, hiring or training personnel, finding necessary facilities and equipment, and deciding on a budget.

Explanation of Problem.   Before being convinced to accept a solution, management must be persuaded that a problem exists. Therefore, a planning proposal includes a detailed explanation of the problem. It describes the current conditions and draws conclusions about the weaknesses in the existing system. Statistical data often provide convincing and objective detail. Therefore, these numbers may be used to show the seriousness of the problem. If writers choose to back up their observations with numbers, they must collect the data carefully under controlled conditions and explain the method of collection in the proposal. They must also report the results of their analysis fairly, even when their findings do not strongly support their viewpoints. If exact numbers are important, statistical data are shown in tables. If a trend showing a significant increase or decrease is important, the data are displayed on a line graph or bar graph. Sometimes only the most important results of a statistical analysis are given in the discussion section. More details, such as raw scores on a questionnaire used in a survey, are put in an appendix. To show the trend toward increased criminal activity in the West Campus area over a five-year period, Lt. Bartles has included a line graph. He introduces the visual aid by explaining what it shows. In addition, he includes data from a survey conducted by the student government association.

Criminal Activity on West Campus

A graph of criminal activity for the past five years shows the dramatic increase on the West Campus. (See Figure 2.) Particularly alarming is the number of assaults on both males and females that occurred last year.

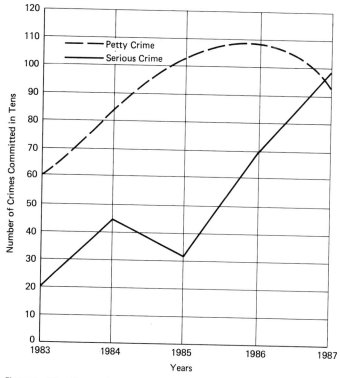

Figure 2:   West Campus Crime Statistics for the Years 1983–1987

Student Response to Student Security Patrol

To determine student attitudes concerning personal safety, 100 students residing in the West Campus dormitory complex were surveyed by four members of the Student Government Association. The survey was conducted after one of the dorm representatives brought the criminal activity in the area to the attention of the Dean of Student Services. The results of that survey, shown below, indicate that more than 35 percent of the students have been victims of some type of criminal activity and most would feel far safer with the Student Security Patrol in the complex each night.

Total Number Surveyed:	100
Total Number of Victims:	37
Total Expressing Fear for Safety:	72
Total Expressing Desire for Increased Patrol:	75

Proposed Solution.   After the problem is explained, a solution is suggested. This information is generally presented in one short paragraph. The remainder of the proposal tells exactly how to implement the solution. Lt. Bartles' proposed solution to the problem on West Campus appears below. Notice how he refers to the statistical data he has presented earlier.

Proposed Solution

In view of the rise in criminal activity and the student response to the survey, I propose that we increase the size of the Student Security Patrol from eight to 15 students for the 1987 Fall Semester and station these students on West Campus between the hours of 11:00 p.m. and 3:00 a.m. Statistics would be kept for the five-month period and a decision for continuing the program considered in January, 1988.

After the solution is given, the time schedule, personnel needs, facilities, equipment, and budget required for implementation are discussed.

Time Schedule.   Like the sales/service proposal, the planning proposal lists the tasks and a time schedule with a completion date for each task. Generally, the information is presented in a table. Bartles' time schedule is shown below.

Time Schedule

An implementation plan for the Student Security Program for Fall Semester, 1987 is shown in the table below.

Table 1:   Time Schedule

Task	Approximate Time in Weeks
Recruit Students	1 Week
Interview Students	1 Week
Train Students	2 Weeks
Total Time	4 Weeks

Because we will begin this program in Fall Semester, students must be recruited and trained in either the last two months of Spring Semester or during the six-week Summer Session.

Personnel.   Personnel requirements, qualifications, and job descriptions are included as appropriate. In Lt. Bartles' proposal, the qualifications of the potential Student Security Patrol members are important.

Qualifications for Student Security Patrol

Juniors or rising seniors should be recruited for the Student Security Patrol. They should have a grade point average of 2.5 or better, be in good health, and be residents of one of the West Campus dormitories. Preference should be given to students enrolled in the Criminal Justice Program. These students have some familiarity with the law and some knowledge of how criminals operate. Student Patrol officers will be paid $4.50 per hour.

Facilities.   A description of facilities is necessary if the proposal requires the use of office or laboratory space, if facilities need to be built or rented, or if existing facilities need to be renovated. If facilities are critical, either a complete description must be included in the proposal or a diagram must be attached. If facilities are to be rented, the location should be identified and a description included in the body of the proposal or the appendix. The location and cost for the new, rented, or renovated facilities must be given. In Lt. Bartles' proposal, facilities are not a consideration.

Equipment.   Equipment includes everything from word processors to flashlights. The equipment may be currently on hand, or it may have to be purchased or leased. If a great deal of equipment is required, it is listed on a table by type, number of pieces required, and cost. Its location is also identified. The equipment that Lt. Bartles requires to implement the Student Security Program is limited. Therefore, a table is not necessary.

Equipment

Each student recruited into the Student Security Patrol program will be furnished with the following items at a cost of approximately $50 per recruit: one three-cell flashlight, one SSP armband, rain gear, a lightweight jacket, and an identification card.

Budget.   When a proposal requires the organization to spend money, the costs are listed and identified. In addition, the writer should suggest where funds could be found to put the program into effect. Totals for personnel, facilities, and equipment must be given and a grand total presented. Lt. Bartles incorporates budget considerations as follows:

Budgetary Considerations

Costs of implementing the Student Security Patrol would be minimal for a five-month period.

Personnel Salaries	$4,008.00
Equipment	250.00
Grand Total	$4,258.00

The money to purchase the equipment may be taken from Budget Code 3000, the Crime Prevention Budget. Money used for salaries may be taken from Budget Code 2009, which is carrying a $10,000 surplus.

Ending Section

The ending section of the proposal sums up the content, draws conclusions, and makes recommendations. The conclusions may be advantages and disadvantages of adopting the proposal. Lt. Bartles summarizes his argument and explains the advantages and disadvantages of his proposal.

Conclusions

The information presented in this proposal shows that criminal activity has increased in the West Campus dormitory complex and that use of the Student Security Patrol has been effective in deterring activity in other areas in the past. It is reasonable to expect that an increase in the number of student officers on patrol can lead to a decrease in crime in the West Campus area. Costs are not prohibitive, and funding for equipment and salaries is available.

Advantages

Using students to patrol the West Campus dormitory complex has several advantages. Uniformed officers are easily recognized and serve as deterring factors only while they are in the vicinity. Plainclothes officers stand out because of their age and style of dress. They, too, have proved ineffective. Also, a lack of officers in the Campus Security Police Department limits the amount of time that foot and mobile units can be stationed in one area of the campus. Finally, using students will leave regular officers free to respond to more serious crimes.

Disadvantage

The primary disadvantage of using students to patrol the area is the loss of personal contact between the Campus Security Police Department officers and the students who live in the dormitories.

Recommendations are the immediate actions that must be taken to implement the proposal. If only one or two recommendations are given, they may be written as a short paragraph. If more than two recommendations are presented, they should be listed. Occasionally recommendations are not necessary; but most of the time, the reader expects to see a strong, specific course of action to take. Since Lt. Bartles has made several suggestions in his report, he writes his recommendations in a list rather than a short paragraph.

Recommendations

I recommend that we increase the Student Security Patrol from 8 to 15 individuals. In addition, I recommend that

1. Upperclass students be recruited no later than April 15 from the Criminal Justice Program and that they have a minimum 2.5 grade point average.
2. The program begin in the Fall Semester, 1987 and be run experimentally for that semester and that statistics be kept for a comparative study.
3. Money already on hand be allocated for this proposal.

Like the sales/service proposal examined earlier, Lt. Bartles' planning proposal cannot show you all the possible variations in submitting suggestions for change to management. Again the information included depends on the needs of the audience and the purpose of the writer. The plan sheet will help you become more familiar with the range of possibilities for planning proposals.

SUMMARY

A proposal is an offer to do something for someone or a suggestion for making a change. Sales/service proposals attempt to sell products or services to customers. To accomplish their goals, they provide a detailed description of the product or service, explain the qualifications of the writer, and tabulate costs. Rather than being sent to customers, planning proposals attempt to convince the management of the writer's company to make some change. They give detailed information about the problem that led to the proposal and explain the recommended solution. Because the sales/service proposal and the planning proposal are longer than the reports discussed in the last chapter, they have front matter and end matter.

An example of a complete sales/service proposal for landscaping and maintaining the grounds of a condominium complex is shown on pages 199–209. The proposal has all the front matter which was discussed in Chapter 7. The cover letter, on letterhead stationery, is a sales pitch from Phillip Stillman, the president of Creative Landscapes, Inc., to Wayne Newburn, the president of the Bellwood Condominium complex. The title page is next. It is followed by a table of contents which lists the major headings and a list of the illustrations found in the proposal. The last section of the front matter is the summary, which gives important details of the proposal, particularly the time and cost factors.

creative landscapes, inc.

January 13, 1988

Mr. Wayne Newburn, President
Bellwood Homeowners' Association
P.O. Box 309, Cameron Station
Raleigh, NC 27605

Dear Mr. Newburn:

The proposal for landscaping and ground maintenance for the Bellwood
Condominium Complex is enclosed. In the proposal, you will find a
description of our landscaping and maintenance services, the proposed
landscape design for the Bellwood Condominium Complex, and a list of
projected costs for landscaping and maintenance services.

Creative Landscapes has been designing and maintaining landscapes in
the Research Triangle Park area for the past six years. We have worked
with major business concerns, developers, and apartment and condominium
complexes to design pleasant and inviting exterior environments for our
customers. Out primary designers are landscape architects, and our
maintenance crews are experienced in lawn and garden upkeep.

I am sure that you will be pleased with our plans for landscaping the
grounds of the Bellwood Condomium Complex. If you have any questions
about the proposal, please call Mr. Sam Chomensky, the designer and
director of your project.

Yours truly,

Phillip Stillman

Phillip Stillman, President

Enclosure

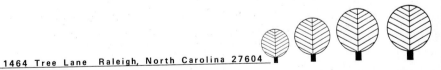

1464 Tree Lane Raleigh, North Carolina 27604

Figure 10-2: Proposal

PROPOSAL FOR
LANDSCAPING AND MAINTENANCE
OF THE BELLWOOD CONDOMINIUM COMPLEX

prepared for
Wayne Newburn, President
Bellwood Homeowners' Association

prepared by
Sam Chomensky, Landscape Architect
Creative Landscapes, Incorporated
Raleigh, North Carolina

January 13, 1988

Figure 10-2 *Continued*

TABLE OF CONTENTS

LIST OF ILLUSTRATIONS

Figure 10-2 *Continued*

SUMMARY

Creative Landscapes, Inc. proposes to landscape the commonly owned and individually owned front areas of the Bellwood Condominium complex for a fee of $12,560.30. The project will be completed in April, 1988. At the request of the Bellwood Homeowners' Association, Creative Landscapes, Inc. will maintain the lawn and gardens of the complex for a period of one year after initial landscaping is completed for a fee of $10,200.00.

iii

Figure 10-2 *Continued*

Introduction

Creative Landscapes, Inc., a landscaping and lawn maintenance firm located in Raleigh, North Carolina, proposes to design, plant, and maintain the grounds of the Bellwood Condominium Complex. When the proposal is approved, Creative Landscapes will begin work within two weeks after receiving the initial down payment as agreed upon in the contract. After completing the landscaping, Creative Landscapes will maintain the grounds for a period of one year, at which time the maintenance contract may be renewed at the discretion of the Bellwood Homeowners' Association and Creative Landscapes.

The design and maintenance personnel at Creative Landscapes, Inc. are all highly qualified. The design group is headed by Joe Kalkhurst, a landscape architect with 15 years' experience in the Raleigh area; and the maintenance group is headed by Worth Shaw, a horticulturist with 10 years' experience. Creative Landscapes has won state and national awards for landscaping in the Raleigh, Durham, Chapel Hill triangle. You can see some of our award-winning designs by visiting International Telex, Inc. in Durham; the President's Inn in Research Triangle Park; Gateway Shopping Plaza in Cary; and Bishop's Hill Condominium complex in Raleigh. The landscaping at each of these facilities is unique, designed to accentuate the architecture of the facilities and to blend comfortably with the surrounding areas. We plan to continue this tradition for excellence in the landscape design for Bellwood Condominium complex.

Landscaping Services

Creative Landscapes provides total landscaping services for its customers. We select and plant trees, shrubs, and flowers;

Figure 10-2 *Continued*

aerate and seed lawns; trim trees and bushes; and remove unhealthy
or unsightly vegetation. The subsections below describe the proposed
design for Bellwood Condominium complex and give the landscaping and
labor costs.

Description and Cost of Proposed Landscaping Design

In keeping with the informal style of the Bellwood Condominium
complex and the landscaping in the surrounding residential areas,
Creative Landscapes proposes to provide a landscape design that is
predominantly natural rather than formal.

Commonly Owned Areas. Creative Landscapes, Inc. plans to place five
natural islands of trees, shrubs, and flowering annuals in the commonly
owned areas of Bellwood Condominium complex. These natural islands will
provide privacy for condominium residents and separate the complex from
the nearby shopping center and heavily traveled streets. Detailed plans
for each of the natural islands will be submitted to the Homeowners'
Association for approval prior to starting the project. We will also
remove the chain link fence and hedge which front Bellwood Drive and
replace them with split rail fencing, shrubs, and flowering annuals. We
plan to leave the existing trees, some of which are over 50 years old,
intact with some minor pruning and shaping. Prior to developing the
islands, we will aerate, reseed, and fertilize the lawn. The figure on
the following page shows the location, shape, and size of the five natural
islands.

The following table shows the approximate cost for creating the
islands, reseeding the lawn, and fencing the perimeter of the lawn. It
lists the cost for each tree, shrub, and flowering annual as well as
grass seed, fertilizer, and fencing for the commonly owned areas.

Figure 10-2 *Continued*

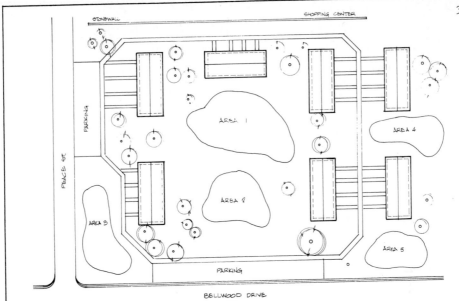

3

Fig.
LOCATION OF NATURAL ISLANDS

Table 1:   Cost of Landscaping Materials for Commonly Owned Areas

Item	Quantity	Description	Unit Cost	Total Cost
1	20	Riverbirch (20 ft.)	$ 49.95	$ 999.00
2	30	Bloodbark dogwoods (5 ft.)	16.45	493.50
3	8	Japanese Maple (6 ft.)	49.95	399.60
4	10	White Pine (20 ft.)	59.95	599.50
5	25	Euphoneyma (12 inches)	4.95	123.75
6	10	Variegated Euphoneyma (12 in.)	4.95	49.50
7	100	Chrysanthemums (rust, gold, orange) (8 inches)	4.95	495.00
8	40	Pine straw (bales)	3.95	158.00
9	50	Bermuda grass seed (pounds)	69.95	69.95
10	100	10-10-10 fertilizer (pounds)	2.95	295.00
11	60	Split rail fencing (sections)	12.50	750.00
				$4434.50

Figure 10-2 *Continued*

4

Individually Owned Front Areas. In the areas in front of each condominium between the building foundation and the sidewalk, Creative
Landscapes, Inc. plans to continue the natural theme of the five islands.
We will plant small trees, shrubs, and a variety of annuals depending on
the size of the area and existing trees and shrubs.

Because so many homeowners have planted vegetables, flowers, and
shrubs in the front areas, we will require permission from the
Homeowners' Association Board to make the changes we feel are necessary.
To obtain cooperation, Sam Chomensky, the landscape architect in charge
of the Bellwood project, will meet with condominium owners to present the
plans for each unit. The cost of materials for landscaping the individually owned areas is shown in Table 2. In accordance with your instructions, these costs will be billed to the Homeowners' Association.

Table 2: Cost of Landscaping Materials for Individually Owned Front Areas

Item	Quantity	Description	Unit Cost	Total Cost
1	200	Hofstra (6 in.)	$ 2.95	$ 590.00
2	100	Variegated Hofstra (6 in.)	2.95	295.00
3	100	Shore juniper (6 in.)	3.95	395.00
4	100	Chrysanthemums (rust, gold, orange)(6 in.)	4.95	495.00
5	24	Blue spruce (2 ft.)	10.95	262.80
6	40	Variegated Euphoneyma (2 ft.)	4.95	198.00
7	60	Sand daisies	3.95	237.00
8	40	Pine straw (bales)	3.95	158.00
9	50	10-10-10 fertilizer (pounds)	2.95	295.00
				$2925.80

Figure 10-2 *Continued*

5

Individually Owned Back Areas. As you suggested in our telephone discussion, we plan to leave the landscaping of the back areas between the foundation and the sidewalk to the discretion of the individual homeowners. Since many of the homeowners have decks and vegetable and flower gardens in the back areas, we think that imposing a uniform plan in the back areas would interfere with the enjoyment that many homeowners find in their own personal gardens.

Labor Cost

In keeping with our standard labor practice, we will charge a flat rate of $200 per day for labor. Based on a 26-day schedule, the projected cost for labor for the project is $5200. The actual cost may vary according to the ease with which we are able to meet our proposed schedule. The final bill will be adjusted to reflect the variance.

Total Cost

The projected total cost for the Bellwood Landscaping project is as follows:

Materials for commonly owned areas	$ 4434.50
Materials for individually owned areas	2925.80
Labor	5200.00
Grand Total	$12,560.30

Method of Payment

Creative Landscapes, Inc. requires a deposit of one-half the projected grand total ($6280.15) upon approval of the proposal. The remaining balance is due upon completion.

Figure 10-2 *Continued*

6

Landscaping Schedule

To have the Bellwood Condominium complex landscaping plan ready for the spring and summer growing season, we need to begin work no later than March 1. The table below shows the schedule we propose.

Table 3: Landscaping Schedule

Task	Time Required in Days	Proposed Date of Completion
Remove chain link fence and hedge	3	March 4
Aerate, seed, fertilize lawn	3	March 9
Install split rail fence	2	March 11
Plant trees, shrubs, flowers in commonly owned natural areas	8	March 22
Plant trees, shrubs, flowers in individually owned front areas	10	April 8

Completion of the landscaping according to this proposed schedule will guarantee a colorful spring, summer, and fall for the Bellwood Condominium homeowners.

Maintenance Service

Creative Landscapes, Inc. operates a maintenance service to insure that the grounds retain their natural beauty after the landscaping has been completed. Our maintenance service includes mowing and trimming the lawn, edging the sidewalks and curbs, pruning bushes and trees, and raking. In addition, we fertilize and control weed and insect problems. We provide all equipment, labor, and supplies for healthy lawn and garden maintenance.

Figure 10-2 *Continued*

7

In the Raleigh area, extensive maintenance is required only from April 1 through November 30 of each year. However, to spread costs out more evenly, we bill on a monthly basis even for those months that do not require services. The cost per month is $850 for a yearly total of $10,200. If the bill is paid in lump sum at the beginning of the year, we allow a 10 percent discount for a yearly cost of $9180. This price is competitive with the other lawn maintenance services in the area.

After seeing the quality of our work in landscape design, we think the Homeowners' Association will want us to maintain the lawns and grounds. Satisfaction is guaranteed. If the Association thinks that we are not fulfilling our contract at any time, Creative Landscapes will release the Association from its commitment.

Conclusion

We at Creative Landscapes, Inc. look forward to working with the Bellwood Condominium Homeowners' Association and the individual homeowners in designing a landscaping plan that will enhance the beauty of the complex itself and provide privacy for the residents. We are more than willing to have our project director available when you present the plan to the Homeowners' Association. Once the plan has been agreed upon and the contract signed, Mr. Chomensky will meet with each homeowner to discuss plans for the individually owned front areas; and we will begin landscaping the complex.

Figure 10-2 *Continued*

ASSIGNMENTS

Application 1:
Revising The Sales/Service Proposal

Read the body of the short proposal shown below. Using the Guidelines for Revision from Chapter 3 and the sales/service proposal plan sheet, examine the format, content, organization, and usage. What essential parts are missing? Could it be better organized? Is there enough information for you to make a decision about the service? Why? Why not? Be prepared to discuss how you might revise the proposal in class.

Subject: Reaves Electrical Co. installs electrical wiring throughout Wake and Johnston Counties. We undertake commercial and residential wiring based on the signing of a contract.

Methods: In order to provide the best service possible, all installers are licensed by the State of North Carolina with at least 5 years experience.

Task Breakdown: The table below states each required task and the approximate number of hours for completion.

Table 1:   Tasks Required

Task	Approximate Hours
1. Removal of present wiring, breaker box, junction boxes, sockets, and switches	6
2. Cutting for the rerouting of new wiring	2
3. Installation of breaker box, wiring, junction boxes, sockets, and switches	8

Table 2:   Costs for Materials

Item	Quantity	Description	Unit Cost	Total Cost
1	1	Breaker Box	$75.00	$ 75.00
2	320 ft	Copper-Core Wire	1.25/ft	400.00
3	6	Light Switches	2.50	13.00
4	3	220-Volt Sockets	5.00	15.00
5	15	120-Volt Sockets	2.50	37.50
6	6	Junction Boxes	1.50	9.00
7	50	Wire Nuts	0.25	12.50
			TOTAL	$562.00

Table 3:   Additional Costs

Description	Costs
10% of cost of materials for transportation and delivery	$56.20

Table 4:   Labor Costs

Position	Hourly Rate	Total Hours	Total
1 Electrician	$18.00	16	$228.00
2 Helpers	7.00	32	224.00
		Total	$512.00

Method of Payment: BMI Electrical Co. requires 50% ($565.10) down payment upon signing of the contract. Final payment ($565.10) must be made upon completion of the job.

Conclusion: BMI Electrical Co. has been in business for the past 13 years. You are invited to call R.L. More at 467-4677 or Henry Davis at 782-6155 to verify our quality of installation.

Application 2:
Writing a Sales/Service Proposal

Write a proposal offering to sell some product or service to a customer. Here are some examples of possible topics:

A new data processing program you designed
A home nursing care service
A new expense accounting procedure
Child care services
A service contract for maintenance of heavy equipment or automobiles
A mechanical or architectural drafting service for large firms
A bid to subcontract the plumbing for an apartment complex
A bid to maintain the grounds and building for an office building
A bid to subcontract the electrical work for an old house or small apartment complex

Begin the proposal by filling in the sales/service proposal plan sheet in this chapter. To be as accurate as possible in describing materials, equipment, and personnel costs, you may have to talk with your curriculum instructor or call local businesses and request the information. Based on the information on the plan sheet, write a first draft. Then revise that draft by looking back at the plan sheet and at the Guidelines for Revision in Chapter 3.

Application 3:
Writing a Planning Proposal

Write a planning proposal suggesting a change in your field of study, your college, or your job. Here are some examples of topics.

Changes in the registration process
Additional space in the student lounge

Larger, more complete athletic facilities
Addition of athletic teams or events
Change in the curriculum
More laboratory facilities
Expanded parking areas
Change in your job shift
Change in job duties
New way of doing your job
Purchase of new books or new magazines for the library.

Fill in the planning proposal plan sheet before you write your first draft.

Sales/Service Proposal
Plan Sheet
LETTER OF TRANSMITTAL

Letterhead

Date

Inside Address

Dear: _____ :
               Customer's Name

BEGINNING
      Purpose of the proposal:

      Basis for your submittal:

REVIEW OF INFORMATION FOUND IN PROPOSAL:

YOUR QUALIFICATIONS TO PERFORM THE JOB:

ENDING SALES PITCH:

               Yours truly,

               _____

               Your Name

Enclosure

TITLE PAGE

Title of the Proposal

Prepared for

Name of Individual and Company
(if applicable) for whom proposal
is being prepared.

Prepared by

Name of Individual and Company
preparing the proposal.

Date

TABLE OF CONTENTS

First-, Second-, and Third-degree Headings	Page Number
_____	_____
_____	_____
_____	_____
_____	_____
_____	_____
_____	_____

LIST OF ILLUSTRATIONS

Number and Title of Tables and Figures	Page Number
_____	_____
_____	_____
_____	_____

SUMMARY

Provide a brief overview of the proposal. Include information about product/service offered, time requirements, total cost. Do not try to write your summary until you have finished the rest of the report.

_____

_____

_____

_____

_____

_____

_____

_____

_____

_____

_____

_____

BEGINNING SECTION

Choose an appropriate heading. The heading"Introduction" is often used.

Purpose:

Location of business:

Guarantee:

DISCUSSION SECTION

Choose appropriate headings for required subsections. Some typical headings are "Description of ____," "Time Schedule," "Required Tasks," "Personnel," "Cost for Materials," "Cost for Labor," "Total Cost," and "Method of Payment." Omit any topics listed below that are not relevant for your report.

Description of product/service (with accompanying drawing or flowchart): (Use a separate sheet of paper if necessary.)

Task Breakdown and Time Schedule:

The schedule for _____
                      (construction/production/implementation)
for _____ is shown below.
     (product/service)

Table   : Schedule of _____

Task	Hours for completion

Total Time Required   _____

We can/will begin work on _____ on _____ .
                           (name of project)   (date)

Project completion date is _____ .
                           (date)

Personnel:

Cost of Materials:

Introductory Sentence: Table   shown below gives the costs of _____ .

Table   : Title

Item	Quantity	Description	Unit Cost	Total Cost

Total Cost of Materials   _____

Other Costs: (Subcontractors, Consultants)

Cost of Labor: (Either flat rate in paragraph form or in a table if large number
                  of individuals involved.)

Table   :Cost of Labor

Position	Hourly Rate	Total Hours	Total

Total Cost of Labor   _____

Total Cost:

The total cost for _____ is as follows:
                        product/service being proposed

Materials:
Other (as applicable):
Labor:
Grand Total:

Method of Payment:

ENDING SECTION

Choose an appropriate heading. If you cannot think of anything more descriptive, you may call the section "Conclusion."

Names of satisfied customers (if any):

Benefits of hiring your company:

Pleasure or convenience customer will receive from product or service:

Actions customer must take to get project started:

Planning Proposal
Plan Sheet
TRANSMITTAL MEMORANDUM

<u>MEMORANDUM</u>

TO:

FROM:

SUBJECT:

DATE:

BEGINNING

    Problem Addressed:

    Recommendations: (very briefly)

OVERVIEW OF INFORMATION FOUND IN THE PROPOSAL

ENDING: POLITE CLOSE
    Offer to provide further information:

TITLE PAGE

_____

Title of

_____

Proposal

Submitted to

_____

Name of Individual

_____

Title of Individual

_____

Company or Department

By

_____

Your Name

_____

Your Title (if applicable)

_____

Name of Company, Institution

_____

City, State

_____

Date

TABLE OF CONTENTS

First-, Second-, and Third-degree Headings   Page Number

_____

_____

_____

_____

_____

_____

LIST OF ILLUSTRATIONS

Number and Title of Tables and Figures   Page Number

_____

_____

_____

SUMMARY

Provide a brief overview of the proposal. Include information about the problem and the recommended solution.

_____

_____

_____

_____

_____

_____

_____

_____

_____

BEGINNING SECTION

Choose a heading that you think is appropriate. Sometimes the heading "Introduction" is used. This section may include subsections with headings "Description of the Problem," "Background," "Scope," and "Purpose." Omit any topics listed below that are not relevant for your report.

Description of Problem/Situation:

Background:

Scope:

    Time Involved:

    Number of People Involved:

    Locations:

    Equipment/Machinery:

    Process/Procedure:

Purpose of Proposal:

DISCUSSION SECTION

Choose headings appropriate for the required subsections. Some commonly used headings are "Existing Conditions," "Proposed Solution," "Personnel," "Facilities," "Equipment," and "Costs." Omit any topics listed below that are not relevant for your report.

Explanation of Problem:

Statistical Data: List the number and title of figures, diagrams, tables, and drawings and indicate whether they are to be included in the discussion section or as appendixes. (Use a separate sheet of paper if necessary.)

Proposed Solution:

Time Schedule:

Table   : Time Schedule

Task	Approximate Time

Total Time _____

Personnel Requirements/Qualifications:

Number of Persons Involved:

Qualifications of Personnel:

Organizational Chart or Flowchart:
(Use separate piece of paper)

Cost:

Facilities:

Description of Facilities:

Diagram of Floor Plan:
(Use separate piece of paper.)

Cost:
Equipment:

Description of Equipment:

Cost:

Table   : Requirements for Equipment

Type	Number Required	Location	Cost

Budget:

Total Cost for Personnel:

Total Cost for Facilities:

Total Cost for Equipment:

Grand Total:

Source of Money:

ENDING SECTION

Choose headings appropriate for the required subsections. Some commonly used headings are "Conclusions,' "Summary," "Advantages," "Disadvantages," and "Recommendations."

Summary:

Advantages:

Disadvantages:

Recommendations:

Introductory Statement:

1.

2.

3.

4.

11

BUSINESS CORRESPONDENCE

When you complete this chapter, you should know how to write routine letters to communicate with customers and other people outside of your company. You should learn about the following formats and types of letters:

"You" attitude
Parts of the business letter
  Letterhead or heading
  Dateline
  Inside address
  Salutation
  Body
  Complimentary close
  Signature block
  Optional parts of business letters
Formats for letters
  Block format
  Modified block format
  Full block format
  Simplified block format
Envelopes
Types of letters
  Inquiry
  Response to inquiry
  Complaint or claim
  Adjustment
  Order
  Resignation

Business correspondence includes letters that are sent to customers and to other groups outside the company. Letters can be written to get information about a new product or service, to soothe angry buyers, to complain about errors made by other companies, or to order equipment and supplies. Because letters go to receivers outside the company, they are usually more formal than memoranda, and they should follow established rules for appearance. This chapter will describe the required and optional parts of a business letter and the acceptable formats. It will also explain some common types of business letters, including letters of inquiry, complaint, adjustment, order, and resignation. The chapter begins with a brief discussion of the "you" attitude, particularly important in business correspondence that is sent to customers.

"YOU" ATTITUDE

Attitude is reflected in the tone used to address the reader of a business letter. The "you" attitude intends to convince the reader that his or her best interests are served by complying with the request or by following the suggestions. The focus of the letter is on "you," the reader, rather than on "we," the writer. The tone is positive rather than negative. Let's look at some examples.

Example 1:

"We" attitude
We would like to invite you to our grand opening sale.
"You" attitude
You are invited to our grand opening sale.

Example 2:

"We" attitude/negative statement
We are sorry that we cannot fill your order by December 30, 1986.
"You" attitude/positive statement
Your order will be filled by January 5 with special delivery to the construction site.

Example 3:

"We" attitude/negative statement
We will not be able to extend your credit any longer.
"You" attitude/positive statement
Your credit may be extended with only a 25 percent payment of your total bill.

In all three examples, the second version is the most likely to communicate effectively with the intended audience. Effective business correspondence never loses sight of its reader and always emphasizes what the company *can do* rather than what the company cannot do.

PARTS OF THE BUSINESS LETTER

Most business letters have seven parts: the letterhead or heading, the dateline, the inside address, the salutation, the body, the complimentary close, and the signature. Placement of these parts on the page depends on the format used. This section will briefly describe those seven parts. Their arrangement will be shown in the next section, which discusses four possible formats of the parts.

Letterhead or Heading

The letterhead or heading is your return address. Most businesses have letterhead stationery which has the name and address of the company printed at the top of the page. Often the company's telephone number and business slogan are included in the letterhead. Examples of letterhead stationery are found later in the chapter. When letterhead is not available, the return address is given in the heading. The heading includes the street address on the first line and the city, state, and zip code on the second line.

Dateline

The dateline is the month, day, and year in which the letter is written. It usually appears two or three spaces below the letterhead; but if the letter is short, more space can be left. If a personal heading rather than a company letterhead is used, the dateline is placed directly under the city, state, and zip code.

Inside Address

The inside address is the name and address of the person who will receive the letter. It is always flush with the left-hand margin. The first line of the inside address is the title and name of the person to whom the letter is written. If the person does not have a title, you may address him or her as "Mr." or "Ms." After the name of the receiver, the name and address of the company are given. The receiver's address should be written in the same way inside in the letter as it is outside on the envelope. Here are some examples. The first and second examples use "Mr." or "Ms." along with a title. The third omits the "Mr." and gives the title on the line below the name.

Mr. Freddie L. Smith, Superintendent
Cuyahoga Falls City Schools
2126 West Lee Avenue
Cuyahoga Falls, Ohio 44223

Ms. Linda Westford, President
Smithwick Furniture Company
P. O. Box 27985
Plainview, New York 11803

Woodrow L. Westmoreland
Chief Purchasing Officer
Eastland Corporation
2929 Williams Road
Haddonfield, New Jersey 08033

If you do not know the name of the person you are writing, you may use the title as the first line. Examples are "Chief of Police" and "Personnel Director." However, it is best to use a receiver's name if possible.

Salutation

The salutation is the greeting line of the letter. It is located two spaces below the last line of the inside address, is flush with the left margin, and begins with "Dear." A colon usually follows the name or title. However, if the letter is informal and you know the receiver well, a comma may be used.

Body

The body of the letter is the message that you want to send. You will learn how to write this most important part later in the chapter.

Complimentary Close

The complimentary close is the final phrase of the letter. It is located two spaces below the last sentence in the body of the letter, either flush with the left margin or slightly to the right of center. The complimentary close is always placed parallel with the dateline. Only the first letter of the first word in the complimentary close is capitalized, and a comma follows the phrase. Standard complimentary closings are "Yours truly," "Sincerely," and "Sincerely yours."

Signature Block

The signature block shows your name written as it should appear on any return correspondence. It includes your signature and a typed version of your name. The typed version of your name is located four spaces below the complimentary close. If you have a title, such as "Purchasing Agent," the title can be typed directly below and in line with the signature line. The title can also be placed on the same line as your typed signature, preceded by a comma. Your signature is written in ink between the complimentary close and the typed version of your name.

Optional Parts of Business Letters

Besides these seven basic parts, optional parts may be included. These are the reference line or block; attention line; subject line; notations for stenographic references, enclosures, and copies; and notations for additional pages.

Reference Line or Block.   Reference lines and blocks are used to list references important to the letter. They may include information about previous phone calls, invoices, files, letters, or documents. Reference blocks may begin with "RE" and run for several lines, if necessary. They appear most frequently under the dateline, but they can also be placed under the inside address.

Attention Line.   Attention lines are used to offer routing information not given in the inside address. They name the individual or department most likely to respond to the letter. Attention lines are begun with the word "Attention" and placed two spaces below the inside address.

Subject Line.   The subject line tells the receiver what the letter is about. The subject line on a letter serves the same function as the subject line on a memorandum. It appears two spaces below the salutation and two spaces above the body of the letter.

Notation for Stenographic References.   A stenographic reference is the initials of the individual who took the dictation and typed the letter. The stenographic reference is located flush with the left margin, generally two spaces lower than the signature line. The writer's initials are capitalized, and the stenographer's initials are typed in lower case.

Notation for Enclosures and Attachments.   Enclosures and attachments are materials which are sent with the letter. As their names imply, attachments are stapled to the letter, while enclosures are "enclosed" in the same envelope. Enclosed or attached items might be brochures, resumes, price lists, or anything else referred to in the letter. The notation lets the receiver know what to expect to find in the envelope. The word "Enclosures" or "Attachments" may be followed by a colon and a number indicating how many items are enclosed. Sometimes the items are listed. The enclosure or attachment notation is flush with the left margin immediately below the stenographic reference if there is one.

Notation for Copies.   Carbon copies or photocopies are duplicates of the letter that are sent to other people. The abbreviation "cc" or "xc" or the word "copy" is followed by the names of any individuals receiving copies. It is located flush with the left margin immediately below any stenographic and enclosure and attachment notations. The abbreviation "bc" on the copies of the letter means that blind copies were sent. In that case, the individual receiving the original letter does not know to whom the other copies have been sent.

Notation for Additional Pages.   When the letter extends to a second page, a notation for additional pages is used. It includes the name of the receiver, the page number, and the date the letter was written on the top line of the page. Either of the two methods shown on the next page is acceptable. In example 1, the name, date, and page are flush with left margin.

Example 1:

Ms. Janie Freeman
June 28, 1986
Page 2

In example 2, the name is flush with the left margin, the page number is centered, and the date is placed as far to the right as possible.

Example 2:

Ms. Janie Freeman   2   June 28, 1986

FORMATS FOR LETTERS

The parts just explained are placed on the page according to the letter format you choose. Four acceptable formats are block, modified block, full block, and simplified block. This section provides examples and descriptions of each.

Block Format

In block format, the inside address, salutation, and the first line of each paragraph are all flush with the left margin. The heading (if letterhead is not used), dateline, complimentary close, and signature are parallel to each other and placed slightly right of the center. Figure 11-1 on page 234 shows a letter in block format.

Modified Block Format

The modified block format is exactly like the block format except that the first line of every paragraph is indented five spaces. Figure 11-2 on page 235 shows a letter in modified block format.

Full Block Format

In full block format, every part of the letter except the letterhead is flush with the left margin. This format is popular because of the ease and speed in typing. Figure 11-3 on page 236 shows an example of a letter in full block format.

Simplified Block Format

The simplified block format omits the salutation and complimentary close. This format can be used when you are writing to a company and do not know who will answer the letter. Like the full block format, simplified block format arranges all its parts flush with the left margin and does not indent for paragraphs. Four lines are skipped between the inside address and the beginning of the body of the letter. Six lines are skipped between the end of the letter and

Graymont Publishing Company

Graymont
Publishing

August 23, 1988

Ms. June A. Nolan
Editor-in-Chief
Harper's Publishing Company
1553 Monticello Road
Montgomery, AL 36108

Dear Ms. Nolan:

This letter is written in block format. The dateline, complimentary
close, and signature block are lined up with each other, slightly right
of the center of the page. Everything else is flush with the left
margin.

Even though the placement of parts varies, the spacing is similar in
all four formats. Within each part and within paragraphs, letters are
single-spaced. Between the inside address and the salutation, the
salutation and the body, and the body and the complimentary close and
between paragraphs, letters are double-spaced. Between the dateline
and the inside address, from two to six spaces can be left. Between
the complimentary close and the typed name, four spaces allow room for
the writer's signature.

Besides the spacing within and between parts, formats for letters share
the same margins. Usually 1 to 1 1/2 inch makes up the left margin. At
least 1 inch makes up the right and bottom margins.

Although block format may be used for letters with personal headings.
this letter is typed on letterhead stationery. The receiver is Ms.
June A. Nolan, Editor-in-Chief for Harper's Publishing Company. The
postal service abbreviation, AL, is used for Alabama.

                              Sincerely,

                              Oscar Lowe

                              Oscar W. Lowe
                              Editor, College Division

1227 Lanham Road East · Orlando, Florida 32809

Figure 11-1: Block Format

```
                                    200 Main Street
                                    Storrs, Connecticut    06268
                                    September 14, 1988



       John Aiken, President
       Eastern Electric Supply Company
       300 Fayetteville Road
       New Haven, Connecticut    06515

       Dear Mr. Aiken:

            This letter is typed in modified block format.  As you can see, it
       is arranged like the last example except that the paragraphs are
       indented five spaces.

            Instead of a letterhead, this example shows a personal heading.  A
       personal heading is used when you are writing for your own business
       rather than your company's business.  You will use a personal heading
       in your letter of application.  You will also use an enclosure notation
       like the one shown below.

                                    Sincerely,

                                    Alan Smith

                                    Alan Smith


       Enclosure:  Résumé
```

Figure 11-2: Modified Block Format

COMMERCIAL   RESIDENTIAL   INDUSTRIAL
DEVELOPMENT   BROKERAGE   APPRAISAL   LEASING   MANAGEMENT

1900 Cameron Street
PO Box 10007
Raleigh, NC 27605
919/821-1350

J W York, CRE, SIR
Chairman, Board of Directors

G. Smedes York, CPM, CSM
President

Hal V Worth, III CPM, CSM
Vice-President

January 25, 1986

In response to: phone conversation, January 20, 1986

John Simpson, Owner
Simpson Electrical Company
1012 Northbook Parkway
Richmond, Virginia 23220

Dear Mr. Simpson:

                Full Block Letter with a Subject Line.

This letter is typed in full block format. This format uses no
indentions for paragraphs, and all the parts are flush with the left
margin.

This example shows the placement of several optional parts. It has a
reference line mentioning a phone call that has some relevance for the
receiver of the letter. It also has a subject line stating what the
letter is about. At the bottom of the letter a stenographic reference
is given, and the word "copies" indicates that copies of this letter
have been sent to the people listed.

Sincerely yours,

Alexander L. Giovanni
Owner

ALG:sm

copies: Alan Ripley
          Maude Gangla

Figure 11-3: Full Block Format

May 15, 1988

RE: Order Number 588642

Rico Supply Company
1456 Wharf Street
San Francisco, CA 94123

Attention: Order Department

This letter is typed in simplified block format. As you can see, the
salutation and complimentary close are omitted. The parts are flush
with the left margin and paragraphs are not indented. Simplified block
format is particularly useful for order letters sent to large, faraway
companies where you do not know who will fill the order.

This letter shows the placement of the reference line, which is
identified in this example with "RE." It also shows the placement of
the attention line, which routes the letter to the proper department.

James Abbott

James Abbott
Head of Purchasing

Capital City Building
The Heart of Downtown Plaza ——————————— 2917 French St.
Iowa City, Iowa 52242

Figure 11-4: Simplified Block Format

the signature line. The simplified block format allows you to avoid salutations such as "Gentlemen," "Dear Sir," or "Dear Madam."

ENVELOPE

The envelope for business letters conforms to the size of the stationery used. Most business envelopes are 8½ by 5 inches. Addresses for both the sender and the receiver are given. Figure 11-5 shows an envelope. The return address for the sender is placed in the upper left corner and the address of the receiver centered. To fit the letter neatly in the envelope, fold it twice. Begin by folding the bottom third up and toward the center, and then fold the top third down and over the bottom third. The receiver should be able to unfold the letter and start reading at the top.

TYPES OF LETTERS

As we mentioned earlier, letters are written for many reasons. Some are sent to sell or to handle transactions with customers, and others are sent to buy products or to get information from other businesses. Depending on their purpose, a number of different types of letters can be identified. This section discusses the contents and organization of six: inquiry, response to inquiry, claim or complaint, adjustment, order or purchase, and resignation. If your job requires you to write other less routine letters, you should consult a business writing textbook for further information.

Before beginning the discussion of the six most typical types of business letters, let's consider some general advice about organization. According to many business writing textbooks, most letters are organized in either a direct

```
Isabelle French
3809 Hampton Court        (Sender's Address)
Cary, North Carolina 27511




                              Mr. Roger L. Wilson
                              Personnel Director
            (Receiver's Address)  Southern Electrical Company
                              1001 Glenwood Avenue
                              Raleigh, North Carolina  27603


```

Figure 11-5: The Business Envelope

plan or an indirect plan. The choice depends on the message being sent. When the receiver will be pleased by the message or when the best interests of the receiver's company require a positive reply, a direct letter plan is used. In this plan, the purpose is stated in the introduction of the letter. An explanation, which provides the necessary details, follows. When the receiver will not be pleased by the contents of the letter or when the receiver is not obligated to reply, an indirect plan is used. In this plan, an explanation is given before the purpose is stated. As their names imply, the two plans have opposite arrangements, as may be seen in the short outlines below.

DIRECT PLAN	INDIRECT PLAN
(Receiver pleased by the message or obligated to reply.)	(Receiver not pleased by the message or not obligated to reply.)
I. Purpose, a clear statement of the main idea.	I. A statement indicating an attempt to comply with or please the receiver.
II. Explanation, details, or questions promised in statement of main idea.	II. Explanation, details leading to refusal or details leading to request. Purpose becomes clear to receiver after the explanation.
III. Polite close.	III. Polite close.

Understanding the direct plan and the indirect plan will help you organize typical letters. However, in the same way that customers differ greatly from each other, the situations that require letters also cover a wide range. In writing letters, your best guide is common sense based on an awareness of the needs and expectations of your intended audience.

Inquiry

The letter of inquiry is written to obtain information. It might be written to a company to find out more about a new product that has just come on the market or to request information about an individual you are planning to hire. Although the circumstances that lead to letters of inquiry are varied, usually a direct plan is best. Figure 11-6 on page 240 shows a letter of inquiry written to get information about a new product that a maintenance supervisor has seen advertised in a brochure. Notice the direct statement of inquiry in the first paragraph and the list of specific questions that follows. The supervisor ends his letter by explaining that he needs the information as soon as possible.

Here are some guidelines for writing letters of inquiry.

○ Begin with a direct statement introducing your inquiry. Follow with a detailed explanation of the inquiry. Include information about how you intend to use the reply. If you want information on a new lathe, tell the reader what you will

Coastal Carolina Electrical Cooperative

227 Front Street   Beaufort, North Carolina 27883

September 3, 1988

Edison Valves
P. O. Box 297, Great Lakes Avenue
Cleveland, Ohio 47967

Attention: Sales Department

As a supervisor in the Maintenance Section at Coastal Carolina
Electric Cooperative, I would like to know more about the valve kit
advertised in your latest brochure. We are considering the
purchase of 12 kits as part of our yearly maintenance program.

Before I make any decisions concerning the valve kits, I need to
know the following information:

1. What is the length of the guarantee, and what parts does the
    guarantee encompass?

2. What is the approximate length of delivery time after the
    valve order has been placed?

3. Which of the brand-name pumps is the valve kit compatible
    with?

4. What would be the cost for an order of 12 kits?

We plan to begin replacement of our valves in January; therefore, I
would appreciate your sending answers to the questions as soon as
possible.

Elliott C. Freberg

Figure 11-6: Inquiry

do with the lathe. If you want information about an applicant for a job, tell the reader what position you are trying to fill. Once they know how the requested information may be used, readers can tailor their replies to your needs.

- If your inquiry requires responses to specific questions, list those questions in the letter. Number each question and double-space between the questions.

- Make the questions as specific as possible. General questions such as "Can you tell me something about your new product?" usually receive general answers that often are not useful to the company. Specific questions such as "What are the capabilities of your new SW435 Lathe?" and "Can it be used to cut patterns on all metals?" will help you get useful information.

- After the list of questions, ask for any further information the reader thinks may be important.

Response to Inquiry

The letter of response to inquiry provides information the writer has requested. Figure 11-7 on page 242 shows the response to the supervisor's inquiry about the valve kits. Again notice the direct plan. After a short sales pitch, the writer answers the questions in the order they appear in the inquiry and ends on a polite offer for more assistance.

Here are some guidelines for responding to letters of inquiry.

- Begin with a direct statement introducing your response. Follow with whatever explanation the reader requested.

- If you are responding to a series of questions, list your answers in the same order as the questions. Give each an appropriate number. Repeat enough of the question in your answers so that the reader will not have to refer to the original inquiry.

- If possible, include a sales pitch for your company. Mention a new product, or enclose a catalog or brochure.

Complaint or Claim

A letter of complaint or claim is written to explain your dissatisfaction with a product or service. Most often, the purpose of this type of letter is to get an adjustment, a refund, or a replacement for defective merchandise or poor workmanship. In writing a letter of complaint or claim, you should keep in mind that good customer relations require companies to make reasonable adjustments. Therefore, you can assume that if your complaint is legitimate and if it is clearly stated, your request will be granted. Figure 11-8 on page 243 shows a letter of complaint. The writer is dissatisfied with a defective pump he has received. He states his complaint directly and explains carefully what appears wrong. He also clearly describes the adjustment he wants.

Here are some guidelines for writing letters of complaint or claim.

- Begin by introducing the complaint or claim. Follow with the details. If possible, briefly explain what is wrong.

Edison Valves

P.O. Box 297 Great Lakes Avenue
Cleveland, Ohio 47967

September 10, 1988

Elliott C. Freberg
Maintenance Supervisor
Coastal Carolina Electric Cooperative
227 Front Street
Beaufort, NC 27833

Dear Mr. Freberg:

We received your letter of September 3, 1988 requesting information about our new valve kits. We are very excited about the response we have had to the redesigned valve kits and think they will work well for your company.

I am answering your questions in the order you asked them.

1. The valve kit is guaranteed to last a minimum of five years if the manufacturer's instructions for installation and maintenance are followed.

2. The approximate delivery date of the valve kit will be four weeks after we receive the order.

3. The valve kit is compatible with the Millstone, Raynor, and Milton multi-stage pumps and the Fremont and Raynor single stage pumps.

4. The cost for one kit is $29.50. An order of 10 kits or more would receive a 10 percent discount so the total cost for 12 kits is $318.60 plus tax and shipping charges.

I am also enclosing a brochure that gives you more information on industry response to our valve. If you have any further questions, call me. I will be glad to have an Edison Valve Company representative give you a demonstration.

Yours truly,

Edmund C. Wilburn

Edmund C. Wilburn
Sales Manager

Figure 11-7:   Response to Inquiry

1383 Evans Drive
Newton, MA 02165
January 12, 1988

George Garcia, Director
Catalog Sales
Automotive Parts, Incorporated
Chicago, IL 60637

Dear Mr. Garcia:

I am returning an Edison Fuel pump, Catalog No. 27619 which I received in the mail today and which I wish to exchange for a Willis fuel pump, Catalog No. 27618.

On January 6, I placed a telephone order with Jane Simpson in your catalog sales department for the Willis pump. When I received the Edison, I was most disappointed because this was the second time in three months that I received an incorrect order.

Since I will need the Willis pump to fix my car prior to returning to school next week, I am requesting that you ship it on one of the overnight express lines no later than Thursday, January 16. If you do not have one in stock, please let me know before January 16 so that I can order elsewhere.

                              Yours truly,

                              Ben Saunders

                              Ben Saunders

Figure 11-8: Claim/Complaint

- State the adjustment you expect directly and clearly. Typical adjustments are refunds, credits to accounts, replacements, or repairs.
- Avoid sounding angry and unreasonable. Assume that the reader will grant the adjustment if the request is stated clearly.

Adjustment

A letter of adjustment is written in response to a claim or complaint. Depending on whether or not you agree to the adjustment, two types of response are possible. A positive response acknowledges that your company is at fault and grants the customer's request. A negative response states that the company is not at fault and does not grant the customer's request. Since these two letters are very different, each one will be looked at separately.

A positive response acknowledges that you will grant the claim or complaint. Because the reader will be pleased by the content, a positive response uses a direct plan. Figure 11-9 shows a positive response to a request for adjustment. The writer immediately states the purpose of the letter—to grant the adjustment. Then he explains briefly what caused the problem. Having granted the adjustment, the writer now uses this opportunity for a sales pitch and encloses a product brochure describing his company's newest tools. Throughout the letter the attitude is pleasant. The writer is neither grudging nor overly apologetic.

Here are some guidelines for positive reponses to letters of adjustment.

- Begin by stating directly that you will grant the request for adjustment. Follow with the details about the adjustment.
- Include a sales pitch, if possible.
- Do not apologize repeatedly, and do not threaten to withhold future adjustments. Be gracious and confident. Also do not promise that such a mistake will never happen again.

A negative response refuses to grant the adjustment. Often the customer is at fault and has made an inappropriate claim. Inappropriate requests for adjustment usually result from misunderstandings. The customer has not properly assembled your product, has misused it in some way, or has not carefully read the warranty. Even though the customer may be wrong, you must try to make the refusal as easy to accept as possible. Techniques of softening a negative response include explaining the reasons for the problem, standing behind a company policy, and offering alternative solutions to the problem. Figure 11-10 on page 246 shows a negative response to an adjustment. The owner of a cleaning service explains her refusal to adjust the bill of a dissatisfied customer. She begins by indicating her concern for customer satisfaction. She then explains why the mildew stains were not completely removed and why the sheets were not changed. She refers to both company policy and a previous conversation with the customer. The refusal of adjustment is not stated until after the explanation. Even though the owner will not refund the customer's

WELLINGHAM TOOL CORPORATION
P.O. Box 2796, Route 3
Bridgeton, New Jersey 08302

August 3, 1984

Mr. Joe Shipp, Foreman
Kennebase Tool and Die Company
216 Point Henry Road
Columbus, Indiana 47201

Dear Mr. Shipp:

We are sending you a brand new Wellingham Socket Wrench, No. 24474 at
no charge as a replacement for the fractured wrench you returned to us
July 26, by overnight parcel service. You should receive your new
Wellingham by Friday of this week.

No matter how careful we are in the manufacture of our tools,
occasionally one that is not up to our high standards will slip by us.
Unfortunately, you happened to receive that one. Our guarantee still
holds. If you have any further problems, please do not hesitate to let
us know.

I am enclosing a brochure of our new series of tools that may be of
some interest to you. Joe Whitson, our Columbus area sales representative, will be delighted to come by and show you the tools at your
request.

Sincerely yours,

Marvin C. Hooks

Marvin C. Hooks
Sales Manager

MCH/jr

Enclosure

Figure 11-9: Adjustment, Positive Response

FEATHER DUSTERS, INCORPORATED
P.O. Box 216
3906 Downtown Boulevard
Raleigh, North Carolina 27605

July 5, 1987

Mrs. Michael Jones
3313 Aligary Court
Cary, NC 27511

Dear Mrs. Jones:

I am happy to respond to your letter of July 3, calling to my attention your problems with the Feather Dusters crew sent to clean your house on July 2. I am sorry that you are dissatisfied with Feather Dusters' first visit to your house.

At the end of every work day, the cleaning crew leaders report to me concerning the status of each house that we are contracted to clean. On July 2, I talked with Sally Johnson, who was in charge of the crew cleaning your house. She indicated that she had run into the same problems you mentioned in your letter. The grouting in the master bathroom had mildew stains that she was unable to remove on a first cleaning, and she was unable to find the sheets which were to be used in the smaller bedroom.

As we discussed on my initial visit to your home, it will probably take several cleanings for us to remove the mildew from the bathroom tiles without using heavy industrial cleaners. Also, as explained in our contract, we change the sheets when fresh sheets are in plain view in the room so that we will not disturb your closets. Sally said she had left a note explaining these two problems to you.

Even though we do not refund payments for work we have completed contractually, I will be happy to send a crew out to remove the mildew and change the sheets on the bed for a small fee. However, I think you will be most pleasantly surprised after our second visit scheduled for next Tuesday. When you return home from work, I believe you will find most of the mildew gone and all the sheets changed. I will inspect your house personally. At that time, if you are not completely satisfied with our work, please call me, and we will see what arrangements can be made.

Yours truly,

Jean Holmes

Jean Holmes
President

JH/ps

cc: Sally Johnson

Figure 11-10: Adjustment, Negative Response

payment, she offers an alternative and promises that the second visit of Feather Dusters will be completely satisfactory.

Here are some guidelines for writing negative responses to adjustments.

- Begin with a positive statement, something that indicates your concern for customer satisfaction. Explain the reasons before you refuse the adjustment.
- When possible, include a company policy, a statement from the warranty, or some clear indication that your company was not at fault.
- When possible, offer an alternative solution. For example, offer to repair broken equipment at cost or offer a discount or a replacement item.
- Use a reasonable tone. Do not apologize, and do not lecture.
- Although your refusal does not have to be stated outright, make certain that it is clear. Otherwise you can expect a second letter from the dissatisfied customer.
- If necessary, abandon the indirect plan and use a direct plan. Do not make the reader think that you are talking down or avoiding the refusal.

Order

An order letter is written to purchase goods or services. This letter is straightforward and impersonal, since the order is usually filled by someone you do not know. Often, instead of a letter, a company will send a printed purchase order form. (See Chapter 9 for an example.) Figure 11-11 on page 248 shows an order letter for books. The writer begins with a direct statement announcing the order and explaining how payment will be made. Then she includes an informal table listing the items, the number she wants, the price for each item, and the total. Finally, the writer gives a date for receiving the items and a method for delivery. Notice that this letter is in simplified block form. It has no salutation or complimentary close.

Here are some guidelines for order or purchase letters.

- State your intention to place an order directly at the beginning of the letter. Follow with a detailed explanation of exactly what you want.
- If you are ordering several items, list these items in a table.
- Include information about the quantity, size, color, style, catalog number, and price, as needed.
- Include information about the method of payment and delivery, if necessary.

Resignation

The letter of resignation is written to inform management that you plan to leave your job. If possible, the letter should be written at least two weeks and preferably 30 days before you plan to leave. In some cases, you may be employed under a contract that requires prior notice of resignation up to 60 days. The letter of resignation should retain the good will of your employer. This

SMITHVILLE TECHNICAL COLLEGE
909 Runnymede Road
Smithville, North Carolina 26639

June 8, 1985

Learning Corporation
2923 Avenue of the Americas
New York, New York 10017

I would like to order several items shown in your Spring Catalog. I would like the materials shipped to me at the address shown above and the invoice forwarded to William Hardman, Purchasing Agent, at the same address.

ITEM	DESCRIPTION	QUANTITY	UNIT PRICE	TOTAL
1	Instructor's Manual, English as a Second Language #2929870, Level I	2	$3.98	$ 7.96
2	Pretests, English as a Second Language, #2929872, Level I	25	.10	2.50
3	Testbooks, English as a Second Language, #2929872, Level I	25	4.25	106.25
4	Posttests, English as a Second Language, #2929871, Level I	25	.10	2.50
				$119.21

Upon receipt of the invoice, Mr. Hardman will send payment in full.

I am most anxious to receive these materials since classes will begin on September 23, 1985. In order to expedite shipment, I am requesting that the materials be sent by United Parcel Service no later than July 1, 1985.

Fran T. Finch

Fran T. Finch, Instructor
General Education Services

Figure 11-11: Order

letter is not the appropriate place to express all the anger you might feel about a company or the people you worked with. Figure 11-12 on page 250 shows a letter of resignation from Gateway Lighting Center. The writer begins this short letter with a compliment to his employer and then explains his reasons for leaving. He states his intention to resign at the end of the second paragraph and asks to use the employer as a reference in the last paragraph.

Here are some guidelines for letters of resignation.

○ When possible, begin with a compliment for your employer. Explain the reasons for the resignation before you make a direct statement of purpose.

○ Be certain to include the date for your last day of work or when the resignation is effective.

○ If you want to use this employer as a reference for future jobs, ask for that reference now.

○ Do not comment about your dissatisfaction with the job or the organization. Such complaints are useless when you are planning to leave.

SUMMARY

Business correspondence includes the letters that are sent to customers and other groups outside the company. More formal than memoranda, letters should follow established rules for appearance. Most have seven parts: letterhead or heading, dateline, inside address, salutation, body, complimentary close, and signature block. Depending on the arrangement of these parts, four formats are acceptable: block, modified block, full block, and simplified block. Six common types of letters are inquiry, response to inquiry, claim or complaint, adjustment, order or purchase, and resignation. According to the expected reaction from the receiver, two general organizational plans are commonly used. When the receiver will be pleased by the contents or is obligated to reply, a direct plan is used. The purpose or main idea is stated at the beginning of the letter and is followed by an explanation. When the receiver will not be pleased by the contents or is not obligated to reply, an indirect plan is used. The explanation is given before the main idea.

3410 Wilkes Drive
Annapolis, MD 21404
August 1, 1988

Mr. Robert Lawson, Personnel Director
Gateway Lighting Center
2600 George Washington Parkway
Annapolis, MD 21405

Dear Mr. Lawson:

I have enjoyed working for Gateway Lighting Center for the past two years. The knowledge and experience I have gained regarding the lighting fixture business should prove to be extremely valuable to me as I pursue my future plans.

As you know, my prior business experience involved customer service work with a wholesale electrical equipment distributor. This is the line of work I enjoy and which appears to have the greatest future career opportunity for me. In this regard, I plan to enroll in the Electrical Installation and Maintenance course at Annapolis Technical College this fall. Therefore, I wish to resign my present position at Gateway Lighting Center effective August 15, 1988.

Thank you for your past consideration and guidance. I would be very pleased to be able to give your name for a future reference.

Sincerely yours,

William R. George

William R. George

Figure 11-12: Letter of Resignation

ASSIGNMENTS

Application 1:
Identifying the Parts of the Business Letter

Name the required and optional parts of the business letter shown in Figure 11-13 on page 252 according to the order of appearance on the letter.

Application 2:
Using Correct Form and Style

Correct the errors in the parts of the letter shown below.

1. Mr. Fred Williams,
    Director of Training
    2126 East Jones Road
    Durham NC 27706

    Dear Fred,

2. Yours truly

    Wilma Woodall,
    President

    WW/LT
    CC

3. Beta Corporation
    1347 Bellwood Avenue
    Raleigh, NC 27606

    Gentlemen:

    Attention: Mr. John Suiter

4. Bill Johnson
    2106 Coley Forest Place
    Chief Engineer
    Engineering Services Inc.
    Seattle, WA 98103

    Dear Bill,

5. Mr. Howard Blanton
    Director of Personnel
    Georgia Peach Growers Association
    Box 276, Route 10
    McDuffie, Georgia

    Gentlemen:

6. Sincerely,

    Raymond T. Snow

    Enclosures

    RTS/agt

7. Northeast Mutual Savings
    P.O. Box 17371
    Montpelier, Vt 05602

    RE: Savings Account Number 27446144

    Dear Mr. Tilliver;

1. *Willingham Travel Corporation*

7739 Long Leaf Pine Road Sanford, North Carolina 27330

2.   January 12, 1988

3.   RE: Phone call about
     Winter Specials Brochure

4. Ms. Elizabeth French
    3304 Hampton Court
    Sanford, NC 27330

5. Dear Ms. French:

    Thank you for your telephone call reminding us to send the
copy of the brochure concerning our Winter Specials to the
Caribbean.

    In addition to the trip featured in the brochure, we have two
weekenders scheduled in February. We will fly you to Bimini on
Friday evening and return late Sunday evening. This is an inexpensive package that just might fit the short "Summertime in
Winter" that you are looking for.

    Susan Edwards will be delighted to answer any questions you
might have about our Caribbean Winter Specials or the February
Weekenders. We look forward to hearing from you.

6.   Yours truly,

7.   Anna G. Grey
     President

8. AGG/ict

9. Enclosures: 2

Figure 11-13: Identification of Parts of Letter

8. Most truly yours,

Edward Stillman, Purchasing Agent

ES:abl

cc: Fred Smith
    Lonnie Rawlings

Enclosures

9. McDonald's Five and Dime
   2726 Front Street
   Lancaster OH 43130

Dear Mr. McDonald:

10. Mr. Rich Naylor,
    Training Center Director
    Molner Corporation
    2763 Fort Virginia Road
    Arlington Vir.

Dear Training Director:

WRITING LETTERS

General Directions

In each of the assignments shown below, Application 1 requires you to revise a poorly written letter. The letterhead, the dateline, and the inside address have been omitted. When you are filling in the plan sheets, you will have to add this information.

Inquiry

Application 1:
Revising a Letter of Inquiry

Revise the letter of inquiry shown below. Use the plan sheet in this chapter and the Guidelines for Revision in Chapter 3. Consider format, content, organization, and usage.

Attention: Sales Director

Dear Sales Director:

My company has won the bid to renovate the Raleigh Cameron Place apartments and convert them to condominiums. Since we prefer to purchase the majority of our appliances and supplies from local suppliers, I need answers to the following questions. What brand names of stackable washers and driers do you carry? What brand-name dishwashers do you carry? What brand-name trash compactors do you carry? Do you carry Formica for kitchen countertops? If so, in how many styles? Do you carry wood-veneer kitchen cabinets?

We will be ordering 40 of each of the above mentioned items in April.

John Greenberg

Application 2:
Writing a Letter of Inquiry

Write a letter of inquiry asking questions about a new product in your field. To learn about the new products in your field, read the advertisements in trade journals, such as *Popular Mechanics* or *Journal of Nursing*. Choose a product that will require you to write a list of questions rather than simply ask for a brochure. Jot down information about the products and the name and address of the manufacturer. Fill in the plan sheet for the letter of inquiry, and use it to write your first draft.

Response to Inquiry

Application 1:
Revising a Letter of Response to Inquiry

Revise the letter responding to the inquiry shown below. Use the plan sheet in this chapter and the Guidelines for Revision in Chapter 3. Consider format, content, organization, and usage.

Dear Ms. Adams:

Thank you for your letter inquiring about Finch's stereo components. Unfortunately no music or department stores in your area sell our equipment. You will have to go to Philadelphia, where three area stores carry Finch's: Garland's Department Store, THE STEREO SHOP, and Music Man's. The cost of the equipment varies according to the quality of the equipment, but you can get a tuner, turntable, and speakers for as little as $350 or for as much as $3,000. Yes, we can ship to you from here if you would like to place your order by mail. It would take approximately two weeks for you to receive the equipment after we receive your order. Thank you.

Bill Geise
Sales Representative

Application 2:
Writing a Letter of Response to Inquiry

Read the letter to the Dean of Students of Akron Area Technical School shown in Figure 11-14 on page 255 and prepare a response to that letter of inquiry. Before you begin a draft, fill in the plan sheet for the response to inquiry.

3210 Weldon Way
Defiance, Ohio 43512
March 4, 1986

Akron Area Technical School
Route 10, Box 200
Akron, Ohio 44319

Attention: Dean of Students

After graduating from high school this spring, I am interested in
attending Akron Area Technical School. Therefore, I would appreciate
your answering the following questions for me.

1. Do you have a one- and two-year program in electronics?

2. What is the average enrollment at the school?

3. Do you have a baseball team, and do you offer baseball
    scholarships?

4. Do you have any on-campus residence halls?

5. What is the cost of tuition for each quarter for an
    in-state student?

6. What is the approximate cost of textbooks per quarter?

I would appreciate your answering these questions as soon as possible.
In addition, please send a college catalog if one is available. I look
forward to hearing from you.

Tony G. Brown

Tony G. Brown

Figure 11-14: Assignment for Response to Inquiry

Claim/Complaint

Application 1:
Revising the Letter of Claim/Complaint

Revise the letter of complaint shown below. Use the plan sheet from this chapter and the Guidelines for Revision in Chapter 3. Consider format, content, organization, and usage.

Attention: Order No. 6159

On March 17, 1985, I purchased from your company one valve-grinding machine, Model No. 680-A. The catalog listed all attachments that came with this machine. I received none of these attachments. Will you please send all attachments which are included with the purchase of this machine.

This machine is used every day in my shop, where I remanufacture cylinder heads. These heads cannot be fixed without this machine. I am enclosing a copy of the list of attachments from the catalog.

Being the largest manufacturer of valve-grinding machines, I hope you see the necessity of the attachments and correct this matter as soon as possible. I will cancel my order if I do not have the attachments three days from the date of this letter, and I will return the valve-grinding machine.

Sincerely yours,

David Wheeler

Application 2:
Writing a Letter of Claim or Complaint

Write a letter of claim or complaint about something that recently caused you a problem. The letter can refer to problems at school or work, such as the registration process, class schedules, or a change in shift or job assignment. Before you begin your draft, fill in the appropriate plan sheet.

Adjustment: Positive Response

Application 1:
Revising a Letter of Adjustment: Positive Response

Revise the positive letter of adjustment shown below. Use the plan sheet from this chapter and the Guidelines for Revision from Chapter 3. Consider format, content, organization and usage.

Dear Freddie:

Well, it looks like you caught us in the wrong this time. We really don't make a whole lot of errors when we do car repairs. In fact, we are almost always right.

Like I said, it looks like we did replace your fuel pump with the wrong size. That's a real shame. All you need to do is bring your car in next week and leave it a couple of days and we'll get everything up to snuff just like I said we would in our phone conversation. You really didn't need to send a letter to our district manager about our little error.

Well, see you next week.

Sincerely,

Dave

Application 2:
Writing a Letter of Adjustment: Positive Response

Write a positive response to the letter of complaint shown in Figure 11-15 on page 258. Before you begin your draft, fill in the plan sheet for a positive response to a letter of complaint or claim.

Adjustment: Negative Response

Application 1:
Revising a Letter of Adjustment: Negative Response

Revise the letter denying the request for adjustment shown below. Use the plan sheet from this chapter and the Guidelines for Revision from Chapter 3. Consider format, content, organization, and usage.

Dear Ms. Davis:

I was sorry to hear of the problems you had on June 23 after Mr. Jonson installed your new telephone. However, the telephone was not installed by a Raleigh Telephone Corporation employee. Mr. Ward Jonson is a contractor and works for himself installing telephones.

Such a situation is highly unusual, but it is part of the chance we take by letting contractors install our telephones. I am sorry, but it is against company policy to guarantee any work done by other installers besides our own. The proper steps you should take would be to call Mr. Jonson and confront him with this problem, since he is responsible. He is liable for this bill. We guarantee the telephone, after installation, for one year against factory defects.

I regret the trouble this situation has caused you and I wish I could be of more help. I hope you enjoy your new phone.

Sincerely yours,

Donald Baker

BURKWELL ELECTRIC
P.O. Box 377767
New Hill, North Carolina 27527

February 17, 1986

RE: Purchase Order 27747-G

Southwest Lighting, Inc.
311 South Street
Raleigh, NC 27603

Several weeks ago, on February 4, I placed an order for 12 cases of
Lithonia Flourescent Light Fixtures, Catalog Number 2373 to be
delivered to our warehouse no later than February 10. It is now
February 17, and I have not received the lights. I need them delivered
within two days, or I will have to place the order elsewhere.

As you know, we were awarded the bids for the lighting in Apple Valley
Shopping Mall. We are under contract to have all the lights installed
by February 22. The painters and finishers are now idle waiting for us
to begin installation so that they can meet their deadlines.

If we fail to meet our deadline, we will be subjected to a $100 per day
penalty. Since the delay is not our fault, we will have no choice but
to pass half of that penalty on to you.

I have confidence that you will be able to solve this problem for us.
Please call me at 475-3103 to let me know the status of the order.

Joseph D. Burkwell
Joseph D. Burkwell

JDL/vc

cc: Elmer Smith, Construction Superintendent

Figure 11-15:   Assignment for Letter of Adjustment, Positive Response

Application 2:
Writing a Letter of Adjustment: Negative Response

Write a negative response to the letter of claim/complaint shown on Figure 11-16 on page 260. Before you begin a draft, fill in the plan sheet for a negative response to a letter of complaint or claim.

Order or Purchase

Application 1:
Revising a Letter of Order or Purchase

Revise the order letter shown below. Use the plan sheet from this chapter and the Guidelines for Revision from Chapter 3. Consider format, content, organization, and usage.

> I will be opening a business office in the Town Plaza Shopping Center in Auburn, Alabama in July of this year. After reviewing your catalog, I would like to order the following furniture to be shipped on July 1, 1986 to Suite 127 in the shopping center. I need 3 desks, catalog number 2745, at $475.00 each; 2 secretarial chairs, catalog number 3343, at $122.50 each; 1 executive chair, catalog number 3444, at $250.00; 3 beige metal 3-drawer file cabinets, catalog number 1011, at $129.60 each; 1 sofa, catalog number 5447-A, at $275.00 and 1 side table, catalog number 5449, at $75.00.
>
> Please bill me at the address noted above.
>
> > Yours truly,
> >
> > Ella Swenson

Application 2:
Writing a Letter of Order or Purchase

Write a letter ordering supplies or equipment for one of the labs on campus or the company you work for. Find out the catalog number, the description, and the cost for each item you want to order. Locate and write down the name and address of the supplier. Before you begin to write your draft, fill in the plan sheet for the order letter.

Resignation

Application 1:
Revising a Letter of Resignation

Revise the letter of resignation shown below. Use the plan sheet from this chapter and the Guidelines for Revision from Chapter 3. Consider format, content, organization, and usage.

390 Elm Tree Lane
Carrolltown, GA 30117
September 2, 1986

Mr. Tom Timulty, President
Alabama Aviation Incorporated
1274 River View Boulevard
Montgomery, AL 36107

Dear Mr. Timulty:

I am writing concerning the Alabama Aviation flight from Atlanta
to Mobile which my wife and I took last week. We were six hours late
reaching our destination. As a result, I missed an important business
seminar I was planning to attend and for which I had paid $300 in
advance. The $300 was non-refundable.

I realize that it was foggy in Mobile, but the least you could
have done was to get us from Atlanta to Montgomery so that we could
rent a car to Mobile.

I would hope that misadventures such as this are not a common
occurrence at your airline. I have full confidence that you will
reimburse me for the seminar and look forward to hearing from you.

Sincerely,

Craig Sighorn

Craig Sighorn

Figure 11-16: Assignment for Letter of Adjustment, Negative Response

Dear Mr. Webb:

This is my letter of resignation from this company. I am tired of having to deal with working two and three hours overtime half the time and I'm really tired of the weekend work. It looks to me like I was the only person ever assigned to work extra hours, since half the people I work with are incompetent and lazy and wouldn't know a lathe if they ever saw one.

Edison Tools said they would pay me what I wanted and let me work regular hours. You have seen the last of me.

Mike Stone

Application 2:
Writing the Letter of Resignation

Write a letter of resignation for a job you have had in the past or one that you currently have. Before beginning your draft, fill in the plan sheet for the letter of resignation.

Letter of Inquiry
Plan Sheet

Letterhead or Heading
Date

Inside Address

Dear _____ :

BEGINNING
   Why you are writing:

   What you want to know:

   How you will use the information:

EXPLANATION OF INQUIRY
   Opening statement:

   Questions you want answered:

   1.

   2.

   3.

   4.

   5.

ENDING: POLITE CLOSE
   Request for further information that the reader thinks is important:

   Action requested:

   Appreciation:

Sincerely,

_____

Your name

Letter of Response to Inquiry
Plan Sheet

Letterhead

Date

Inside Address

Dear _____ :

BEGINNING
    Acknowledgment of receipt of request:

    Restatement of original request (briefly):

COMPLIANCE WITH REQUEST
    Opening statement:

    List of answers to questions:

    1.

    2.

    3.

    4.

    5.

ENDING: POLITE CLOSE

    Offer of further assistance:

    Goodwill closing:

Sincerely,

_____
Your name

**Letter of Claim/Complaint
Plan Sheet**

Letterhead or Heading

Date

Inside Address

Dear _____ :

BEGINNING
General statement of problem:

Action you want taken (briefly):

EXPLANATION OF CLAIM OR COMPLAINT
Facts about problem:

ENDING: POLITE CLOSE
Action you want taken (including deadlines, if applicable):

Goodwill statement:

Yours truly,

_____

Your name

Letter of Adjustment
Positive Response
Plan Sheet

Letterhead

Date

Inside Address

Dear ——————————— :

BEGINNING
    Acknowledgement of claim:

How you or your company will solve problem (grant adjustment):

EXPLANATION OF ERROR
    Why or how error occurred:

ENDING: POLITE CLOSE
    Expression of appreciation to customer:

    Goodwill closing:

Yours truly,

———————————
Your name

Letter of Adjustment
Negative Response
Plan Sheet

Letterhead

Date

Inside Address

Dear _____ :

BEGINNING
Acknowledgment of claim:

EXPLANATION OF REFUSAL
Details about cause of the problem or error:

Indication that customer was in error:

REFUSAL TO GRANT CLAIM
Statement of refusal:

Offer of alternative solution to problem (if possible):

ENDING: POLITE CLOSE
Request for response to offer (if necessary):

Goodwill closing:

Sincerely,

_____
Your name

Letter of Order or Purchase
Plan Sheet

Heading or Letterhead

Date

Inside Address

BEGINNING
  Purpose of letter:

  Where order is to be delivered:

EXPLANATION OF ORDER
  Introductory statement:

  Table listing items you wish to order:

Item	Description	Quantity	Unit Cost	Total Cost
1			$	$
2				
3				
4				
5				
			Grand Total	$

  Where bill is to be sent:

ENDING: POLITE CLOSE
  Method of shipment desired:

  Need for items:

  Goodwill closing:

_____

Your name

Letter of Resignation
Plan Sheet

Heading

Date

Inside Address

Dear _____ :

BEGINNING
   Positive statement about work experience:

EXPLANATION OF RESIGNATION
   Why you are leaving:

Effective date of resignation:

ENDING: POLITE CLOSE
   Request for reference in the future:

Sincerely,

_____
Your name

12

MANUALS

When you complete this chapter, you should know the types of manuals used most often in business and industry and in service institutions and be able to write informal technical descriptions and instructions. You should learn about the following topics:

> Policy manuals
> Administrative manuals
> Standards
> Technical manuals
> Procedures
> User's manuals
> Writing informal technical descriptions and instructions
>> Informal technical descriptions
>> Informal technical instructions

Manuals provide guidelines for the efficient and consistent operation of a company or agency and equipment or instruments. Depending on their audience and purpose, manuals range from very formal policy manuals which define the overall goals and objectives of a company to informal user's manuals which explain how to operate a car. They vary in length from a highly complex, 400-page technical manual which describes an instrument and control system to a two-page user's manual that explains how to hook up the component parts of a home stereo system. In this chapter, policy and administrative manuals, standards, technical manuals, procedures, and user's manuals are described. At the end of the chapter, an explanation of how to write informal technical instructions and descriptions is presented.

POLICY MANUALS

Policy manuals broadly define the overall guidelines for the manner in which a company or agency conducts business. They generally include the following sections:

> Purpose
> Goals and objectives
> Organization and administration

The purpose section gives the reason the company or agency was formed and explains its commitments. The goals and objectives section explains how the purpose will be achieved. The organization and administration section defines the authorities and responsibilities of the company's primary officers. Sometimes a brief history of the company is included in policy manuals.

Policy manuals are written by upper-level management and approved by the company president and board of directors. Most employees review the policy manual when they enter employment with the company, but the manual is primarily written for upper-level managers directly responsible for implementing policy. Here are a purpose statement and several of the objectives from a policy manual used in a community college. Notice that the manual does not explain or suggest methods for implementing the objectives. That information is given in administrative manuals.

1.0 PURPOSE

The purpose of Altahanna Technical College is to offer academic, cultural, occupational education, and training opportunities from basic educational through two-year technical programs to anyone of eligible age who can learn and whose needs can be met by the College. The College strives to fill the manpower needs in our society. Altahanna Technical College is fully committed to the Open Door policy and aims for the total development of each student. The President reviews the stated purpose and objectives of the College annually and makes recommendations to the Board of Trustees.

2.0 OBJECTIVES

2.1   To provide occupationally oriented curricula for those students who wish to enter employment with one year or less of vocational training.

2.2   To provide occupationally oriented curricula for those students who wish to enter employment after two years of technical education.

2.3   To provide single or combination courses needed by adults in the community to update their occupational capabilities to meet the challenges of a changing technological society.

2.4   To provide courses for those individuals whose formal education stopped short of elementary grade completion or high school graduation.

2.5   To provide specialized training for employees of new and/or expanding industry.

2.6   To provide general education courses for the social, cultural, and personal development of those individuals wishing to continue their education beyond high school.

2.7   To provide for the needs of those persons who desire to remove academic deficiencies so that they may enter regular curriculum programs.

2.8   To provide guidance and counseling services to all students.

2.9   To provide community educational services for individuals and organizations, including speakers, displays, resource personnel, or materials, as requested.

2.10 To provide low-cost tuition and fees and financial assistance.

2.11 To provide an effective articulation with community educational, business, governmental, and industrial institutions.

The style is formal, and it makes the goals and objectives impersonal and official sounding. Expressions such as "occupationally oriented curricula" and "effective articulation" are not easy to understand, but they sound very official. These types of expressions appear frequently in policy manuals.

Once a company's or agency's policies are established, the responsible officers or managers write administrative manuals to explain how their sections or divisions operate.

ADMINISTRATIVE MANUALS

Administrative manuals explain how the goals and objectives described in the policy manuals are to be met. They usually include the following information:

> Introduction
>   Purpose
>   Applicability (audience)
>   Objectives
> Organization
> Functions
> Duties and responsibilities
> Departmental guidelines

The introductory section of an administrative manual defines the reason the manual has been written, identifies the employees to whom the guidelines apply, and states the objectives of the department. The organization section includes a departmental organizational chart. Then it describes the functions of the department and the duties and responsibilities of the staff. Departmental guidelines include procedures that define how the department operates to implement the overall policy of the company.

Administrative manuals are usually written by a department head with the aid of his or her staff. Depending upon the purpose of the manual, the audience may be limited to employees in the department, or it may include all company employees. For example, the employee relations department of a company may be responsible for writing and issuing an employee handbook that explains criteria for employment and promotion in the company, conduct expected of employees, and employee benefit programs. In addition, the department may have its own administrative procedures that apply only to those employees in the employee relations department. The section of the administrative manual shown here is a detailed explanation of the hours of work and overtime pay for the employees of a large printing company.

9.0 HOURS OF WORK AND OVERTIME COMPENSATION

9.1 GENERAL

Company employees are to perform their duties within the established 40-hour work week and will be paid not less than the minimal hourly wage. The annual monthly salary rates represent the employee's straight-time pay for a standard 40-hour work week.

9.2 OVERTIME COMPENSATION

Compensation in the form of compensatory time off or monetary payment is required for hours worked in excess of 40 within a work week, except for those employees classified as executive, administrative, or professional who are exempt from the hours of work and overtime pay standards. Any non-exempt employee shall be given time off on the basis of 1.5 hours for each hour worked beyond 40 during a work week, but such time off must be taken within 30 days from the date the overtime is performed or by the end of the following pay period. If compensable time off is not given by the end of the pay period following the 30-day period, the overtime pay at 1.5 times the regular pay rate will be reported for inclusion in the next regular paycheck. The hourly rate of pay is determined by dividing the annual salary by 2080 hours (52×40).

9.3 DEFINITIONS

The following definitions apply to accounting for hours of work:

9.3.1 Work Week—The regular recurring period of 40 consecutive hours which may begin any day of the week and any hour of the day but must in each case be established in advance and is intended to be permanent. The beginning of the work week can be changed but not to evade the policy.

9.3.2 Hours Worked—Time which an employee is required or permitted to be on duty.

9.3.3 Overtime—Hours worked in excess of 40 during the work week.

9.3.4 Unauthorized Work—Hours worked by an employee without the employer's permission or contrary to instructions and without the employer's knowledge of such practice.

9.3.5 Compensatory Time Off—Time away from the employer's premises or the prescribed workplace granted for the purpose of compensating the employee for overtime.

9.4 SUPERVISORY RESPONSIBILITIES

9.4.1 Supervisors shall hold the hours worked by non-exempt employees to the established 40-hour work week. Unauthorized work is not permitted. Any work in excess of 8 hours in a day should be planned to give equal time off during the work week to avoid overtime work.

9.4.2 Overtime for any employee must be authorized prior to occurrence by the President or the responsible Vice-President. The practice of overtime work will be subject to review by the Office of the President.

9.4.3 Overtime will not be authorized as a matter of convenience for the employer or employee but only where excessive hours are necessary to meet emergency demands. It is the responsibility of the supervisor and employee to administer work time in the best interest of the company.

9.4.4 When authorized overtime occurs, the supervisor must give the employee scheduled compensatory time off within the required time limit. Due to budgetary limitations, any monetary payment for overtime must be approved by the President.

9.4.5 The supervisors shall see that the Time Record is kept by each non-exempt employee on a daily basis and will certify the correctness of reported hours worked.

9.5 TIME RECORD

9.5.1 All non-exempt employees are required to record daily the hours worked and report this on the appropriate Time Record (Form 96 or time clock punch card). The record is to be turned in to the supervisor at the end of each month, pay period, or upon termination. It is to be certified by the supervisor and forwarded to the Personnel Records Office.

A copy of Form 96 (Time Record) is included for reference.

9.5.2 When overtime occurs and compensatory time off is scheduled, the time off shall be reported on Form 114 (Application for Leave). The employee should indicate the date, hours, and total hours of compensatory time taken and the balance of hours remaining due. The time taken should be referenced to the actual occurrence of overtime shown on Form 96 (Time Record) or Time Card.

As you can see, employee and supervisor responsibilities are explained in detail in this section of the administrative manual. Any required forms, such as time sheets, are included in the administrative manual, and instructions for completing the forms are given. Employees usually receive copies of administrative manuals to keep for reference while they are employed.

Like policy manuals, administrative manuals are written in a formal style. Rather than personal pronouns "you" and "I," they use impersonal nouns, like "employee" and "employer." They also use authoritative helping verbs, such as "must," "will," and "shall." The sentences are long and complex.

The terms are carefully, if not clearly, defined. Again the purpose is to be official.

Policy and administrative manuals give overall guidelines and outline specific personnel and departmental procedures. As mentioned earlier, they explain how the company or agency conducts business. The remaining manuals that will be discussed are technical and relate to standards, equipment, and operations.

STANDARDS

Standards are documents that establish engineering and technical requirements for processes, procedures, practices, and methods. Their major purpose is to control variety and ensure consistency. Standards may cover "materials, items, features of items, engineering practices, processes, codes, symbols, type of material, definition and classification of defects, and standardize the marking of materials, items, parts, and components of equipment." [1]

Standards govern everything from how a procedure will be written to methods for testing concrete. They are published by a variety of interested parties. Companies publish their own standards. Regulatory agencies, such as the Nuclear Regulatory Commission, which publishes standards for the construction and operation of nuclear power plants, define requirements for the industries they govern. Societies, such as the American Society for Testing and Materials, publish standards that are used by business and industry to ensure that products meet minimum requirements for efficiency and safety.

An example of a standard is our monetary system. To establish control and consistency in the purchase of goods and services in the United States, the federal government has devised a system made up of metal coins—the penny, nickel, dime, quarter, and half-dollar—and paper—the one-, five-, 10-, 50-, 100-, 500-, and 1000-dollar bill. Each of these coins and bills has a specific value. A dollar in the hands of an automotive technician in Detroit has the same worth as a dollar in the hands of the president of the United States. Published standards usually include the following information:

> Scope and applicability
> References
> General concepts or significance of the standard
> Definitions of terms

Depending upon the type of standard being discussed, other information may also be included. Some standards, such as those published by the American Society for Testing and Materials, may include sections describing

---

[1]United States. Department of Defense. *Standardization Policies, Procedures and Instructions.* Washington, D.C.: Government Printing Office, n.d.

the material being tested and the manner in which test data were collected and analyzed. On the other hand, the *National Electrical Code Handbook* has sections called "articles" which govern electrical safety requirements for wiring design and protection, wiring methods and materials, and equipment.

The scope limits the discussion of the standard to a specific area. In a Department of Defense (DoD) manual which outlines the safe handling, storage, and disposal of ammunition, the scope is defined as follows: [2]

> The provisions of this manual apply to contractor-operated plants and cover all DoD purchases and contracts for ammunition, explosives, and related dangerous materials.

The reference section lists the documents which have been used to establish the standard. In describing the Electrical Safety Standard for storage of ammunition, the Department of Defense manual mentioned above references the National Fire Protection Association standards, the National Electrical Code, and the standards of the Underwriter's Laboratories, Inc.

The general concept or significance of the standard is a purpose statement which gives the reason for establishing and following the standard. Depending upon the design of the standard, the purpose statement may come before the scope. In the DoD manual, the purpose statement comes first.

> The purpose of this manual is to set forth safe practices and standards for all work performed in connection with DoD contracts involving ammunition, explosives and related dangerous materials. This manual also prescribes safe methods, practices, and standards for insuring continuity of production, safeguarding personnel, and preventing property damage at contractor-operated plants.

The definition section is an explanation of the terms used throughout the manual to ensure consistent understanding. In the DoD manual, "ammunition" is defined as follows:

> All components and any explosives case or contrivance prepared to form a charge, complete round, or cartridge for cannon, howitzer, mortar, or small arms, or for any other weapon, torpedo warhead, mine, depth charge, demolition charge, fuse, detonator, projectile, grenade, guided missile, rocket, pyrotechnics; and all chemical agents, fillers, and associated dangerous materials.

Standards are usually written by engineers or other content specialists in technical fields. The audiences using standards range from design engineers to medical laboratory technicians to architects to sanitation engineers. Generally anything that affects health, safety, efficiency, and quality is governed by a standard.

[2]United States. Department of Defense. *Contractor's Safety Manual for Ammunition, Explosives and Related Dangerous Materials.* Washington, D.C.: Government Printing Office, 1968.

TECHNICAL MANUALS

Technical manuals describe equipment and systems, explain how they operate, and provide instructions for their maintenance. Technical manuals include the following information:

> Descriptions
> Specifications
> Principle of operation
> Instructions
>   Initial hookup
>   Maintenance and repair

A technical description usually consists of a photograph or drawing of a piece of equipment or a system accompanied by text explaining the major parts. In technical manuals, a technical description introduces the item to the reader. Figure 12-1 shows the technical description of the Spec 200 210S Series Indicator[3], a part of a highly complex electronic process control system. Notice that this section is labeled "Technical Information." The photograph in Figure 1 shows the electronics technician exactly what the front and back of the indicator look like. Figure 2 shows a signal distribution module which is used with each indicator. The written text gives an overall description of the indicator, its function, its major parts, and optional parts that may be furnished by the manufacturer at the request of the buyer.

The second major section in the technical manual lists technical specifications, usually called "tech specs" in industry. Tech specs have two purposes. They serve as the guidelines by which the buyer purchases the equipment to meet a required need. They also provide the buyer with the range of limitations or tolerances within which the equipment may be operated safely and efficiently. The specifications for the Spec 200 210S Series Indicator are shown in Figure 12-2. Note that the model number is given and that those criteria such as mounting equipment, electrical classification, power requirements, and accuracy are listed and defined. The manufacturer of the equipment bases the tech specs on tests that are conducted by the company's design engineers. The technician uses the tech specs to ensure that the equipment functions within the design tolerances.

The principle of operation of the equipment is the third section that generally appears in a technical manual. This section is usually a brief description of how the equipment works. The discussion of the principle of operation of the 210S Indicator shown in Figure 12-3 explains the operation of the indicator in a paragraph accompanied by a simplified drawing. Notice that no attempt is made to avoid technical terms. The writer assumes that the reader is familiar with electronics and has worked with other indicators. Technical manuals are not intended for the untrained customers described in Chapter 2.

---

[3]All materials relating to the Spec 210S Series Indicator are used by permission of The Foxboro Company, Foxboro, Massachusetts.

<table>
<tr><td>**Technical Information**</td><td>**TI**
210-100
March 1972</td></tr>
</table>

SPEC 200 INDICATOR

Standard Display

Figure 1. 210S Series Indicator

Figure 2. Signal Distribution Module

GENERAL

SPEC 200 210S Series Indicators provide accurate indication of one or two measured variables. The dual indicator version is shown in Figure 1. Fluorescent-colored pointers and easy-to-read 4-inch measurement scales permit fast, sure reading. A wide selection of easily changed, standard scales is available. Each pointer is positioned by a voltage-to-position drive unit. The operation of the drive units utilize the unusual characteristics of a modern "memory" alloy.

Each indicator occupies one space in a SPEC 200 shelf, and connections are made via a plug to a cable. Figure 2 shows a signal distribution module which is used with each indicator. Signal distribution modules mount in an associated nest (located in the same enclosure as the shelf) or in a remote location. Terminals are provided for connection of measurement input signals and optional circuits.

REFERENCE DOCUMENT TI 220-160

Indicators can optionally be furnished with alarms and/or alarm lights. Also optional is a sequence alarm with logic output to a remote horn circuit. This provides absolute alarming for up to two variables. In an alarm condition, the internal alarm lights flash on and off, and, if provided, the remote horn circuit is energized. When acknowledged by a TEST/ACKNOWLEDGE push-button on the front of the indicator, the horn circuit deenergizes; the lights stay on, but stop flashing. When the alarm condition is corrected, the lights go out. Connections to operate remotely located lights in the flashing sequence are available when this option is specified.

Figure 12-1: Description of SPEC 210S Series Indicator

SPECIFICATIONS

Model Number:
210S-1 Single Pointer Indicator
210S-2 Two Pointer Indicator
  -A Dual Absolute Alarm
  -L Two Internal Alarm Lights
  -D Dual Absolute Alarm prewired to Internal
     Alarm Lights
  -G Dual Absolute Alarm with Common
     Flasher and Internal Lights for sequence
     alarming (prewired, includes Test/Ack
     Push-button)
  +DSP or +DIO Signal Distribution Module

Note 1: To purchase Signal Distribution Module
    separately, specify 2AX+DSP.
Note 2: For plug/cable assembly to interconnect
    shelf and signal distribution module, specify
    Cable Assembly 2KBL-( ). Fill in length in
    feet desired.

Mounting Equipment:
Occupies one space in SPEC 200 shelf (see TI 200-275)

Electrical Classification: Ordinary Locations

Intrinsic Safety: See TI 200-255

Power Requirements:
+15 V dc ±5% at 60 mA per pointer
-15 V dc ±5% at 60 mA per pointer
Note: Additional power requirements for optional
internal alarms and/or alarm lights are given in
TI 220-150.

Input Signal(s): 0 to 10 V dc

Input Resistance: 100 kilohms minimum

Accuracy: Less than ±0.5% of input span

Repeatability: Less than 0.1% of input span

Dead Band: Less than 0.2% of input span

Dial: 4-inch scale length

Supply Voltage Effect:
Less than ±0.5% of input span for a ±5% change within
normal operating limits

Ambient Temperature Range: +40 to 120°F (+5 to 50°C)

Ambient Temperature Effect:
Less than ±0.5% of input span for a 50°F (25°C) change
within normal operating limits

Figure 12-2: Technical Specifications for the SPEC
210S Series Indicator

After the technical description, specifications, and principle of operation are presented, the information for using the equipment becomes very specific. Installation and maintenance instructions, accompanied by technical drawings, provide the technician with the information necessary to install and maintain the equipment properly.

Technical instructions explain how to perform a specific operation or process. They include any special techniques required to accomplish the procedure. If the instructions pertain to a complex piece of equipment, they are often accompanied by figures which allow readers to see how to perform the task correctly. Figure 12-4 on pages 280–282 shows the instructions for wiring and calibrating the 210S Series Indicator. Notice that a photograph and a general description of the equipment are given first. Then, under separate headings, the instructions for correctly wiring and calibrating the indicator are included. Figures accompany each of the sections, and the tools or specialized equipment required to calibrate the instrument are included. Because the ini-

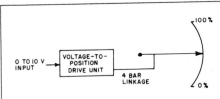

Figure 12-3:   Description of Principle of Operation
of SPEC 210S Series Indicator

Figure 3. Simplified Operational Diagram

PRINCIPLE OF OPERATION

As shown in Figure 3, the 0 to 10 volts dc signal is applied to the input terminals of the voltage-to-position drive unit. The high torque rotary motion at the output shaft (approximately 7.5 degrees) is directly proportional to the magnitude of the input signal. A conventional four-bar linkage transmits and amplifies the 7.5 degree motion to 22.5 degrees of arc, necessary for full scale pointer travel. When two-pointer indicators are involved, two separate drive units are used. For complete information on the voltage-to-position drive unit, consult TI 220-160.

tial wiring is less complex than the calibration, the procedure for wiring is written in paragraph form. Because the calibration requires steps to be performed in a certain sequence, the steps are listed in order and numbered.

Technical manuals are generally written by technical writers and the engineers who helped design the equipment. The photographs and drawings are produced by professional photographers and technical illustrators. The manufacturer of the equipment is responsible for providing the purchaser with a technical manual so that the equipment may be used and maintained correctly. As a technician, you will not be responsible for writing technical manuals; however, your job requires you to be able to read and interpret them.

PROCEDURES

Procedures outline the correct method for performing a required task. Operating procedures for equipment are adapted from the instructional sections of technical manuals. When a company purchases a piece of equipment and the accompanying technical manual, a technician may be required to write a more specific set of instructions or procedures for troubleshooting, maintenance, and repair to ensure that each person who works on the equipment does so in exactly the same way. Sometimes, a technician or engineer may find that the process described in the equipment technical manual does not exactly fit the company's requirements. Then he or she changes the manufacturer's manual to meet the company's needs in an operating procedure.

Operating procedures written for a particular company generally have fewer illustrations and more specific instructions than those in the manufacturer's technical manual. They include the following information:

Purpose statement
References (if applicable)

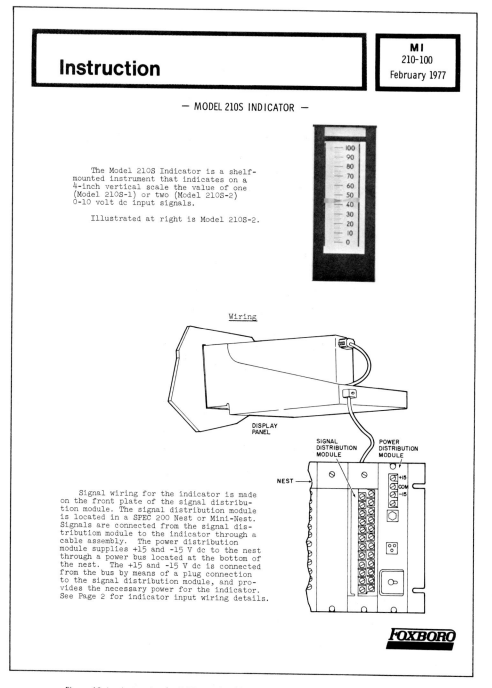

Instruction

MI
210-100
February 1977

— MODEL 210S INDICATOR —

The Model 210S Indicator is a shelf-mounted instrument that indicates on a 4-inch vertical scale the value of one (Model 210S-1) or two (Model 210S-2) 0-10 volt dc input signals.

Illustrated at right is Model 210S-2.

Wiring

DISPLAY PANEL

SIGNAL DISTRIBUTION MODULE

POWER DISTRIBUTION MODULE

NEST

+15
COM
-15

Signal wiring for the indicator is made on the front plate of the signal distribution module. The signal distribution module is located in a SPEC 200 Nest or Mini-Nest. Signals are connected from the signal distribution module to the indicator through a cable assembly. The power distribution module supplies +15 and -15 V dc to the nest through a power bus located at the bottom of the nest. The +15 and -15 V dc is connected from the bus by means of a plug connection to the signal distribution module, and provides the necessary power for the indicator. See Page 2 for indicator input wiring details.

FOXBORO

Figure 12-4:   Instruction for Wiring and Calibrating the SPEC 210S Series Indicator

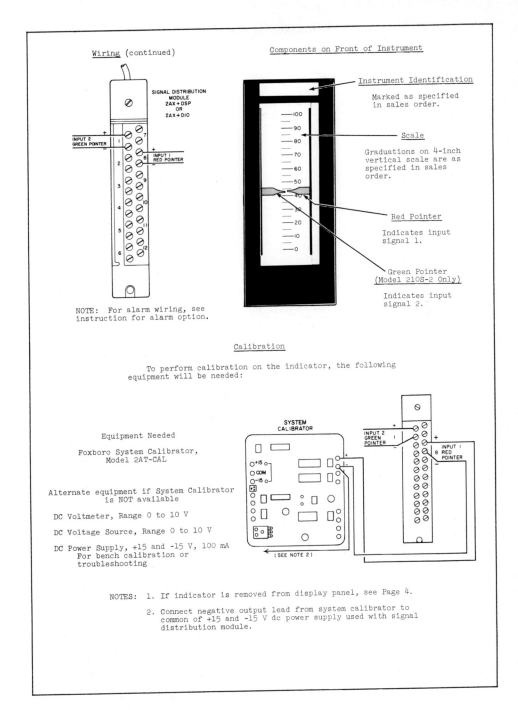

Wiring (continued)

Components on Front of Instrument

Instrument Identification

Marked as specified in sales order.

Scale

Graduations on 4-inch vertical scale are as specified in sales order.

Red Pointer

Indicates input signal 1.

Green Pointer (Model 210S-2 Only)

Indicates input signal 2.

NOTE: For alarm wiring, see instruction for alarm option.

Calibration

To perform calibration on the indicator, the following equipment will be needed:

Equipment Needed

Foxboro System Calibrator, Model 2AT-CAL

Alternate equipment if System Calibrator is NOT available

DC Voltmeter, Range 0 to 10 V

DC Voltage Source, Range 0 to 10 V

DC Power Supply, +15 and -15 V, 100 mA For bench calibration or troubleshooting

NOTES: 1. If indicator is removed from display panel, see Page 4.

2. Connect negative output lead from system calibrator to common of +15 and -15 V dc power supply used with signal distribution module.

Figure 12-4: *continued*

Calibration

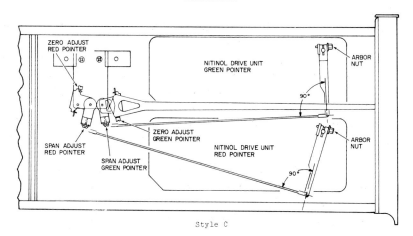

Style C

1. Connect system calibrator to input terminals for pointer to be calibrated. See Page 2.

2. Adjust system calibrator output for a signal of 5 volts.

3. Check for 90° angle on pointer linkage. If necessary, loosen arbor nut and adjust lever for 90° angle.

4. Adjust system calibrator output for a signal of 0 volts.

5. Rotate zero adjustment screw so that pointer is at 0% of scale.

6. Adjust system calibrator output for a signal of 10 volts.

7. Rotate span adjust screw to bring pointer halfway towards 100% of scale.

8. Repeat Steps 4 through 7 until pointer reads correctly when 0 and 10 volts are applied.

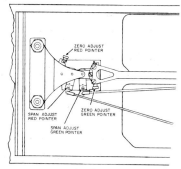

Styles A & B

Figure 12-4: *continued*

Precautions (if applicable)
Procedure

The purpose statement explains why the procedure has been written. It is usually no more than one or two sentences long. The reference section refers the reader to the technical manuals, schematics, diagrams, or textbooks used in writing the procedure. General precautions in following the procedures are addressed, if applicable. The procedure section is a step-by-step set of instructions for the troubleshooting, maintenance, or repair of the component, equipment, or system described in the purpose statement. It may also explain the correct performance of a defined task.

Procedures are usually written by senior-level technicians who have experience with the process being described. The language is technical and presumes the audience, the employee who performs the job, is a highly trained, experienced technician.

Procedure writers usually follow this sequence of steps:

1. They gather and read all required sources of information (technical manuals, drawings, textbooks).
2. Based on the reference documents, they write a draft of the procedure.
3. They field-test the procedure for technical accuracy and sequence.
4. They ask a lower-level technician to field-test the procedure. Procedure writers follow the technician in the field test and make notes when problems occur or directions seem unclear.
5. They rewrite the procedure and have a lower-level technician field-test a second time. Again, they make notes when problems occur.
6. They revise the procedure as necessary. Then procedure writers field-test and revise a third time.

Generally three field tests will identify the problems and provide the information required to write a well-organized, accurate procedure. At entry-level positions, technicians should be able to identify poorly written procedures and be prepared to offer suggestions for their improvement. Figure 12-5 on page 284 shows the first page of a procedure describing the correct method for making an unoccupied bed in a hospital. Although this may seem to be a simple task, 36 steps are required to make the bed correctly. Notice the headings and numbering system. These special features of technical writing are described in Chapter 7.

USER'S MANUALS

User's manuals explain the operation of a piece of equipment to the purchaser. Like technical manuals, user's manuals accompany new equipment. However, this equipment will be operated not by trained technicians but by untrained customers. For example, the owner of every new automobile receives a booklet which describes how to operate and service the car. This same car is also de-

Making an Unoccupied Bed

1.0   Purpose

This procedure describes the correct method for making an
unoccupied bed. Since the patient spends an inordinate amount
of time in the bed, a well-made bed is of paramount importance
in increasing patient comfort during the period of
confinement.

2.0   Precautions

Micro-organisms move through the air and are transferred from
one surface to another. Following the basic principles of
asepsis is critical to control the contamination of oneself
and the environment.

3.0   Materials Needed

Mattress pad
Bottom sheet
Rubber or plastic draw sheet
Cloth drawsheet
Top sheet
Blanket
Spread
Pillow cases
Laundry bag

4.0   Procedure

4.1   Raise the bed to an appropriate height and lock wheels to
      prevent movement.

4.2   Remove any attached equipment and place side rails in
      DOWN position.

4.3   Remove cases from pillows and place in laundry bag.
      Place pillow on beside table.

4.4   Loosen the spread, blanket, top and bottom sheets from
      the mattress, moving around the bed from head to foot on
      one side and foot to head on the other side.

4.5   Gather linens loosened in Step 4.4 by pulling in from
      corners and place in laundry bag.

4.6   WASH YOUR HANDS to avoid contamination of clean linens.

4.7   Place mattress pad on bed, securing it smoothly.

Figure 12-5: Procedure for Making a Bed

scribed in a series of technical manuals intended for automotive technicians. User's manuals usually include the following information:

Introduction
Operation
Description
Maintenance
Specifications

The introduction explains the purpose of the manual, describes the contents, and introduces the product. The operation section describes how the equipment operates and explains the correct method for using the equipment. The description section identifies the major parts of the equipment. The maintenance section gives the manufacturer's recommendations for servicing the equipment. The last section, specifications, defines the tolerances to which the equipment has been manufactured.

Technical writers usually write user's manuals. They translate the highly technical information in technical manuals into language a customer can understand. User's manuals are much less formal than the other manuals discussed because they need to be "user friendly." "User friendly" is a term from the computer industry that describes computer software which is easy to use.

This is the foreword from a manual accompanying a new car. Even though the sale has been completed, the writing is persuasive with a clear "you" attitude. Notice that a special service manual may be purchased if the new car owner is knowledgeable enough to perform his or her own maintenance. The service manual is more formal and less friendly than the user's manual.

Before you start driving your new Bearcat, please read through this instruction book carefully. It contains all the information you need to be able to drive and service your vehicle in the best possible way. By following the instructions given in this book, you will find that your Bearcat will come up to all the expectations concerning economical operation and excellent performance that you have every right to expect of a top-quality vehicle.

This instruction book is not intended to be a comprehensive technical manual and does not claim to make the reader into a perfect car mechanic. It will, however, show you how to look after your vehicle so that trouble in the future can be avoided. The better you know your Bearcat, the better service it can give you. Even for an experienced motorist, this book can contain some valuable information.

For a more detailed mechanical description and repair procedures, we refer you to the special service manual for the car.

WRITING INFORMAL TECHNICAL DESCRIPTIONS AND INSTRUCTIONS

Unless you are a technical writer, you will generally not write the formal descriptions and instructions that appear in technical manuals. However, even as an entry-level technician, you should know enough about the basic characteristics of each so that you can determine when they are correctly written. Later, when you become a senior-level technician or a lead, you will have to prepare operating procedures based on the information in technical manuals. In addition, your explanations to customers, supervisors, and new trainees may require you to prepare informal descriptions and instructions. This section discusses how to write short descriptions and instructions and provides examples of each.

Informal Technical Descriptions

A technical description explains what a tool or piece of equipment looks like. It gives an overall view of what is being described and detailed information about the major parts or sections. The description is specific and precise. It provides exact dimensions and weights as well as the shape, the color, and the materials the item is made of. The intended audience of the description determines the amount of detail included as well as the words used. An audience of customers who want to understand the general characteristics of an item will require much less detail than an audience of technicians who have to repair the item. As was pointed out previously, user's manuals are much less detailed and much simpler than technical manuals.

The informal technical description is divided into three major sections: the beginning section, or introduction; the description of the item's major parts; and the ending section, a brief discussion of the item's operation. A diagram with major parts labeled is usually included. The description is organized so that the audience can "see" the item. Depending upon the object, descriptions move from left to right, top to bottom, outside to inside, or inside to outside. The location of a part is identified by using such words as "below," "above," "to the left," and "beneath." Then the audience can see the placement and the relationship of the part to other parts. Comparisons are also helpful in technical descriptions. For example, to describe an oscilloscope screen to a customer, an electronics technician may compare the oscilloscope screen to the screen on a small television set.

Beginning Section.   A technical description begins with a sentence definition. The definition includes the brand name and model number of the item. Then the item as a whole is described—dimensions, shape, material, color, and unusual qualities. The last sentence of the beginning section lists the major parts in the order they will be described.

Description of Parts.   The second section of the informal technical description gives the characteristics of each major part. This section is made up of a series of short paragraphs, each describing one part. The description includes the part's size, shape, material, color, and location. The paragraphs are generally only three or four sentences long.

Ending Section.   The ending section of the technical description is a brief statement of how the various parts work together.

The examples in Figures 12-6 and 12-7 show two different types of technical descriptions. Figure 12-6 on pages 288 and 289 is a description of the *outside* of a Wilson Volt-ohm-milliameter (VOM). The writer describes the VOM from the top down, beginning with the meter scale and ending with the terminals. The attached sketch of the VOM is referred to in the first paragraph. Figure 12-7 on pages 290 and 291 is a description of the *inside*, the internal parts, of a Kassin headlamp used on a forklift. The sketch is shown immediately after the major parts are named in the first paragraph. Notice that the major parts are numbered both on the sketch and in the written description. The writer describes the Kassin headlamp from the internal housing assembly to the external retaining ring. Both descriptions are intended for trained audiences. The description of the VOM is aimed at students enrolled in an electrical installation and maintenance curriculum; the description of the headlamp is directed at students enrolled in a heavy equipment repair curriculum.

Informal Instructions

Technical instructions tell how to do something, how to perform an operation or process. They include any special techniques required to accomplish the task. Like technical descriptions, technical instructions are designed to meet the needs of a particular audience. Instructions prepared for customers are much simpler than those prepared for technicians. In fact, there are certain tasks that untrained individuals should not attempt to do. Technical instructions have three major sections: a beginning section, or introduction; a list of steps; and an ending section, or summary.

Beginning Section.   The beginning section gives information necessary to start the procedure. Unless the process is very common, the first sentence is usually a definition. Then the purpose of the process, its importance, special skills and knowledge, and any necessary equipment and preparations are explained.

Steps.   The second section gives the steps for completing the procedure. These steps are numbered sequentially and written as direct commands. Notes and warnings are included as necessary. As shown in Figure 12-9, sketches and diagrams may also be included. Direct commands make the instructions easy to follow. They make the users feel that you are standing over their shoulders, watching them perform the process. Although they are easy to read, direct commands are very authoritative. In writing direct commands, omit the subject and focus the attention on the verb. If possible, begin each step with an action verb.

1. Open the door.
2. Turn on the light.
3. Attach red wire A to the terminal.

The Volt-Ohm-Milliameter

The Wilson Volt-ohm-milliameter (VOM) is a multipurpose instrument
designed to measure voltage, current, and resistance. Current passes
through the instrument, activating a meter, which provides a direct
reading of the quantity being measured. Shown in the attached figure,
the Wilson is a black, plastic, rectangular device. It weighs 500 gm
and measures 15 x 9 x 3.2 cm. The black plastic casing houses the
multiple meter scale, a pointer, the range select switch, the zero-ohms
adjust potentiometer, and the terminals to which the input leads, or
probes, are attached.

The meter scale, measuring 9 x 6.5 cm, is located in the upper
half of the instrument case. The background is white and has five scales
printed on it. The first scale at the top, printed in black, measures
ohms. The second scale, printed in red, measures voltage. The third
scale, printed in black, measures ac voltage. Directly below the ac
voltage scale is a fourth scale, printed in green, which measures low ac
voltages. The fifth scale, printed in black, measures decibels.

The black pointer is 5.3 cm long and has an 80 degree arc. Depending
on the variable selected for measurement, the pointer swings through a
proportional section of its arc to indicate the reading volts, amps,
ohms, or decibels.

The range select switch, measuring 5.5 cm in diameter, is a circular
switch located directly beneath the meter scale. It is used to select the
variable and the specific range to be measured.

The zero-ohms adjust potentiometer is located directly to the left of
the range select switch. It is used to reset the ohm-meter function
of the VOM to zero whenever resistance ranges are changed. It is
bright red.

Four input terminals connect the probe leads to the VOM circuitry.
One input terminal--the common, or negative terminal--is located

Page 1 of 2

Figure 12-6: Informal Technical Description

directly under the zero-ohms adjust.   The other three--dc, 1.2 KV,
Output +. and V-Ω-A+--are located to the right of the range select
switch.

The probe leads are two insulated wires, one red and one black,
which provide input from the circuit being analyzed.   They are 84 cm
long.   The leads are connected to the input terminals.

To use the VOM, the technician determines the variable to be
measured and sets the range select switch.   The probe leads are plugged
into the appropriate terminal and connected to the circuit.   Then the
desired value is read on the meter scale.

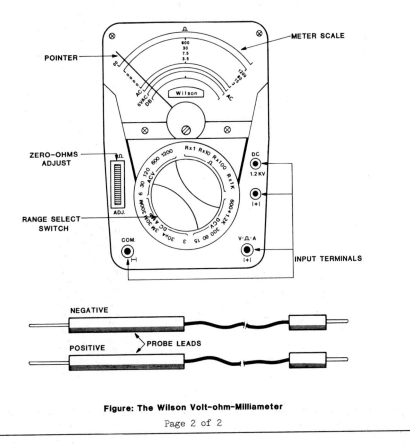

Figure: The Wilson Volt-ohm-Milliameter

Page 2 of 2

Figure 12-6: *continued*

The Kassin Headlamp

The Kassin Headlamp, Model 17A, is a headlight used to provide auxiliary lighting for the operation of diesel-powered forklifts. It is mounted six inches above the forklift beam and provides forward illumination to a range of 150 feet and peripheral illumination to 27 feet. The three major parts are the lamp housing assembly, the sealed incandescent lamp, and the retaining ring. These parts are shown in the figure below.

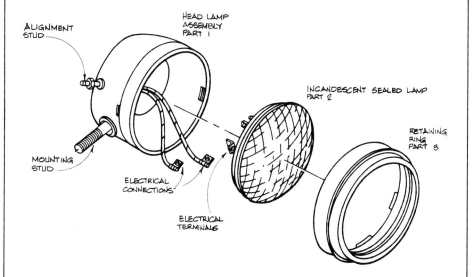

Part 1. LAMP HOUSING ASSEMBLY. The lamp housing assembly is circular with a diameter of 4 1/2 inches and a depth of 3 inches. The 1-inch outerlip has two 3/4 inch slots for mounting the retaining ring. The assembly provides support for the sealed incandescent lamp and serves as a means of attaching the lamp to the forklift. The magnesium housing shell holds the carbon steel mounting and alignment stud and

Page 1 of 2

Figure 12-7: Informal Technical Description

two copper electrical connections. The alignment stud controls and fixes the direction of the headlamp beam.

Part 2. SEALED INCANDESCENT HEADLAMP. The sealed incandescent headlamp is a circular glass-sealed beam unit 4 inches in diameter and 2 inches deep. It has three electrical terminals at the back of the headlamp. The lens pattern is standard 77A-5. The sealed beam output is nominally 8750 beam candle power with an expected life of 2000 operating hours.

Part 3. RETAINING RING. The retaining ring is 4 1/4-inch molded polycarbonate ring with an internal, weather-tight seal. It is used to hold the headlamp in place and provide moisture protection for the lamp and lamp housing assembly by means of two notched tabs which snap into the slots in the outer lip of the housing assembly.

For correct assembly, the three electrical terminals are connected to the electrical conductors according to Technical Specifications sheet 09755. The sealed incandescent headlamp is then placed in the housing assembly and the retaining ring snapped into place. The complete assembly is then bolted to the forklift.

Figure 12-7: *continued*

Notes are information that is not part of the action but that the user should know in order to better perform the procedure. To separate them from the direct commands, notes are often put in parentheses, with the word "Note" written in capital letters at the beginning. For example, in the instructions for installing a Schrader Valve shown in Figure 12-8, the author tells the technician how much sanding should be done before the line is punctured. He gives this information in a note. In the instructions for making the Super Duper Paper Plane shown in Figure 12-9, the author reminds his audience to make sure the sides of the paper are perfectly aligned before folding.

Warnings or cautions are also included when a part of the procedure may be dangerous to the technician or damage the equipment. Warnings or cautions appear immediately before the step to be performed, or they may be included in the step. In the instructions shown in Figure 12-8, the writer thought that a technician should be warned that soldered metal can cause severe burns. Therefore, he included a warning statement. To make it easy to see, the warning is centered and capitalized.

Drawings or diagrams show what the equipment looks like during disassembly or reassembly from one step to the next. They are generally not included in short instructions dealing with simple equipment. However, in longer procedures explaining assembly or repair of complex equipment, flow paths, or troubleshooting techniques, drawings or photographs may be included. The figures are numbered, titled, and placed near the step they illustrate.

Ending Section.   The ending section is usually one or two sentences summing up the procedure.

Figure 12-8 on pages 293 and 294 shows a set of instructions for installing a Schrader Valve. Students learning to repair air conditioners and refrigerators make up the intended audience. Customers, such as untrained homeowners, should not attempt to install a Schrader Valve. Figure 12-9 on pages 295–298 shows a set of instructions for making the Super Duper Paper Plane. These instructions explain how to recreate a prize-winning design from Auburn University's annual paper airplane contest. The writer claims that, with a little help from an updraft, this plane will fly a mile. Notice the drawings that he uses to help his audience follow the steps.

SUMMARY

Manuals provide guidelines for the operation of companies or equipment. Policy manuals define the manner in which a company or agency operates. Administrative manuals explain how company goals and objectives are met. Standards establish engineering and technical requirements to ensure consistency in the production of goods and services. Technical manuals describe equipment and systems, their operation and maintenance. Procedures list the correct methods for performing a required task, and user's manuals explain the opera-

INSTALLING A SCHRADER VALVE

Soldering a Schrader service valve into a refrigeration line is a relatively simple process that allows a set of refrigeration gauges to be attached to the line. These gauges enable the technician to check the pressure of refrigerant in a cooling system at the point of attachment. The skills required are a knowledge of basic refrigeration and gas welding. The equipment needed includes an oxyacetylene torch, flux, sandpaper, silver brazing rods, a Schrader Valve, a hole punch, and water and a sponge. Before attempting to install the valve, check all tools and equipment to be sure they are fully operational. Insure that the system is disconnected and free of refrigerant and the area selected for work is properly ventilated.

1) Clean the line of all grease and dirt. Make sure that the surface is dry.

2) Sand area clean. (NOTE: Sand until the original metal color shines through.)

3) Puncture the line. Make sure the stem of the valve will slide into it easily.

4) Apply soldering flux to the base and around the sanded area on the line.

5) Light and adjust the oxyacetylene torch until a blue-tipped flame appears.

6) Apply the flame to the line until the flux begins to run.

7) Apply silver brazing rod tip to the area between the valve-seat and the line while still applying heat.

8) Apply constant heat until the silver solder begins to run completely around the base of the seated valve and the opening is completely filled with solder.

WARNING

WHEN CLEANING EXCESS SOLDER FROM THE BASE OF THE VALVE, DO NOT TOUCH SOLDER OR METAL. METAL IS STILL HOT AND SEVERE BURNS WILL RESULT.

9) Turn off torch and remove excess solder by wiping with rag briskly.

Page 1 of 2

Figure 12-8: Technical Instructions

10) Check to insure a good quality weld.

11) Dip sponge into water and rub line and valve repeatedly until both are warm to the touch.

12) Insert the valve stem and partially charge the system while checking for leaks.

If no leaks are found, charge the system to capacity and allow it to run continuously for 45 minutes. Check for leaks again. If none are found and the pressure is gauged properly, the valve is correctly installed.

Figure 12-8: *continued*

INSTRUCTIONS FOR THE SUPER DUPER PAPER PLANE

The Super Duper Paper Plane is designed to fly farther than any other paper plane in the air today. To make this magnificent glider, all you need is an 8 1/2 x 11 inch sheet of paper. The Super Duper Paper Plane is guaranteed to give hours of enjoyment to all kids eight years and older.

To make this plane, you will fold and unfold the paper several times. Construction of the plane takes 10 easy steps. Read each step all the way through before proceeding. Your plane will be sleek, with broad flat wings and wing tips to control your flight.

1. Fold the sheet of paper in half lengthwise from right to left. (Note: Make sure that each side is lined up perfectly.) Crease the paper and unfold.

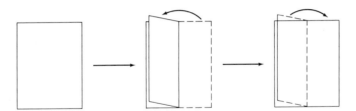

2. Fold each top corner of the page along the center line so that the top edges of the paper lie directly against each other. Crease the folds. The top portion now forms a <u>triangle</u>.

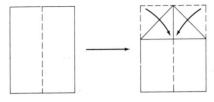

Figure 12-9: Instructions

3. Fold the top of the page down, making the crease at the bottom edge of
    the flaps.

    (Note: Make sure that the tip of the <u>inverted</u> <u>triangle</u> lies on the center
    line.)

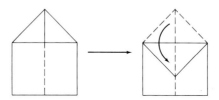

4. Turn the paper over from the right to left. Fold it in half lengthwise,
    right to left, along the center line.

    The <u>inverted</u> <u>triangle</u> should be on the <u>outside</u> of the fold.

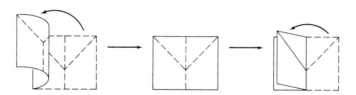

5. Now you must remove a portion of the top left corner. At about 3/4 inch
    to the right of the left side, tear downward about 3/4 inch until just
    past the diagonal flat. Remove the piece by tearing a straight line to
    the left.

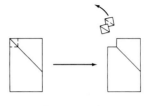

Page 2 of 4

Figure 12-9: *continued*

6. Unfold the top half of the paper to the right. The <u>inverted</u> <u>triangle</u> is now showing again.

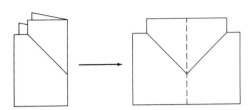

7. Again fold each top corner of the page along the center line so that the top edges of the paper lie directly against each other. Crease the folds.

The top portion of the paper now forms a second <u>triangle</u>, and the <u>inverted</u> <u>triangle</u> lies within and below the torn out portion.

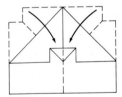

8. Fold the tip of the <u>inverted</u> <u>triangle</u> upward and crease at the flap junction. Both <u>triangles</u> now point in the same direction.

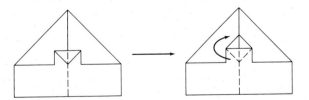

Figure 12-9: *continued*

9. Fold the paper in half lengthwise along the center line so that the triangles and flaps are on the outside.

10. Turn the paper so that the center line is now on the bottom with the tip of the <u>upper triangle</u> pointing to the left.

    Fold the upper half of the paper down, making the crease 1 inch from the bottom. Fold the bottom 1/2 inch of the wing upward. Turn the paper over and fold the other half down and bottom tip up to match the first side.

    (Note: Hold the plane's body between two fingers; adjust the wings to make them flat and the tips straight up.)

    Your Super Duper Paper Plane is now ready to fly.

Figure 12-9: *continued*

tion of equipment or instruments to customers. When they occupy senior or lead positions, technicians may have to write the manuals described above. At an entry level, they are responsible for using and suggesting changes and improvements in manuals and for writing informal technical descriptions and instructions.

ASSIGNMENTS

Application1:
Reading Manuals

Read the excerpts below. Answer the questions that follow each excerpt. Write down your answers.

A. This excerpt is from a student handbook at a technical college. It explains the school's policy on registering vehicles.

Automobiles, Motorcycles, and Bicycles

Registration of automobiles, motorcycles, and bicycles should occur at the beginning of fall quarter for all students. Students entering the college at other quarters will register their vehicles during academic registration for that quarter.

Students who bring unregistered cars or cycles on the campus after any registration period must register them with campus security. Failure to register a vehicle, to use a proper decal, or to park in the proper zone will constitute a violation and subject the violator to certain penalties. See "Rules and Regulations for Traffic and Parking."

Write down the answers to these questions.

1. When will most students register their vehicles?
2. When should the students who do not enter at fall quarter register their vehicles?
3. What actions mentioned here are considered violations?

B. These standards are from the Department of Defense manual mentioned earlier. They give the requirements for the exteriors; interior walls, roofs, and ceilings; and the floors and work surfaces in facilities that house ammunition.

Associated Standards For Facilities

a. Building Exteriors. Exterior wall and roof coverings of operating buildings should be noncombustible and, wherever possible, should be of frangible or "breakaway" construction. The buildings should not be provided with basements and should not be more than one story high, except where necessitated by process requirements.

b. Interior Walls, Roofs, and Ceilings. Interior wall surfaces and ceilings of operating buildings where loose, finely divided explosive materials may be present shall be smooth, free from cracks and crevices, fire resistive, and if painted be covered with a hard-gloss paint to minimize accumulation of dust and to facilitate cleaning. There should be no horizontal ledges upon which dust may accumulate; but if any exist, they shall be beveled or kept clean. Wall joints and openings for wiring and plumbing shall be sealed to prevent the entry of dust into concealed space. Roofs and walls shall be as light in weight as practicable and constructed and supported so that they will vent an internal explosion. Exception is made in case of fire walls and substantial dividing walls.

c. Floors and Work Surfaces. Floors and work surfaces in hazardous locations shall be constructed to facilitate cleaning and shall have no cracks or crevices in which explosives may lodge. Subfloors, finished flooring, and work surfaces should not wrinkle or buckle under operating conditions. Where washing is required, surfaces must be capable of withstanding repeated applications of hot water. Nonsparking floors and work surfaces are required in all locations where exposed explosives and/or hazardous concentrations of flammable vapor or gas are present. When grounding is necessary, conductive floors (mats or similar static dissipating floor surfaces), table tops and other work surfaces shall be provided. Cove bases at the junction of walls and floors are preferred. Exposed nails, screws, or bolts in work surfaces shall be avoided.

Write down the answers to these questions.

1. What are two requirements for the exterior walls and roof coverings?
2. How high should the building be?
3. What are three requirements for interior wall surfaces and ceilings of buildings that may house loose, finely divided explosives?
4. Why should the builder avoid horizontal ledges and seal wall joints and openings for wiring and plumbing?
5. Why should roofs and walls be as lightweight as possible?
6. What are two requirements of floors and work surfaces?
7. Where are nonsparking floors and work surfaces required?

C. This excerpt lists the specifications for a car stereo system.

Specifications

Audio Amplifier Section

Maximum Power Output	8 watts per channel
Continuous Power Output	3 watts per channel into 4 ohms, 100–20,000 Hz at no more than 0.8% T.H.D.
Load Impedance	4 (4 Ω –8 Allowable)
Tone Control Range (Bass)	$\pm$ 10dB at 100Hz
(Treble)	$\pm$ 10dB at 10KHz
Frequency Response	40–20,000 Hz
S/N Ratio	60 dB

Radio Section

Frequency Range (FM)	87.5−108.0 MHz
(AM)	530−1,620 KHz
(FM TUNER)	
Usable Sensitivity	17.2 dBf (2.0uV/75)
50 dB Quieting Sensitivity	19.5 dBf (2.6uV/75)
Alternate Channel Selectivity	65 dB
(400KHz)	
Frequency Response	40−15,000 Hz
Stereo Separation	30 dB
Capture Ratio	2.0 dB
(AM TUNER)	
Sensitivity	20 uV
Selectivity	35 dB

Cassette Deck Section

Wow & Flutter	0.15% (W.RMS)
FF & REW Time	130 sec (C−60)
Frequency Response	50−13,000Hz($\pm$3dB)
S/N Ratio	52 dB
Stereo Separation	40 dB

General

Power Requirement Operating Voltage	DC 14.4V (11−16V Allowance)
Grounding System	Negative Ground
Dimensions (W × H × D)	
Chassis	178 × 50 × 130 mm
	(7 × 2 × 5⅛ in)
Nosepiece	105 × 42 × 35 mm
	(4⅛ × 1¹¹⁄₁₆ × 1⅜ in)
Control Shaft Pitch	130 mm (5⅛ in), 140 mm (5½ in),
	148 mm (5¹³⁄₁₆ in)
	—6-Position Allowable—
Gross Weight	1.6 kg (3.6 lb)

Write down the answers to these questions.

1. How many major divisions are there in the specifications? Name them.
2. What is the Bass Tone Control Range? Treble Tone Control Range?
3. What is the signal to noise (S/N) ratio of the audio amplifier? The cassette deck?
4. What is the AM frequency range of the stereo?
5. What is the usable sensitivity of the FM tuner?
6. How long does it take to rewind (REW) the cassette tape.
7. What are the dimensions of the chassis in millimeters? In inches?
8. What is the gross weight of the system in kilograms? In pounds?

D. This excerpt is from procedures that explain how to clean glassware in a medical laboratory.

Cleaning of Routine Glassware

1. Collect dirty glassware at a designated collection point in the blood banking section of the laboratory until an appropriate lull in the day's work allows time for it to be cleaned.

2. Transport glassware to a sink in the laboratory and rinse with cold running tap water until all serum and blood clots are removed. Scrub the glassware with a soft hair or synthetic nylon brush. During this procedure the blood clots are collected in a beaker and then discarded. (NOTE: Steel brushes and abrasives erode and scratch glass and should not be used in cleaning.)

3. Soak all glassware in hot detergent solution overnight. The solution is hot at the outset of the soaking period but cools to room temperature during the soaking process.

4. The following morning, rinse the tubes three times in cold running tap water and once in distilled water.

5. Place the tubes in wire baskets and put in a drying oven at 100–120°C for 3 hours.

6. Remove from the oven, cool, and replace in proper drawers, cabinets, and racks in the blood bank section of the laboratory. At this point, equipment which requires sterilization should be prepared for that procedure.

7. At regular intervals routine glassware should be soaked in sulfuric acid potassium dichromate solution and given a thorough cleansing. The pipette tips should be tipped up and kept up throughout the cleaning process.

Write the answers to these questions.

1. Where should dirty glassware be collected?
2. How should serum and blood clots be removed?
3. How long should the glassware soak in the detergent solution?
4. After the soaking, how many times should the tubes be rinsed in cold tap water?
5. How long should the tubes be placed in the drying oven? How hot should the oven be?
6. How often should routinely used glassware be soaked in sulfuric acid potassium dichromate solution?

Informal Technical Description

Application 1:
Revising the Informal Technical Description

The technical description shown on the next page was intended for students enrolled in a criminal justice curriculum. Read it carefully, and then see if you can draw a sketch of the item described from the information given. What is missing from the description? What are the errors in format and usage? Be prepared to discuss your evaluation of the description in class.

Intoxilyzer 4011 AS

The Intoxilyzer 4011 AS measures the alcohol in a person's breath by detecting the decrease in intensity of infrared energy by passing light through the breath sample. It weighs 20 pounds, is 20 by 5 inches in size at the base, and stands 9 inches to the top. The Intoxilyzer 4011 AS is made up of hard steel and painted black. The Intoxilyzer 4011 AS consists of six major parts: on/off switch, zero adjust knob, mode select knob, breath tube, pump tube, and digital display.

The zero adjust knob is round and ½ by 1 inches in size. The zero adjust knob is black at the base and it has a silver top. This knob also depresses allowing movement of numbers in the digital display from the negative or positive position.

The on/off switch is located on the face of the Intoxilyzer 4011 AS. It is about ½ inch long and made of steel. The on/off switch is a two-position toggle switch that applies AC power to the instrument.

The mode select knob is made and designed the same as the zero adjust knob. The only difference is it does not depress. It is a rotary switch that selects the mode of operation for the instrument. The four positions are zero set, air blank, breath, and calibrate.

The breath tube is about 20 inches long and 1/4 inch in diameter. The tube is made out of reinforced plastic and is grayish in color. The breath tube is located at the base on the left-hand side of the instrument. This tube is what the subject actually blows his or her breath into. This tube is stored within the instrument when not in use.

The pump tube is about 12 inches long by 1.4 inch in diameter. The pump tube is made out of clear plastic. It is located right beside the breath tube. It is connected to the internal air pump. It is used to purge the sample cell and perform calibration tests.

The digital display is located on the face of the Intoxilyzer 4011 AS. It is 1½ inches in length and 1 inch in width. When the instrument is turned on the digital display is luminous. The digital display is a three-digit numeric read-out with a decimal point in front of the first digit.

Application 2:
Writing the Informal Technical Description

Write an informal technical description of a piece of equipment, tool, or instrument used in your field of study. Specify the intended audience. Before you begin your draft, fill in the plan sheet, and make a rough sketch of the item, labeling those parts you plan to discuss.

Informal Technical Instructions

Application 1:
Revising Informal Technical Instructions

The instructions on page 304 were written for students training to be medical laboratory technicians. Revise them based on the plan sheet in this chapter. First, identify and number the steps. (There are nine.) Then, mark out any unnecessary words.

How to Take a Blood Sample

Taking a blood sample is a procedure used to draw blood for analysis by a laboratory technician. Although it is a fairly easy task, you should have some knowledge of the needle and syringe and its use. Before taking a sample, you need a small rubber hose, some alcohol-soaked cotton balls, and a needle and syringe and you should explain to the patient what you are planning to do. First, tie the rubber hose (tourniquet) on the patient's arm approximately three inches above the elbow. With the arm straightened out and extended, have the patient tighten his fist. (WARNING: If the patient has long nails, give him a small object such as a wadded tissue to grasp.) Next, locate the protruding vein with your forefinger. After you have found the vein, cleanse the area with a cotton ball. Then inject the needle into the vein. (WARNING: Be sure not to inject the needle completely through the vein.) Pull back on the plunger with your thumb until 10 cc's of blood are in the syringe. Loosen the tourniquet with your free hand and place an alcohol-soaked cotton ball over the needle and vein and remove the needle from the vein. Finally, tell the patient to bend his elbow up tightly to prevent unnecessary bleeding. After performing these steps, put the blood in a test tube with the donor's name on the label and take the tube to the laboratory where prescribed tests are made.

Application 2:
Writing Informal Technical Instructions

Write informal technical instructions for a process or procedure used in your field of study. Specify the intended audience. Before you begin your draft, fill in the plan sheet.

Technical Description
Plan Sheet

BEGINNING SECTION

Item: Brand Name and Model Number

Sentence Definition:

Overall Dimensions: Height: Weight:

Shape:

Color:

Material:

Unusual Qualities:

Parts: The _____ has _____

major parts: _____,_____,_____,

_____,_____.

Drawing of item:
(Use separate sheet of paper.)

PARTS

Each part is described in a paragraph. Add or delete sections as necessary.

			Material (Texture) (Color)	Location
Part 1	Function	Size	Material (Texture) (Color)	Location
Part 2	Function	Size	Material (Texture) (Color)	Location
Part 3	Function	Size	Material (Texture) (Color)	Location

Part 4	Function	Size	Material (Texture) (Color)	Location

Part 5	Function	Size	Material (Texture) (Color)	Location

ENDING SECTION: OPERATION

Parts work together in the following way:

Technical Instructions
Plan Sheet

BEGINNING SECTION

Name of Process:

Sentence definition of process (if necessary):

Theory of operation (if applicable):

Purpose:

Importance:

Special skills or knowledge needed:

Tools and equipment needed:
Preparations:

STEPS

Steps are listed sequentially. They are stated as direct commands. Include notes, warnings, and drawings as necessary.

1.

2.

3.

4.

5.

6.

7.

8.

9.

10.

11.

12.

ENDING SECTION: SUMMARY

Write a statement summing up the process.

13

APPLYING FOR THE JOB

In this chapter, you should learn how to apply for a job. You should learn the following steps:

> Writing the résumé
>   Arrangement of information
>   Types of information
> Writing the letter of application
> Filling out the application for employment
>   General information
>   Personal data
>   Education and training
>   Work history
>   References
> Following up

Applying for a job requires you to find a company which needs your services and for which you wish to work. Many resources are available to help in your search for the ideal employer. Help-wanted ads appear in local newspapers and in technical and trade journals. The Employment Security Commission lists many jobs available, and the student service offices at technical colleges frequently help students find appropriate positions. Instructors and classmates also are excellent sources of information. Once you have found an available opening, you can begin the application process. In this chapter, we will explain how to write a résumé and letter of application, fill out an application form, and follow up on the application.

WRITING THE RÉSUMÉ

A résumé is a formal document used to present qualifications for employment to a prospective employer. When sent with a letter of application, the résumé, also called a personal record or data sheet, is often your introduction to an employer. It is used by the potential employer as a screening tool to determine which applicants will be called for an interview. It is very important, then, to prepare a good résumé before you begin to look for a job.

The résumé contains personal data and information about your education, work experience, and references. In its final perfect form, it may be copied so that it does not have to be retyped each time it is sent out. Once copies on high-quality bond paper are made, one is included in each letter of application for employment. You should also keep a copy of the résumé in your wallet for help in filling out application forms.

Arrangement of Information

Many types of arrangements may be used for a résumé. Information about your education and work or volunteer experience should be arranged so that your best qualifications are emphasized.

Arrangement 1. The most common technique for arranging a résumé is to provide a detailed explanation of previous employment and education. This information is presented in two separate sections. Applicants with no previous employment in the field should describe their education first so that a prospective employer can see immediately that they are well trained for the position. Applicants with extensive work experience should discuss their employment history first. The information in both sections is arranged in reverse chronological order. The most recent job should appear at the beginning of the section discussing employment history. The most recent degree or certification should appear at the beginning of the section discussing education. Several examples of this arrangement are shown later in the chapter.

Arrangement 2. Another technique that may be used in arranging the résumé is to divide experience and education into skills areas. In this type of presentation, the information is presented in broad headings such as "Organization," "Supervision," "Leadership," "Maintenance," and "Operation." This arrangement allows applicants to emphasize particular strengths and skills that would not be easily seen in any other format. It is often effective for applicants with several years of work experience in various positions. It also is a good technique for applicants with very little paid work experience but a great deal of volunteer experience, such as involvement in local hospitals and youth and senior citizen programs. This arrangement is particularly useful to women who have not been employed but who have been active in the community. Figure 13-1 shows a résumé of a woman who has worked at a paid job only briefly but who has done much volunteer work.

```
                          DATA SHEET
                              OF
                        CAROLYN SEAWELL
                       3639 EDENTON STREET
               SANFORD, NORTH CAROLINA  27330
                         (919-362-4700)

Objective:   Entry-level position as a digital electronics technician.

                          EDUCATION

Smithville Technical College, P.O. Box 1679, Smithville, NC  26639

Diploma:  Digital Electronics Repair, 1985

Special courses at Smithville Technical College:  Accounting I, 1971;
Accounting II, 1971; Marketing, 1972; English Composition, 1972;
Technical Math I, 1973.

Sanford Senior High School, 2713 Broad Street, Sanford, NC  27330

Diploma:  College Preparatory Program, 1970

                       WORK EXPERIENCE

Clerk/typist, Phillips Hardware Store, 326 Broad Street, Sanford, NC
27330.  June 1970 - December 1972.  Responsible for general office
work, answering telephones and typing business letters.

                    SUPERVISORY EXPERIENCE

Girl Scout leader, NC Council of Girl Scouts, Sanford, NC
September 1978 - September 1984.  Responsible for leadership of twelve
Girl Scouts for six years.  Arranged field trips, taught lessons,
guided in earning badges.

Member, Women's Auxiliary, Sanford Memorial Hospital, Sanford, NC
December 1980 - January 1982.  Responsible for running hospital gift
shop three days each week.  Purchased supplies, supervised two paid
clerks, and handled accounting for gift shop.

Volunteer, Hopeline, Sanford, NC July 1979 - November 1980.
Responsible for answering telephones and referring potential suicide
victims to appropriate personnel and agencies.

                       CLUB ACTIVITIES

Member and Vice President, Women's Club of Sanford, Sanford, NC
August 1974 - present.  Participated in Women's Club activities.  As
Vice-President, responsible for planning all monthly program
presentations.

Coach, Phillips Hardware Softball Team, June 1970 - December 1972.
Responsible for obtaining funds for uniforms and transportation and
scheduling all softball games.

                         REFERENCES

Furnished on request.
```

Figure 13-1:   Résumé Emphasizing Volunteer Experience

Arrangement 3.   A third technique for arranging the résumé is to have a one-page abbreviated summary of work and educational history attached to an expanded discussion of duties and responsibilities. The abbreviated format allows an employer to check quickly the applicant's work and educational history. Then the employer can read the more detailed information if the candidate seems appropriate for the job. This résumé format is used only by individuals who have had a great deal of work experience. Figure 13-2 shows an example of this arrangement. Notice that the first page briefly mentions relevant work experience and education. The second and third pages give the details.

Types of Information

The following sections discuss the eight types of information found on résumés: heading, goals and objectives, work experience, education, awards, honors, memberships in professional or civic organizations, special licenses, and references.

Heading.   The heading is placed at the top of the page. It includes your full name, your current address, and your telephone number with the area code.

Goals and Objectives.   The objective states the position you are applying for. Examples are "Entry-Level Position for Management Trainee," "Position as First-Class Instrument and Control Technician," or "Executive Secretary."

Work Experience or Employment History.   The section on work experience includes a short description of current and past jobs. It lists previous employers, their addresses, the dates of employment, and the positions held. It also has a brief job description or a discussion of the duties and responsibilities of each position. The work experience section begins with the job last held and moves backward in time from that point. A series of part-time or temporary jobs may be grouped under a section called "Part-Time Employment" or "Summer Employment."

Educational Data or Academic Preparation.   The section on educational data or academic preparation lists educational institutions you have attended and the addresses. It also includes dates of attendance, the type of degree received, the date it was received, the major course of study, and possibly some mention of specialized training. The last school you attended is named first, and the dates are listed backward in time. You should not list degrees further back than high school or GED. This section may also mention special courses that do not lead directly to a degree or special schools, such as military schools or management training programs.

Awards and Honors.   Awards and honors, such as membership in the National Honor Society, Dean's List at your school, Student of the Year award, and

DAVID M. LEVY
P.O. Box 1193
Cary, North Carolina 27511
919 469-2634

RELEVANT EMPLOYMENT

ORGANIZATION AND SUPERVISION

Supervisor, Instrumentation and Control – Training and Qualification
Program Development Group, Carolina Power and Light Company,
New Hill, North Carolina, 1984–1985

Lead Instructor, Instrumentation and Control Training Group –
Consumers Power Company, Midland, Michigan, 1981–1982

Lead Electrical Operator – Navy Nuclear Prototype (S8G) Ballston Spa,
New York, 1980–1981

OPERATIONS AND MAINTENANCE

Electrical Operator – Navy Nuclear Prototype (S8G) Ballston Spa,
New York, 1978–1981

Electrical Operator and Engineering Laboratory Technician – USS
Hawkbill (SSN 666) Western Pacific, 1975–1978

TRAINING

Nuclear Instructor – Midland Plant Training Department, Consumers
Power Company, Midland, Michigan, 1982–1984

RELEVANT EDUCATION

MILITARY TRAINING

Navy Nuclear Power School, 1975
Engineering Laboratory Technician School, 1975

PROFESSIONAL TRAINING

Instrumentation and Controls, General Physics Corporation, 1982
Bailey 820 School, Bailey Controls Corporation, 1982
Foxboro SPEC 200 School, Foxboro Corporation, 1982

ACADEMIC

Completed Freshman year at University of Kentucky, Lexington, 1971

Figure 13-2: Expanded Résumé

Expanded Resume: DAVID M. LEVY

EMPLOYMENT

ORGANIZATION AND SUPERVISION

Supervisor, Instrumentation and Control - Training and Qualification Program Development Group - Carolina Power and Light Company, New Hill, North Carolina, 1984-1985. Directed a four-person team in developing Job Task Analysis, Qualification Criteria, Training Needs Analysis, and Training Materials for CP&L Nuclear Instrumentation and Control Technicians at three nuclear power plants.

Lead Instructor, Instrumentation and Control Training Group - Consumers Power Company, Midland, Michigan, 1981-1982. Established goals and action plans for the I&C training group during the establishment of a nuclear training center for three nuclear plants.

Lead Electrical Operator - Navy Nuclear Prototype (S8G), Ballston Spa, New York, 1980-1981. Supervised a shift electrical group for operations, maintenance, and production training.

OPERATIONS AND MAINTENANCE

Electrical Operator - Navy Nuclear Prototype (S8G), Ballston Spa, New York, 1978-1981. Staff electrical operator during final phases of plant construction and acceptance testing.

Electrical Operator and Engineering Laboratory Technician - USS Hawkbill (SSN 666), Western Pacific, 1975-1978. Qualified electrical and mechanical areas for operations and maintenance of propulsion plant. Performed chemistry monitoring of primary and secondary systems. Performed radiological control functions for plant operations and maintenance.

TRAINING

Nuclear Instructor - Midland Plant Training Department, Consumers Power Company, Midland, Michigan, 1982-1984. Developed and conducted training in the areas of safety, plant systems, and instrumentation and controls. Designed laboratory trainers for FOXBORO SPEC and BAILEY 820 control systems with interconnection capabilities to the QUINTECH training system.

Figure 13-2: *continued*

DAVID M. LEVY
Page 2

EDUCATION

MILITARY TRAINING

Solid State Generator Regulator School, 1977
Variable Speed Motor Control School, 1977
Engineering Laboratory Technician School, 1975
Navy Nuclear Power School, 1975
Navy Electricians Mate "A" School, 1973

PROFESSIONAL TRAINING

Management By Objectives, Consumers Power Company, 1983
Foxboro SPEC 200 School, Foxboro Corporation, 1983
Understanding Microprocessors, Movanics Corporation, 1983
Digital Troubleshooting, Movanics Corporation, 1983
Bailey 820 School, Bailey Controls Corporation, 1982
Diesel Generator Controls, Transamerica Delaval, 1982
Design for Results (JTA and training material design),
    Consumers Power Company, 1982
Instrumentation and Controls, General Physics Corporation, 1982

ACADEMIC

Completed Freshman year at University of Kentucky, Lexington, 1971

Figure 13-2: *continued*

athletic honors or letters, are included in this section. The award or honor, the place received, and the date are listed.

Organizations.   This section describes your membership in professional and civic organizations. These organizations include business or social fraternities, student government associations, and professional organizations or clubs. The names of the organizations, the dates of membership, and any offices held are listed.

Special Licenses and Certifications.   This section lists licenses or certifications, such as an FCC license, certified automotive technician, or registered nurse. The section identifies the license, the date of issuance, and the certifying agency.

References.   In the past, résumés listed names, positions, and professional addresses of three individuals who could attest to the applicant's character and ability. Recently, most résumés have replaced this list with a statement that references will be furnished upon request. Whether you list references on your résumé or not, you should consult these people before forwarding their names to companies.

Figures 13-3 and 13-4 show typical résumés. Figure 13-3 shows a résumé in which education is most important. Figure 13-4 on page 318 shows a résumé in which work experience is most important.

WRITING THE LETTER OF APPLICATION

The letter of application is a business letter which explains or "covers" the résumé. It discusses classroom training and work experiences that may be especially relevant to the employer. It is a sales letter, intending to persuade the company that you are the best person for the job. Before you write your letter, you should research the job and the company. The more you know about the job, the better you will be able to point out how your education and experience qualify you for the position. Researching the company also lets you decide if you really want to apply for the job. Advice about how to research a company and a job is found in Chapter 14. As you conduct your research, find out the name of an individual to address your letter to rather than sending it to a box number. This specific routing will ensure that the letter reaches the correct destination. The letter of application follows the rules for business correspondence.

Regardless of your qualifications, most companies are not willing to hire new employees without a face-to-face meeting. Therefore, the purpose of the letter of application is to request an interview. Since the receiver of your letter is not obligated to grant you an interview, the letter is organized in an indirect plan. The request for the interview is in the last paragraph. Here are some guidelines for writing the letter of application.

```
Resume of William David Johnson
         2727 East Lane Street
         Winston-Salem, NC  27106
         919-633-6464

Objective: Position as an Air Conditioning/Heating Technician
           with a large firm.

                          EDUCATION


1984-1985  Forsyth Technical College, 4713 Guess Road
           Winston-Salem, NC  27107

           Diploma: Air Conditioning, Heating, and Refrigeration

1980-1983  Forsyth Consolidated High School, Winston-Salem, NC 27106


                       WORK EXPERIENCE


1983-1985  Stock and checkout clerk, Wiggins grocery, 2306 Main Street,
           Winston-Salem, NC  27106.  Responsible for stocking shelves
           and serving as a checkout clerk 25 hours per week after school
           and on weekends.


1981-1983  Busboy, Freddy's Fast Foods, 316 Raleigh Avenue,
           Winston-Salem, NC 27106.  Responsible for cleaning tables 20
           hours per week after school and on weekends.


                    ACTIVITIES AND HONORS


1985  Dean's List, Forsyth Technical College

1984  President, DECA Club, Forsyth Consolidated High School

1984  Member, Amateur Radio Club, Forsyth Consolidated High School


                          REFERENCES


Furnished on request.
```

Figure 13-3: Résumé Emphasizing Education

ROSCOE WOODARD
1001 Mountford Avenue
Raleigh, NC 27603
919 828-9364

Employment

October 1979 to   Baker Heating and Air Conditioning Company
March 1982   Highway 42 West, Wilson, NC 27839
                   Supervisor: George Baker
                   Position: Sheet Metal Mechanic
                   • Installed heat-vent and air-conditioning
                     systems
                   • Installed and set plenums, turning vanes,
                     and duct work
                   • Installed and set air-handling units
                   • Wired controls
                   • Tested equipment

August 1974 to   Evans Heating and Air Conditioning Company
September 1979   1204 Downing Street, Wilson, NC 27839
                   Supervisor: Fred King
                   Position: Heat and Air Conditioning Mechanic
                   • Installed heat pumps
                   • Installed heaters and controls
                   • Troubleshot systems and made needed repairs
                   • Ran refrigeration lines

Military Experience

November 1968 to   United States Marine Corps
May 1979   Position: Industrial Maintenance Mechanic
                   • Maintained electrical and mechanical equipment
                   • Troubleshot mechanical and electrical systems
                     and made needed repairs
                   • Conducted preventative maintenance schedule

Education

September 1983 to Diploma: Industrial Maintenance, 1985
August 1985   Diploma: Electrical Installation and Maintenance, 1985
                   Certificates: Plumbing and Welding, 1984
                   Wake Technical College, Raleigh, NC 27603

February 1969 to   Certificate: Industrial Maintenance
August 1969   U.S. Marine Corps Engineers
                                  School, Camp Pendleton, CA 40549

HONORS AND ACHIEVEMENTS

    Deans List (3.5 GPA) Wake Technical College, 1983 - 1985

    Honorable Discharge, Sergeant, 1979

REFERENCES

    Furnished upon request

Figure 13-4: Résumé Emphasizing Work Experience

- Begin the letter by naming the position you are applying for and the way you found out about the position.

- In the second paragraph, point out items of educational interest that appear on the résumé. Mention the program you are enrolled in and the degree you will obtain. Include important course work that relates to the job you are applying for, and describe your skills using specialized machinery and equipment.

- In the third paragraph, explain how your work experience has qualified you to work for the company. Include this discussion of work experience whether or not the jobs are directly related to the job you are applying for. Prior work experience shows ambition and responsibility, especially if you have supported yourself. If the prior work experience is in the same field as the position applied for, relevant duties of the job should be discussed. If your work experience is particularly impressive, the order of the second and third paragraphs may be reversed.

- In the last paragraph, confidently summarize your qualifications for the position and request an appointment for an interview. You may also include the date you will be available for employment.

Figure 13-5 on page 320 shows a letter of application from a student with little relevant work experience. Figure 13-6 on page 321 shows a letter of application from someone with a great deal of work experience and recent formal training.

FILLING OUT THE APPLICATION FOR EMPLOYMENT

The application for employment is a form used by companies to document employee qualifications and past history. Some companies request that you fill out an application before an interview. Others have you fill it out when you come in for an interview. Once you are hired, the application is kept on file until you leave the company.

Filling out an application accurately and legibly is extremely important, for you are generally required to sign a statement that the information supplied is complete and true. Sometimes people have been rejected as potential employees because of careless errors or inadequate information supplied in their application forms. Most applications are divided into the same sections as the résumé: personal data, educational and work experience, and references. You should follow the guidelines stated below when you are filling out your application.

General Information

- Read the directions carefully and follow them.

- Answer truthfully. If a company is interested in hiring you, the references will be checked. If you have falsified the application, you will not be hired.

- Type the application if a typewriter is available. If you do not type it, be sure to use dark blue or black ink.

- When you are asked for addresses or locations of schools, references, and for-

Route 10, Box 12
Miami, Florida 33168
October 15, 1988

Brent Williamson
Personnel Director
Southern States Industries
4210 West Ninth Street
Miami, Florida 33169

Dear Mr. Williamson:

Please consider me for a position as a machinist with your company. Mr.
Don Chesson, my machinist instructor, informed me that you were planning
to conduct interviews next week and recommended that I send you a resume.

I will graduate from the Machine Shop Practices program at Dade Technical
College on November 14, 1988. While in school, I have taken courses in
all machine operations and worked on machinery common in industry as well
as small shops. The last three months of my schooling have allowed me to
work with new computer-operated machines. Also included in the
curriculum were courses in blueprint reading, communications skills, and
math.

My father has a small machine shop in the garage at our home. I have
worked with him throughout high school and during my breaks between
quarters at Dade Tech. In addition, I have been employed part time at
McDonald's as a busboy for the past two years to earn money for school.

Because of my classroom training and my work with my father, I believe
that I meet your requirements for the position and look forward to an
interview. I will be available for employment November 15, 1988.

                              Sincerely,

                              Russell Pappendick

                              Russell Pappendick

Enclosure: Resume

Figure 13-5: Letter of Application for Employment

2611 Church Lane
Media, PA 19063
January 11, 1988

Mr. Roger James, Personnel Director
Williams Engineering Corporation
Dept. R0111
P. O. Box 2193
Boston, MA 02106

Dear Mr. James:

According to your advertisement in the January 11, 1988, News and
Observer, you will soon be holding local interviews for positions at
your various project construction sites. I am particularly interested in employment as a Buyer or Quality Control Inspector.

I have almost 10 years of experience in the electrical field dealing
with electrical contractors and electrical equipment manufacturers. My
work experience includes building electrical apparatus from the initial
engineering blueprints, purchasing, and overseeing shipment to the job
site.

In addition to the experience I have gained while on the job, I have
just received my diploma in Electrical Installation and Maintenance
Program from Media Technical College. This one year program has
provided me with classroom training equivalent to that of a journeyman
electrician.

Based on my prior knowledge of electrical construction and my diploma
from Media Tech, I am confident that I qualify for the position of
either Buyer or Quality Control Inspector. I am enclosing a copy of my
resume covering my complete work experience and educational background
for your consideration. Please include my name on your list of
applicants when you schedule interviews for these positions.

Sincerely,

Dennis L. Reed

Dennis L. Reed

Enclosure

Figure 13-6: Letter of Application for Employment

mer places of employment, give the street, city, state, and zip code. Since a prospective employer may write letters to find out more about you, you should provide appropriate and correct addresses. It is very irritating to a personnel director to have a request for information returned because of an incorrect address that you have provided. This carelessness can cause delays in the hiring process and keep you from being considered for employment.

○ If you make an error in filling out the application, erase the error or mark through it with a single line, and write the correction in directly above or beside the error. If you make an error that is not easy to correct, get another application to fill out. Do not turn in a sloppy application form.

○ Do not leave blank spaces on the application. The blank implies that you have overlooked the space. If a question does not apply to you, write in "does not apply" or "not applicable." If you come across an entire section that does not apply to you, write "does not apply" in the first blank of the section. You do not need to repeat "does not apply" in every space.

○ When an application asks for a specific job title, state one such as "machinist," "clerk-typist," "medical laboratory technician," "chemical engineering technician."

Personal Data

○ You are not required by law to answer personal questions, such as those about age, race, sex, religious preference, and marital status. In most instances these questions no longer appear on company applications or employment forms. When they do appear, answer them as you choose. However, many businesses will not process your application if all questions are not answered.

○ Fill in your full name. Do not use initials unless you are requested to do so.

○ Give a permanent address and a mailing address. If the two addresses are not the same, be sure to fill in both blanks. If they are the same, all you need to write is "Same as above" in the permanent address blank.

Education and Training

○ Give the names and addresses of the schools you have attended and the dates of attendance. The date usually includes the month and year.

○ Identify the type of degree you hold. Usually degrees are divided into four categories: certificates for any program of study less than a year; diplomas for programs of study lasting a year; associate degrees for programs lasting two to three years; and bachelor's degrees for programs lasting four years.

○ State your major, your primary course of study. Examples are Nursing, Computer Technology, Electronics Servicing, Secretarial Science. If there is a section entitled "minor," write N/A in the blank.

○ If necessary, state your grade point average and the grade point average base. For example, you might have a 3.24 GPA on a base of 4.0.

○ When the company asks you to list special courses, fields of work for which you are licensed, registered, or certified, or machines you are able to operate, be sure to fill these blanks in even though all of your answers may not apply to the job you are seeking. Information of this type serves to distinguish you from other individuals applying for the same position and shows special skills and knowledge that you have. You do not need to list all the courses in your program of study; but if you have taken extra course work, extension courses, or correspondence courses, list them. Do not list such machines as car or lawn mower that are pieces of equipment most people can operate, but do list such equipment as bulldozer, milling machine, oscilloscope that most people are unfamiliar with.

Work History

- Under the heading "Current or Last Employer," fill in the name of the company you are working for or have worked for, not the name of your supervisor or the personnel director. Usually, the form will have another space for the name of your supervisor.

- Often you are asked to state the salary you were paid when you entered employment with a company and the salary you were earning when you left. Providing information about previous salaries always poses a problem. You may have been earning more in your former job than the company you are interviewing with is willing to pay, or you may have been earning a salary much lower than the company had planned to pay you. You may leave the spaces blank, you may fill them in accurately, or you may give a range that your salary falls in. If you do not fill in the salary, you run the risk of not having your application processed.

- You are also sometimes asked to write in the salary you will accept if you are employed by the company. Prepare yourself to answer this question before you fill out the application or go in for an interview. You can usually find out the pay scale for persons in your field by calling the Employment Security Commission, checking the help-wanted section of the local newspaper, or talking with your curriculum instructor.

- On most applications, you will be asked the reason you had for leaving previous jobs. Write "fired" only if you were. Usually people resign or are asked to resign. Some more acceptable and typical reasons for leaving a job include "moving to another location," "split shift," "better opportunity," "go to school." If you are still employed at a company, state "currently employed" or "presently employed."

References

When you are asked to list references, you are usually limited in the names of people you may enter. Generally your employer is trying to find out about your character and abilities. Therefore, you should list teachers, guidance counselors, older friends of yours or your family, or your minister. Do not list relatives or close friends. Before you put anyone's name down, be sure to get permission.

Figure 13-7 on pages 324–326 shows a typical application blank. Notice that it is long and requires you to provide specific information, including information about your health.

C. C. MANGUM, INC.

ccm
Since 1927
Raleigh, N.C.
GRADING · PAVING

APPLICATION FOR EMPLOYMENT

Position
Desired: _____

Salary Expected: _____ Referred by: _____

Availability Date _____ Regular _____ Part Time _____

EQUAL EMPLOYMENT OPPORTUNITY

C. C. Mangum, Inc. is an equal opportunity employer. All conditions of employment are adminis-
tered without regard to race, sex, color, age, religion or national origin.

C. C. Mangum, Inc. adheres to an approved affirmative action policy which will employ and advance qualified disabled veterans, veterans of the Vietnam Era and Handicapped persons. This
Affirmative Action Program is voluntary and all information shall be kept confidential and used
only in accordance with Section 402 of the Vietnam Era Veterans Readjustment Assistance
Act of 1974 and Section 503 of the Rehabilitation Act of 1973.

Any refusal to provide this information will not result in any adverse treatment of your application or employment. If you would like to benefit under this program, please check one:

Disabled Veteran _____ Vietnam Era Veteran _____ Handicapped _____

Are you at least 18 years old? _____ 21 years old? _____

Are you a United States Citizen? _____

If not a U. S. Citizen, do you hold a valid work permit? ___ _____

EDUCATION AND TRAINING

	Name	City & State	Major/ Course	Dates Attended	Degree Obtained	Class Standing
High School or Equivalent						
College						
Graduate						
Other						

LIST ANY OTHER SKILLS, TECHNICAL TRAINING, OR PROFESSIONAL CERTIFICATES.

_____

SPECIAL ACTIVITIES — Include: High school, college, community activities, memberships in professional
societies and associations. **Exclude:** Any organization which may reveal race, creed, color or national origin.

_____
_____

FORM 81-16 CCM REV. 7/84   Pittman Printing Co. — Raleigh, N.C.

Name _____
Last

Address _____
Number   First   Street   Middle

City _____   Date _____
State _____   Mo   Day   Yr
Zip _____

Social Security No. _____

Telephone No. _____
(where you can be reached)

Previous addresses within last three years

Address
City
County
State
Zip

Address
City
County
State
Zip

OFFICE USE ONLY

Reporting Date _____

Classification _____

Rate of Pay _____ HRLY _____ WKLY

Figure 13-7: Application for Employment

Do you have a North Carolina Driver's License?   YES☐   NO☐

Driver's License Number _____ Expiration Date _____

Chauffeur's License Number _____ Expiration Date _____

Has your license ever been revoked or suspended?   YES☐   NO☐

If "YES", explain _____

In what other states have you held an operator's license? _____

State _____ License Number _____

State _____ License Number _____

Have you ever had a surety bond?   YES☐   NO☐

Cancelled? _____

Refused? _____

Have you ever been convicted of a crime?   YES☐   NO☐

If "YES" explain _____

Have you received Unemployment benefits within the last 60 days?   YES☐   NO☐

Have you received Social Security benefits within the last 60 days?   YES☐   NO☐

If "YES", explain _____

Have you ever received worker's compensation benefits?   YES☐   NO☐

What is the longest period of time you have missed from work due to sickness or injury? _____

EMPLOYMENT HISTORY

List below the names of all former employers. Begin with most recent employer and work back. Include U. S. military service.

FROM Mo./Yr.	TO Mo./Yr.	EMPLOYER NAME & ADDRESS	TYPE OF BUSINESS	NAME & TITLE OF SUPERVISOR	BRIEF JOB DESCRIPTION	SALARY	REASON FOR LEAVING/DISCHARGE

LIST ALL VEHICLE ACCIDENTS INVOLVED IN DURING THE PAST THREE YEARS.

NATURE OF ACCIDENT	DATE	ANY INJURY OR FATALITIES?

LIST ALL VIOLATIONS OF MOTOR VEHICLE LAWS OR ORDINANCES (OTHER THAN PARKING) FOR WHICH YOU WERE CONVICTED OR FORFEITED BOND OR COLLATERAL FOR LAST THREE YEARS.

Employees may be asked to accept assignments at other work locations when required.

I understand that misrepresentation in this application will justify cancellation of this application, or dismissal if hired. If I am employed, it will be for a specified trial period. Permission is granted to C. C. Mangum, Inc. to verify any statement herein contained.

ACKNOWLEDGEMENT

_____   Signature of Applicant _____   Date _____

Interviewed by _____   Dept. _____   Date _____

Figure 13-7:   *continued*

Pre-Placement Medical Questionnaire

C.C. MANGUM, INC

Restricted and Confidential Information

Name	Date	City	State & Zip

Street Address

Position Applied For	Department

	Yes	No
1. Do you have impaired hearing or any speech difficulty which might affect the use of the telephone or transcribing equipment?	☐	☐
2. Do you have impaired vision that eye glasses do not correct?	☐	☐
3. Have you had a contagious disease in the past two weeks?	☐	☐
4. Do you have chronic bronchitis, recurrent asthma, or any other lung disease which requires special work areas?	☐	☐
5. Are you taking any medication or injections on a regular basis which might have an effect on specific job assignments?	☐	☐
6. Do you have a recurring skin disorder or sensitive skin which would prevent you from working with certain materials (for example, carbon paper, cleaning fluids, detergents)?	☐	☐
7. Do you have any muscle weakness, paralysis, back disorder, or deformity that might have an effect on specific job assignments?	☐	☐
8. Have you ever been told you had an abnormal heart or needed treatment for heart disease or high blood pressure?	☐	☐
9. Within the past three months, have you had any problems with your internal organs (for example, kidney, bladder, prostate, uterus, or heart)?	☐	☐
10. Within the last six months, have you suffered from dizzy spells, black outs, fainting, or convulsions?	☐	☐
11. Have you any emotional disorder, learning disability, or excessive fear which might prevent you from working in certain situations or locations?	☐	☐
12. Is any special treatment or surgical operation planned in the near future?	☐	☐
13. Do you have any handicaps which could cause you difficulty in a specific task or require special accommodations in your work environment?	☐	☐

C.C. Mangum, Inc. is a government contractor subject to Section 503 of the Rehabilitation Act of 1973. We are committed to hiring qualified handicapped individuals. If you have a physical or mental impairment which substantially limits your activities, please tell us. Also, we'd like to know about any work you cannot perform because of your handicap and any accommodations we can make to help you perform your work satisfactorily and safely. The law does not require you to share this information.

I certify that all the information I have given in this questionnaire is accurate and complete.

Signed _____Date_____

Interviewer: _____

Examination Waived ☐   Examination Necessary ☐

Interviewer's Signature_____

Form 81-18 CCM   Pittman Printing Co.—Raleigh, N.C

Figure 13-7: *continued*

FOLLOWING UP

If you have not heard from a company approximately two weeks after mailing a letter of application for employment, call the personnel director, and ask about the status of the position you applied for. Indicate that you would like to come in for an interview, and be prepared to state times you would be available. Again, sell yourself. Let the personnel director know that you are still interested in the job and believe that you could be a good employee. The telephone call serves as a polite reminder to the personnel director that you are available. It will also often get you in for an interview.

SUMMARY

Applying for a job usually requires you to prepare a résumé, to write a letter of application, and to fill in an application blank. A résumé is a formal summary of experience, education, awards and honors, organizations and activities, licenses, and references. The letter of application, which accompanies the résumé, "covers" the résumé and points out items of special interest to the potential employer. The job application is the formal document kept on file by the company to attest to your qualifications to do the job. Like the résumé, it is a record of your important qualifications.

ASSIGNMENTS

The Résumé

Application 1:
Revising a Résumé

Revise the résumé shown here. Use the plan sheet from this chapter as a guide. Consider whether or not you would call the individual for an interview.

Résumé of
Edward Lee Wilson
919-773-0661

Objective: To become maintenance director of a medium-sized company.

Education:

1. I have attended Alamance Community Technical College for two years. I have a certificate in plumbing and a certificate in welding and a diploma in EIM and a diploma in Industrial Maintenance. 1983-1985

2. I graduated from Alamance Senior High School in 1983.

Experience:

1983-1985 Cook at Big Boy's Drive-In. Responsible for all fast-food preparation and keeping the kitchen cleaned up on second shift.
1982 Life guard at the Alamance County Public Swimming pool for 3 months.
1981 Changed tires part time at Phillips Tire Center for one month.
1981 Pumped gas at Quick Market for one month.
1981 Cleaned up at Smith's Super Market for two months.
1980 Stacked shelves at Smith's Super Market for three months.
Hunting and Fishing are my favorite hobbies.

Awards:

I won a letter for the Soccer Team and for the football team my senior year at Almance Senior High School.
I was a member of the OECA club and a Student Government Member.
Dean's List at Alamance Community Technical College in Plumbing.

Application 2:
Writing your Résumé

Based on what you have learned in this chapter, prepare a résumé that you could use if you were looking for a job. Begin by filling in the sections on the plan sheet that apply to you. Make sure that you have the correct dates and complete addresses for your employers and schools. Then transfer the information in your plan sheet to an unlined sheet of paper in the format in which you would like the résumé typed.

Letter of Application

Application 1:
Revising a Letter of Application

Revise the letter of application shown here. Use the plan sheet from this chapter and the Guidelines for Revision in Chapter 3. Would you call this individual for an interview? Why or why not?

> 2739 Hope Church Road
> Burlington, NC 27716
> July 18, 1988

Personnel Department
IRC Corporation
Box 27369
Winston-Salem, NC 27106

Dear Personnel Director:

I would like to apply for a job with your company. I heard that you had a lot of openings and I am going to graduate soon.

I have been at Alamance Community Technical College for the past two years. The first year I studied plumbing and welding. The second year I studied Electrical Installation and Maintenance so you can see there is a lot of stuff I can do to help you out at your company if you have a job that calls for my skills. I am sending you a résumé too.

I have worked at our local Big Boy Drive-In as a cook for two years while I have been in school so I know what hard work means and I'm not afraid to work hard.

Yours truly,

Ed Wilson

Application 2:
Locating a Job

Using any or all of the sources of job information mentioned at the beginning of the chapter, list three jobs in your area that you feel might be good prospects. Find out the name of the personnel director of the company and the correct company address.

Application 3:
Writing Your Letter of Application

Write a letter applying for one of the jobs you have located. Begin by filling in the plan sheet. Refer to jobs and courses of interest to the employer. Then transfer the information from your plan sheet to unlined paper. Refer to Chapter 11 to ensure that your letter follows the rules of business correspondence. Like the résumé, this letter will be typed.

Application for Employment

Application 1:
Obtaining Application Forms

Call three companies to whom you might consider applying for a job when you graduate and ask them to send you an application for employment. Some companies do not like to send out application forms if they do not plan to hire an individual, so it might be necessary to explain to them the reason for your request. After you receive the forms, note special problems that could arise if you were to fill each one out, and be prepared to discuss how you would go about completing the form with the class.

Application 2:
Filling Out Application Forms

Fill in the blank form shown in this chapter or one of those obtained in your previous assignment. Use dark blue or black ink. You may assume that you have graduated from your program. While you fill in the form, refer to the guidelines in this chapter. Check the form carefully before you submit it to your instructor.

Resume Plan Sheet

Resume
of
Your name in capital letters
Street address
City, State, Zip code
Area code   Telephone number

EDUCATIONAL HISTORY (Begin with your current or most recent degree)*

Name and address of college:

Dates of attendance:
Degree received:
Major course of study:

Relevant specialized training:
Name and address of high school or GED:

Dates attended:

Special Schools, Military Schools, Seminars

(If you need more space, use a separate sheet of paper.)
Name of school/seminar:
Sponsor:
Dates of attendance:

EMPLOYMENT HISTORY (Begin with your current or most recent job.)
(If you need more space, use a separate sheet of paper.)
Title of your position:
Name and address of company:
   (If extra space needed for address here and below, use an extra sheet
   of paper.)
Dates of employment:
Duties and responsibilities:

NOTE: Reverse the order of educational history and employment history if
employment is more impressive.

Title of your position:
Name and address of company:
Dates of employment:
Duties and responsibilities:

<u>Part-time Employment (if any)</u>
(If all your jobs have been part time, fill in the
top section under Employment History.)

Title of your position:
Name and address of company:
Dates of employment:

Title of your position:
Name and address of company:
Dates of employment:

AWARDS AND HONORS
(If you need more space, use a separate sheet of paper.)
Name of award:
Place received:
Date:

PROFESSIONAL ORGANIZATIONS AND CIVIC ORGANIZATIONS
(If you need more space, use a separate sheet of paper.)
Name of organization:
Dates of membership:

LICENSES
(If you need more space, use a separate sheet of paper.)
Name of license:
Issuing agency:
Date of issuance:

REFERENCES

Furnished on request.

Letter of Application for Employment
Plan Sheet

                                                        Heading

                                                        Date

Inside Address

Dear _____:

BEGINNING
    Name of position applied for:
    How you found out about opening:

EXPLANATION OF EDUCATION AND WORK EXPERIENCE*
    (Include only information that is relevant to the job you are applying for.)
    Degree, courses, projects, special schools:

    Equipment, machinery you can operate:

    Previous jobs:

    How previous jobs relate to position:

ENDING: STATEMENT OF REQUEST
    Reasons you feel qualified (summary):

    Request for interview:

    Date of availability for employment:

                                                        Yours truly,

                                                        _____

                                                        Your name

Enclosure

*NOTE: Reverse the order of employment and education if employment is
more impressive.

14

INTERVIEWING FOR THE JOB

When you complete this chapter, you should know how to interview successfully for a job. You should learn about the following topics:

Purpose of the interview
Forms of communication
  Verbal communication
  Nonverbal communication
Preparing for the interview
  Self-assessment
  Job assessment
  Company assessment
The interview process
Following up

If your letter of application and résumé are successful, you will be asked to interview for a job. The job interview offers you a chance to get acquainted with the company while the company also gets to know you. It is the second major task in the job search process. This chapter explains the purpose of the interview, effective forms of communication to use in the interview, preparation for the interview, phases of the interview, and follow up to the interview.

PURPOSE OF THE INTERVIEW

Most companies, particularly large ones, have established practices that they follow when hiring new employees. They generally advertise a position in trade journals and local newspapers and request the submission of a résumé by a specific date. After that date, the letters of application and résumés are reviewed. The four or five applicants with the most appropriate skills and experience are selected for interviews. The interview is a formal face-to-face meeting. It serves two purposes. First, it gives the company the opportunity to verify the technical qualifications listed on the résumé and to evaluate the applicant's personal qualities. Second, the interview gives the applicant the opportunity to evaluate the company as a potential employer.

The following qualities are usually assessed during an interview: appearance, enthusiasm, alertness, ability to communicate, confidence, poise, and sense of humor. Besides these qualities, interviewers evaluate a candidate's general knowledge, technical knowledge, use of proper grammar and diction, level of maturity, mannerisms, and personality. An individual's success in the interview depends on how well he or she shows the interviewer these qualities. Both verbal and nonverbal communication skills are important.

FORMS OF COMMUNICATION

As we explained in Chapter 1, communication may be verbal and nonverbal. Verbal communication includes speech and writing. Nonverbal communication includes appearance, facial expressions, gestures, posture, and tone and pitch of voice.

Verbal Communication

Your letter of application and your résumé have shown the company that you can express yourself in writing. The job interview gives you the opportunity to demonstrate your skills in spoken communication. The speaking skills used in a successful job interview are unique. In casual conversation with your friends, you do not need to consider word choice and diction. In a formal presentation, you have an opportunity to prepare in advance. The job interview is both casual and formal. You can prepare for some questions; but for others you cannot. A few general guidelines may make the interview easier and more successful.

- Answer questions honestly. If you do not know the answer to a question, admit your lack of knowledge. If the question concerns an important aspect of the job you are applying for, indicate your willingness to learn.
- Use the appropriate level of technical language. If the interviewer is as technically qualified as you, adjust your technical language to meet his or her expectations.

○ Choose your answers carefully. Answer questions accurately and completely. If necessary, pause briefly and get your thoughts in order before you blurt out an answer.

○ Avoid the use of slang and interrupting words such as "uh," "you know," "ok," and "See what I mean."

○ Use correct grammar and pronunciation. "Ain't" should not be used in job interviews.

○ Ask that a question be repeated if you do not fully understand it. Asking questions is better than rambling along with unrequested information.

Nonverbal Communication

Nonverbal communication is just as important as verbal communication in the interview process. Throughout the interview, the interviewer is watching your behavior as well as listening to what you have to say. Whether you are aware of it or not, you reveal a great deal about yourself through your appearance, facial expressions, gestures, posture, and tone and pitch of voice.

Appearance.   Appearance is affected not only by your age, sex, and race—physical characteristics that are relatively unchangeable—but also by your hair style, clothing, cleanliness, accessories, and jewelry. Appearance is the first basis on which you are evaluated, since companies have an image that they expect their employees to project.

The type of job you are applying for determines your attire. You normally wear clothing similar to that which is actually worn on the job. For example, you should not wear a three-piece business suit when you apply for a job at a construction site. But you should wear clean, neatly pressed slacks and a nice shirt. Administrative or supervisory jobs require a business suit and tie and navy, gray, or camel blazer. Jobs in which you are constantly meeting the public, such as sales and some service jobs, also require a coat and tie. Three-piece business suits are generally worn when applying at banks, insurance offices, or stock brokerage firms. No matter what the job applied for, women should wear conservative skirts, jackets, or dresses and low-heeled, dark shoes. They should not wear slacks or pants suits. Accessories should be limited and blend in with the overall attire.

Elaborate or exaggerated hairstyles should be avoided by both men and women. Exotic perfumes and lotions and extremely unusual or gaudy jewelry should also be avoided. Before the interview, men should find out the company's attitude about beards, mustaches, and long hair.

Facial Expressions.   Facial expressions include the movements of your face that reveal your inner thoughts and emotions. The face is an outward register of the emotions. You smile or laugh when you are happy, frown when you are unhappy or puzzled, cry when you are sad, bare your teeth in rage when you are angry, lower your eyelids and slightly bow your head when you feel guilty, and yawn when you are bored. Along with your posture, your facial expressions, particularly your eyes, indicate alertness, enthusiasm, and interest. These are the qualities you want to display during the interview.

Besides maintaining facial expressions that indicate your intelligence and interest in the job, you should maintain eye contact with the interviewer throughout the interview. This suggestion does not mean that you should get into a staring contest. You should generally shift your gaze away from the interviewer's eyes when you are thinking of answers to questions. But when you greet the interviewer, listen to the questions, give your answers, and close out the interview session, you should maintain direct eye contact.

Gestures.   Gestures are body movements used to emphasize speech. Most gestures involve the arms, hands, and head. A tilt of the head to the left or right accompanied by a slight frown indicates puzzlement. An up-and-down nod indicates agreement with what is being said and is an offer of encouragement to continue. During the interview you should use those gestures that are natural to you. You should not try to add new ones because they will appear unnatural.

One of the most important gestures you make in the interview is the handshake. In a handshake, the arm should extend from the shoulder, and the grip should be firm. A handshake is not a contest to see who has the most muscle, nor is it offering your hand like a dead fish.

Some gestures are so much a part of an individual's body language that they have become nervous mannerisms. These include jiggling the feet up and down, swinging a leg rapidly back and forth, putting the hands to the mouth, twirling a strand of hair, playing with keys or change in a pocket, or constantly straightening a crease in a pair of pants or a skirt. Mannerisms of this type are distracting. You should identify these distractions and try to eliminate them, particularly during the interview.

Posture.   Posture is the manner in which you sit, stand, and walk. It indicates how you feel about yourself. The person who is self-confident and poised stands and sits tall, with shoulders back, head raised, and eyes forward. Leaning slightly forward while seated indicates interest in what is being said. Although you must not appear rigid and unnatural, you do not want to walk into an interview with slumped shoulders and bowed head nor sprawl in a chair with your legs stretched out and your spine suspended in the air.

Tone and Pitch of Voice.   Tone of voice is the manner in which information is presented. Pitch is the variation in sound from high to low. Tone may be sarcastic, breathy, angry, babyish, dejected, monotonous, or lively depending on how you want your message to be received. Moderate variations in tone and pitch make your information interesting and pleasant to the ear and indicate enthusiasm and alertness.

Other Nonverbal Behaviors.   Three nonverbal behaviors that do not fit any particular category should be avoided. Two of these, chewing gum and smoking, are obviously rude. Chewing gum is extremely distracting and unpleasant. Once a socially acceptable habit, smoking is now becoming unacceptable. Many companies have either banned smoking in company facilities or set aside limited smoking areas. The third nonverbal behavior you need to be aware of is sound. Sighs, groans, giggles, or loud laughter are not acceptable in the job interview. Sighs and groans indicate a negative outlook, and giggling and loud laughter make you appear immature and out of control.

One last form of nonverbal behavior, silence, is a technique that is often used by interviewers to test the applicant's self-confidence and poise. Because applicants are already nervous, they fear silence and will continue to talk when they have already answered a question. After you have given an answer to a question, you should be prepared to sit quietly until the next question is asked. This ability to sit still shows maturity as well as poise and self-confidence.

As you can see, appropriate verbal and nonverbal behavior is critical in the job interview. In the next section, we are going to give you some guidelines for preparing for the interview. These guidelines should make the process easier and prevent some of the problems that contribute to inappropriate performance.

PREPARING FOR THE INTERVIEW

Adequate preparation for the job interview includes assessing yourself, the job you are applying for, and the company. The company has already begun its assessment of you through the résumé, letter of application, and letters of recommendation. Company personnel are prepared for the interview. Interviewers have in mind, or sometimes on paper, the questions they plan to ask. They know how you compare with the other individuals they plan to interview. Although no prospective employee knows ahead of time exactly what a company expects, failure to assess the situation adequately can cost the offer of a job.

Self-Assessment

In preparing for the interview, the first step is to look at yourself from several different perspectives before you go to the job interview. When you wrote your résumé and letter of application, you indicated your goals and objectives. Think again about these and have answers in mind concerning your short- and long-range goals.

Review your course of study. Get your college catalog and go over the descriptions of courses you have taken. List the types of specialized equipment or instruments you are able to operate. Then jot down the actual hands-on practical laboratory experiences you have had, types of reports you have written, and special or elective courses you have taken. Be prepared to talk about how these contribute to your overall abilities to do the job. Next, review your employment history and be prepared to discuss duties and responsibilities and former employers.

Evaluate your strengths and weaknesses and be prepared to talk about them. Pay particular attention to how you have overcome what you might have once considered a weakness. The more you know about yourself, your goals, your education, and your former work experiences, the easier it will be to answer the interviewer's questions.

Another point to remember is to take a positive tone in the interview. You will be asked some questions to which you will be tempted to respond in a very negative manner. For example, if you hated your last boss and thought he was an incompetent supervisor, you do not need to complain about him to the interviewer. Without compromising your honesty and integrity, you may comment instead that his supervisory style was a little different from what you were used to. You may also say that the course you liked least in school was math but you buckled down and studied hard and pulled your grades up. In both cases you have turned a potentially negative point into a positive one. In doing so, you have presented yourself in the best light.

A final self-assessment is to consider the questions most commonly asked during the interview. These questions generally fall into three categories: education, experience, and personal information. Listed below are the general questions that fall in each of these categories. We suggest that you rehearse your answers aloud and either audio- or videotape yourself to see how well you come across.

Education.   Some of the most commonly asked questions concerning education are listed below.

1. Why did you choose to attend your college?
2. Why did you choose your particular course of study?
3. What did you like most about your college? Course of study? Why?
4. What did you like least about your college? Course of study? Why?
5. What courses did you make the best grades in? The poorest? Why?
6. Do you think your training has prepared you for this job? In what way?
7. Who was your best instructor? Describe him or her.
8. What clubs did you belong to?

Work Experience.   Some of the most commonly asked questions about previous work experience are listed below and on the next page.

1. What was your last job? Describe it.
2. What did you like most about your last job? Least?
3. Who is the best person you ever worked for? Describe him or her.
4. Why did you leave previous job(s)?
5. How did your previous jobs help train you for this one?
6. Did you work as a member of a crew? Alone? Which do you prefer?
7. Did you help finance your education?
8. What professional groups or organizations do you belong to?

9. What types of equipment or machinery have you worked with? Repaired?
10. Can you explain a specific process or procedure from your field of work?

Personal.   Some of the most commonly asked personal questions are listed below.

1. Will you tell me about yourself? (Keep the answer to this question related to the job you are applying for.)
2. What are your short-range goals? Long-range goals?
3. Do you work better as a team member? Alone? Why?
4. What are your major strengths? Weaknesses?
5. What can you contribute to this company?
6. Do you think you are successful? Why? What personal characteristics have contributed to your success?
7. What do you do in your leisure time?
8. Why do you think you would like this job?
9. Why do you think you would like our company?
10. Who has been the most important person in your life? Why?
11. Are you willing to relocate? Travel?
12. What will you be doing 10 years from now? Twenty-five years?
13. Do you plan to continue your education?
14. What salary would you expect if you were hired?
15. Do you read books? Magazines? Name them.
16. What is your greatest achievement?
17. What gives you the most satisfaction in life?

These questions may be stated differently. However, this is the general information you will be asked to provide in an interview.

Job Assessment

The second step is to assess the job you are applying for. You need to know exactly what the job duties and responsibilities are. Help-wanted ads generally offer only a brief description of the position and degree or experience requirements. You need to know how your education and experience relate to the position. To find out specific requirements, ask individuals who are currently employed to describe the job for you. If necessary, call or go by the company personnel office and ask for a copy of the job description. At the same time, try to find out if shift work is involved. It is better to decide before the interview if you are willing to work any one of three shifts and if you are willing to work rotating shifts.

Company Assessment

The third step is to research the company. Many companies hand out brochures which give a general history of the company and the benefits of working there. If a brochure is unavailable, you should find out how long the company has been in business and what its major products and services are. You should find out if the company has prospects for growth, if its current financial status is stable, and if the company is a national or international firm. You should also be aware of where various subsidiaries are located. Company policy may require automatic transfer after a period of time. You need to be able to state not only if you would be willing to transfer but also what your choice of location might be.

You should also be aware of general company policies and benefit plans. You should find out how the company evaluates employees for promotion and whether or not it promotes from within the organization. You need to know, too, if new employees have to work through a probationary period and what the terms of the probation are. Company benefits, such as education, insurance, dental and health programs and their cost, should be examined. Sources for this type of information include company employees, trade journals, the local Chamber of Commerce, and newspapers. If you are unable to find out all you need to know prior to the interview, jot down questions to ask while you are in the interview.

It is also helpful to find out how the company conducts interviews. Very frequently you will interview with at least two individuals and sometimes more. One person will be your direct supervisor. This is the individual to whom you would report on a daily basis. The direct supervisor is interested in what you know about the job and how you would fit into the group. Another interviewer might be the manager to whom your supervisor reports. He or she might not be as concerned about your technical abilities as the direct supervisor, but the manager is evaluating how well you fit into the group and meet the overall company requirements for employees. Sometimes, you will be interviewed by a panel of three or more individuals. The panel interview allows you to be evaluated by a small group meeting together. The meeting saves time for both you and the company.

Finally, you should double-check the time and location. You might drive or ride to the company to see how long it takes you to get there. In addition, you need to check on the availability of parking spaces and bus services. If you have to walk or drive a long distance to the interview, you need to allow extra time.

If you have assessed yourself, the job, and the company prior to attending the interview, you will be far more comfortable when the interview actually takes place. The better prepared you are, the better you will respond to the interviewer's questions. The better you respond, the more likely you are to get the job.

THE INTERVIEW PROCESS

Interviews generally go through three phases: beginning, middle, and closing. The beginning, or introductory phase, is a period of getting acquainted. You are generally called into or taken to the interviewer's office and introduced. Greet the interviewer by name with a firm handshake. Remain standing until you are invited to sit down. If the interviewer is seated when you enter the room and does not offer to shake hands, you may sit down immediately. After the initial greeting, the introductory phase is fairly casual. It is made up primarily of general conversation designed to put you at ease and to let you and the interviewer get acquainted. Very frequently, the interviewer will describe the type of individual the company is seeking for the position, give a description of the duties and responsibilities of the job, and a brief history of the company and its goals. Even though this phase of the interview is fairly casual, it is extremely important to create an immediate good impression. You are being evaluated on your appearance, handshake, and general ability to communicate. You should take the opportunity to emphasize those qualities that fit the job you are interviewing for.

The second phase of the interview is generally a question-and-answer period. The interviewer is interested in finding out more about your education and previous work experience. He or she is interested in your skills and abilities, your personal preferences, and your knowledge of the job and company. You need to be able to tell the interviewer why you have applied for this particular job with this organization and clearly show why you are the best-qualified candidate for the position. You must be able to tie your skills to the job you are applying for and demonstrate that you are motivated and capable and that you exhibit the general employee image that the company is seeking.

After the question-and-answer phase of the interview, the interviewer will often begin the third phase, the closing. During this phase, the interviewer describes company benefits and policies and offers you the opportunity to ask questions concerning the job and the company. Prior to leaving the interview, you should request some indication of what to expect next. You should ask when you will know the company's decision about hiring you. In addition, if this is the only interview you will have with the company, the salary for the position must be determined. Salary determination can be a very delicate matter. Most of the time, an interviewer will explain the salary scale during the interview and give you a close approximation of the salary you would be making. If the question of salary is not addressed and this is the only opportunity you will have to interview with the company, you should ask. Then you will be able to make a decision about accepting employment with another company. At the close of the interview, thank the interviewer for the opportunity to talk with him or her and leave. Sometimes you might be offered a job during the interview. Therefore, you should be prepared to accept the position or give the interviewer a specific time when you will let the company know your decision.

Immediately after the interview is over or sometimes during the interview itself, the interviewer makes notes to write an assessment of you as a potential employee. Very frequently, a checklist and rating scale is used. After all applicants are interviewed, their overall scores may be compared and the individual with the highest score hired. Examples of two types of interview rating sheets are shown in Figures 14-1 on pages 343 and 344 and 14-2 on page 345.

INTERVIEW EVALUATION SHEET

Name of Candidate _____   Position Applied For _____

Date_____   Interviewer_____

Directions: Check the appropriate block for each of the categories listed
below.

Personal Appraisal

	Excellent(4)	Good(3)	Acceptable(2)	Poor(1)
General First Impression	_____	_____	_____	_____
Personal Appearance	_____	_____	_____	_____
Posture	_____	_____	_____	_____
Body Movement/Gestures	_____	_____	_____	_____
Initiative in Conversation	_____	_____	_____	_____
Ability to Express Self	_____	_____	_____	_____
Tone of Voice	_____	_____	_____	_____
Eye Contact	_____	_____	_____	_____
Total	_____	_____	_____	_____

Technical Appraisal

	Excellent(4)	Good(3)	Acceptable(2)	Poor(1)
Ability to Express Career Goals	_____	_____	_____	_____
Ability to Answer Questions Concerning Academic Preparation	_____	_____	_____	_____
Ability to Answer Questions Concerning Prior Experience	_____	_____	_____	_____
Ability to Ask Intelligent & Pertinent Questions Relative to Job/Company	_____	_____	_____	_____
Total	_____	_____	_____	_____

Figure 14-1:   Interview Evaluation Sheet

Character Appraisal

Personality	Poise and Manner	Maturity
Strong(2) _____	Confident(2) _____	Advanced(2)_____
Average(1) _____	Average(1) _____	Average(1) _____
Passive(0) _____	Nervous(0) _____	Immature(0)_____
Timid(-1) _____	Overbearing(-1)_____	
Total _____	_____	_____

Grand Total _____

Comments _____

_____

_____

Recommend _____   Do not recommend _____

_____
Interviewer   /   Date

Figure 14-1: *continued*

INTERVIEW RATING SHEET

Applicant's Name _____   Position _____

Directions: Circle the number from 1 to 5 that most accurately reflects
your assessment of the applicant. Five reflects the highest possible
score and one the lowest.

Relaxed	5	4	3	2	1	Tense
Excellent eye contact	5	4	3	2	1	Avoids eye contact
Appropriate gestures	5	4	3	2	1	Excessive or unrelated gestures
Appropriate tone and pitch	5	4	3	2	1	Inappropriate tone and pitch
Comments honest and direct	5	4	3	2	1	Comments whiny, sarcastic
Strong personality	5	4	3	2	1	Timid personality
Poised	5	4	3	2	1	Nervous, jittery
Advanced maturity	5	4	3	2	1	Immature
Appropriate posture	5	4	3	2	1	Poor posture
Initiates conversation	5	4	3	2	1	Comments only when questioned
Discusses course work well	5	4	3	2	1	Cannot discuss course work
Knowledgeable about prior jobs	5	4	3	2	1	Unsure of prior job duties
Appropriate self-esteem	5	4	3	2	1	Downgrades self
Enthusiastic	5	4	3	2	1	Dull, bored

Total Score _____

Comments: _____

_____

_____

Recommend for position: _____ yes   _____ no

_____
Interviewer   /   Date

Figure 14-2: Interview Rating Sheet

Notice that the majority of the checklist categories are based on personal qualities discussed earlier in the chapter. Notice also the importance of effective verbal and nonverbal communication.

FOLLOWING UP

Approximately one week after the interview, if you have not been notified of the company's decision, call or write the interviewer and politely ask about the status of the position and when you can expect a decision to be made. A request of this type is not an imposition. The interviewer will understand that you need to know this information in order to plan for your future.

SUMMARY

The job interview is a face-to-face meeting between an applicant for a job and a potential employer or representative of the company. To do well in a interview, you must be aware of how to communicate effectively, both verbally and nonverbally. You must prepare for the interview by assessing yourself, the job, and the company. Self-assessment includes a review of goals and objectives, course of study, and prior work experience. It provides answers to commonly asked questions. Job assessment is researching the job to determine duties and responsibilities. It helps you decide how your education and experience fit these duties and responsibilities. Company assessment provides information about the history of the company, its policies and procedures, and its method of conducting interviews. The interview process begins with a period of getting acquainted. It then moves to a question-and-answer period. During this second phase, the interviewer assesses the applicant's knowledge and experience. Finally, the interview process closes with an explanation of company policy, benefits, and hiring practices.

ASSIGNMENTS

Application 1:
Analyzing behavior

To get some idea of how important nonverbal behavior is in communication, go to your student lounge or to a busy fast-food restaurant and observe the posture, gestures, eye contact, facial expressions, appearance, and nervous mannerisms of two or three individuals. Watch them for 10 or 15 minutes. Make notes on the behavior and be prepared to discuss it with the class. You must be a polite observer and not stare at individuals or invade their privacy.

Application 2:
Preparing for the interview

Using the help-wanted ads in your local newspaper or a trade journal, find a job you might be interested in applying for. Bring the ad with you to class. Then assess yourself, the job, and the company.

First, call the company and ask for a more detailed description of the job duties and responsibilities if these are not clearly indicated in the ad. Call the Employment Security Commission, or ask you curriculum instructor about the average salary you could expect if you were to take that job. Second, assess yourself in relationship to that particular job. Determine how your education and past work experiences fit the job description. List course work that is directly applicable to the job. Jot down your strengths and weaknesses. Third, assess the company. If possible, talk to one of its current employees and find out about the company history, its products and services, and benefits. If you do not know a current employee, call the Chamber of Commerce or visit your library and find out as much as possible about the company.

Finally, look over the most commonly asked questions listed in this chapter. Read each question and answer it aloud into a tape recorder. Then play the tape back and make notes on how you can improve your responses.

Application 3:
Interviewing

With the help of your instructor, videotape yourself being interviewed by a fellow student. Dress as you normally would for the interview. Afterwards, replay the videotape. With your instructor's help, use one of the interview evaluation sheets shown in this chapter to assess your performance. If videotaping the interview is impossible, go through the interview with a fellow student in front of the class. Have one or two of your fellow students and your instructor evaluate you, using one of the interview evaluation sheets. After the evaluation, take notes on how you can improve your performance.

15

COMMUNICATION WITH INDIVIDUALS

When you complete this chapter, you should know how to perform some important oral communication tasks with individuals on the job. You should learn about the following tasks:

Listening to others
Orienting new employees to the work force
Training co-workers
  Defining the job
  Demonstrating the job
  Letting the employee perform the job
  Evaluating job performance
Giving explanations to supervisors and customers

The most frequent form of spoken communication is one-on-one, face-to-face conversation. Often considered relaxation or recreation off the job, conversation on the job has practical goals. It ensures that the company functions efficiently and that customers are satisfied with products and services. This chapter will discuss some typical conversations on the job, some with co-workers and new employees and others with supervisors and customers. You will learn how to listen attentively, how to help new employees adjust to the job, how to conduct on-the-job training, and how to justify time and money to supervisors and customers. Before beginning this chapter, you should review the communication process and its components described in Chapter 1.

LISTENING TO OTHERS

Because speech is the most frequently used form of communication on the job, effective listening skills are essential for all employees. Listening is more than just hearing what is said. It is paying close attention to understand the message being sent by the speaker. Six techniques may be used to develop more effective listening skills: concentrating, avoiding interruptions, showing interest and alertness, being patient, providing an appropriate response, and asking questions.

- ○ *Concentrating.* Concentrating requires you to direct your attention to the speaker. Private thoughts, such as worrying about how to pay next month's bills, interfere with the ability to concentrate. External distractors, such as phones ringing and doors slamming, also interfere with concentration. Unless you listen carefully, this interference can cause you to only partly understand the message. In that case, you may misinterpret what the speaker wants you to do.

- ○ *Avoiding Interruptions.* Avoiding interruptions requires you to allow the speaker to finish a statement before you ask questions or make comments. If allowed to complete the statement, the speaker may answer your questions or be so clear in the presentation that the comments are unnecessary.

- ○ *Showing Interest and Alertness.* Showing interest and alertness requires you to carefully consider the speaker's message and make direct eye contact to indicate your involvement.

- ○ *Being Patient.* Being patient requires you to listen attentively. Patience is particularly important in working with new employees in orientation and on-the-job training. When you are impatient with new employees, you can cause them to lose confidence and harm their future performance.

- ○ *Providing an Appropriate Response.* Providing an appropriate response requires you to let the speaker know how the message has been interpreted. The response may be verbal or nonverbal.

- ○ *Asking Questions.* Asking questions helps to ensure that the message being sent is correctly interpreted. Asking questions also shows that you are interested in the topic.

Effective listening is an important part of the communication process. Listening attentively to new employees, co-workers, supervisors, customers, and clients is essential in accomplishing tasks in business and industry.

ORIENTING NEW EMPLOYEES
TO THE WORK FORCE

The first day of a new job can be confusing and uncomfortable. Most companies, particularly large ones, recognize the difficulties individuals have in coping with the problems of starting a new job, meeting new people, becoming familiar with the ways in which the company operates, and even learning how to get around in a new building. Very rarely is an individual expected to be very productive during the first week or two of employment.

At the same time, new employees are wondering about how they will fit into the work force. No matter how many questions they have asked during the interview and no matter how familiar they are with the way the company operates, new employees may still have doubts about the wisdom of accepting a position with the company. Very often the attitudes that employees will demonstrate for the rest of their employment are established during the first one or two weeks at a new job. Therefore, it is very important that they be properly oriented to the work force.

Some large companies have formal orientation programs with a structured format that new employees follow. An experienced individual from the work crew, or sometimes the supervisor, will guide the employees through the complexities of employment with the company. Smaller companies generally do not have formal orientation programs. Instead, they provide informal orientations for new employees. The process of orientation, whether formal or informal, usually includes the following components:

- *Introduction of New Employees to Key Members of the Work Force.* Rather than being left to wander around meeting company employees at random, new employees are assigned to an experienced employee who will introduce them to other staff members. Generally, new employees report to the supervisor on the morning of the first day of employment. At that time, they are introduced first to the members of the group with whom they will be working. They will also meet secretaries, clerks, members of the typing pool, and other personnel who will aid them in getting their job done.

- *Completion of Company Forms.* Part of the first week's orientation includes learning to complete the company's forms. Although the forms vary from company to company, new employees fill out federal and state income tax withholding forms, insurance forms for health and dental benefits, and forms for retirement and stock options. They are also shown how to fill out time sheets, purchase order forms, requisitions for materials and supplies, and other items such as trouble tickets and work order forms.

- *Orientation to the Company Layout.* Often a tour is provided to show new employees how to get from one place to another in the work location. The tour may include short stops at office areas, supply rooms, copy rooms, break areas, lunchrooms, restrooms, and the coffee room. Sometimes the tour encompasses the whole company. The tour is important to new employees because it helps them achieve a sense of independence.

- *Orientation to Company Policies.* In addition to being introduced to members of the work force and company layout, new employees need to know the company's policies concerning break times, overtime, proper attire, vacation time, sick leave, and safety requirements. A quick review of the company's policy and administrative manuals helps new employees know where to find answers that are critical to job performance and evaluation.

- *Orientation to the Work Area.* Orientation also helps new employees become familiar with the area in which they will perform their job. At a minimum, new employees are shown the location of equipment, machinery, tools, and supplies.

Without an orientation similar to the one described above, new employees have to waste valuable time trying to find out how to function in the new work situation rather than being productive. Experienced employees should be patient in orienting new employees to the company so that they can become productive members of the work force as soon as possible.

TRAINING CO-WORKERS

One of the most important tasks in any company or agency is to train new employees for the job they have been hired to do. The new employees usually have training and prior work experience that fit the needs of the company; but each company has its own special way of doing things and its own equipment, procedures, and operating rules and regulations. Therefore, once employees have been oriented to the company, they must then be oriented to the job. Many companies have on-the-job training programs with new employees assigned to a more experienced employee to learn how to perform job tasks satisfactorily. On-the-job training is conducted not only for new employees but also for employees who move to another department or another job within a unit. Like orientation, on-the-job training is best conducted on a one-to-one basis.

The federal government began developing on-the-job training programs during World War II, when civilians were trained to produce goods and services for the defense of the country. In that program, it was found that individuals learn best when as many of their senses as possible are involved in the learning process. The most rapid and accurate learning takes place when individuals see a job demonstrated and then perform the job themselves. They should explain each step aloud as they perform the operation. In learning the job in this way, they incorporate sight, hearing, and touch. For example, an employee learning how to use a lathe would first hear and see an instructor demonstrate the correct use of the lathe. Then the employee would perform the operation just demonstrated. While performing the operation, the employee would talk through each step. He or she would identify the parts of the lathe, explain the function of each part, and then use the lathe to machine a simple part while the instructor watches. Because the World War II program was so successful, it has been further refined. The concepts of on-the-job training have been incorporated in the currect technical training in the Armed Services as well as in many businesses and industries.

Current on-the-job training programs have four major phases: defining the job, explaining and demonstrating the job, allowing the employee to perform the job under direct supervision and then alone, and evaluating employee performance.

Defining the Job

The most important step in any on-the-job training program is defining the job. Defining the job means stating the activity the employee is expected to perform and the level of accuracy or speed required. For example, one of the many tasks required of a good executive secretary is the ability to type a minimum of 60 words per minute with no more than one error. Other performance requirements might include taking dictation, transcribing dictation, answering the telephone correctly, making travel arrangements, and organizing conferences.

To define the job of the employee, many companies and agencies have developed task lists which detail all of the job responsibilities for each classification of personnel working in the company. Separate task lists describe the job duties of a clerk, those of a senior technician, and those of a supervisor. Under each task the basic concepts an individual must master and special hands-on skills are given. A task list for an electrician in a steel mill may have as many as 100 separate tasks. Each one of these has sets of smaller tasks that are required to perform the job. The on-the-job training worksheet on calibrating overcurrent trip relays shown on Figure 15-1 gives an example of a task and the steps necessary in completing the task. Notice that the task is defined, and the tools, equipment and supplies, and safety precautions necessary to perform the job are stated. Defining a job in such detail tells employees exactly what is expected. It lists the skills and knowledge they must have to perform well.

If your company does not have a task list and you are responsible for helping to train new employees, you will have to develop your own definition of the job. The definition should include any requirements for special tools or equipment. Then you should list the major steps or the procedures required to complete the job. The final document that you create is similar to the technical instructions and descriptions explained in Chapter 12.

It is important to begin on-the-job training with a simple task. A new employee will not be able to troubleshoot a complex piece of equipment or take care of all the needs of a patient in the Intensive Care Unit on the first work day. As the employee becomes more familiar with the work environment and the job requirements, you may move steadily toward more complex tasks.

Demonstrating the Job

Demonstrating the job is showing the employee how to follow the procedure correctly. After you have defined the job and written the step-by-step instructions for getting it done, you should explain the instructions aloud to the new employee. Then you should demonstrate exactly how the job is done. Again, you should explain what you are doing at each critical point along the way. Repeat warnings and cautions when you are demonstrating the job. Emphasize those points where special precautions are required to perform the task safely.

After you have demonstrated the task, have the employee talk through the entire process with you before trying it alone. If time permits, the new employee can then act as the instructor, giving you directions, warnings, and cautions while you perform the task. Letting the employee instruct allows you to check his or her mastery of the procedure and offers a second chance for the employee to see the task performed.

Delaney Steel Mill
On-The-Job Training

Electricians

TRAINEE
NAME _____

SSN _____

DATE COMPLETED _____

EVALUATOR _____

Calibrating Over-Current Trip Relays

DESCRIPTION OF UNIT: The current trip relay is a device used to provide current protection for various 4160 volt distribution components. The unit measures system currents and energizes the appropriate circuit breaker trip coil when current exceeds specified values.

TOOLS/EQUIPMENT NEEDED: Andex Relay Tester, Model 14

REFERENCES NEEDED: Andex Instruction Manual 1001

SUPPLIES NEEDED: None

PRECAUTIONS: The electrical system must be shut down prior to calibration in compliance with appropriate technical specifications.

ACTIONS: NOTES:

1. Obtain testing clearance from
    shift supervisor.

2. Remove front cover of relay and
    pull circuit connecting plug
    from relay housing.

Figure 15-1:   On-The-Job Training Work Sheet

3. Unlatch and remove relay from housing.

4. Check relay for accumulation of dirt and debris. Check for proper alignment of moving parts. Adjust clearance as necessary.

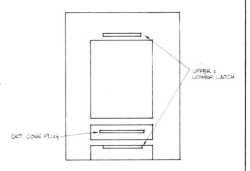

RELAY ASSEMBLY

5. Reinstall relay in relay housing.

6. Insert test jack into connecting plug location.

7. Make test connections according to Andex Relay Tester specifications.

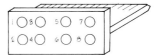

8. Perform time-delay functional test in accordance with Andex Instruction Manual 1001. Adjust as required.

9. Perform instantaneous functional test in accordance with manual. Adjust as required.

Figure 15-1: *continued*

Letting the Employee Perform the Job

The third step in training new employees is to let the employee perform the job under your supervision. The new employee should tell you exactly what is being performed and why. In that way, the senses of touch, sight, and hearing are used; and you can pick up potential errors in performance before the employee actually does the procedure alone. During this phase of training, it is important to remember that the new employee is uncomfortable and somewhat insecure. You must use a positive attitude in pointing out errors so that the employee does not become defensive or frustrated.

After the initial show-and-tell performance, let the employee try to perform the job alone, with you as a silent observer. After the employee has completed the job, you should again explain the reason for the procedure and recommend ways for improving performance. You should then repeat the correct method for accomplishing the task. Afterwards, leave the area and allow the employee to attempt the job alone. Be certain that the employee knows where you or other experienced employees will be in case problems arise. You should continue to supervise performance until you and the new employee are sure that the job can be performed without your direct supervision. By starting with a simple task, you help a new employee build confidence in his or her abilities to perform alone. Then you are able to begin training on the more complex tasks.

Evaluating Job Performance

The fourth step in training a new employee to do a job is evaluating job performance. Depending upon how the company operates, evaluation may be nothing more than telling an employee that he or she is doing a good job at each step along the way. It may also be a formal evaluation that rates the employee on each task. Some companies require evaluation each day; others, every six months; and still others, yearly. In on-the-job training, you will be required to assess the performance of the new employee. You must determine whether or not this new employee has the potential to become an effective member of the work force.

Performance may be assessed in a variety of ways. Sometimes you may write a short paragraph or make a list of the tasks a new employee has accomplished each day and state how well or poorly those tasks have been performed. If the company has a comprehensive on-the-job training program, you may use an evaluation sheet similar to the one for calibrating over-current trip relays. Each task that the employee is required to perform is evaluated on a separate training evaluation report. Other evaluation sheets list a variety of tasks that a new employee is required to perform competently. Figure 15-2 on pages 356 and 357 shows a comprehensive job training task listing and evaluation form.[1]

[1]Used by permission of Glenn Kaminsky, Division Chief, and the Boulder, Colorado Police Department.

BOULDER POLICE DEPARTMENT

DAILY OBSERVATION REPORT NO. _____

TRAINEE'S LAST NAME, FIRST INITIAL   BADGE NO.   FTO'S LAST NAME, FIRST INITIAL   BADGE NO.   DATE

RATING INSTRUCTIONS: Rate observed behavior with reference to the scale below. Comment on the most and least satisfactory performance of the day. Comment on any behavior you wish, but a specific comment is required on all ratings of "2" or less and "6" and above. Check "N.O." box if not observed. If trainee fails to respond to training, check "N.R.T." box and comment.

WATCH WORKED:

FTO PHASE:

RATING SCALE

NOT ACCEPTABLE BY FTO PROGRAM STANDARDS   ACCEPTABLE LEVEL   SUPERIOR BY FTO PROGRAM STANDARDS

------> 1   2   3   <4>   5   6   7   <------

ASSIGNMENT OR REASON FOR NO EVALUATION

		1	2	3	4	5	6	7	N.O.	N.R.T.		R.T.
	1-	1	2	3	4	5	6	7	[ ]	[ ]	**APPEARANCE** 1 GENERAL APPEARANCE	
											ATTITUDE	
	2-	1	2	3	4	5	6	7	[ ]	[ ]	2 ACCEPTANCE OF FEEDBACK - FTO/PROGRAM	
	3-	1	2	3	4	5	6	7	[ ]	[ ]	3 ATTITUDE TOWARD POLICE WORK	
											KNOWLEDGE	
											4 KNOWLEDGE OF DEPARTMENT POLICIES AND PROCEDURES	
	4-	1	2	3	4	5	6	7	[ ]	[ ]	REFLECTED BY VERBAL/WRITTEN/SIMULATED TESTING	
		1	2	3	4	5	6	7	[ ]	[ ]	REFLECTED IN FIELD PERFORMANCE	
											5 KNOWLEDGE OF CRIMINAL STATUTES	
	5-	1	2	3	4	5	6	7	[ ]	[ ]	REFLECTED BY VERBAL/WRITTEN/SIMULATED TESTING	
		1	2	3	4	5	6	7	[ ]	[ ]	REFLECTED IN FIELD PERFORMANCE	
											6 KNOWLEDGE OF CITY ORDINANCES	
	6-	1	2	3	4	5	6	7	[ ]	[ ]	REFLECTED BY VERBAL/WRITTEN/SIMULATED TESTING	
		1	2	3	4	5	6	7	[ ]	[ ]	REFLECTED IN FIELD PERFORMANCE	
											7 KNOWLEDGE OF TRAFFIC CODES	
	7-	1	2	3	4	5	6	7	[ ]	[ ]	REFLECTED BY VERBAL/WRITTEN/SIMULATED TESTING	
		1	2	3	4	5	6	7	[ ]	[ ]	REFLECTED IN FIELD PERFORMANCE	
											8 KNOWLEDGE OF CODES OF CRIMINAL PROCEDURE	
	8-	1	2	3	4	5	6	7	[ ]	[ ]	REFLECTED BY VERBAL/WRITTEN/SIMULATED TESTING	
		1	2	3	4	5	6	7	[ ]	[ ]	REFLECTED IN FIELD PERFORMANCE	
											PERFORMANCE	
	9-	1	2	3	4	5	6	7	[ ]	[ ]	9 DRIVING SKILL: NORMAL CONDITIONS	
	10-	1	2	3	4	5	6	7	[ ]	[ ]	10 DRIVING SKILL: MODERATE AND HIGH STRESS CONDITIONS	
	11-	1	2	3	4	5	6	7	[ ]	[ ]	11 ORIENTATION/RESPONSE TIME TO CALLS	
	12-	1	2	3	4	5	6	7	[ ]	[ ]	12 ROUTINE FORMS: ACCURACY/COMPLETENESS	
	13-	1	2	3	4	5	6	7	[ ]	[ ]	13 REPORT WRITING: ORGANIZATION/DETAILS	
	14-	1	2	3	4	5	6	7	[ ]	[ ]	14 REPORT WRITING: GRAMMAR/SPELLING/NEATNESS	
	15-	1	2	3	4	5	6	7	[ ]	[ ]	15 REPORT WRITING: APPROPRIATE TIME USED	
	16-	1	2	3	4	5	6	7	[ ]	[ ]	16 FIELD PERFORMANCE: NON-STRESS CONDITIONS	
	17-	1	2	3	4	5	6	7	[ ]	[ ]	17 FIELD PERFORMANCE: STRESS CONDITIONS	
	18-	1	2	3	4	5	6	7	[ ]	[ ]	18 INVESTIGATIVE SKILL	
	19-	1	2	3	4	5	6	7	[ ]	[ ]	19 INTERVIEW/INTERROGATION SKILL	
	20-	1	2	3	4	5	6	7	[ ]	[ ]	20 SELF-INITIATED FIELD ACTIVITY	
	21-	1	2	3	4	5	6	7	[ ]	[ ]	21 OFFICER SAFETY: GENERAL	
	22-	1	2	3	4	5	6	7	[ ]	[ ]	22 OFFICER SAFETY: SUSPECTS/SUS. PERS./PRISONERS	
	23-	1	2	3	4	5	6	7	[ ]	[ ]	23 CONTROL OF CONFLICT: VOICE COMMAND	
	24-	1	2	3	4	5	6	7	[ ]	[ ]	24 CONTROL OF CONFLICT: PHYSICAL SKILL	
	25-	1	2	3	4	5	6	7	[ ]	[ ]	25 PROBLEM SOLVING/DECISION MAKING	
	26-	1	2	3	4	5	6	7	[ ]	[ ]	26 RADIO: APPROPRIATE USE OF CODES/PROCEDURE	
	27-	1	2	3	4	5	6	7	[ ]	[ ]	27 RADIO: LISTENS AND COMPREHENDS	
	28-	1	2	3	4	5	6	7	[ ]	[ ]	28 RADIO: ARTICULATION OF TRANSMISSIONS	
											RELATIONSHIPS	
	29-	1	2	3	4	5	6	7	[ ]	[ ]	29 WITH CITIZENS IN GENERAL	
	30-	1	2	3	4	5	6	7	[ ]	[ ]	30 WITH ETHNIC GROUPS OTHER THAN OWN	
	31-	1	2	3	4	5	6	7	[[	[ ]	31 WITH OTHER DEPARTMENT MEMBERS	

_____ MINUTES OF REMEDIAL TRAINING TIME (EXPLAIN REMEDIAL PLANS)

Figure 15-2: Training Evaluation Form

THE MOST SATISFACTORY AREA OF PERFORMANCE TODAY WAS RATING CATEGORY NUMBER _____

A SPECIFIC INCIDENT WHICH DEMONSTRATES TODAY'S PERFORMANCE IN THIS AREA IS: _____

_____

_____

_____

_____

THE LEAST SATISFACTORY AREA OF PERFORMANCE TODAY WAS RATING CATEGORY NUMBER _____

A SPECIFIC INCIDENT WHICH DEMONSTRATES TODAY'S PERFORMANCE IN THIS AREA IS: _____

_____

_____

_____

_____

DOCUMENTATION OF PERFORMANCE AND COMMENTS:

CAT. NO.

____   _____

____   _____

____   _____

____   _____

____   _____

____   _____

____   _____

____   _____

____   _____

____   _____

____   _____

____   _____

____   _____

____   _____

____   _____

_____   _____
RECRUIT OFFICER SIGNATURE   TRAINING OFFICER SIGNATURE

REVIEWED BY _____

10/30/81

Figure 15-2: *continued*

Over 1200 separate tasks were identified by the Boulder Police Department as skills or knowledge that a police officer must have to perform effectively on the job. These were grouped in the 31 actual jobs and knowledges that police officers use most frequently. Then the 31 jobs and knowledges were divided into five major areas: Appearance, Attitude, Knowledge, Performance, and Relationships. An evaluation form and rating scale were designed. The rating scale of 1 through 7 was used to reflect recruit performance. A rating of 1 is unacceptable; 4 is acceptable; and 7 is superior. A rating of 2 or 3 reflects the gradations between unacceptable and acceptable behavior. A rating of 6 or 7 reflects gradations between acceptable and superior behavior. Guidelines for evaluating each of the 31 criteria were established. For example, in evaluating Knowledge items, the police trainee is judged on both written and field performance. The criteria required for item 5, "Knowledge of Criminal Statutes," are shown below:

5. *Knowledge of Criminal Statutes*—Evaluates recruit's knowledge of criminal statutes and ability to apply that knowledge in field situations.

Reflected by Testing

(1) Unacceptable—When tested, verbally or written, answers with 20% or less accuracy.

(4) Acceptable—When tested, verbally or written, answers with 70% accuracy.

(7) Superior—When tested, verbally or written, answers with 100% accuracy.

Reflected in Field Performance

(1) Unacceptable—Does not know the elements of basic sections of the codes. Does not recognize criminal offenses when encountered or makes mistakes relative to whether or not crimes have been committed and, if so, which crimes.

(4) Acceptable—Recognizes commonly encountered criminal offenses and applies appropriate section of the code. Knows difference between criminal and noncriminal activity.

(7) Superior—Has outstanding knowledge of the criminal codes and applies that knowledge to normal and unusual criminal activity.

The performance section of the evaluation considers the trainee's ability to perform on the job. The criteria for item 21, "Officer Safety: General," are very detailed. They let the trainee know exactly what to expect during the evaluation process.

21. *Officer Safety: General*—Evaluates the recruit's ability to perform tasks without injuring self or others or exposing self or others to unnecessary danger/risk.

(1) Unacceptable—Fails to follow accepted safety procedures or to exercise officer safety, i.e.
A. Exposes weapons to suspect (baton, mace, handgun, etc.).
B. Fails to keep gun hand free during enforcement situations.
C. Stands in front of violator's car door.
D. Fails to control suspect's movements.

    E. Does not keep suspect/violator in sight.

    F. Fails to use illumination when necessary or uses it improperly.

    G. Fails to advise dispatcher when leaving police vehicle.

    H. Fails to maintain good physical condition.

    I. Fails to utilize or maintain personal safety equipment.

    J. Does not anticipate potentially dangerous situations.

    K. Stands too close to passing vehicular traffic.

    L. Is careless with gun and other weapons.

    M. Stands in front of doors when knocking.

    N. Makes poor choice of which weapon to use and when to use it.

    O. Fails to cover other officers.

    P. Stands between police and violator's vehicle on car stop.

    Q. Fails to search police vehicle prior to duty and after transporting suspect.

(4) Acceptable—Follows accepted safety procedures. Understands and applies them.

(7) Superior—Always works safely. Foresees dangerous situations and prepares for them. Keeps partner informed and determines the best position for self and partner. Is not overconfident. Is in good physical condition.

Police officers must be able to communicate effectively with the variety of individuals they meet. Therefore, trainees are evaluated on their successful communications with three groups of people: citizens in general, ethnic groups other than their own, and other department members. The criteria for evaluating item 29, "Citizens in General," are shown below:

Relationships

29. *With Citizens: General*—Evaluates the recruit's ability to interact with citizens (including suspects) in an appropriate, efficient manner.

(1) Unacceptable—Abrupt, belligerent, overbearing, arrogant, uncommunicative. Overlooks or avoids "service" aspect of the job. Introverted, insensitive, and uncaring. Poor non-verbal skills.

(4) Acceptable—Courteous, friendly and empathetic. Communicates in a professional, unbiased manner. Is service oriented. Good non-verbal skills.

(7) Superior—Is very much at ease with citizen contacts. Quickly establishes rapport and leaves people with feeling that the officer was interested in serving them. Is objective in all contacts. Excellent non-verbal skills.

By using this detailed training task list with guidelines for evaluating each of the skills and knowledges, both the trainer and the recruit can identify problems. Then steps can be taken to help the recruit become a competent member of the police force.

GIVING EXPLANATIONS TO SUPERVISORS AND CUSTOMERS

Being able to explain actions, events, or situations to supervisors and customers or clients is also a critical part of your job. As discussed in Chapter 2, you are required to adjust your language according to the needs and expectations of a particular audience. In spoken communication, you are likely to be face-to-face with your audience. Therefore, you must maintain a professional demeanor no matter how upset or frustrated you feel about a particular situation.

To prepare an effective explanation for a supervisor or a customer, you should follow three steps.

1. Provide a quick summary of the problem so that the supervisor or customer has an overview of the situation.
2. Present the facts of the situation in a logical and orderly sequence.
3. Draw a conclusion and make recommendations for actions that should be taken.

Presenting information in an orderly manner increases the clarity of your message. It also increases your credibility.

Supervisors are concerned with circumstances which may cause disruption of the work flow. These circumstances might include an employee's need to be away from the job on personal business, a personality conflict between members of a crew, an injury, or a lack of adequate staff or equipment to do a job. For example, Joe and Harold are members of the same work crew. For the past six weeks, Joe has been consistently late to work, has disappeared from the work area for extended periods of time, and has tried to start arguments with other members of the crew. The supervisor of the work crew calls Harold aside to ask why the crew is behind in its work. How should Harold answer that question? Instead of blaming the delay on that "bum," Joe, Harold should explain that the work crew has not always been at full force. He should tell the supervisor that all the crew members are not carrying out their assigned duties. He should avoid name-calling and finger-pointing. Harold's explanation includes facts. It does not include value judgments. Based on the facts that Harold provides, the supervisor is responsible for finding out who is doing what and for taking action.

In addition to reporting to supervisors, employees in service industries such as air conditioning installation and repair, plumbing installation and repair, nursing, or television sales and repair must deal with customers or clients. They need to be able to explain what they are doing, why they are doing it, and how much the services will cost. A patient who has been placed on a highly restrictive diet and enforced bed rest is likely to be much more agreeable about complying with the physician's regimen if he or she fully understands the reasons for the limitations. The physician generally tells the patient the reasons for the actions prescribed, but patients often want more details, which the nurse may be requested to provide.

When a customer complains about the bill for tuning his engine, aligning the front end, and inspecting his car, the automotive technician has to explain the process used to do those tasks. Certainly, the customer could have done the job at one-fourth the cost, but this price does not include compensation for highly skilled labor. Although customers do not mind paying for parts, they often resent paying $25 to $30 an hour for labor. Rarely do they take into consideration that what they are paying for is skill and knowledge. By explaining the sequence of steps used to identify and correct the problem, technicians may be able to appease angry customers. Since customers or clients are what keeps a service industry functioning, technicians must be able to listen attentively, communicate well, and remain professional at all times.

SUMMARY

Communicating with individuals on the job includes listening effectively, providing orientation and on-the-job training, and explaining to supervisors and customers how time and money have been spent. Effective listening includes concentrating, avoiding interruptions, showing interest and alertness, being patient, providing appropriate responses, and asking questions. Proper orientation helps a new employee begin work as soon as possible and sets the stage for a productive career with the company. Proper on-the-job training leads to safe and efficient performance. It has four major phases: defining the job, demonstrating the job, letting the employee perform the job, and evaluating employee performance. Besides communicating with co-workers, technicians also have to participate in face-to-face conversations with supervisors and customers. During these conversations, they often have to justify or explain procedures used on the job.

ASSIGNMENTS

Application 1:
Orienting a New Student to Your College Campus

Jot down in brief phrases or sentences exactly what you would do if you were assigned to orient a new student to your college campus. Include the names of individuals you would introduce the new student to, the forms you would show to the student (for example, a registration form and a grade report), the specific locations on campus you would visit, and the important rules and regulations you would discuss (absence policy and dress code).

Application 2:
Training a New Student

Using the guidelines on training co-workers, demonstrate with a fellow student the process of on-the-job training on a specialized tool, piece of equipment, or procedure from your curriculum. Prepare a job task sheet with instructions, and demonstrate the correct technique for accomplishing the job.

Application 3:
Providing Explanations

Using an incident or situation that might arise in your field of study, you and another student prepare a short role-playing presentation, with one of you being an unhappy customer, a frightened client, or an angry supervisor and the other being the technician who has to offer an explanation of the situation. Brief examples of possible roles are listed below.

Customer extremely unhappy about total cost of repair bill to fix a leaking pipe under the house.

Patient fearful of having blood drawn for tests.

Supervisor upset because job assignment for the day is not completed.

16

COMMUNICATION IN WORK GROUPS

When you complete this chapter, you should know how to perform some important oral communication tasks with your work group. You should learn about the following topics.

Work groups
  Characteristics of the work group
  Responsibilities of group members
Group dynamics
  Supportive groups
  Destructive groups
Group meetings
  Environment
  Territoriality
  Eye contact
Some methods of effective communication in group meetings
  Informative presentations
  Problem-solving presentations

Groups are formed whenever two or more people come together with a common interest. People form groups naturally, as pleasant ways of spending leisure time. They also form groups deliberately, as ways of getting work done on the job. The purpose of this chapter is to offer advice about how to communicate effectively in work groups. The chapter begins by describing the characteristics and responsibilities of work groups and then discusses group dynamics and appropriate behavior in formal and informal group meetings.

WORK GROUPS

Work groups are composed of people who associate with each other to accomplish some task on the job. Like battalions in the military, these groups are deliberately formed. Common responsibility rather than friendship holds the group together. The members of the work group are responsible for performing tasks assigned to them by their employer. Whether they like each other or not, they must cooperate to get their job done. Your success on the job may be tied to your ability to communicate effectively in performing tasks with your work group and in attending and participating in group meetings.

Characteristics of the Work Group

Work groups have three characteristics. First, they are highly structured. Each member is assigned a certain role. Second, each member is expected to do his or her share of the work. Everyone must achieve a certain standard to stay in the group. Third, each member must behave according to the rules set by the group or by the company that employs the group. This section discusses these three characteristics.

The first characteristic of work groups is that they are structured. Structure is the defined relationship among the members of the group. This relationship is based on the role or position that an individual occupies within the group. Each group member's role is clearly shown on a company's organizational chart. Figure 16-1 is an organizational chart for a training center in a

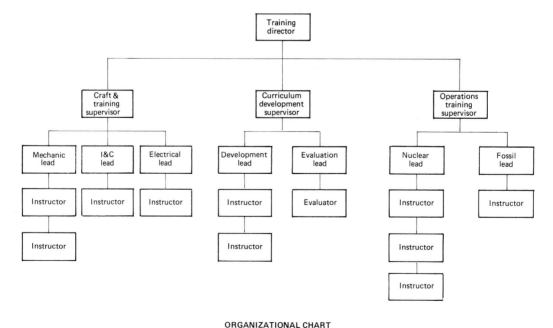

ORGANIZATIONAL CHART

Figure 16-1:   Organizational Chart

public utility. The training director, shown at the top of the chart, holds the highest position. The three supervisors hold the second-highest positions and are equal in position and rank. The leads are at the third level in the hierarchy, and the instructors are at the fourth level.

The position a person occupies within a group is usually based on seniority, skill in performing a job, or special expertise in the technical aspects of a job. The supervisors or leaders of a work group have usually been employed longer than the members of the group they supervise. The first-class mechanic or senior technician has special skills that are necessary in getting the job done. The specialist who is called in to troubleshoot difficult problems usually has special training in repairing a particular item. Each individual has a role to play, and rank and status are based on that role. If any member of the group oversteps the bounds of the assigned status and rank, problems occur in the work group. A third-class technician should not tell the crew members what to do, because that action would violate the rank and status of the head of the crew. It would cause problems not only for the head but for all the other group members as well.

A second characteristic of work groups is that a standard of performance is required of each group member. As discussed in Chapter 15, employees are evaluated on their ability to perform those tasks that are a requirement of the job classification. Each company sets standards that it expects employees to obtain, whether welding on an assembly line, repairing computer terminals, or taking dictation. When a high standard of performance is achieved, the employee is usually granted a pay raise, bonus, or promotion. When individuals either do not or cannot live up to the expectations of the job, the result is the reverse.

A third characteristic of groups is that a standard of conduct is required of each group member. Most companies have policies that dictate the conduct their employees must exhibit on the job. They will not tolerate behavior that causes conflict or interferes in accomplishing work safely and efficiently. An individual who consistently comes to work late, drinks a couple of beers at lunch, or argues with the other group members will eventually be fired, transferred, or offered the opportunity to resign.

Responsibilities of Group Members

Once work groups have been defined and once rank and standards of performance and conduct have been determined, members of the work group have two major responsibilities: to accomplish the goals of the company and to get along with the other group members.

The first and most important responsibility is to accomplish the goals of the company. To accomplish these goals, work groups usually meet weekly or sometimes daily to determine the jobs to be done and to assign each group member a task in accomplishing the job. Again, communication plays an important role. If each group member does not fully understand what must be done to accomplish the job, both the individual and the group suffer. For example, at a crew meeting, the crew leader explains to the group that the procedure manual for repairing centrifugal pumps will have to be revised because of recent modifications made to the pump. A senior mechanic is assigned to rewrite the procedure within two days and check it out with two first-class mechanics as they tear the pump down before putting it into service. The senior mechanic does not meet the two-day deadline, and the two first-class mechanics are involved in working on the turbine and forget their assignment. To meet the production schedule, the pump is put on line and immediately malfunctions. The second-class mechanic assigned to repair the pump follows the out-of-date procedure and causes the pump to become totally incapacitated. The modifications have to be redone, and the pump is out of service for two additional weeks. Production levels decline. The supervisor reprimands the head of the crew for poor management. The crew leader reprimands the senior mechanic for failing to accomplish assigned tasks. Each member of the crew, management, the company, and the stockholders suffer because the goals of the company have not been met.

The second major responsibility of the group is to maintain good interpersonal relationships. No job can be accomplished if there is disagreement about the goals and tasks. Differences of opinion should be discussed openly and agreement reached. If necessary, the group members must be willing to compromise. Every member of the group must be given the opportunity to participate, and individual feelings must be taken into consideration. Unless members of a group feel that they have taken a part in determining goals and tasks and unless all members understand their roles, conflicts will occur in the group. The goals of the group, as well as those of the company, will not be accomplished effectively or efficiently.

Therefore, it is essential to understand the characteristics and responsibilities of the group and to follow company standards of performance and conduct. Employees should know exactly what these expectations are. Once you are employed, talk with those individuals who can tell you what you must do to be a successful employee and an effective member of the work group.

GROUP DYNAMICS

Group dynamics are the ways in which group members interact with each other. The dynamics of a group are determined by the group leader, the communication styles of the various members of the group, and the process of communication that occurs within the group. Based upon these criteria, groups tend to be either supportive or destructive. Two crews of mechanics employed by the same company may work side by side but behave very differently because of the way members interact with each other. Membership in a supportive or destructive group influences the manner in which group members communicate. In turn, the amount of openness allowed in communication influences the accomplishment of the goals of the group and the company. Supportive and destructive groups are described in this section.

Supportive Groups

In supportive work groups, the members share a sense of equality, understanding, and loyalty to each other and the group as a whole. They work together in achieving group goals, and each member feels a sense of personal worth. Because of this support, members of the group trust each other. As a result of this trust, the members cooperate and get the job done. They communicate honestly and openly. Cooperation and open communication lead to a productive and efficient work group.

Destructive Groups

On the other hand, destructive groups are usually inefficient. Members of the group feel isolated from each other and avoid contributing to group discussions for fear of appearing dumb. Instead of being supportive, they are very defensive in their behavior. Rather than leading to cooperation, the destructive climate leads to an unhealthy competitiveness. Each group member seeks control and superiority. In turn, this need for control and superiority leads to conflicts and a general feeling of dissatisfaction and causes a decline in the productivity and efficiency of the work group. Destructive groups hamper good working relationships and make meeting the goals of the company difficult.

GROUP MEETINGS

Group meetings are gatherings of the individuals who make up a work group. Depending on their purpose, these gatherings can be formal or informal. In a formal meeting, a speaker stands in front and talks. Group members are primarily responsible for careful listening. In an informal meeting, group members exchange ideas freely rather than listening quietly to a leader. Regardless of the formality, physical surroundings are important influences on the success of the meeting. In addition, nonverbal communication is used to reinforce a message or to send a silent reply. This section discusses the effects of environment, the human need to maintain personal space, and the use of eye contact.

Environment

Environment is the space in which a meeting takes place. It is everything in the space that might have some effect on the individuals participating. Environment includes lighting and noise level as well as wall color and room size. The environment is important in influencing the interactions of the individuals involved. Unpleasant, ugly, or noisy environments lead to poor communication and negative interaction. On the other hand, pleasant environments lead to more cooperative, energetic, and positive responses. As you may have noticed, executive offices and board rooms are usually spacious, elegantly decorated, and softly lit. Major decisions affecting an entire company and its work force are made in these offices, so the environment must be made as pleasant as possible. A pleasant environment leads to agreement, a sense of well-being, and individual importance.

Seating arrangement is especially important in establishing the overall environment of a meeting. Some of the common seating arrangements are shown in Figure 16-2. The seating arrangements move from the most formal (*a*) to the least formal (*e*). Arrangement *a* is generally used in a formal presentation such as a lecture in a classroom, where the leader is clearly identified and is physically separated from the group. In arrangement *b* the leader usually is seated at the head of the rectangular table and again is usually clearly identified and slightly separated from the group. In arrangement *c* the leader generally sits at the end of the U-shape and again is separated from the group. In arrangements *d,* the square, and *e,* the circle, the leader is difficult to identify. The seating arrangement in both situations is equal, and the leader is not separated from the group members. The informal seating arrangements in *d* and *e* lead to more involvement among individuals. When group members face each other, eye contact occurs easily, and information may be readily exchanged. In addition, the group members are more likely to take turns in presenting information. A sense of equality can be established among group members simply on the basis of seating arrangement.

Territoriality

Territoriality is the human tendency to protect personal space or territory. In formal group meetings where an individual presents information from behind a podium at the front of the room, certain group members will choose to sit in the back of the room. Others sit at the front close to the speaker. Still others sit at a middle distance. When formal meetings are held on a regular basis, members tend to claim the same seat they occupied as much as a month before.

Territoriality also occurs in small, less formal group meetings. Individuals stake a claim to their space and defend it with markers, such as pencil and paper, a jacket, a sweater, or a coffee cup. When a meeting adjourns for a coffee break and someone else occupies a previously occupied seat, the original "owner" will usually claim the seat from the intruder. Territory should not be invaded or taken, since it serves to establish an individual's place.

Eye Contact

As mentioned in Chapter 14, the face, especially the eyes and the area around the eyes, is the most obvious indicator of emotion. In small group meetings, eye contact is one of the most important means of communicating. Eye contact is important in a variety of circumstances. When speakers seek a response for a comment they have just made, they look to others to see if their message has been received and interpreted correctly. Listeners establish eye contact to signal

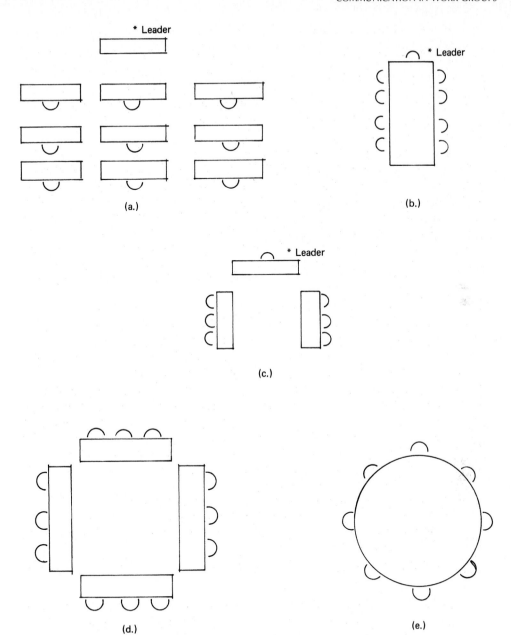

Figure 16-2:   Seating Arrangements

that the communication channel is open and they are prepared to receive information. People also try to establish eye contact when they need attention, involvement, or inclusion in the group.

In a different situation, direct eye contact may be used to produce anxiety in group members. An instructor staring directly at a rowdy student for longer than 10 seconds will usually cause the student to become anxious and change his or her behavior. In a group meeting the leader may maintain extended eye contact with a group member to signal dissatisfaction with the group member's performance or behavior.

Eye contact is generally absent when an individual wants to conceal some negative emotion or feeling concerning the message being sent. Students usually lower their eyes when an instructor asks a question which they cannot or do not want to answer in the classroom. Group members may doodle or stare into space when they want to indicate noninvolvement in a meeting. Eye contact is also generally absent in competitive situations, particularly when the individuals involved dislike each other or when a meeting becomes tense because of the topic under discussion. Group members will avoid eye contact with each other and with the leader to keep from taking part in the discussion. Meetings may suddenly become very silent, with group members busily fussing with coffee cups or pencils when they do not want to be involved. Eye contact is also absent when one member of the group begins to speak for an extended period of time. This evasion indicates noninvolvement and boredom on the part of the individuals participating in the group.

SOME METHODS OF EFFECTIVE COMMUNICATION IN GROUP MEETINGS

Most group meetings in business and industry are held for two primary reasons: to give employees information or to solve problems. The type of meeting being held determines the style of communication to be used.

Informative Presentations

Informative presentations are held to let employees know of a change in jobs, company policy, procedure, or company benefits. They are held to describe a new piece of equipment and explain its operation. Informative presentations are also used to keep members up to date on what is occurring in the company at a particular time. These meetings are often fairly formal, with a designated leader separated from the group by a podium or desk. Group involvement, other than to listen, is not expected. The group leader must ensure that the correct message is being sent and that it is received and interpreted correctly.

An effective informative meeting requires careful planning. A series of steps should be followed to ensure that the meeting is a success. These steps include planning an agenda, preparing note cards and visual and audiovisual aids, arranging the seating, and presenting the material effectively.

Planning an Agenda.   An agenda is an ordered listing of topics to be discussed. It also generally includes the time and location that the meeting will be held. Copies of the agenda are forwarded to group members by memorandum approximately one to two weeks in advance so that they will know what to expect when they attend the meeting. An agenda is similar to a shortened version of the course outline or syllabus that instructors give students on the first day of class.

Preparing the Presentation.   After the agenda has been completed, the individual responsible for the meeting should plan the presentation. The speaker should jot down notes about the topics to be covered and design visual and audiovisual aids.

The notes should be written on 3-× 5-inch cards, with the key topics to be addressed jotted down on each card. They should be arranged so that the speakers have only to glance at the note card to see the topic to be discussed. Then speakers can direct eye contact to the members of the group to see how the message is being received. The notes should be brief so that speakers will talk to the audience rather than read from the cards. When speakers try to write all their information down on paper, two major problems result. First, they read aloud from the text and lose eye contact with the audience. Second, they lose their place in the text, stumble, and waste time. An example of an effective 3-× 5-inch card with an outline is shown below.

PURPOSE: To Explain New Company Benefit Package

I.   Health Insurance

    A.   Preventive Care Concept

        1.   Choose doctors on approved list

            a. Take care of all general medical needs
            b. Make referrals to specialists

To use an outline and note cards, speakers must know the content well. Key words and phrases will not help speakers remember unfamiliar information.

In organizing the presentation, speakers should first clearly state the purpose of the meeting and then organize the information in a logical manner. Any general statements must be backed up with facts. For example, in an informative presentation describing a new health insurance plan, a supervisor makes the general statement, "It's the best plan money can buy." To convince the employees in the work group about the value of the plan, the supervisor must back up that statement with facts about the deductible and the plan's coverage. At the end of the presentation, speakers should restate the purpose of the presentation and summarize the main points.

As explained in Chapter 8, visual aids include drawings, charts, graphs, tables, samples, or pieces of equipment that the audience needs to see to understand the presentation. Audiovisual aids use a combination of sight and sound. The most common audiovisual aids are videotapes. Audiotapes, which allow the audience to hear but not to see, are also sometimes used. Below is a list of the common aids used to enhance presentations.

Transparencies. Transparencies are thin pieces of plastic used to show drawings or tables with an overhead projector on a screen. Simple and inexpensive to make, they are especially effective in showing organizational charts, diagrams of equipment components, and schematic diagrams. Transparencies are not effective for showing movement or change unless special polarizing devices are attached to the overhead projector.

Slides. Slides are pictures or drawings shown on a screen with a slide projector. Although they are more expensive to make than transparencies, they can show a specific piece of equipment, condition, or location in color. However, slides cannot show movement or change.

Audiotapes. Audiotapes are magnetic tapes on which sound is recorded and played back on a tape player. Audiotapes are effective when the audience needs to hear a particular sound, such as sirens or warning bells. They may also be very effective in presenting interrogation techniques taught in criminal justice courses and explaining various types of verbal behavior. Long audiotapes should be avoided because the audience will become bored very quickly.

Videotapes. Videotapes are magnetic tapes used to record moving images with accompanying sound. They are most effective in presenting movement, such as the operation, assembly, or disassembly of equipment or appropriate techniques and procedures for performing a job. They are very ineffective for showing lectures. Videotapes are expensive to make because of the initial equipment purchase. However, if a company has the necessary equipment on hand, the cost is minimal for the production of high-quality videotapes.

Equipment Mock-ups and Cutaways. Equipment mock-ups are replicas of pieces of equipment generally made out of a much lighter material than the original. They are used to demonstrate the component parts or the operation of a piece of equipment or item. Cutaways are replicas of the interior of a piece of equipment or any other item.

Equipment. Using and demonstrating the equipment you are discussing is very effective. The major limitations are the size, expense, and mobility of the equipment.

Charts and Drawings. When transparencies, slides, or videotapes are unavailable, enlarged charts and drawings or flipcharts are effective. They are very inexpensive to make, but they may require the attention of an experienced artist.

Arranging Seating. Since discussion is often not important in an informative meeting, the seating should be arranged so that each member of the group is facing the speaker. This arrangement allows for eye contact in only one direction, from speaker to audience to speaker. Even if a question-and-answer period follows an informative presentation, the questions are generally directed to the speaker rather than to another member of the audience. The formality of the meeting is maintained regardless of the informality of the question-and-answer session.

Making the Presentation.   Careful preparation will lead to effective presentations. Here are six tips for making presentations:

- Stand up straight, and use gestures that are natural to you when you speak. Do not grip the podium or use it as a barrier to hide behind.
- Establish eye contact with your entire audience. Do not focus on a spot immediately above everyone's head, or direct your attention to one person in the audience. Instead, move your gaze from person to person so that all group members feel that they are involved.
- Speak loudly and clearly enough for the entire audience to hear and understand you.
- Vary the tone and pitch of your voice rather than speaking in a monotone.
- Use correct grammar and pronunciation. Audiences lose confidence in leaders who misuse everyday terms or mispronounce technical words.
- Do not fiddle with pointers, pencils, rubber bands, or chalk, and do not jingle change in your pocket. These movements are very distracting and focus the audience's attention on objects rather than information.

Problem-Solving Presentations

Problem-solving meetings are more informal than informative meetings. Group participation is important for reaching a mutually agreeable solution to the problem under discussion. Again, to let the group know what to expect, an agenda may be sent to each participant prior to the meeting or introduced at the beginning of the session. The leader is responsible for the agenda.

Arranging Seating.   To get the most active and equal group participation, the seating arrangement in a problem-solving session should be U-shaped, square, or circular.

Taking Turns.   One technique to ensure the participation of each group member in problem-solving sessions is turn-taking. The leader should ask the opinion of those group members who are hesitant to speak up. Then once a decision is reached, all members feel that they have had a part in the decision-making process. This involvement helps to ensure future cooperation.

Making Decisions.   The decision-making process, which the leader must direct, includes the following five steps:

1. *Defining the Problem.* The group determines what is wrong and states the problem in clear terms.

2. *Analyzing the Problem.* To analyze a problem, the group must determine the cause of the problem.

3. *Deciding a Method of Solving the Problem.* Various methods of solving the problem must be discussed, and comments obtained from each group member.

4. *Making a Decision.* After the alternative methods of solving the problem have been discussed, a simple, realistic solution must be proposed.

5. *Taking Action.* Exactly what to do in solving the problem must be determined. Short-term and long-term action plans must be stated so that each group member knows the direction to take once the meeting is over.

An effective method for ensuring that all the aspects of the problem-solving process are covered is to use a decision-making worksheet. Figure 16-3 shows a completed decision-making worksheet for solving the problem of training 200 electronics technicians in the use of a new microprocessing system.

After a specified period, the group meets again to evaluate the action taken. If necessary, it repeats the entire problem-solving process. It revises schedules and makes new decisions.

SUMMARY

A work group is composed of two or more individuals who come together to do a job for the company that employs them. Membership in a work group requires each individual to perform his or her role according to the standards of performance and conduct expected by the company. Depending on the openness of the communication and the trust that is established, groups may be either supportive or destructive. To get information about how to complete a required task or to learn about changes in company policy, employees attend group meetings. These meetings may be primarily informative or problem-solving. In informative meetings, groups members are not usually actively involved. They simply listen. In problem-solving meetings, group members actively work together to overcome some difficulty that has occurred on the job.

ASSIGNMENTS

Application 1:
Observing Group Communication

Sketch the seating arrangement and make notes on the nonverbal behavior you observe in one of your classes. Pay particular attention to the territoriality and eye contact in the classroom setting. Then, make the same observations in a laboratory setting where two or more individuals are working together on an assignment. Be able to discuss the differences in the verbal and nonverbal behavior you have observed in these two very different situations.

```
                        DECISION-MAKING WORKSHEET


Definition of problem:  Lack of training facilities and instructors to
    meet the training needs of 200 electronics technicians at three
    separate plant sites.


Analysis of the problem:

    1.  200 techs to train

    2.  1 year to accomplish all training

    3.  Training for each tech is 4 weeks long

    4.  Need 2 additional micro system troubleshooting trainers

    5.  Need 2 more instructors

    6.  Need to schedule around vacation time, holidays

    7.  Not enough space available at training center


Possible methods of solving the problem:

    1.  Run double shifts January-June to avoid majority of vacation
        holidays

    2.  Check with plant management about shutting down plants for one
        month to train all techs in three shifts (100 for Raleigh
        plant, 50 for Lewisville, 50 at Research Triangle Park); would
        take us 3 months total time

    3.  Obtain funding for trainers or build them ourselves

    4.  Borrow two foremen or engineers to aid in instruction

    5.  Run training 1 shift per day for entire year


Solution to the problem:

    1.  Run double shifts Jan-June.  7 a.m.-3 p.m.; 3 p.m.-11 p.m.

    2.  Purchase 2 micro system troubleshooting trainers

    3.  Train 2 engineers as instructors rather than pulling foreman out
        of plants

    4.  Rent two rooms at Research Triangle Park Convention Center,
        centrally located
```

Figure 16-3: Decision-Making Worksheet

Actions:

	Short-term Action Items	Person Responsible
1.	Present proposed training program to Training Director on October 1	Ella Hollowell
2.	Call plant managers and arrange a meeting to discuss training program no later than October 10	Ella Hollowell
3.	Call Engineering Division to request two engineers as instructors for six months no later than October 15	Fred Willis
4.	Send in purchase order for micro system troubleshooting trainers no later than October 12 (after program approval by plant managers and training director)	Ben Williamson

	Long-term Action Items	Person Responsible
1.	Schedule shift training and notify plants of dates, personnel involved no later than December 10	Eric Holmes
2.	Arrange for a rental of classroom facilities at RTP no later than December 10	Eddie Allen
3.	Set up classrooms and lab facilities at RTP no later than December 28	Eric Holmes
4.	Train engineers in appropriate instructional techniques	Fred Willis

Figure 16-3:   *continued*

COMMUNICATION IN WORK GROUPS   377

Application 2:
Presenting Information

Choose a process, procedure, or piece of equipment used in your field of study and prepare to present an informative discussion. Ensure that your presentation is suitable for your audience. Make appropriate note cards and prepare at least one visual aid. If possible, have your instructor videotape your presentation so that you may see how effective you are in communicating technical information.

Application 3:
Evaluating the Informative Presentation

Using the evaluation form shown in Figure 16-4 on page 378, evaluate the informative presentation of one of your classmates or your own videotaped presentation. Discuss methods for improving the presentation.

Application 4:
Solving Problems

Divide into small groups in your classroom and prepare, as a group, a solution to a problem that is occurring at your college. The problem may be long lines at registration, inadequate cafeteria facilities, lack of parking, or extended curriculum hours. Using the decision-making worksheet in Figure 16-5 on pages 379 and 380, go through the steps described in the problem-solving process and discuss the problem and your group's solution with the class as a whole.

EVALUATION FORM

INFORMATIVE SPEECH

NAME _____   TOPIC _____

DATE _____

Directions: Circle the number that indicates the performance of the

    topic under consideration with 5 being the highest points awarded

    and 1 being the lowest.

NONVERBAL BEHAVIOR

Seating arrangement appropiate for type of presentation.	5	4	3	2	1
Note cards used effectively.	5	4	3	2	1
Visual aids appropriate to topic.	5	4	3	2	1
Gestures natural and appropriate.	5	4	3	2	1
Eye contact established with entire audience.	5	4	3	2	1
Posture erect.	5	4	3	2	1
Tone and pitch of voice appropriate.	5	4	3	2	1

CONTENT

Purpose stated clearly.	5	4	3	2	1
Facts presented to backup general statements.	5	4	3	2	1
Organization easy to follow.	5	4	3	2	1
Visual aids incorporated at correct times.	5	4	3	2	1
Correct use of grammar/diction/ technical terminology.	5	4	3	2	1
Summary of key points provided.	5	4	3	2	1

        TOTAL POINTS_____   GRADE_____

Figure 16-4: Informative Speech Evaluation Form

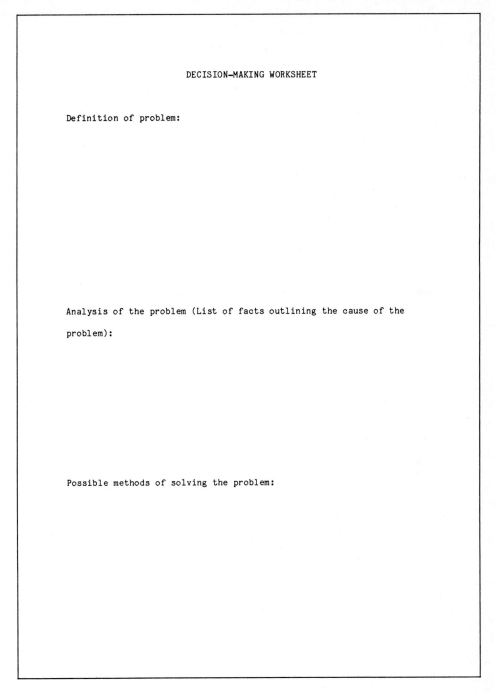

Figure 16-5:   Decision-Making Worksheet

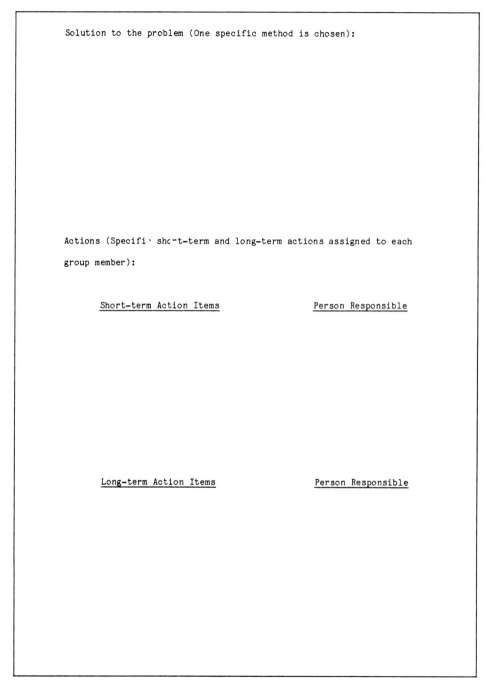

Figure 16-5: *continued*

Appendix A

CONVENTIONS OF STANDARD WRITTEN AMERICAN ENGLISH

Conventions associated with written language are the rules which determine appropriate or "correct" form and style. Although our language has all kinds of conventions, the ones examined here are important to writing in the same way that table manners are important to eating. Communication can occur without following these rules of etiquette, but it will be messy and time-consuming. This appendix discusses the rules for punctuation and capitalization and the appropriate use of numbers and abbreviations.

PUNCTUATION

Speakers indicate emphasis by pauses and gestures or by changing the tone of their voices. However, since writers are not face to face with their audiences, they cannot give these physical signals. Instead, they use punctuation, a group of devices that indicate these pauses and emphasis in writing. Common punctuation marks are

    periods[.]
    question marks[?]
    exclamation points[!]
    semicolons[;]
    colons[:]
    commas[,]

apostrophes[']
dashes[--]
parentheses[( )]
quotation marks[" "]
italics (underlining)[_____]

Periods

1.   Use a period to mark the end of a sentence.

When the clutch is disengaged, the engine can run. However, the car does not move forward or backward unless it is put in gear.

2.   Use a period after some abbreviations. However, no periods are used after abbreviations for government agencies, associations, service organizations, unions, and other similar groups.

Mr.   EPA
Ms.   AFL-CIO
R.N.   NCAA

When a sentence ends in an abbreviation, only one period is used.

Question Marks

Use a question mark to show the end of a question.

Do you like your new job in Florida? Have you found a place to live yet?

Exclamation Points

Use an exclamation point after a group of words or a sentence that expresses strong feeling.

The car won't start again! This is the third time this week!

Like interjections, exclamation points are not often used in formal writing. They are appropriate in letters to your friends but not in memoranda to your supervisor.

Semicolons

Semicolons can be used between ideas of equal importance that are expressed in the same form.

1.   Use a semicolon between closely related main clauses that are not connected with coordinate conjunctions. Coordinate conjunctions are "and," "or," "but," "for," and "nor."

Some people believe that fuel switching will save them money; others think that switching will stop the knocking in their engine.

2.   Use a semicolon to separate items in a list that contains confusing commas. The items must be equal in form and importance.

The students provided the food for the faculty picnic: hot dogs, which were moldy; bread, which was stale; and soft drinks, which were flat.

3.   Semicolons *cannot* be used in the following ways:

To separate a subordinate clause from a main clause

Not Correct

Jan is responsible for all the household chores; although she works 40 hours a week and earns more money than her husband.

Correct

Jan is responsible for all the household chores although she works 40 hours a week and earns more money than her husband.

If you cannot insert a period between two clauses, you cannot use a semicolon. Commas separate some subordinate clauses from main clauses; others require no separation.

To separate a salutation from the body of a letter

Not Correct

Dear President Oleski;

Correct

Dear President Oleski:

Colons

A colon is used to announce specific information that supports a general statement.

1.   Use a colon to signal a list that follows a main clause.

On your next trip to the store, please buy these items for me: a bar of soap, a pound of bacon, a dozen eggs, and a loaf of bread.

Unless the list is preceded by a main clause, a colon cannot be used.

Not Correct

The new officers for the organization are: Jane Waters, President; Sam Elridge, Vice-President; Bernice Allen, Secretary; and Amy Pitts, Treasurer.

Correct

The new officers for the organization are Jane Waters, President; Sam Elridge, Vice-President; Bernice Allen, Secretary; and Amy Pitts, Treasurer.

2.   Use a colon to signal a word, phrase, or clause that explains a general statement.

In this sentence, the dime is what the man is looking for. By setting it off from the sentence with a colon, the writer emphasizes its importance.

Reaching to the bottom of his pocket, the man finally found what he was looking for: his last dime.

A colon shows that meaning moves from general to specific.

Commas

Their placement not determined by "where you pause," commas have many uses. They can separate a list of equal, or coordinate, items and a subordinate item from the clause or word it modifies.

1.   Use a comma to separate main clauses joined by a coordinate conjunction.

This sentence has two main clauses joined by "and."

The ignition system causes an electric spark to occur in the cylinder, *and* the spark sets fire to the fuel-air mixture.

2.   Use commas to separate items in a list or series.

In this sentence a series of nouns is separated with commas.

Machines can change *the size, direction, or speed* of the force we apply.

In this sentence a series of verbs is separated with commas.

Kaplan Plants, Inc. *selects, places, and maintains* the plants it rents.

Even though there is a coordinate conjunction, the comma before the last item helps to prevent misunderstandings.

3.   Use a comma to separate an introductory expression of more than five words from the subject of the sentence.

In this sentence two prepositional phrases, seven words, appear before the subject of the sentence.

Because of his fear of the dark, the child wanted to sleep with his parents.

4.   Use a comma to separate an introductory expression that contains a verb or verbal from the subject of the sentence.

This sentence is introduced with a verbal phrase. The verbal is "hunting."

> *After hunting ducks on the salt marsh near the Pamlico River for most of the weekend,* Jake was too tired to work on Monday.

This sentence is introduced with a subordinate clause.

> *Even if you hold an ionization smoke detector close to your body for eight hours a day through a year,* you will receive only one tenth as much radiation as you can get on one round-trip airline flight across the United States.

5.   Use commas to set off nonessential elements from the rest of the sentence. Although they often add clarity, nonessential elements can be removed from the sentence without changing the meaning. Nonessential elements can be words, phrases, or clauses, and they can function as adjectives or adverbs.

In this sentence the nonessential element is a "which" clause modifying "heavy equipment."

> Heavy equipment, *which includes bulldozers and cranes,* may be difficult to repair.

In this sentence the "which" clause is essential. If the "which" clause is removed, a meaningless statement results: "Machines are called hydraulic machines."

> Machines *which are operated by liquids under pressure* are called hydraulic machines.

In this sentence a nonessential appositive (a renaming noun) is set off.

> Barbara, *the crew leader,* hated to ask the crew members to work overtime on special holidays.

In this sentence the appositive is essential, and it is not set off. "William Shakespeare" is an appositive that renames "poet."

> The poet *William Shakespeare* never owned a car.

But: When "the poet" and "William Shakespeare" change places, the appositive is nonessential. Then it is set off. The name "William Shakespeare" is more specific than the description.

> William Shakespeare, *the poet,* never owned a car.

6.   The comma has other uses:

To set off comparative or contrastive elements
Comparisons are often set up with the prepositions "like" and "unlike."

Unlike his old tennis shoes, John's new tennis shoes felt stiff and hard.

To set off the names of people when you talk to them directly

Mr. Holmes, this is an offer you can't afford to pass up.

To set off direct quotations

Barbara, the leader of the work crew, said, "Give me an intelligent technical school graduate, and in three months I'll give you a first-rate electrician."

To separate the parts of dates

July 4, 1775

To separate the parts of addresses

714 West Main Street, Hertford, North Carolina

To separate a name from a title

Julian Erwin, Captain, United States Army

7.   The comma *cannot* be used to separate a compound verb in a predicate from its subject.

Not Correct

As part of his exercise program, Alvin ran two miles every day, and walked one.

Correct

As part of his exercise program, Alvin ran two miles every day and walked one.

Dashes

1.   Use dashes to set off nonessential elements that you want to emphasize. Sometimes the same element can be set off with dashes, commas, or parentheses. The decision about which punctuation to use depends on the emphasis you want to give the element.

In this sentence the nonessential element gives the percentage to further explain the number.

One estimate indicates that almost 31,000 Americans—15 out of every 100—suffer from allergies.

2. Use dashes to set off nonessential elements that are already punctuated with commas.

In this sentence the dashes set off a list of machines.

Simple machines—levers, inclined planes, pulleys, wedges, and wheels—were used by early civilizations.

When you are typing, a dash is made by hitting the hyphen key twice.

Parentheses

Use parentheses to enclose nonessential elements that define terms or act as afterthoughts. In the same way that dashes make elements stand out, parentheses tuck them away.

One estimate indicates that almost 31,000 Americans (15 out of every 100) suffer from allergies.

Parentheses are used to enclose full names for government agencies, companies, or anything else that is abbreviated.

The EPA (Environmental Protection Agency) gets support from environmentalist groups such as the Sierra Club.

Quotation Marks

1. Use quotation marks to enclose words copied directly from a book, newspaper, magazine, or any other printed material.

In *The Handbook of Nonsexist Writing*, Miller and Swift say, "The social movement to achieve rights and opportunities for women equal to those of men, whether one agrees or not, is an historic fact."

2. Use quotation marks to enclose words written down exactly as another person said them.

The new supervisor yelled to the crew: "Watch out on the scaffolding over there!"

3. Use quotation marks to enclose titles of articles or poems or anything published as a part of another book or magazine.

Brown's article, "The Changing American Family," was published in *Newsweek* last month.

4. Use either quotation marks or italics to set off words used as words. If the manuscript is typed or handwritten, underline the word.

Correct

The word "love" has different meanings for different people.

Correct

The word *love* has different meanings for different people.

In the United States, commas and periods are always put inside quotation marks. Other kinds of punctuation are placed according to the meaning of the sentence.

Italics and Underlining

Words, phrases, or sentences that are underlined in a typed or handwritten manuscript are italicized in printed material.

1. Underline titles of books, newspapers, magazines, pamphlets, radio and television shows, long poems, plays, and the names of computer software programs.

Alex reads his favorite newspaper, *The New York Times*, every morning. He watches *60 Minutes* every Sunday night.

2. Underline the names of spacecraft, aircraft, ships, and trains.

Orman's mother once crossed the ocean on the *Queen Mary*.

The *Orient Express* is a famous train.

3. Underline words and phrases for emphasis.

I said that I would *not* recommend you for a raise.

The same expression is almost never set off by both underlining and quotation marks.

Apostrophes

1. Use apostrophes to make the possessive forms of nouns.
Nouns that name human beings can be made possessive.

John's new car

Nouns that name animals can be made possessive.

the dog's collar

Some nouns that cannot own anything have possessive forms. Words that name periods of time and those that describe amounts of money can be possessive.

today's date
week's work
a dollar's worth

2.   Make most singular nouns possessive by adding -'s.

Oscar's books
owner's profits

If it ends in -s, make the plural noun possessive by adding -'.

boys' books
teachers' classrooms

If it does not end in -s, make the plural noun possessive by adding -'s.

women's shoes
fish's breeding grounds

An exception to this rule is the commonly used possessive "its." "It's" is the contraction for "it is."

Regardless of whether a noun is singular or plural, if it ends in -s, the possessive can usually be formed by adding -'.

boss'
Jones'

3.   Use apostrophes to show contractions. Apostrophes can show that letters have been left out. Although contractions are often used in speech, they are seldom used in technical writing.

do not	don't
cannot	can't
it is	it's

CAPITALIZATION

Capitalization is generally used to indicate proper nouns, nouns that name specific people, places, or things. It is also used to indicate the first word of a new sentence. Below are a few rules relating to capitalization.

To decide whether a noun is proper or common, use the "a/an" rule. If you can place "a" or "an" before the word and then substitute the expression in a sensible sentence, the word is a common noun and should not be capitalized.

1.   Names of people are capitalized. When they accompany a proper names, titles are also capitalized.

Susan Markham
Dr. Hoggard

2.   Names of places are capitalized.

The Alamo
Alexander City, Alabama

3.   Names of events are capitalized.

World War II
Superbowl

4.   Names of companies are capitalized.

Norfolk and Carolina Telephone and Telegraph Company
Nabisco

5.   Names of brands are capitalized.

Quaker State Motor Oil
Crayola Crayons

6.   Names of hotels, apartments, and other buildings are capitalized.

Holiday Inn
Empire State Building
Shamrock Apartments

7.   Directions are capitalized only when they refer to sections of the country or the world.

Elmer lived in the *Northeast,* just outside of Boston.
The *West* and the *Southwest* are growing rapidly.

8.   Holidays, days of the week, and months are capitalized. Seasons are not capitalized.

Easter
Sunday

July
fall

Christmas gives us a pleasant break in *December*, the beginning of *winter*.

9.   Nations and languages are capitalized.

England—English
France—French

10.   The first word in a quotation is capitalized.

During his inaugural speech, John Kennedy said, "Ask not what your country can do for you; ask what you can do for your country."

11.   The important words in a title and the first and last words are capitalized.

The police officer is writing her first novel: *It Happened One Day on the Way to the Subway.*

12.   The first word of each sentence is capitalized.

A dog's best friend is man; if owned by a woman, the dog's best friend is woman.

13.   School subjects are capitalized only when they are derived from proper nouns or when they name specific courses and specific institutions.

Physics 201—physics courses

But

English 100—English courses (See 9.)
French 100—French courses

14.   Schools, colleges, and departments are capitalized.

Smith Technical College
Department of Electrical Engineering
School of Business

15.   Abbreviations for academic degrees are capitalized.

B.A.
A.A.

16.   Names of airplanes, railroads, trains, and steamships are capitalized.

The *USS North Carolina* is a famous warship.

17.   Names of planets are capitalized.

Mars
Jupiter

18.   Names of churches and clubs are capitalized.

First United Methodist Church
Jaycees
Society of Automotive Engineers

ABBREVIATIONS

Acceptable abbreviations can be easily understood by your audience. However, if your readers are not familiar with a particular abbreviation, you should not use it. Below are a few rules pertaining to the use of abbreviations.

1.   Military rank and civilian titles can often be abbreviated. However, when these ranks or titles are used alone without names, they cannot be abbreviated.

Dr. Felton is the new resident at the hospital.

But

The hospital hired a new *doctor* for the emergency room.

2.   Government agencies and private companies can be abbreviated as dictated by the particular agency.

Environmental Protection Agency—EPA
Minnesota Mining and Manufacturing—3M

Notice that not all abbreviations are followed by periods.

3.   The Post Office has approved this list of abbreviations for states and territories. They should be used with zip codes.

Alabama	AL	Montana	MT
Alaska	AK	Nebraska	NE
Arizona	AZ	Nevada	NV
Arkansas	AR	New Hampshire	NH
California	CA	New Jersey	NJ

Colorado	CO	New Mexico	NM
Connecticut	CT	New York	NY
Delaware	DE	North Carolina	NC
District of Columbia	DC	North Dakota	ND
Florida	FL	Ohio	OH
Georgia	GA	Oklahoma	OK
Guam	GU	Oregon	OR
Hawaii	HI	Pennsylvania	PA
Idaho	ID	Puerto Rico	PR
Illinois	IL	Rhode Island	RI
Indiana	IN	South Carolina	SC
Iowa	IA	South Dakota	SD
Kansas	KS	Tennessee	TN
Kentucky	KY	Texas	TX
Louisiana	LA	Utah	UT
Maine	ME	Virginia	VA
Maryland	MD	Vermont	VT
Massachusetts	MA	Virgin Islands	VI
Michigan	MI	Washington	WA
Minnesota	MN	West Virginia	WV
Mississippi	MS	Wisconsin	WI
Missouri	MO	Wyoming	WY

NUMBERS

There are many conflicting rules about when to use figures or words to stand for numbers. The most important consideration, however, relates to clarity: if words are easier to understand, use words; if figures are easier to understand, use figures. Here are a few rules to help you decide how to express numbers.

1. Most of the time, figures are used for numbers above nine.

2. Figures are always used in these expressions:

Dates	May 25, 1987
Measurements	6 × 12 inches
Percent	16%
Policy Numbers	Policy No.: 3456729
Serial Numbers	#3412
Telephone Numbers	212-345-8954
Time	9:00
Weight	3 lb. 6 oz.
Quantities with whole numbers and fractions	1 ½

3. Figures should not be used at the beginning of a sentence.

Nineteen people came to the party.

4. When two numbers appear together in a sentence, write one in words.

Horace bought *twelve 2- × 4-ft* boards.

5.   Numbers can be made plural by adding -s.

The *1920s* were times of change in the United States.

6.   A noun that names a whole measurement is singular when the measurement is considered one unit; it is plural when it refers to separate items.

Ten pounds is too much weight to lose in a month.

After three months of diet and exercise, the *10 pounds* I gained at Christmas have finally come off.

7.   Columns of numbers are aligned to the right or over a decimal point.

```
  10.250
   4.564
 101.000
2431.432
```

Appendix B

COMMON PROBLEMS WITH WRITTEN ENGLISH

This appendix discusses some typical problems with standard written American English: problems with sentence construction, problems with agreement of subjects and verbs, unclear pronoun reference, problems with agreement of pronouns and antecedents, problems with the forms of verbs, and misplaced modifiers.

PROBLEMS WITH SENTENCE CONSTRUCTION

Problems with constructing sentences take two forms. The first, an incomplete sentence punctuated as if it were complete, is called a *fragment*. The second, two or more sentences combined incorrectly, can be either a *comma splice* or a *fused sentence*.

Fragments

A *fragment* occurs when a group of words is incorrectly punctuated as a sentence. Fragments can be corrected by connection with another sentence or by addition or deletion of words.

1. Fragments can be phrases or other groups of words that lack complete subjects and verbs.

Not Correct

The group of words, "Sitting under the tree," is not a sentence.

When we crossed the state line into Alabama, we saw a restored 1956 Chevy. Sitting under a tree.

Correct

The fragment can be connected with the sentence before.

When we crossed the state line into Alabama, we saw a restored 1956 Chevy, sitting under a tree.

2.   Fragments can be subordinate clauses. In this case, they have complete subjects and verbs, but they begin with subordinate conjunctions that made them dependent on another clause for meaning.

Not Correct

This fragment is a subordinate clause. Even though it has a subject "he" and a verb "was," it is introduced with "because," a subordinate conjunction.

Because he was the Best Man in our wedding.

Correct

This fragment can be corrected by the addition of a main clause.

Because he was the Best Man in our wedding, we have always felt especially close to Zack.

3. Special fragments are formed when semicolons are used incorrectly. Since semicolons act like periods, they cannot be used to separate lists or subordinate clauses from main clauses.

Not Correct

The subordinate clause at the end cannot stand alone as a sentence.

Soybean protein is often used as a substitute for meat, eggs, and fish; although it is not as nutritious as the protein derived from animals.

Correct

A comma or, in some cases, no punctuation separates subordinate and main clauses.

Soybean protein is often used as a substitute for meat, eggs, and fish, although it is not as nutritious as the protein derived from animals.

Comma Splices and Fused Sentences

A *comma splice* occurs when two main clauses are weakly separated with a comma. A *fused sentence* occurs when no punctuation at all separates the two main clauses.

Not Correct

Since a comma separates the main clauses, this sentence is a comma splice.

Reginald was caught sneaking away from work at 4:00 Friday afternoon, he was immediately fired.

Correct

Reginald was caught sneaking away from work at 4:00 Friday afternoon; he was immediately fired.

Not Correct

Since no comma is present, this sentence is fused.

Some workers prefer to receive pay for their overtime others want vacation days.

Correct

Some workers prefer to receive pay for their overtime; others want vacation days.

Four ways of correcting a comma splice or a fused sentence are as follows:

1.   Insert a coordinate conjunction ("and," "or," "but," "for," "nor") and a comma.

Not Correct

This fused sentence has two main clauses. The first describes the crew, and the second describes the crew leader.

The crew preferred working overtime for three weekends rather than changing shifts the crew leader agreed.

Correct

The fused sentence can be corrected by inserting a comma and "and."

The crew preferred working overtime for three weekends rather than changing shifts, and the crew leader agreed.

2.   If the two clauses are closely related and this relationship is clear,
insert a semicolon.

Not Correct

This comma splice has two main clauses. The first describes the death
rate for smokers who smoke less than a pack a day, and the second describes
the death rate for those who smoke more than a pack a day.

> The death rate for those who smoke less than a pack a day is four times
> higher than for nonsmokers, for those who smoke more than a pack it is seven
> times higher.

Correct

The comma splice can be corrected by inserting a semicolon.

> The death rate for those who smoke less than a pack a day is four times
> higher than for nonsmokers; for those who smoke more than a pack it is seven
> times higher.

3.   If the two clauses are not closely related, insert a period.

Not Correct

This fused sentence has two main clauses. The first describes the temporary elimination of overtime, and the second suggests that a fourth part-time
worker will be needed.

> By hiring three part-time workers, we have eliminated overtime for the past
> six months in January, however, we may need to hire a fourth part-time
> employee.

Correct

The fused sentence can be corrected by separating the two clauses with
a period.

> By hiring three part-time workers, we have eliminated overtime for the past
> six months. In January, however, we may need to hire a fourth part-time
> employee.

4.   If one clause seems to modify or explain the other, revise the sentence. Make one clause subordinate.

Not Correct

This fused sentence has two main clauses. The first describes the closing of the stores, and the second explains the reason for the closing.

Four stores in the mall have closed recently they had poor sales.

Correct

The second main clause can be made subordinate to the first.

Because they had poor sales, four stores in the mall have closed recently.

Application 1:
Correcting Fragments, Fused Sentences, and Comma Splices

Each of these items contains a fragment, a fused sentence, or a comma splice. Correct the errors.

1. Exposure to a current of only 25 milliamperes can be fatal exposure to 100 milliamperes is likely to be fatal.
2. Quickly and carelessly built, this house is poorly constructed, the foundation and the floors are already cracked.
3. Tighten the drill securely in the chuck with the key provided; never with pliers or a wrench.
4. All machines operate according to only two basic principles; namely the lever and the inclined plane.
5. One smoke detector gives more protection than no detector two detectors, if properly installed, provide a more reliable early warning than one.
6. Some consumers mistakenly believe that the cover on a power line will protect them from electrocution. For example, while painting or working on the house.
7. Regardless of the old stories, poisonous mushrooms will not turn a silver coin black, they also will not turn dark when they are soaked in salt water or turn milky when they are left in vinegar.
8. Locate the antenna a safe distance from power lines. A horizontal distance from the base to the power line of at least twice the length of the antenna.
9. The beverages drunk with the average fast food meal often have lots of calories depending on place of purchase and size, a milkshake can add 400 to over 800 calories to a meal.
10. Twenty years ago about one out of every seven dollars spent eating out went to fast-food restaurants today fast-food restaurants are getting two out of every five dollars spent eating away from home.

PROBLEMS WITH SUBJECT-VERB AGREEMENT

A verb should "agree with" its subject in *person* and *number*. Verbs have different forms depending on whether the subject is "I," "you," or a person or item and on whether they are singular or plural.

1.   A third-person singular noun is usually accompanied by a verb that ends in -s. In speech, this final -s is often dropped, but dropping this -s is not allowed in writing.

Not Correct	Correct
he run	he runs
she see	she sees
it consist	it consists

2.   Some nouns have irregular plurals. Taken from other languages, these words have not been changed to accommodate English spelling.

Singular	Plural
criterion	criteria
medium	media
crisis	crises

The *criterion* for choosing the beauty contest winner WAS simple: Pick the prettiest girl in the group.

The *criteria* for hiring new employees WERE decided before the company began interviewing.

A few of these words are now accepted as either singular or plural. For example, "data" is now used as a singular collective noun or as a plural noun.

3.   Some nouns have singular forms that appear plural. Most *indefinite pronouns* are singular. Indefinite pronouns include "everyone," "everything," "anybody," and other words that do not refer to an identifiable person or object.

Everyone IS ready to work.

Collective Nouns can be either singular or plural. Collective nouns refer to groups of items or people. When the writer wants to refer to the group as a whole, the collective noun is singular. When the writer wants to refer to the individuals who make up the group, the collective noun is plural.
In this sentence the collective noun is singular.

The *crew* BEGINS its next job Thursday.

In this sentence the collective noun is plural.

The *crew* PICK UP their paychecks from the supervisor.

4.   Compound subjects can be either singular or plural, depending on the conjunction used. If an adding conjunction is used, for example "and," the subject is plural.

John and Mary WERE HIRED recently by Northern Telecom.

If a disjoining conjunction, for example "or" and "nor," is used, the verb agrees with the part of the subject closest, regardless of whether that word is singular or plural.

In this sentence, both "principal" and "teachers" are subjects. The one closest to the verb is "teachers."

Neither the *principal* nor the *teachers* ENJOY going to school on Saturday.

If the order of the two subjects is reversed, the subject closest to the verb is singular.

Neither the *teachers* nor the *principal* ENJOYS going to school on Saturday.

Expressions such as "as well as" and "in addition to" are not conjunctions. Therefore, they cannot be used to make compound subjects. In this sentence the subject is "cost."

The increasing *cost* of energy along with tax incentives from the federal government IS likely to encourage homeowners to add insulation to attics, walls, and below floors.

5.   Interruptors and unusual subject-verb order can make the subject difficult to identify.
In this sentence the subject is "dress" and the verb is "was thrown."

THROWN in the corner in a heap WAS Alice's new *dress.*

6.   The verbs in relative clauses (wh- clauses) agree with the noun the clause modifies. The pronouns "who," "which," and "that" serve as subjects of the adjective clauses they announce. These pronouns take on the characteristics of the nouns they refer to.
In this sentence "which" refers to "law" and is singular.

The changing of heat energy to mechanical energy is explained by a law of physics *which* STATES that gas will expand when heated.

In this sentence "who" refers to "employees" and is plural.

The new employees, *who* WERE not certain about how the company operated, refused to join the union.

Application 2:
Correcting Subject-Verb Disagreements

Each of these sentences has an error in subject-verb agreement. Correct those errors.

1. Sue and Eileen has received pay raises each year for the last five years.
2. The training building was the area where classes in welding and machine shop was held.
3. The entire group were expelled after the Dean of Students found out about the cheating on the math exam.
4. The multimeter measure the current flow in many electronic devices.
5. A UL-approved trouble light, along with sunlight or a garage light, usually provide sufficient lighting for most automotive repair work.
6. Neither the principles behind the automatic transmission nor the routine maintenance required to keep it working correctly are mysterious.
7. Although there is little research on the long-term effects of drinking herbal teas, much evidence suggest serious short-term effects.
8. Either malfunctioning electrical appliances or faulty wiring usually cause home fires.
9. Friction between two surfaces depend upon the nature of the materials and the size of the forces pushing them together.
10. Found among herbs is nature's strongest poisons.

PROBLEMS WITH PRONOUN REFERENCE

A pronoun must connect clearly with the noun it refers to. The noun a pronoun refers to is its antecedent.

In this sentence "he" refers back to "boy," and "it" refers back to the "fire truck." "Boy" is the antecedent for "he," and "fire truck" is the antecedent for "it."

The little *boy* loved his *fire truck*. *He* played with *it* constantly.

1. A pronoun cannot refer to two different nouns.

Not Correct

In this sentence "it" can refer to both "Carnation" and "diet drink."

Carnation advertised its new low-calorie diet drink. *It* received praise from many groups of dieters.

Correct

Depending on what the writer means, two corrections for this sentence are possible.

Carnation advertised its new low-calorie diet drink. *The company* received praise from many groups of dieters.

Carnation advertised its new low-calorie diet drink. *The diet drink* received praise from many groups of dieters.

2.   Like other pronouns, the pronouns "this" and "which" must refer to nouns. They cannot refer to an entire sentence or a phrase.

Not Correct

The "this" in the second sentence does not refer to a noun in the first sentence.

> After spending 20 years on the same job, Alan was promoted to crew leader. This made him happy and his family proud.

Correct

The correction requires that "pronoun" be added.

> After spending 20 years on the same job, Alan was promoted to crew leader. The promotion made him happy and his family proud.

Not Correct

The "which" clause does not modify "Group B" or any other noun in the first part of the sentence.

> After three years of testing, Group A had fewer cavities than Group B, which means that the toothpaste used by the first group is more effective than that used by the second.

Correct

Again some rewriting is necessary

> After three years of testing, Group A had fewer cavities than Group B. These results mean that the toothpaste used by the first group is more effective than that used by the second.

As you can see, the corrections for reference errors sometimes require that words be inserted and new breaks for sentences be created.

Application 3:
Correcting Reference Errors

These sentences have reference errors. Revise them to eliminate the errors. Rewrite only as necessary.

1. The Rams play the Steelers next week. Last year this game took them to the Superbowl.
2. They say that "Love is blind."
3. Ann will be promoted next week, which means that she will also get a raise.
4. The old coat lay on the chair. It belonged to my grandfather.

5. Tom spent Christmas day at work, which shows that he is a workaholic.

6. Matches that are discolored or damaged may have been exposed to dampness. This can make them more likely to fall apart when struck.

7. In less than an hour, you can easily replace worn friction pads, which is the most common disc brake maintenance.

8. Since Jan was two inches taller than her date, this meant that she could not wear high heels.

9. Freestanding electric heaters should have tip-over switches to shut off the current if the unit is knocked over. This helps to prevent fire if the heater falls against fabric or other flammable material.

10. Gasoline gives off vapors which are heavier than air, which means that the vapors can flow along the floor or even down stairs.

PROBLEMS WITH PRONOUN-ANTECEDENT AGREEMENT

A pronoun should "agree with" the noun that serves as its antecedent. If the noun is plural, the pronoun should also be plural. If a noun is singular, the pronoun should be singular.

1. Singular pronouns refer to most indefinite pronouns.

Each of the flowers can be planted in *its* own pot.

2. Plural pronouns refer to compound antecedents joined by "and."

Paul and Mike decided to combine *their* training in electrical installation and maintenance and air conditioning and refrigeration repair to open *their* own business.

3. Singular pronouns refer to companies, colleges, and universities.

Everett and Lowe Lumber Company is the area's largest retail lumber business. *It* is located near the river.

4. Singular pronouns refer to collections of people or items considered single groups.

That *crew* is the laziest in the plant; *it* never finishes a job on time.

Application 4:
Correcting Pronoun-Antecedent Disagreements

These sentences have errors in pronoun-antecedent agreement. Correct each error.

1. General Motors is a good company to work for. They have an excellent benefits package.

2. Everyone bought the roses for their date from the same flower shop.

3. The choir has been invited to sing at the White House. They leave for Washington next week.

4. Anyone who tries to get their own way all the time is mean and uncaring.

5. Don't leave an electrical appliance plugged in while repairing them.

6. Although the sheriff is primarily responsible for law enforcement, they often also give assistance at accidents and at other emergencies.

7. Nobody would quit a job that they enjoy and that pays well.

8. Since the primary job of a smoke detector is to awaken a sleeping person and warn them of danger, it is important to put the detector as close to the bedroom as possible.

9. Union City Technical College finally raised enough money to expand their campus.

10. On Christmas a person can relax and do whatever pleases them.

PROBLEMS WITH VERB FORM

Regardless of how you speak or how you hear other people speak, verbs must be written in the forms allowed in standard written American English. Some problems occur when writers leave the -ed off the past tense of verbs. Other problems occur when they use the wrong form of an irregular verb. Some common irregular verbs are "begin," "break," "bring," "catch," "do," "drink," "drive," "eat," "go," "know," "lie," "run," "see," "take," and "write." You can consult a dictionary for the past and perfect forms of these and other irregular verbs.

Application 5:
Correcting Verb Form Errors

These sentences have verb form errors. Correct each error.

1. The draftsperson has drew a complete set of plans for Mike's new house.

2. Susan become a registered nurse when she passed her State Board Examination.

3. Ann has been playing so much racquetball that she has develop strained tendons in her elbow.

4. We stood behind the bulldozer as it begun clearing the land for the housing development.

5. You should lie technical manuals and parts on a clean table or workbench.

6. After 10 years of training in guerilla warfare, Ames lead his first mission against the terrorists.

7. Cams are use to change rotary motion into linear motion.

8. Work is done when resistance is overcame by a force acting through a measurable distance.

9. Jan had lain the silverware on the table and left to answer the phone.

10. By the time she was 10, the genius had wrote her first novel.

PROBLEMS WITH MODIFICATION

Modifiers function as adjectives or adverbs. The most common problems with modification relate to the form and position of the modifiers. Readers must be able to decide easily how the modifiers go with the rest of the sentence.

    1.   Misplaced modifiers can be moved to a more appropriate position.

Not Correct

In this sentence the subordinate clause "when it burns" seems to say something about the movement in the pistons. The subordinate clause is misplaced.

> The fuel-air mixture expands greatly in the cylinder, and the pressure created moves the piston *when it burns.*

Correct

This version connects the subordinate clause clearly to the expansion of the fuel-air mixture.

> *When it burns,* the fuel-air mixture expands greatly in the cylinder, and the pressure created moves the piston.

Not Correct

In the sentence babies are compared to peanut butter and other sticky substances. The prepositional phrase "Like peanut butter and other sticky substances" is misplaced.

> *Like peanut butter and other sticky substances,* babies can choke on large pieces of meat.

Correct

This version makes the comparison clear; peanut butter and other sticky substances are compared with meat.

> *Like peanut butter and other sticky substances,* large pieces of meat can cause babies to choke.

Not Correct

In this sentence the technicians seem to be constantly stuck in a open position. The verbal phrase is misplaced.

> The valves were major problems for the technicians, *constantly stuck in open positions.*

Correct

This version makes the verbal clearly modify "valves."

Constantly stuck in open positions, the valves were major problems for the technicians.

2.   Limiting modifiers must be placed next to the words they modify. Limiting modifiers include words like "only," "even," "almost," "just." These expressions establish conditions.

Not Correct

In this sentence the "only" is misplaced. It should modify $12.00.

The family *only* had $12.00 to buy food for the rest of the week.

Correct

This version puts "only" in its correct place as close to the word it modifies as possible.

The family had *only* $12.00 to buy food for the rest of the week.

Application 6:
Correcting Misplaced Modifiers

These sentences have misplaced modifiers. Correct each sentence, rewriting only when necessary.

1. Herman only visits his mother at Christmas. (Hint: Herman visits his mother once a year, no more.)
2. Mary prepared the sketches for her supervisor drawing and then making blueprints of them.
3. The repair person found that the word processor needed a new chip troubleshooting the system.
4. Precooked food may undergo further preparation once it is received by the restaurant which includes multiple heatings and cookings.
5. Minerals are absorbed in the intestines and transported in the blood to other parts of the body like other essential nutrients.
6. Used safely, we benefit greatly from electricity; but defects or improper use can cause tragedy.
7. With no loss Pascal discovered that a pressure applied to any part of a confined fluid is transmitted to every other part.
8. Walking has been widely practiced as a recreational and fitness activity throughout history unlike tennis, running, skiing, and other more recent activities.
9. The small child looked so sad and tattered that Jenny almost gave him her entire salary for the week. (Hint: Jenny gave the child some money.)
10. Thrown by the neighborhood bully, the windowpane shattered when the rock hit it.

Appendix C

LANGUAGE OF EQUAL TREATMENT

The United States promises its citizens equal opportunities. Race, sex, and other physical characteristics are not supposed to affect a person's chances for success in our democratic society. However, even as our country has grown greater and stronger and as opportunities have increased, women and minorities have not enjoyed the equal treatment guaranteed by their citizenship. They have been the victims of race and sex discrimination. Being thought of as incompetent, helpless, and inferior, women and certain minorities have been encouraged to perform only the lowest-paying jobs while being excluded from jobs with power and prestige. This discrimination is reflected in the language used to describe women and minorities, especially in discussions of their performance in the workplace. To help bring about the social change that is long overdue, you should stop using language that encourages this discrimination. Here are some ways to make a language of equal treatment.

1. *References to images of women and minorities as inferior should be avoided.* Images of the flighty, helpless female rob women of a chance to compete equally with men for jobs. Images of blacks and Puerto Ricans as shiftless criminals also exclude them from chances for power and prestige. Numerous other images—for example, jokes about Jews and Poles—influence the treatment received by certain groups of Americans in the United States. Possibly the most harmful image of all, however, is that of the white male as always successful, strong, and resourceful.

2. *People should not be described by their physical characteristics when the discussion is about professional qualifications or achievements.*

> *Not:* Lance Elmore III is the best CPA in the firm, and his wife, Linda, is a gorgeous blonde.

> *But:* Lance Elmore III is the best CPA in the firm, and his wife, Linda, is the firm's best lawyer.

> *Not:* I'll have my girl send the information you requested.

> *But:* I'll have my assistant send the information you requested.

Not	*But*
authoress	author
poetess	poet
stewardess	flight attendant
woman doctor	doctor
male nurse	nurse
woman astronaut	astronaut
black college professor	college professor
Puerto Rican lawyer	lawyer

3. *"Man" words should be eliminated from the language.* Some people argue that the word "man" includes both men and women. However, the fact is that when most people read "man," they think male, not female. It is difficult to hire a woman as a fireman, policeman, or mailman. Words with "man" in the beginning as well as the end should be avoided.

Not	*But*
mankind	humanity, humans
manmade	synthetic
manpower	work force
mailman	letter carrier
policeman	police officer
salesman	salesperson
chairman	chair
the best man for the job	the best person for the job

4. *The use of the pronoun "he" to refer to both men and women should be avoided.* In the same way that "man" words are supposed to include women as well as men, "he" is supposed to refer to both sexes. However, the pronoun "he" excludes women.

Consider this example. You might write

> The electrician should always have his toolbox in the back of his truck.

But would you write

The nurse should always have his first aid kit in the back of his car.

Not likely. Instead you probably would write

The nurse should always have her first aid kit in the back of her car.

As you can see, in everyday use "he" is not used consistently to refer to both sexes. When the reference is to a person in a traditionally male occupation, "he" is used; however, when the reference is to a person in a traditionally female occupation, "she" is often used. The implication is that all electricians are male and all nurses are female.

One way of avoiding discrimination is to use "he or she" rather than "he" to refer to a person in a position that could be held by either a male or a female. However, the best correction is to make the noun referred to plural and to use "they."

Not: Everyone brought his tools to lab.

But: Everyone brought his or her tools to lab.

Better: All the students brought their tools to lab.

5. *Reference to the marital status of women along with other kinds of unequal reference should be eliminated.* One title, "Mr.," applies to all men, married or single. For women, however, "Miss" and "Mrs." have been used to identify women according to their marital status. The implication is that married women are different from single women and that they should be treated differently by employers. Now "Ms." has been widely adopted to avoid this unnecessary identification.

When a title is known, the "Ms." is often dropped. For example, Elizabeth Byrd has recently received a Ph.D. in physics and is a professor at MIT. She may be referred to as "Dr. Byrd," "Professor Byrd," or "Ms. Byrd." However, even though she is married, she should not be called Mrs. Byrd unless she asks for that title.

In addition to being classified as married or single, women are often referred to by their first names, while men mentioned in the same discussion are called by their last names. This unparallel reference reflects unequal treatment.

Not: Captain John Smith and Alice

But: Captain John Smith and Dr. Alice Ward

Some women today prefer to use initials. Until recently only men signed their initials rather than their first and middle names.

| G. M. Anderson | Gail May Anderson |
| S. C. Toland | Susan Christine Toland |

INDEX